THE KAISER

A LIFE OF WILHELM II,
LAST EMPEROR OF GERMANY

BY JOACHIM VON KÜRENBERG

Translated by
H. T. RUSSELL *and* **HERTA HAGEN**

With a Foreword, Notes, and Appendix by
QUINCY HOWE

SIMON AND SCHUSTER
NEW YORK, 1955

LIBRARY OF CONGRESS CATALOG CARD NUMBER: 55-8807
DEWEY DECIMAL CLASSIFICATION NUMBER: 92
MANUFACTURED IN THE UNITED STATES OF AMERICA
BY AMERICAN BOOK—STRATFORD PRESS, INC., NEW YORK

CONTENTS

vi · **Contents**

viii · **Contents**

FOREWORD TO THE
AMERICAN READER

THE AUTHOR *and the subject of this book lie two worlds and two wars away from the United States at mid-century. The first of these wars ended the world in which Imperial Germany reached the summit of its glory. The second ended the world in which Europe formerly played as commanding a role as Germany had once played in Europe. Joachim von Kürenberg is a survivor of the world of Kaiser Wilhelm II and comes from the same Prussian aristocracy to which the Kaiser himself belonged. He is therefore able to recapture the atmosphere of a vanished time and an extinct society that already seem as far away as the France of Louis XIV or the England of the first Elizabeth. A member of the court of Louis XIV, turned loose in twentieth-century America, would not be likely to win many political converts. A contemporary of Queen Elizabeth I would need to be able to do more than speak English to gain acceptance for his views. But if a survivor of either of these two periods were able to communicate with us, we should certainly want to listen and probably try to learn. Because of the speed at which contemporary history moves, we sometimes take for granted the many survivors of earlier times still in our midst, only to come upon a book like this biography of the Kaiser in which one of our own contemporaries re-creates a world that is already one with Nineveh and Tyre.*

For this life of Wilhelm II dwells chiefly on the golden age before the first World War and covers the years that followed in the light of what happened during the preceding half century. The German title, War Alles Falsch?, *explains why. It means "Was Everything Wrong?" and the Kaiser inscribed the words on a photograph of himself that he gave to Kürenberg in 1935. The two men met shortly before the first World War, during which Kürenberg served with a number of German diplomatic missions abroad. The books he subsequently wrote on Krupp, Queen Victoria, and Johanna von Bismarck attracted the Kaiser's interest and led him to name this fellow aristocrat from East Prussia as his official biographer, giving him exclusive access to source material and encouraging conversations of extraordinary frankness. Kürenberg criticizes the Kaiser's vanity, indecision, and superficiality. He told him to his face that he should have led his troops in battle and not sought refuge in Holland in November 1918. But he praises the Kaiser's personal qualities—his courage, energy, and sincerity; he admires his devotion to family, fatherland, and God. Clearly everything cannot have been wrong with the Kaiser and his Empire.*

Kaiser Wilhelm II belonged to the Protestant branch of the House of Hohenzollern. For more than four centuries, his ancestors had been Kings of Prussia, and some of them—notably Frederick the Great—had helped to make Prussia the foremost of the many North German principalities. But Prussia and Germany made their most spectacular advances during the first fifty years of the Kaiser's life and the first twenty-five of his reign. Indeed, during that half century, the power of Germany in Europe and the power of Europe in the world went forward together. The first World War halted this process; the second World War reversed it. Although the Kaiser held the title of Supreme War Lord throughout the first World War, he contributed little to Germany's victories—or defeats. And although he lived to see Hitler crush France and overrun Western Europe, he passed the last two decades of his life observing the history of his times, but playing no part in its making.

The opening chapters of Kürenberg's biography of the Kaiser rank with the opening chapters of the Duke of Windsor's A King's Story. *Both give charming—even touching—pictures of the early tribulations of a boy born to kingship. But it was not the discipline to which young Wilhelm was subjected that stirs our pity so much as the irrelevance of what he learned. The Duke of Windsor has long recognized how much his early education handicapped him in the world of his manhood. The Kaiser never achieved that self-awareness, even in his last, long years of exile. Some biographers have traced the Kaiser's tragedy back to his withered left arm and to his dominating British mother. But the Kaiser's tragedy—unlike Brutus's—did not lie in himself but in his stars. Both Theodore and Franklin Roosevelt overcame severe physical handicaps, and not all dominating mothers are the daughters of Queen Victoria. In a different setting, the Kaiser might have overcome these early influences —just as the Roosevelts might have left no footprints on the sands of time if they had had to contend against the stupefying atmosphere of an imperial court.*

The most revealing and engrossing chapters of Kürenberg's biography depict the years of Bülow's chancellorship. And because Kürenberg deals with personalities rather than policies, he depicts Bülow as more a knave than a fool. Moreover, if Kürenberg did not share Bülow's anti-British prejudices, he might have made more of the malign influences these prejudices had on the impressionable Kaiser. Although the Kaiser resented his British mother and hated his British uncle, Edward VII, he loved his British grandmother, Queen Victoria, who died in his arms and treated him as her favorite grandchild. The Kaiser may not have been the brainiest, the ablest, or the most talented ruler who ever sat on any throne, but he possessed a complex and even a subtle nature. His attitude toward the English vacillated between love and hate, between respect and suspicion. He took pride in his British ancestry and described himself as half English, but Bülow played exclusively on his hatred and suspicion of the English, never striving, as a wiser and more understanding statesman might have done, to encourage the love and respect for his mother's country that formed a no less essential part of the Kaiser's nature.

Kürenberg's life of the Kaiser teaches one abiding lesson about its own time and about ours. What was wrong about the Kaiser and the Germany over which he ruled was not the folly of the one or the wickedness of the other. What was wrong was the irrelevance of the values by which the Imperial Court and all the other ruling groups in Germany lived—the professors as well as the soldiers, the businessmen as well as the diplomats. These values were not inherently or absolutely wrong. The trouble was that they did not apply to the world of 1900. And Kürenberg brings this out, not by castigating the Kaiser, but by presenting him in a favorable light. It is easy, in the light of what we now know, to throw stones at both the Kaiser and his biographer. But if we translate into the language of our own time this account of the Kaiser, we may recall that we live in glass houses, too.

It is the biographer's prerogative to fix the limits within which he treats his subject, and Kürenberg decided to make this a one-volume treatment of the Kaiser's life rather than a more extended treatment of the Kaiser's times. After all, he had new and first-hand information to impart on the subject of the Kaiser, whereas his German readers were already well posted on the Kaiser's times. But American readers know less of Bismarck and Bülow, of Prince Eulenburg and Baron Holstein, of Czar Nicholas and Emperor Franz Joseph, of Bosnia, Herzegovina, Algeciras, and Agadir. To supply some of the information that Kürenberg assumed his German readers already knew, I have therefore, at the instance of the American publishers, added a number of factual footnotes and an appendix. The footnotes explain themselves. The appendix consists of ten brief essays, nine of them biographical, that are intended to supply only such factual and interpretive matter as may aid the American reader of this book to see some of the topics it covers in fuller perspective. For instance, the appendix notes on Bismarck and Bülow were prepared primarily to give further information on some of the events that happened under their chancellorships. They are not put forward as rounded character sketches of those two men, much less as thumbnail histories of their times. But it is hoped that the material about them and other personalities will make the biography itself more understandable and enjoyable to the American reader. In one instance, that of Sir Edward Grey, I have also made so bold as to call attention to some of the facts of his life that do not square with the interpretation that both the Kaiser and his official biographer chose to give them.

January 1955   QUINCY HOWE

Three months after Mr. Howe wrote his Foreword news came of Mr. von Kürenberg's death in Europe at the age of sixty-two.

INTRODUCTION

"War *alles falsch?*" ("Was everything wrong?"). These are the words written by Kaiser Wilhelm II on November 15, 1935, across a photograph of himself that he gave me as a present after my first visit to Doorn.[1]

I had written books that had interested the Kaiser because they dealt with various aspects of events within the period covered by his reign—for instance, my *Holstein, l'Eminence grise* (foreign affairs); *Russia's Road to Tannenberg* (conduct of the war on the eastern frontiers); *Menzel, "His Little Excellency"* (art); *Krupp, Kampf um Stahl* (the struggle for steel); *The Empress of India* (relations with his grandmother and uncle in England); and *Johanna von Bismarck* (his friendship, and breach, with the family of the Prince Reich's Chancellor). The description of the central figure in all the events treated of in those books, namely that of Wilhelm II himself, had remained unwritten.

This task, the writing of the first German biography of the Kaiser, presented itself to me as almost a self-evident necessity and all the more so because a farrago of brochures and pamphlets about the last Monarch of the German Reich had been appearing in foreign countries without a single one of his former subjects taking up a pen to defend the Kaiser against these malevolent concoctions, originating for the most part in sensation-mongering and backstairs gossip.

Something must needs be inserted here by way of explanation. Most of the personalities named in this biography are known to me

[1] The explanation of this apparently cryptic inquiry is to be found in the circumstances under which it was made. The exiled Kaiser bitterly resented the way in which his life and actions were depicted after his downfall, and the almost unanimous chorus of execration for which he was the target. Having found his biographer (and he could have made no better choice) he looked to him to carry out his undertaking to "deal justly" with his case and—since no other procedure was possible in defense—to present to the court of world opinion a reasoned plea in mitigation. *War alles falsch?* means "Did I then never do anything right?" (*Trans.*)

personally. I was introduced to the Kaiser for the first time when I was a young Guardsman in Potsdam, so that I got to know Court life in the days of Wilhelm II, both in Potsdam and Berlin, from my own experience.

At the beginning of the 1914–1918 war I was posted by Cabinet Order to the then important Embassy in Constantinople, which was staffed by Baron Wangenheim and Herrn von Kühlmann, von Neurath and Humann. From there I went to Rome—but only for a short time—to the Ambassador Prince Bülow—whose guest I was, after the war, in his Villa Malta, where I could see and talk with him for weeks on end.

When Italy came into the World War, I was attached to the Embassy in Vienna, where Baron von Tschirschky und Bögendorff watched over German interests in the Metternichgasse. Ten years previously he had countersigned the Treaty of Björkö, and Holstein had been ousted. I have to thank him for much material used in Holstein's biography and also in this work. During my stay in Vienna I also made the acquaintance of the old Emperor Franz Joseph, and was even received by him in private audience on February 18, 1915.

After 1918 all these impressions were reinforced by detailed study of materials that came to hand. They have since found their ultimate destination in my books mentioned above.

The Keepers of the State Archives in Berlin and Potsdam, the Library of the Berlin University and numerous other universities have generously, and with a full understanding of what was needed, placed much more material at my disposal. To all who have assisted me in my task sincere thanks are given.

After such a voluminous mass of materials had been gathered together from personal experience and from what had been heard and read, and this had been further supplemented by contributions offered by the Kaiser's contemporaries, the final touch—taken from life itself—was still lacking to make it all a living thing: personal intercourse with the Kaiser in Doorn.

While I was yet in doubt as to whether such a meeting was possible, there came from Doorn the invitation that provided an opportunity of putting to the Kaiser himself questions that had lately arisen, and others dealing with matters that were of importance but were obscure.

My questions were always frankly answered, at first with three persons present, for the Kaiserin Hermine was bidden to the earlier conversations.

Answering the Kaiser's inquiry as to how I intended to write his biography, I replied with one word—*gerecht*! (justly!). Perhaps that one word caused the Kaiser to make me his biographer. "So far," he said bitterly, "I have noticed very little doing of justice. What has been written about me up to now is for the most part distorted, false or silly—a lot of it was even cribbed from the comic papers! The worst behaved of all was that man who, without ever having spoken to me or met me, poured out rubbish about me as out of a bucket. This creature is now living in Switzerland—I can only feel sorry for the gallant Confederates! Others have done much the same sort of thing, they were not much better."

This first meeting in Doorn had already established a contact that was never afterward to be broken—despite some malevolent attempts. When strolling in the garden or talking in Kaiserin Hermine's salon, and above all in the "tower," I had ample opportunity of studying the Kaiser and of inducing him to give explanations that often were quite new and highly informative. I reproduce his corrections even where they appear to conflict with other versions.

Time and again, in the heat of wordy warfare—both of us being temperamental and impulsive—we came near to the limits of our endurance. Then a frigid dismissal would put an end to the discussion. This, however, did not prevent a friendly note's being found lying on the table the following morning with an invitation to continue the walks and talks.

In order to confirm me in my position as his biographer the Kaiser himself chose the title of the German edition of my biography. Shortly before his death he read the Swiss edition, then in course of production. It has already been translated into five languages. He did not by any means agree with all of it; nevertheless he appended as a conclusion, "It does at least endeavor to depict my life and my times with accuracy and justice."

I did in fact try to avoid any Byzantine glorification of Wilhelm II and above all to provide no material for monarchist propaganda. The only thing that fascinated me was the problem of representing the changeable and inconsequent personality of the Kaiser, so difficult to grasp, in a way free from both false adulation and malicious distortion. The epoch of the last German Empire seems, moreover, to be interesting enough, in its pomp and glory, but also in its Prussian simplicity, to ensure its own viability.

After every interview with the Kaiser I made careful notes. These are interspersed in the text and incorporated in such a way that the Kaiser himself always gets a hearing. Pros and cons are often confronted directly, so that the reader must determine which was wrong and which was right. To assist him in forming his judgment of innocence or guilt the opinions of the Kaiser's colleagues, friends, relatives and enemies are interwoven, so that the picture is, as it were, built up by reflections from many mirrors and becomes more recognizable.

The story told in this present biography is that of the Kaiser's life, not of his time. Were it intended to write this latter, many bulky volumes would be needed to cover the lifetime of Wilhelm II in its political and economic developments. It could then provide only a background which, if meant to conduce to a better understanding of the principal character, would be more brightly illumined. It remains, however, the firm intention of the biographer to keep the figure of the person he depicts consistently to the fore and to prevent its being ousted from its privileged position by the play of events and changes of scenery that occur around it, or by the going and coming of other characters.

A first biography of this kind—moreover, one of a man whose personality is so productive of disputes as Kaiser Wilhelm's undoubtedly was—cannot (and this must be stressed particularly) lay claim to completeness. Let a saying of Napoleon III serve as a device to this arduous task—*Historical truth is no less sacred than Religion.*

Hamburg
  Oevelgönne, Villa Parva
    January 27, 1951

Kaiser Wilhelm II

Princess Victoria of England, widowed consort of Kaiser Friedrich III, mother of Wilhelm II

Kaiser Wilhelm I holding his great-grandson. On his right the Crown Prince, later Friedrich III, on his left the latter's son, later Wilhelm II

The Kaiser when he was a Lieutenant of the 1st Guard Regiment

Prince Bernhard von Bülow

Archduke Franz Ferdinand of Austria-Este

Kaiser Wilhelm II, with the Kaiserin Auguste Viktoria, Prince August Wilhelm and Prince Oskar *(Picture Post Library)*

Generals von Hindenburg and Ludendorff on the former's seventieth birthday

Chancellor von Bethmann-Hollweg (in uniform) with Vice-Chancellor Dr. Karl Helfferich (right) and the Foreign Secretary Gottlieb von Jagow in the garden of the Chancellory at the outbreak of war

Wilhelm II, with Admirals von
Tirpitz and von Holtzendorf,
on the Imperial yacht *Hohenzollern*, Kiel Week, 1910

Wilhelm II with Czar Nicholas II of Russia

Prince Max von Baden and his family *(Picture Post Library)*

Doorn House, front view *(Picture Post Library)*

Potsdam. Neues Palais

Wilhelm II in the reading room of Doorn House, with Princess Hermine and her daughter, Princess Henriette *(Picture Post Library)*

1. THE SAPLING

ON MARCH 4, 1859, the ancient table around which the Hohenzollerns had transacted their important family business ever since the time of the Great Elector of Brandenburg, and at which many a momentous agreement had been signed, was moved into position before the altar, lavishly bedecked with flowers, in the private chapel of the Crown Prince's palace.

On this historic table stood baptismal accessories which again dated back to the days of the first king. They were covered by a silver-brocaded cloth, worked with black eagles that 158 years before, at the coronation in Königsberg, had for the first time figured as the emblem of the High Order of the Black Eagle, instituted on that occasion. Above table and altar hung the purple canopy with its gold-embroidered Prussian crowns whose pearls and precious stones glittered and flashed in the candlelight.

Once again did the Lord Chamberlain von Wedel examine the golden vessels, satisfy himself that the Jordan water was in its place, and rectify the position of the red portfolio with its impressed crown in which lay the parchment that was to testify that on this day Prince Friedrich Wilhelm Victor Albert of Prussia had been the recipient of Holy Baptism.

Then Consistory Councilor Strauss entered the chapel to deposit his Bible on the altar and run over again in his mind the theme of his baptismal sermon.

Through the main door came the rumbling sound of the State coaches, the slamming of carriage doors and the hoofbeats of horses on the stone pavement.

Below, in the Princess's salon, the nearest relatives were already assembling. Some of them may have shared the thoughts of the clergyman who, standing with folded hands before the altar, was giving thanks to God for having once again extended His favor to the Royal House.

1

Who would have thought it possible, thirty-five days previously, that the nineteen-year-old mother would come safely through the ordeal of such a birth, or that the child—supposed at first to be dead—would still be living? Only when it was at last certain that all had gone well was the signal given with a handkerchief to the officer waiting on the castle bridge. Then the saluting battery that had taken up its position in the Lustgarten informed the people of Berlin by its rolling salvos that the Princess of Prussia had given birth to a son, an heir to the Throne.

The clink of a saber made the preacher look up. It was General von Wrangel, in his Königsberg Cuirassiers' uniform, come to make sure where his place in the chapel would be during the ceremony. On January 27 he happened to be in the palace when the gunfire announced the happy event. In his own casual way he had smashed a window in the ground floor of the palace and shouted breezily to the closely packed crowd of people gathered by the pavement, "It's a prince, and a hefty recruit into the bargain!"

But Wrangel was wrong. This Prince would never be a real soldier—he was a cripple. Not until three days after birth was the infirmity definitely established. The left arm was stunted—undeveloped. Mindful of this, Consistory Councilor Strauss reflected, "The future King of Prussia a cripple!" Nervously he pulled out his handkerchief and mopped his damp forehead.

Chairs were being pushed about. The Hereditary Grand Duke of Mecklenburg-Strelitz and the Prince of Hohenzollern came in and fell to talking of the little candidate for baptism. "I may remind you," said the Grand Duke, "that Prince Regent Wilhelm, at his birth, was thought to be dead. Today he is over sixty and in perfect health!"

The taciturn Prince of Hohenzollern nodded in assent. He, the representative of the senior and Catholic line, kept his own counsel. True, his line had Portuguese, Spanish and French blood in their veins, but that foreign blood was at least sound.

None of the Sigmaringens or the earlier Hechingens had been a cripple, or mentally afflicted like King Friedrich Wilhelm IV of Prussia, who, suffering from melancholia, had had to be put under the surveillance of mental nurses in the Orangery at Potsdam. Might that also be the fate of the newborn child? Was it not an injustice of history that this junior unsound Berlin line, apostates from Catholicism, should be allowed to reign at all?

Just then, while the first guests were assembling in the chapel, the invalid King, great-uncle of the infant to be baptized, was driving with his Queen through the park of Sans-Souci on that sunny spring day. As though to give the lie to his physicians, when the Queen mentioned the baptism's taking place in Berlin, he replied clearly and coherently, "How nice, Elisabeth!"

More guests arrived and were taking their places before the altar under the directions of the Court Chamberlain. Then the signal was given to the Prince Regent's palace over the way. Offering his arm to his wife, the Princess Augusta, the Prince crossed the square on foot. As they entered the chapel the organ began to play. At the altar the Prince of Prussia (it was only later that he received the title of Crown Prince) greeted his relatives in his capacity of happy father. Behind him stood Prince Karl (who was generally disliked), and the Princes Friedrich-Karl, Albrecht (father and son), Alexander, Georg and Adalbert of Prussia; the Grand Duke and Duchess of Saxe-Coburg, and the Hereditary Grand Duchess of Mecklenburg-Strelitz.

It was only a small gathering that watched the ceremony, smaller than had been hoped for, for Grandmother Victoria, Queen of Great Britain, was absent, as were also her Coburg-born Consort, Prince Albert (whose name, by the way, was one of those to be given to the infant), and the representative of the once friendly Court of the Czar.

Next came the Mistress of the Robes, Countess Perponcher, with the child. The little Prince wore a white jacket with a long train supported by two Maids of Honor. Then the Prince Regent took his grandson in his arms, and it was in his grandfather's arms that little Fritz (as he was to be known until he reached the age of six) received baptism.

At the same time the Princess Royal, as people had got into the habit of calling Princess Victoria of Prussia, appeared in the annex to the chapel to take charge of her small son after the reception, and for them both to be blessed by the clergyman.

A blessing lay too on that spring of 1859, for thanks to the calm and steady regency of the future King Wilhelm I, Prussia in those early months began to recover her strength. The evil memories of

Olmütz were slowly fading, a new era of German unification was in
the making, overshadowed by the vague shape of Bismarck,[1] envoy
to the Diet. On March 5, 1859, the day after the baptism, Bismarck
was appointed Prussian Ambassador in St. Petersburg, and a new
era dawned.

The black and white flags were fluttering gaily over the Linden
thronged with people. Over in Cölln a huge transparency had been
erected at the Town Hall depicting Borussia and Britannia engaged
together in the planting of a young sapling in the golden rays of a
rising sun.

2. THE BONBONNIÈRE

FROM THE TIME OF Friedrich Wilhelm III there had been a
large window in the palace on Unter den Linden consisting of a
single pane of glass, and from it one could see clearly the new guard-
house, the arsenal and down the wide street as far as the castle
bridge. There were lots of things to see—cabs with their drivers in
varnished top hats and in the afternoon the strolling promenaders
making their way to Claus's Coffee House in the Tiergarten. But it
was even better in the evening, when the lamps were all lit and
people were hurrying into the near-by Court Opera House or driving
on to a reception at Grandpapa's house, the big house with the eagles
on the roof.

From this window little Fritz gathered his first impressions of the
world, and for him it meant just what it had meant for his grandfather and his great-uncle, who, as children, fifty years before, had
squatted by that same window.

Another important event was the visit to Grandmamma Augusta.
With "Dokka" (as little Fritz called his governess, Fraülein von
Dobeneck) leading him by the hand, he crossed over to the Prince
Regent's palace into the Bonbonnière where his grandmother had
her salon.

Princess Augusta, who two years after the birth of little Fritz
had become Queen of Prussia, exerted a lasting influence on the

[1] *See* Appendix, page 435.

early years of her grandson's youth, all the more easily because the young Princess Royal was more a wife than a mother and remained so as time went on. Thus it came about that the grandmother conceived a special affection for her grandson, and by her special kindness to the boy endeavored to compensate him for the estrangement between him and his mother.

Queen Augusta, formerly the Duchess Augusta of Saxony and Princess of Saxe-Weimar, was not exactly looked upon as an amiable or sweet character at the Court of Berlin. She was generally regarded as cold, conventional, scheming and intellectually arrogant. She was prone to insisting haughtily and much too frequently on the fact that her grandfather, the celebrated Grand Duke Karl August, had been one of the most prominent German princes of his time, head and shoulders above the dozens of other princes of Germany in wealth of ideas and true national sentiment, quite apart from his friendship with Goethe and his advancement of the latter.

Grandmamma Augusta was always glad to refer to Goethe. She spoke of him as "her teacher, on whose knees she had been rocked." Now it was the turn of little Fritz to be rocked on her knees. She was proud, too, of her descent, on her mother's side, from the Grand Duchess Maria Paulovna of Russia, a descendant of the Czar Paul I. Mention of this ancestry used to cause quite understandable surprise among visitors to the Bonbonnière, for it was well known that this "brute with a death's head" had been a lunatic, and most people would be glad not to have him figure in their pedigree.

When the little Prince heard the word Bonbonnière he thought of sweets, pralines and fondants, things he never got from his parents but which were given him all the more freely by his kind grandmother, who was herself fond of sweetmeats. Her pastrycook, Olivier, was a master hand at *petits fours* and the *Gothaer Kranz* that had to be made exactly in accordance with the recipe of Frau Superintendent Herder from Weimar. Naturally "Dokka" had to turn a blind eye, for what would their Royal Highnesses say if they learned that their Fritz was being pampered with dainties?

It was in the Bonbonnière that the Princess Augusta used to receive her talented visitors. Among the frequenters of her salon were Ernst Curtius with the head of an artist and the dreamy eyes of a seer, Hofmann the discoverer of aniline, and before these the old Alexander von Humboldt whose brother Wilhelm once said about the Princess, "She has a firm character. Through her shrewd eyes speaks a lively and penetrating mind which one cannot but admire!"

3. HINZPETER

SOON AFTER coming to Berlin the Princess Victoria, obsessed by the idea of arranging everything according to English standards of hygiene, had half the palace reconstructed in order, as she said, "to let light and air into the house." Bathrooms, at that time almost unknown in Berlin, were installed. Never had such a luxury been available in the palace of the Prince Regent, who once a fortnight used to borrow from the Hôtel de Rome over the way a big wooden tub and, after using it, have it rolled back across the street by a manservant. The improvements concerned the nursery in particular, for the Princess wished that Fritz should have the most thorough schooling in the best atmosphere.

The choice of a teacher presented the young mother with many difficult problems, for she realized that because of her Fritz's willful character there could be no question of any but an experienced, conscientious and strict person for the post.

After a good deal of humming and hawing, Georg Hinzpeter, from Bielefeld, was appointed as tutor to the now seven-year-old Prince, in the spring of 1866. Though only thirty-nine, Hinzpeter had a very mature personality; he was highly educated, not devoid of partiality and ambition. He laid down from the first his principles for the upbringing of his charge. They were embodied in the *mot d'ordre* —"Prussian frugality!—Renunciation!—Hardening of the body!— Diligent study!"

As a tutor he was averse to giving any praise and so was very severe in criticism and reproof when superintending the performance of allotted tasks. Lessons began in summer at 6 A.M., and in winter at 7 A.M., and ended only just before the evening meal, after two breaks, a short one for lunch and an hour for exercise.

Soon after taking over his duties Hinzpeter could see that his pupil was not easy to handle—that he was, in fact, a difficult proposition. Later, he put this in writing:

"Of the union between Guelph obstinacy, easily transformed into energy, and Hohenzollern idealism coupled with willfulness, there was born on January 27, 1859, a human being with a peculiarly strongly marked individuality, which, never having really been modified by anything, and resisting the most powerful exterior influences, developed consistently in its originality."

It was therefore Hinzpeter's duty to be severe, especially as the stubbornness mentioned above showed itself offensively during the first lessons, the intention being to oppose the tedious, didactic pedant by boyish resistance.

The curriculum of instruction drawn up by Hinzpeter met with the immediate approval of the parents, who were glad to have made such a good choice. The emancipated mother felt that they were on common ground when Hinzpeter proposed to rely only on the Bible and a hymnbook for religious instruction: "Fritz must not become priest-ridden!"

Besides the cultivation of the mind, and especially tuition in the English and French languages, Hinzpeter was charged with the physical training of the Prince, by riding, swimming and fencing.

On walks or rides, on a trip from Reinhardsbrunn to the Heuberg, or during an excursion to the Black Forest accompanied by the young Grand Duke Friedrich of Baden, the pedagogue was always close beside the pupil, ready with comments and remarks calculated to stimulate his thoughts. Thus, Hinzpeter utilized the occasion of a tour in the Swabian Jura and a visit to the little castle of Hohenzollern to tell the young Prince the story of his ancestors from the glorious days of past ages onward, and in so doing to hold before him a picture of the immeasurably onerous responsibilities that one day would fall upon him and must be discharged by him in accordance with the five-hundred-year-old Hohenzollern traditions.

During the height of summer the little Prince found he could not follow these endless lectures simply because he was thirsty—but the pedagogue paid no attention. He wanted to accustom his pupil to self-discipline, even at that early stage. Seventy years afterward that pupil could recall how, at that time, every bottle of lemonade on a huckster's stall seemed far more desirable to him than any of the paragons conjured up by Hinzpeter, such as Joachim Friedrich, Nestor and Hector, or the ancestral Irontooth.

Wherever they happened to be, Hinzpeter was always the lecturer and instructor. If they were strolling up and down the Tannenallee in the park of Charlottenburg in front of the mausoleum of his great-great-grandparents, Hinzpeter would take the opportunity of bringing to life the marble effigies of the dead, chiseled by the master hand of Christian Rauch, and of reminding the Prince that he was privileged by fate to be the successor to such great forefathers.

The precepts "that must always be followed" bequeathed in the form of a parchment scroll by Alcuin, Charlemagne's tutor, to his pupil, were also inculcated by Hinzpeter upon his young charges:

> That which pretends to appear big, is always small; that which boasts of its strength, tries to cover up its well-known weakness by noise. He who is secure in himself, loves peace, for he has no occasion to disturb it. He who wantonly seeks to disturb the peace is unsure of himself and dares not remain at peace himself!

Despite his rebellion against the authority of his inconvenient mentor, Fritz made good progress. He had already learned to read and write from the student-teacher Schüler, so that Hinzpeter was in a position to report that he had completed his elementary schooling. He produced a new and wider plan of education at the palace and this was approved without question by the parents.

The seven-year-old boy could not appreciate his tutor's sound teaching at its true worth. Only later did he understand and admit that Hinzpeter's counsel had always been good—better in any case than that given him subsequently by his own entourage.

4. IN THE PARK OF SANS-SOUCI

KAISER WILHELM II, grown old and speaking of the days of his youth, said, "A great city, with its sea of stone, far removed from nature, is not for young people. Our joy was always great when in the spring we removed to Potsdam. For weeks before it happened we looked forward to the moment when the great business of the move to the Neues Palais—to freedom—should begin. Potsdam became my second and beloved home. I was happy there. I often cast my mind back to the simple little room with its round window on the second floor—it is a sweet but sad memory!"

Little Fritz's playground at Potsdam was laid out on spacious lines and full of splendors that in part dated back to the time of the Great Frederick. There were the Temples of Friendship and Antiquity, the flower terrace of the Orangery over which there spread in autumn a wonderful golden-brown carpet of leaves interspersed with great violet asters. Then there was the Roman Bath and the Chinese Pavilion with its strange pigtailed, grinning Mongols and yawning, greeny-gold dragons; the Great Fountain and a steep flight of steps at Sans-Souci, which to the boy seemed like a sanctuary.

One day his father took him into the little Schloss to show him the rooms in which his great ancestor had lived. The little Prince followed him on tip-toe, for even the parquet floor seemed to him so venerable that he scarcely dared to set foot on it. From the side of the drive leading to the "Vigne," as Frederick the Great called his hermitage—he seldom referred to it as Sans-Souci—the Ruinenberg can be seen. Behind it stretched the Bornstedter Feld, the great training ground of the Potsdam garrison. Here, on the slopes of the Ruinenberg, the young Prince found a fine playground for games of "Robber and Soldier," and a smaller piece of ground where he could play at "Maneuvers" with other boys of officers' families from Potsdam, such as Rex Haenisch, Mortimer von Rauch and Eugen von Roeder. A variation of these games was enjoined when Poultney Bigelow, a young American, took part. Then they went on the warpath—exactly as the Mohicans did over in Delaware.

Those hours of freedom on the Ruinenberg could not, however, be allowed to encroach upon the hours of study—Hinzpeter saw to that. Nor were duties of a social character to be neglected. Into this category fell visits to his great-aunt and great-great-aunt, who resided on the periphery of the park of Sans-Souci.

After the death of Friedrich Wilhelm IV the widowed Queen Elisabeth continued to live at the Orangery which held for her so many sad memories. The gray-haired Kaiser described her later in Doorn [1] as "an old lady who, in spite of her lovable character, in-

---

[1] Dutch village near which Kaiser Wilhelm II lived in exile from 1920 until his death in 1941.

spired everyone with the greatest respect." In her drawing room she had a wooden model of "the Heavenly Jerusalem," provided with removable cupolas, which must have made a special impression on the boy, since seventy years afterward he remembered every detail of that wooden wonder.

Of the Princess Liegnitz, by birth a Countess Harrach too, the Kaiser had an excellent recollection. "Among the relatives that I used to visit as a youngster I often think of her. She was the second wife of my great-grandfather Friedrich Wilhelm III. I remember her as a sunny, gentle, kind old lady who won the admiration of all the members of our House. My parents were greatly attached to her and often sent me to her with flowers. She lived in a villa called after her near the entrance to the park. All her life she kept her difficult position with the utmost tact and thereby won the love and respect of everyone."

Thus the early years of the little Prince passed between the Villa Liegnitz and Sans-Souci. He could not have anticipated then that sixty years afterward he would be calling his step-great-grand-mother and Friedrich Wilhelm III as chief witnesses for himself in connection with the formalities of the second marriage that he was contemplating in his old age.

5. THE "LONG STABLE"

IT WAS the beginning of great times that opened soon after the birth of Prince Wilhelm, as he was called after attaining the age of seven. In 1862 Bismarck was called to the Ministry of Foreign Affairs and the office of Minister President. Two years later Austrian regiments were tramping through Berlin with drums beating and trumpets sounding, to march together with Prussian troops to the attack on Denmark. A few weeks later they marched back again, victorious, with the captured *Danebrog,* which, after being displayed at a parade by the Prince's palace, was brought to the arsenal.

Within two years the Prussian Army was on the move again, but this time it was against Austria, who week after week suffered fresh reverses until the final decision was reached at Königgrätz.[1] Linked with the name of the battle rang another name, that of the victor, the Army Commander, the Crown Prince.

Full of youthful enthusiasm the young Prince awaited the homecoming of his father from the field. Sounds of cheering from the direction of the Brandenburger Tor announced his approach. Then the tall figure on horseback came in sight. At the palace he swung himself lightly from the saddle to greet his wife and children. Something new about his father caught the little Prince's attention—it was the blue cross hanging below the long sandy side whiskers, the *Pour le Mérite,* the victory badge of Königgrätz.

The rejoicings of the homecoming were interrupted by the death of little Prince Sigismund. The disconsolate mother had to suffer for the first time the loss of a child, and what is more, of one that she declared to be her favorite child. Usually well able to control her emotions she was now, as she said herself, almost out of her mind.

"Times of brass" such as those between 1864 and 1870 required that the future King of Prussia should soon begin his military training. Captain von Schrötter of the Guards Field Artillery Regiment was appointed as his military tutor. So there was an end to playing at soldiers and the stern Prussian service began.

Prince Wilhelm was now nine years old and in a few months' time he would, according to the traditional practice of the House of Hohenzollern, enter the Army with the rank of Lieutenant. "I did not have an easy time; my mother saw to that," the aged Kaiser confessed in Doorn. "Like every 'rooky,' early every morning while it was still dark I had to be in the Long Stable, the Drill Hall of the 1st Regiment of Foot Guards where we practiced *Griffe kloppen* (the manual exercise) and were taught to march. People may laugh at it today, but it was then a good way of inculcating discipline, which is as necessary now as it ever was where good order has to be maintained. I can still see my sergeant-major with the fat notebook stuck between the two top buttons of his tunic. He used to make me fall in, and examined my dress to see if any powder from the white belt had fallen on my blue regimentals, or if any greasy polishing paste had got through the button stick onto the red binding. To this

[1] Bohemian town of predominantly Czech population where the Prussians overwhelmed the Austrians in 1866. Also known as Sadowa.

day I remember the smell of that "Cupid Paste"! Then I had to be fitted with a high helmet—it was far too big for me, so they had to have one specially made. I also learned to beat a drum. My instructor was a Sergeant Klee who treated me just the same as the other drummers. Of course it is a Potsdam tradition that Prussian princes on duty are not spared anything. Like every other Grenadier recruit, I, with my nine years, had to train on the Bornstedter Feld and take part in the *Up!* and *Lie Down!* with the usual assault on 'Angermann's Coachhouse.' "

It was a world almost unchanged from that of the Great Frederick or even from that of his father. It was in the Long Stable that the Potsdam *Wachtparade* (nickname given to the Prussian Army) was first taught. People laughed at it at the time because of its rigid drill movements, until Rossbach and Leuthen had shown that rigid drill movements were not to be derided. The men in the Long Stable were not the same, but the picture had scarcely altered, so it would not have seemed very surprising had the door opened suddenly and the Great King or his father, alive and in the flesh, stepped into the Drill Hall. Neither of them would have had far to go, for they both rest under the chancel of the Garrison Church only a few paces distant.

If Von Schrötter, his military tutor, contributed a good deal to awaken in the Prince a devotion to soldiering, it was really his grandfather, King Wilhelm, who first implanted in the boy the love of arms, of the vocation of the officer and of the Army. "From my earliest youth," said his grandson afterward, "the exalted gentleman followed my military career with unceasing care and kindness."

In order to see his grandson more often and to give him instruction, the King often invited him to a meal in his writing room, where they both ate at a rickety little card table and the Prince got only a sherry glass of champagne. The grandfather was fond of telling stories of the past, about the events of the wars in Schleswig and Bohemia, or of his own baptism of fire at Bar-sur-Aube, more than fifty years before. He insisted upon personally conducting the ceremony of commissioning his young grandson as Lieutenant, on January 27, 1869, when, in accordance with the tradition of his House, he conferred on him the High Order of the Black Eagle.

When the Prince stood before his Supreme War Lord for the first time in the uniform of a Lieutenant in the 1st Regiment of Foot

Guards the King looked at once delighted and serious. He addressed him as the youngest Lieutenant, admonishing him that as such he must do his duty as his father and forefathers, being Prussian officers, had always done.

"With this, my commissioning, my youth was ended," declared the old Kaiser afterward in Doorn; "I was no longer allowed to visit the Christmas Market in Berlin, nor play with tin soldiers, nor attend the performances for children at Renz's Circus."

Three months after being commissioned Prince Wilhelm took part in his first Review. The troops paraded in the Potsdam Lustgarten and the 1st Regiment of Guards led the March Past, with the little Prince bringing up the rear as a *serre-file* officer. Standing surrounded by the colors of the famous regiments the old Ruler smilingly returned the salute of his youngest Lieutenant. As the drums rolled, the regimental march struck up and the peal of bells from the tower of the Garrison Church joined in with its warning note *Üb immer Treu und Redlichkeit.*[2]

The Duke of Argyll, brother-in-law of the Crown Princess Victoria, who at this parade met his nephew Wilhelm for the first time, expressed his opinion of him as follows:

"This little Prince Wilhelm may possibly become the best king that Prussia has had since Frederick the Great—provided he lives!"

6. ILLNESS AND TREATMENT

THIS APPREHENSION on the part of the Duke of Argyll— "provided the Prince lives"—was not unfounded. The Court doctors were afraid that the crippled arm might impede the circulation of the blood, affect the whole system, and involve grave consequences. They advised electrical treatment, which was given, but with little success. The patient himself said afterward about this:

"In consequence of an injury sustained at birth and overlooked at the time the arm was retarded in its development. In those days medical science did not possess the orthopedic equipment with which

[2] "Always be faithful and sincere," beginning of a church hymn, played at the full hour.

such a condition could today be remedied. In any case I was treated in all sorts of ways that could only be regarded now as amateurish. The only result was that I was made to suffer great torture."

Though the right arm became all the better developed and stronger, as does happen in such cases, the Prince could not make it compensate for the enfeebled left, nor succeed in learning to ride his pony. Hinzpeter was determined not to tolerate this failure of his pupil. The old gentleman of Doorn commented thus on the matter:

"It often happens that in our old age we judge more leniently the schoolmasters and fellow pupils, our relations and our enemies who seemed odious to us when we were young, and we may even forgive them because we realize that they did not mean badly at the time. Hinzpeter was a really good fellow. Whether he was the right tutor for me, I dare not decide. The torments he inflicted on me, especially in this pony riding, must be attributed to my mother. The thought that I, as heir to the Throne, should not be able to ride, was to her intolerable. But I felt I was not fit for it because of my disability. I was worried and afraid. When there was nobody near I wept."

About what took place in the sidetracks of Sans-Souci Hinzpeter reported:

"A groom had to lead the Prince's pony on a leading rein, as his sense of insecurity caused him unconquerable anxiety. As long as this persisted there could be no question of his learning to ride. It had to be overcome at any cost. But as neither groom nor riding master was able to achieve this, it was left to the tutor alone to assert his now absolute moral authority, lifting the weeping Prince onto the stirrupless pony, deaf to all his prayers and tears, pitilessly insisting on practice of the various paces, and mercilessly hoisting him back into the saddle when he fell off, which he did continually, until at last, after weeks of pain and trouble, the indispensable sense of balance, so difficult to acquire, was attained."

During this time of his grievous affliction the Prince found solace in books. He read a great deal of English, for he had learned to speak that language very early, from his mother. She gave him copies of the works of Charles Dickens, Walter Scott and Byron. In Byron he found the bitter complaint, so intelligible to himself—"Ah! I would give my all not to have this deformed foot. Every day it reminds me that I am a cripple!"

When the doctors thought a cure necessary for the Prince, Hinz-

peter and his pupil went to Bad Rehme, the present-day Oeyn-
hausen. With them in the Prince's party were Mortimer von Rauch
and the two Bunsen brothers.

In Rehme the first symptoms of an ear trouble showed themselves.
"The Prince has suffered considerably from pain in the ear," so
Hinzpeter described it in a report to the parents in Potsdam. "The
complaint is of a scrofulous nature." One of the Court physicians
expressed himself more pessimistically later—he strongly advised
the general manager of the Gotha Life Insurance not to issue a policy
on the life of Prince Wilhelm. "I cannot recommend the Prince to
you. I cannot answer for his expectation of life, for the discharge
from the ear is incurable and will one day affect the brain."

Hinzpeter, fated to spend sleepless nights wrestling with the
vision of the mentally deranged Friedrich Wilhelm IV, with the
ghost of the mad Czar Paul and the spirits of a whole bevy of his
little charge's unsound forebears in the Low Countries, did not lose
heart. In a letter, hitherto unpublished, to a factory manager in
Bielefeld he expressed his own confidence in the future:

"In any case, children often develop in a wonderful way and quite
differently from what is expected, or is very often feared, and
this is so even where they are afflicted with some bodily defect.
Caesar and Nelson are surely to be regarded as world heroes and
as such will be recognized in world history, yet they were demon-
strably epileptics."

7. THE SEA

In JULY 1869 Prince Wilhelm had his first glimpse of the
sea—the North Sea. A trip was made to Heligoland, where the British Governor Maxse insisted on showing the little grandson of his
great Queen round the island himself. Outside in the roads there
lay only a few English patrol boats. In Wilhelmshaven he saw a real
warship for the first time. It was the *König Wilhelm*, the largest unit
of the Prussian Fleet. The impression made on the young Prince
after visiting this "floating fortress" was a lasting one, yet the

"fortress" offered only the romantic allure of a frigate with a few guns stuck into her.

This adventure was given wider scope by a trip to Cannes, then only a little fishing village which, however, had been discovered by Lord Brougham and was already patronized by "Uncle Bertie." To each of them a statue was erected by the grateful population of Cannes.

They put up in the Hôtel de la Méditerranée together with relatives from Darmstadt and The Hague, and toward Christmastime were joined by the Prince's father, who was on his way home from the festivities at the opening of the Suez Canal and wished to be with his children—three sons and a daughter—for the feast.

The father never tired of telling his attentive audience of children about his travels in Egypt and Palestine, how the first ship to pass the Canal—with himself on board—traversed the waterway between wide stretches of sandy desert, how he had climbed the Pyramid of Cheops and seen the mummies of the Pharaohs in Cairo. Then about the days spent by the Sea of Genezareth (Tiberias) and a vivid description of the holy places of Bethlehem and Golgotha.

He often took his two sons, Wilhelm and the eight-year-old Heinrich, about with him. They visited the Jardin des Hespérides, la Croisette and the port, going by boat from there to the Iles de Lérins. It is said that the "Man in the Iron Mask" was confined in the fort on the island of Ste. Marguerite, a mysterious prisoner whom his guards addressed only after removing their hats, and who was served at table on gold plate.[1]

So romantic an island means much to young people especially as here were to be seen Algerian Spahis in their white *burnous*, with pitch-black eyes, who were part of the garrison. Three years later these Spahis were mounting guard over the disgraced Marshal Bazaine, who had played such a sorry and tragic part in the defense of Metz against the Prussians.

[1] Evidence sufficiently conclusive to establish the identity of this unfortunate individual is still to be sought. The extraordinary precautions taken indicate that he must have been a personage of great importance and one whose "liquidation" was inadvisable. Two speculations hold the field: (*a*) that he was an inconvenient twin brother of Louis XIV, to be treated with the deference shown by the story of the gold plate and doffed hats; (*b*) that he was an Italian diplomat accused of treason by that King and imprisoned at Pignerol (Pinerolo) in Piedmont, then under French domination. He was, in any case, ultimately transferred to the Bastille in Paris. (*Trans.*)

The run back to Cannes was highly unpleasant, for a violent mistral was blowing and made the little vessel roll heavily. Prince Wilhelm was seasick, and even long afterward, when he was an Admiral, he never quite overcame the tendency if the weather was rough.

After Christmas the parents returned to Berlin, while Wilhelm and Heinrich stayed on at the Villa Gabriella with Hinzpeter for a few months. During this time they paid a visit to the naval base of Toulon, where they saw the powerful armored ship *La Provence*, double the size of the old *König Wilhelm*. A year before Wilhelm had seen, at Krupp's, the largest steam hammer in Europe. Naturally he asked Hinzpeter why Prussia did not build ships like *La Provence*. Hinzpeter explained that Prussia, being a land power of the first order and having the best-trained army in Europe, had no need for a great fleet. France and England, being sea powers, had to have strong fleets. They also had an opportunity in Toulon of seeing the snow-white pleasure yacht *Aigle* in which the Empress Eugénie [2] had just returned from the Suez Canal festivities.

Varied and interesting as the experiences of those eight months on the Riviera had been, both the Princes were now feeling anxious to return to Germany. They greeted with joy Hinzpeter's decision to set out in May on the homeward journey to Potsdam.

In the summer they went again to the seaside—to Wyk on Föhr, where Friedrich Wilhelm IV's screw yacht *Grille* lay. She was far nicer than the old sailing frigate *Royal Louise*, a present from King William IV of England to Friedrich Wilhelm III and now stationed on the Jungfernsee at Potsdam.

In the *Grille* her Captain, Ratzeburg, a jovial and kindly man, allowed the young people to romp about on deck and below, to ask questions which he, an old seadog, sometimes found it not easy to answer. These questions were mostly put by Prince Wilhelm, for Heinrich, the younger one, was not particularly thirsty for knowledge and was even rather indolent, a matter which caused Hinzpeter and the parents some concern. Nevertheless Heinrich did learn in the *Grille* the elementary principles of seamanship which later on provided a foundation for his career in the Navy.

The Princes also learned the flag alphabet and signaling, and at the same time were instructed in the use of the compass. Their playmates in Wyk were Ernst and Hermann von Salza, both of whom

[2] Wife of Emperor Napoleon III of France.

were to accompany the Princes on a trip in the gunboat *Blitz*, commanded by Kapitän-Leutnant (Lieutenant Commander) Glomsda von Buchholtz.

On board this vessel their interest was above all else concentrated on the gun which a short time before had become rather famous for having fired a warning shot across the bows of a British steam trawler. The skipper of the trawler had not considered it necessary to dip his ensign in salute to the Prussian warship. After that unmistakable reminder, however, the Englishman made amends for his negligence, greatly to the satisfaction of the Prussian crew.

It may be that it was here on board *Blitz* that an association of ideas first occurred to the young Prince Wilhelm—if you are concerned for your honor, you must have a gun, a warship, a fleet . . . especially for use against England!

After this cruise Prince Wilhelm stayed on for some time at Wyk. He liked to visit the quiet farmhouse of the painter Magnussen, who taught him to sketch. In contradistinction to his mother, who painted landscapes in England, Spahis in Ste. Marguerite and still life in Potsdam, her son preferred subjects other than the mallows and sunflowers that flourished on the island of Föhr—sailing boats, frigates, warships (little ones like the *Blitz* and bigger ones too) and, finally, fleets.

"Uncle Bertie," afterward King Edward VII, heard from his sister, the Crown Princess Victoria, about "William's progress." He praised "William" and urged him to persevere. But he had no inkling of the fact that this nephew of his was already dreaming of building a German Navy—for use against England!

8. IMPERIAL ROMANTICISM

ONE EVENING in 1936, in the tower at Doorn, the Kaiser talked about his father and the year 1870: "I remember very well his coming into our room one morning and saying to Mlle Darcourt, with every sign of excitement, '*Eh, mademoiselle! Vos compatriotes ont perdu la tête! Ils veulent nous faire la guerre!*'"

The same morning the Crown Prince summoned his eldest son

and explained in a few words that for the third time it was war . . .
and this time against France. He, his father, was to be the Commander of the newly formed Southern Army, and would be taking
over that command within the next few days.

Firm as a rock was the young Prince's confidence that his father
would soon return home victorious. Pleased at this assurance of his
pupil, Hinzpeter strove to make clear to his little charge the gravity
of the moment, the blamelessness of Prussia for its occurrence and
the "aggressive attitude of France." He hung up in the schoolroom
a large map of France—so sure was he that the fighting would take
place on the far side of the Rhine—on which to make clear at a
glance the deployment and lines of advance of the German armies.

Wörth! The first important success in the struggle! With its name
was coupled, in all the special editions of the newspapers throughout Germany, the name of the Army Commander. When the news
came, Unter den Linden was transformed into a sea of flags. Enthusiastic crowds rushed to the palace, where the Kaiserin Augusta,
visibly affected, appeared at a window. Then they rushed on farther,
to the palace of the Crown Prince where, however, everyone seemed
to be asleep behind the curtained windows.

Seemed to be! For in reality everyone was up and doing. The
Crown Princess Victoria was sitting at her worktable writing to her
husband, Hinzpeter was studying the latest reports in the schoolroom, while the young Princes, hiding behind the window curtains,
listened to the uproar in the street until in the joy of victory they
started a wild battle of their own, with the cushions.

After that they quietly got dressed, tiptoed down the stairs to the
door that opened onto the Oberwallstrasse, which stood open and
unguarded. From there it was only a few steps to the Linden, where
they hastily gathered up the copies of the special newspaper editions
that lay about on the ground and hurried back with them to the
palace. When the news items had been thoroughly studied, the sheets
were soaked with hair oil and set alight to provide a festive illumina-
tion for their bedroom. In the schoolroom their tutor knew nothing
of this unauthorized outing or of his pupils' bonfire.

Successes at Nancy, Bar-le-Duc and Bar-sur-Aube followed. It
was in this district that their grandfather had fought more than fifty
years before, as a Lieutenant. Captured French standards and flags
were brought to the palace, and Hinzpeter held forth to the young

Prince on the high honor it was to belong to an army with such a victorious record.

But he was not allowed to remain ignorant of the other side of war. The Crown Princess removed to the Taunus with her children, to establish and manage a hospital in Homburg vor der Höhe. In that hospital Prince Wilhelm visited the victims, the wounded, the mutilated and the dying.

News of a fresh victory was filtering into Homburg. This time the Princes were asleep, but even the thick ivy-clad walls of the old castle could not exclude the clamorous voices in the street. They were singing the *Wacht am Rhein!* A leap, and they were at the window. Below them they saw, like a huge glowworm, a torchlight procession that was approaching, hemmed around by jubilant masses of people all shouting the same word, a place name that only a few hours before scarcely anyone in Germany had heard of . . . Sedan! [1]

The ensuing historical events—the entry of the German troops into Paris, the proclamation of his grandfather as Emperor of Germany at Versailles, and the conclusion of peace, were things whose political consequences and material effects were beyond the comprehension of the eleven-year-old boy. But he heard the salvos and the maroons that heralded the peace, the cheering of exultant people and the name of that other emperor, Napoleon, now a prisoner in the hands of his grandfather. With this name and that of his father, the Crown Prince, were recalled also the names of the great paladins, Bismarck, Moltke [2] and Roon,[3] who in the imagination of the young Prince attained the stature of the giants of the legendary Germanic ages.

Nevertheless there was one definite conclusion that Prince Wilhelm could draw from all these victories—after his grandfather and his father, he would become not only King of Prussia but also German Emperor.

For the reception of the new Kaiser and the Crown Prince, the Princes accompanied their mother, Grandmother Augusta and Aunt

[1] Town in northern France where Prussians won decisive victory in 1870 and where Guderian's tanks broke through French lines in 1940.

[2] Count Helmuth von Moltke (1800–1891), Prussian Field Marshal who commanded the victorious Prussian armies in the war against France in 1870.

[3] Field Marshal Albrecht von Roon (1803–1879), chief organizer of the Prussian armies that defeated Denmark, Austria, and France.

Luise (Grand Duchess of Baden) to meet the triumphant party at Potsdam. It was the sixteenth of June, 1871; the Crown Prince had been parted from his family for a whole year. The entry into Berlin was at once simple and splendid, the city being now exalted to the status of capital of the Reich. To his great delight Prince Wilhelm participated in the ceremonial entry, riding behind his father and by the side of his uncle, the Grand Duke of Baden, on a little piebald pony.

A tumultuous welcome greeted the aged Kaiser as, with his son, the paladins and the Army leaders, he rode through the Brandenburger Tor. The dream of the patriots—the unification of Germany, which the Wars of Liberation had failed to bring about—was now achieved.

The cavalcade rode between lines of captured French guns and *mitrailleuses* down Unter den Linden as far as the Lustgarten, where stood the memorial to Friedrich Wilhelm III, still shrouded in a covering veil. As guns thundered in salute, the veil fell from the equestrian statue of the unfortunate King, and the Kaiser, his son, saluted it with his sword.

Fifty-six captured French standards and flags were laid round the plinth of the monument—by way of satisfaction for Saalfeld, Jena, Memel and Tilsit.

The twenty-first of March (1871), which was also the eve of Kaiser Wilhelm's seventy-fourth birthday, had been fixed for the summoning of the newly constituted Reichstag. Prince Wilhelm was present at the opening ceremony in the White Hall. The assembled Federal princes were painfully surprised to find that the ancient throne of the German emperors, brought specially from Goslar for the occasion, had been set up by the side of the chapel. They saw in this a challenge, a claim by the Hohenzollern to an overriding authority that in their view ran counter to the new Constitution of the Reich. This envisaged only a Kaiser and Federal princes, all with equal rights, not an Emperor in the sense of the Middle Ages of the time of the Goslar Palatinate.

The wave of excitement died down when it was understood that Kaiser Wilhelm had known nothing at all about the fetching of the throne and that this had been arranged by the Crown Prince Friedrich alone. Following his bent for romanticism he had hit upon the idea of enhancing the significance of this first official act of the new Kaiser by providing a venerable if stony witness thereto, one that was both solemn and appropriate to the occasion.

Gustav Freytag, the writer, appears to have been in part responsible in this matter. He had always exerted a detrimental influence on the Crown Prince by encouraging his romantic proclivities.

It had also been Freytag who at Christmas 1870 had suggested to the Crown Prince that he ought to join with the Federal princes in proclaiming, not a Kaiser, but a hereditary German King. Then each of the Federal princes would be accorded the status of Herzog (Duke), like the former Dukes of Saxony and Swabia. A plan of this kind, which the Crown Prince had never taken seriously, would have been indignantly rejected by King Ludwig II of Bavaria, in spite of the bent for romanticism which he shared with the Crown Prince.

Prince Wilhelm also became acquainted with Freytag, who soon (and deservedly) achieved fame as the author of *Bilder aus der deutschen Vergangenheit (Pictures from the German Past)*. Nevertheless, he was disappointed in the man—whose bourgeois manners and whose Silesian dialect, perhaps, and his vague way of speaking and expressing himself, proved repellent to the Prince.

Freytag's influence, however, continued to be felt in the palace of the Crown Prince. Books recommended by the writer were in favor, such as that sumptuous work of the historian Bock, in which the romance of the Middle Ages comes to life again and the story of the treasures of the old Empire is told in inspiring language.

The young Prince read that book, whose content aroused romantic leanings in the eleven-year-old boy, already inclined to flights of the imagination, and gave him false ideas that by no means operated for his good.

Between the pages of Bock's work his father had inserted numerous slips of paper, with notes supplementing the various chapters. These were based upon his own research in various churches and burial places and in the castle of Nuremberg. The latter the Crown Prince declared to be the proper place for the preservation of the relics of the Old Reich, which in his opinion had been wrongfully retained in the Secular Treasury of the Imperial Palace in Vienna.

Enmeshed in the past, in the history of the German people of the Holy Roman Empire, the Crown Prince went so far, to the aston-

ishment and anger of Bismarck, as to voice again—in spite of unfavorable experiences—his fantastic ideas for the future: that, with
reference to the Staufen Emperor Friedrich II [4] and to the Habs-
burg Friedrich III,[5] he should become known as Kaiser Friedrich
IV at his accession.

9. THE MONK AND THE SIBYL

ONE FINE AUTUMN DAY IN 1872 the Crown Prince ordered
his shooting brake and took his wife, his two sons and Hinzpeter
for an excursion. The boys would greatly have preferred to go
shooting, for Prince Wilhelm had that season shot his first pheasant
and experienced the joys of the chase. But their father had other
plans for that day—he wanted to inspect the ruined monastery of
Lehnin in order to decide after a personal survey whether later on,
when he became Kaiser, he should have the monastery rebuilt.

Lehnin had been once the Mother House of four Cistercian
houses in the March, and so was the oldest and most venerable of
them all. Hinzpeter had for years been familiar with its history, so
for this occasion he became the guide. He told of the legendary
founding of the monastery and gave a description of the various
buildings that now lay in ruins, overgrown by barberries and ivy. A
few ancient gravestones showed that eleven Ascanian Margraves
and three Hohenzollerns had been buried there.

The fact that three ancestors had found their last resting place in
Lehnin determined the Crown Prince to have something done at
once. Having summoned the President of the District Council to
meet him in the "King's House," which once provided lodgings for
princely guests, he gave him instructions to begin by having all the
rubbish removed and the heaps of ruins made tidy. He was not to
incur any great expense.

However, what the Crown Prince proposed to do about the restoration of the monastery was not entirely due to his piety or his
romantic bent. Rather did it concern the *Vaticinium Lehninense*, the

[4] 1194–1250; crowned Holy Roman Emperor in 1220.
[5] 1415–93; crowned Holy Roman Emperor in 1452.

Lehnin Oracle, written by a Brother Hermann and foretelling for the Hohenzollerns their destinies for hundreds of years to come.

The Hohenzollerns knew yet another oracle, the prophecies of the so-called "Sibyl of Silesia." Around 1807 she must have enjoyed the highest repute, for in that disastrous year for Prussia Queen Luise paid a visit to this fortuneteller.

What the Sibyl told the Queen was attested and handed down:

The Queen's eldest son (*Friedrich Wilhelm IV*) would be "of little importance" to his country. (*He died insane in* 1861.)

But the second son (*Wilhelm I*) would unite the Germans. (*He became Emperor of Germany in* 1871.)

He who came next (*Friedrich III*) would have only a short reign. (*He reigned for three months.*)

His son (*Wilhelm II*), "bearing a mark," would follow, and under him Germany would experience a catastrophe. "On fleeing to a wood in Upper Lusatia this last of the Hohenzollerns will cry out in lamentation—'Where is my country? What has become of my people?' "

Apart from the last sentence, the prophecy of the Sibyl of Silesia was to be exactly fulfilled.

Hinzpeter, the Westphalian Calvinist, would have nothing to do with all this. He once said in a letter "prophecies are nothing but mental aberrations." Parson Flesch of Lehnin undertook to give them a commentary on the *Vaticinium*. The surroundings were well adapted to make the parson's exposition a living thing. Here in the Zauche the first Zoller had planted his banner in the sandy soil, the old "sandbox" of the Reich. It is a peculiar tract of country, rich in lakes, pine trees . . . and legends. The tall tree trunks and, seen between them, the arched windows of the old monastery walls were tinged with dull red in the afterglow of sunset. Pious monks used to sing their Vespers up there. They say that even today, Valentine, the last Abbot, appears on the wall by night, with his pointed cap and his buttons as big as hens' eggs, and that in winter too one can see, on the ice of the monastery pond, the hind (*lanye* in the Slavic language) that seems to have given Lehnin its name.

And there is another ghostly apparition that lives here in Lehnin (though some say it comes from Orlamünde)—the White Woman, who always appears in the Berlin Schloss whenever a Hohenzollern is about to die. The Great Elector (of Brandenburg), however, had to see her twice; he died only after her *second* appearance.

Parson Flesch knew the verses of the *Vaticinium* by heart. At the request of the Crown Prince he recited some passages from it during an evening stroll round the lake, beginning with the sonorous Leonine verses from the year 1235 [1] in which they were recorded. Translated from the Latin they run:

> *Jetzo mit Kummer, Lehnin,*
> *Dir sing ich die künftgen Geschicke,*
> *Welche geoffenbart mir der Herr,*
> *Der Alles erschaffen!*

This may be crudely paraphrased in English by:

> *'Tis with grief and bitter sorrow*
> *Lehnin, that to thee I sing*
> *Of what our fate shall be tomorrow,*
> *Revealed me by the Heavenly King*
> *Who created everything!*

After sixty such verses the prophetic monk alludes to the first Hohenzollern to appear in the March—the Burgrave Friedrich of Nuremberg:

> *Klimmst Du aus Niedrigkeit nun*
> *Durch zwei der Burgen berühmt auf,*
> *Zündest den Krieg sofort an,*
> *Nur im Namen prahlend mit Frieden!*

Which may likewise be paraphrased as:

> *If now from lowliness you seek to climb*
> *Because in two towns famous for a time,*
> *At once the dogs of war you will unleash*
> *And ruin bring, whilst still you prate of Peace!*

So the prophecy goes on for hundreds of years until it ends with words that ring out like a sworn affirmation:

[1] According to new research, it may have been composed as late as 1620 by an unknown author; both date and contents are subjects of fierce controversies.

> *Dico tibi verum!*
> *Und nun sage ich Dir die Wahrheit!*
>
> *And now I tell you the Truth!*

the "truth" being the end of the Hohenzollern overlordship after exactly 500 years. Reckoning from 1414, the year 1914 would correspond to that of the predicted downfall.

It seems that Brother Hermann of Lehnin was not very far out.

10. THE PRINCESS ROYAL

THE CROWN PRINCESS VICTORIA had her studio in the arch connecting the first floor of the Crown Prince's palace with her own adjoining palace. Its windows looked out on the Linden and the Oberwallstrasse, thus receiving light from two sides. Her library was there also. The books, on open shelves, were almost exclusively English.

Here Prince Wilhelm used to read aloud to his mother from the latest publications, while she sat at her easel; in English, of course, for his mother had no liking for any other language.

Her kitchen was English, the menus were written in English and the menservants were English. She called herself "Vicky" and her sons "William" and "Henry." Her code in all things was that of the Court of St. James and she would tolerate nothing that ran counter to her English ideas.

This consciousness and striving were permanent characteristics of the Crown Princess; she kept them so much in the foreground that she tended to eclipse her husband, the heir to the Throne. This predominance was viewed with increasing apprehension in Conservative circles. People listened with displeasure when the Crown Prince paid homage to English liberal institutions and recommended them as an example to Prussia.

The Junkers (minor nobility and squirearchy) held "the Englishwoman" responsible for this deviation and the attitude of their Crown Prince and made no secret of their antipathy to the Princess.

She felt hurt by their affronts and spoke disdainfully of the "needy gentry," a miserable lot who did not impress her at all. "There's more silver in Birmingham than in all Prussia taken together!"

Such flippant remarks brought Bismarck into the field. Soon after the wedding of the Crown Prince he wrote to a friend: "Royal weddings usually mean that the House from which the bride comes exerts an influence in the House into which she enters, and not vice versa. All the more often is this the case when the fatherland of the bride is the more powerful and has developed a stronger sense of nationality than that of the husband." Later, he gave it as his conviction that "The Crown Princess has never given up looking on England as her fatherland."

She herself looked on Bismarck as her archenemy; she openly showed that she hated him with all her heart. She never dissembled it. If she was defeated in a dispute with him, she shed, as she confessed herself, "enough tears for Bismarck's sake to fill buckets."

She credited him with every kind of malignity, especially in any matter touching herself. She believed blindly all that anyone told her about him, even to his having alluded to her as "that English mare who is now corrupting the whole breed." If he ever really did say such a thing, it must have been among intimate friends and inspired by champagne!

In defense of the Princess it must be said that she came from an environment very different from the Court of Berlin, which was wholly strange to her, and to a Prussia whose manners and customs were quite unlike those of England. Her position was made all the more difficult by the fact that she brought with her a very poor sense of adaptability to circumstances and that her character was, as even her friends recognized, extremely complex.

She always retained her astonishingly good memory. Her knowledge of literature and her excellent education went with an energy and an ardent temperament that easily led her into outbursts, especially in argument, which she always tried to dominate, brooking no contradiction. Above all, she was uncompromisingly determined to exercise authority! Did the chance of doing so come her way she knew no fear. Frankness was her finest attribute. Always an honorable adversary, she was a good hater. She had a horror of hypocrisy in politics. Though she was English, "cant" was foreign to her nature.

Her manner was assured but often haughty, and what she said was well considered. She spoke German, French and Italian fluently.

As a good Englishwoman she loved sport, especially swimming and riding, also driving. Strict and energetic, she grasped things quickly and was unsparing of relentless criticism whether in matters of politics or art. She had a predilection for aphorisms, which she rated as valid axioms: "Any style is good if it is clear," or "Politics are a business fit only for people who have seen the world!"

Despite her firmly held and loudly proclaimed affectation of superiority, the Crown Princess could be in two minds. Her brother "Bertie" (afterward King Edward VII), pointing out this trait, said of her: "When Vicky was in Germany she praised everything English, but when she was at home Berlin was the only place for her!"

The longer she lived in Germany the more stiff and statuesque she became. A Berlin sculptor likened her to the Madonna of Giovanni Pisano, behind whose marble mask lay hidden the true face of a distracted woman.

This mask, always kept ready for defense, made it difficult to maintain social relations with her. As she herself declared, she felt at ease only when at home, or perhaps in the Schleinitz salon. The Schleinitz family belonged to the Bismarck-Fronde (the anti-Bismarck party), the husband, coming from the old school of Manteuffel, was Minister of the Royal Household and lived in the palace at 73 Wilhelmstrasse. Marie von Schleinitz, generally called Mimi, was an enthusiastic dilettante in science and art who understood how to gather to her salon a circle of such important people as Helmholtz, Mommsen, Menzel and Richter, and to canvass for Richard Wagner and his projected Festival Playhouse in Bayreuth.

"At Mimi's I have found my oasis in Berlin—there at least people think broad-mindedly and freely." Prince Wilhelm did not like this salon, and because of his distaste for it he wavered more and more between the Fronde and Bismarck, consequently between the liberal and freethinking camp of his parents' Court and the Old Prussian Court of King and Kaiser.

If serious clashes were avoided this was mainly due to the fact that the Crown Prince endeavored to steer tactfully, to be appeasing and conciliatory, with a hint of how difficult things were in Berlin for his wife, who was always being misunderstood.

Prince Wilhelm showed himself less adaptable. He would never put up with being "schoolmistressed" by his mother on the lines of the recipe of old Queen Victoria. Although the Prince of Wales was now nearly forty years of age, his mother treated him as a minor whose place it was to remain silent and do as he was told.

When the Crown Princess tried to apply similar principles she was met with opposition by her eldest son. Surprised at this, she had to recognize that he would not allow himself to be led as hitherto. Her thin lips twitched with anger and she nervously stroked her smooth hair when speaking of "William"—that "obstinate donkey," who was being "nothing but spiteful and stubborn." In her rage she forgot herself and hurt the Prince's feelings by interjecting an unkind remark about his crippled arm.

A young man with an infirmity of that kind, and moreover one that is clearly visible, suffers severely from every humiliation; he anticipates it before it is uttered. If one's own mother looks on one as a cripple how much more must others do so. The Prince became suspicious of people, and lost self-confidence because of his inferiority complex.

To fight against this feeling he tried early to make others forget his disability by dazzling them with a display of extravagant mannerisms. The Prince of Wales, "Uncle Bertie," that keen observer, noticed this in Potsdam and said that his nephew William was always attempting to spread his tail like a peacock and that if he could not do so, he felt put upon and miserable.

The older Prince Wilhelm became, the stronger grew his mother's aversion to him. She found him "far too independent for his years, too disobedient, and not at all disposed to accept instructions." To her vexation she was compelled to recognize that her influence over "William" was steadily decreasing and even tended to disappear altogether. "If your father should die before I do," she once declared bitterly, "I shall leave at once. I will not remain in a country where I have had nothing but hatred and not a spark of affection!"

When, sixty years afterward, Wilhelm II was speaking (in Doorn) about his mother, it could happen that in his excitement very bitter remarks escaped him. But if he was speaking composedly about her he did so with a deep sense of devotion, and often with an almost exaggerated respect. Then he would use such expressions as "that unique woman," and even "the great Kaiserin."

From Arthur Ponsonby's publications we know that the Kaiserin
Friedrich (as she was soon to be called) was indeed a unique
woman, uncommonly talented, intelligent and highly cultivated, with
much capacity for politics and statecraft. Bismarck's fear of her was
well founded. She was a strong personality and had in her everything
needed to make a great Empress. That it was not given her to become one was the tragedy of her life.

11. CASSEL AND SCHEVENINGEN

AT THE AGE OF FOURTEEN, Prince Wilhelm, thanks to the
solid and comprehensive education already given him, had far out-
distanced those as old as himself. Nevertheless his parents decided
not to have him confirmed until he was fifteen, as in their view his
moral preparation could not be sufficiently well grounded before
that. This time Grandmamma Augusta also had a say in the matter.
She wished to ensure that his religious instruction, hitherto treated
as of only secondary importance, should not be cut too short. She
often invited her grandson to Babelsberg to put him through his
paces and satisfy herself personally as to the progress of the candidate.

The confirmation took place on September 1, 1874, in the Peace
Church at Potsdam. "Uncle Bertie" was present, representing Queen
Victoria. He made a great impression with his air of a man of the
world and his conspicuous elegance. The Kaiserin Augusta disliked
and avoided him, calling him disdainfully a *bon vivant*.

After the confirmation the question arose as to which Gymnasium
(grammar school) Prince Wilhelm should attend. It was not only a
matter of choosing the institution, for the right headmaster had to be
sought, one that satisfied all the requirements laid down by the
Crown Princess. In the end the choice fell upon Cassel and Headmaster Doktor Vogt, who was recommended by Hinzpeter as the
very man that was needed. The Crown Princess agreed, especially
"because in the Schloss Wilhelmhöhe, where Wilhelm would stay in
the summer, there was plenty of light and air."

Prince Heinrich was to accompany his elder brother to Cassel.

But while Wilhelm went to the Gymnasium, Heinrich would only attend the Secondary Modern School, as this seemed to offer a better guarantee of practical training for a future naval officer. So it was said! In reality this decision was determined by the indolence of Heinrich who, in spite of private "coaching," could make no progress at the Gymnasium.

The Princes were to be accompanied by Hinzpeter, who was appointed their Civil Governor, and by Major General von Gottberg as Military Governor. Very soon the two Governors were at loggerheads and waged war on one another.

On September 12, 1874, the Princes moved into the so-called Princes' Court in the Königstrasse at Cassel, which was to be their winter quarters. By the Crown Princess's wish Prince Wilhelm was "to sit on a bench with the sons of the citizens of the town." This gave rise to some awkwardness on either side, which was thus described by Hinzpeter:

"Both the teachers and the pupils felt quite uncomfortable at first, as the new fellow pupil seemed to be an altogether incalculable quantity, a heterogeneous element. However, this did not last for long, since the Prince, as is his way, accepted the situation as it stood with a good heart, feeling and behaving here in the Gymnasium just as he did later as a university student and a young officer.

"The other pupils soon discovered that despite his always maintaining a tactful reserve that discouraged any undue familiarity, the Prince could be and would be a good comrade. Always ready to fall in with their plans and activities, he was filled with a sincere aspiration to compete with them on an equal footing, renouncing all privileges.

"As in principle he was neither prompted nor restricted in his choice of closer acquaintances he made friends with a few congenial personalities, which allowed him to have a little circle of companions. The whole situation in this respect resolved itself naturally, and therefore with good results, in a way that was scarcely to be expected."

This sociability on the part of the Prince was not confined to the Gymnasium but was extended to the Cassel Military Academy, where Prince Wilhelm, accompanied by Hinzpeter, often attended sporting events, without, however, being allowed to take part in them. Visits to the Court Theater and to the houses of some officers' families, provided interludes in the otherwise monotonous days of schooling.

As an especially notable figure in Cassel society, mention must be made of the officer commanding the 83rd Infantry Regiment, Colonel von Oettinger. Four years before this he had had to conduct Napoleon III [1] from Cassel to Wilhelmshöhe, and had after that often been in the company of the captured Emperor, so that he could tell many interesting stories about him.

The summer holidays brought everyone to Wilhelmshöhe. Even the heat of August is tolerable there in the park and by the waterfalls. But if it rained, Prince Wilhelm would bury himself in his favorite books, among which were Georg Ebers' *Uarda* and *Le fond de la mer*. This description of life on the bed of the ocean revived afresh his longing for the sea. In the end his parents acceded to the pleading of the boy and permitted a journey to the North Sea, to Scheveningen.

From his window he could look out over the sea and note the vessels that were leaving for all parts of the world. There were English flags, Danish and Dutch flags, but no "black-white-red" flags. He could not but think of his ancestor, the Great Elector, who, here in Holland, began the building of the Brandenburg fleet. Off Scheveningen, too, once used to ride the fleet of the Dutch sea hero, Michel de Ruyter, who, when dying, declared contentedly: "With a few, but good, frigates, manned by reliable seaman, we succeeded in ruling the seas of the world and abating the pride of England!"

12. THE VICTOR OF WÖRTH

BETWEEN Nedlitz and Bornimer Amt lies the village of Bornstedt, close to the Crown Prince's country estate. Just as King Friedrich Wilhelm III used to enjoy the time he could spend in Paretz, far from the life of the Court, so, too, his grandson loved to pass delightful days, with his family around him, in idyllic rural Bornstedt, close to, but remote from, Potsdam.

---

[1] French Emperor who abdicated after victory of Germany in Franco-Prussian War.

In Bornstedt the Crown Prince was, and meant to be, an ordinary human being and a landowner, riding round his fields in the morning, or strolling with the Crown Princess by his side through the plots of the kitchen garden. Then he usually wore an open *litevka* and smoked a rather short pipe, which had been his constant companion on active service in war.

He was beloved by the farmers of the neighborhood. They called him "distinguished" and "knightly." The ladies were of the same mind. The Empress Eugénie, despite her aversion for Prussia, spoke of him as "a fine handsome man, nearly a head taller than the Emperor (her husband), slim and fair, with a reddish beard, a true German as depicted by Tacitus. He is courteous and chivalrous, but not without some traits *à la Hamlet*." To this she added: "The Germans are an impressive breed! Louis even says that they are the race of the future—but I will never admit that!"

The Empress Eugénie's remark about traits *à la Hamlet* seems to indicate acute perception. The Crown Prince, now nearly fifty, felt depressed, superfluous, and he chafed at being unemployed. Lack of any useful part to play—for his aged father still excluded him from all affairs of State—made him moody and ill-humored. In his anxiety he started a number of projects, which were never carried out. Some ten years older than his brother-in-law "Bertie," he had, like the latter, the not very pleasing prospect which falls to the lot of many heirs to thrones—the prospect of having to wait, being made to look on, while another, aged seventy, eighty or even ninety, continues to reign. The impatient heir slips into the Opposition, and is used by the Opposition as a weapon against the ruler.

When the Crown Prince looked back over his career, he found, in his frequently recurring fits of self-depreciation, but little that could entitle him to claim a place in the Valhalla of the Hohenzollerns. The further his victories at Königgrätz and Wörth receded into the past, the less stimulating was his retrospective view of them. When the former Chief of his General Staff, Count von Blumenthal, claimed the credit for the success at Königgrätz for himself, he freely conceded it. When he had first heard of the claim, he had been beside himself with rage. Afterward he was fair-minded enough to recognize his General Staff as the real architects of the victory.

With the Hohenzollerns a precedent often repeated itself in a remarkable way whereby a grandfather transmitted his character attributes to his grandson. The Crown Prince had much in him of Friedrich Wilhelm III, above all his good nature, his indulgence, but also his tendency to melancholia. In their virtues they resembled each other, but as Goethe says, "with those virtues they cultivate at the same time their defects."

His greatest fault, in the eyes of men who were solicitous for the Crown Prince, was his irresolution and his readiness to yield to a wife who dominated him. As a good husband he may have been guided by the desire to avoid trouble within his own family. Gustav Freytag cannot sufficiently praise this submissive attitude: "His devotion and subordination to his beloved wife were complete. This love was the highest and most sacred thing in his life, and filled it entirely. She dominated his younger days, the confidante of all his thoughts and his counselor. The layout of a garden, the decoration of a dwelling, the upbringing of the children, opinions on people and events, were all decided by him in conformity with her personal wishes. Whenever he could not go all the way with her, or when his inner instinct discountenanced some particular course of action, he was deeply unhappy and ill at ease with himself. She had come to him from an exalted station and in addition to her rich, natural talents, her lofty mind and quickly comprehending brains, she had received, as the favorite child of her father, an intellectual equipment gathered from an extensive and varied range of formative subjects."

So powerful an influence wielded by a wife, and a foreigner at that, was bound to excite mistrust and opposition. So the cleavage widened between the Friedrich party and the Bismarck-Fronde on the one side and Government officials and officers on the other. Quarrels, such as frequently occur in social organizations and lead to painful episodes, began to figure in the *chronique scandaleuse* of High Society in Berlin.

Prince Wilhelm, too, was willy-nilly drawn into these squabbles and endeavored to avoid taking sides. His mother did not appreciate at all his having taken up this very proper attitude; on the contrary, she suspected that "William" had already made his choice, decided against his parents and gone over to Bismarck and the Old-Prussian party.

These suspicions made the Crown Prince himself mistrustful and, as Bismarck declared, jealous. So it came to an estrangement be-

tween father and son, with frequent scenes by the exasperated par-
ent, who in his fury uttered curses against his son, which must have
wounded him grievously. One thing that was said was "that it
would be a better arrangement if fate were to decree that his brother
Heinrich should one day mount the Throne, since he had a better
character."

Vituperations and insults of this kind were usually uttered in the
presence of the mother. She would have her satisfaction. She used
to punctuate the words of her husband with energetic nods of her
head and signify her approval, for to her mind "William" could
never be "carpeted" often enough.

Once the Prince was alone with his father and had a chance of
speaking his mind undisturbed they got on quite well together. "I
can come to an understanding with my father," the Prince confessed,
"but with my mother I find it difficult."

13. THE ACCOLADE

OUT OF SEVENTEEN candidates for the final examination at
the Cassel Gymnasium, Prince Wilhelm passed tenth. On January
25, 1877—two days before his eighteenth birthday, the passing-out
ceremony for the boys of the top form was held in the Great Hall.
Hinzpeter was there to take part. He had reached his appointed
goal—his task was ended. He would now take his leave of the
Prince and return to his home in Bielefeld.

In accordance with the laws of the House of Hohenzollern, Prince
Wilhelm would attain his majority at the age of eighteen. On the
morning of January 27, which the Prince spent in Berlin, the
British Ambassador, Lord Odo Russell, by command of Queen
Victoria, invested him with the mantle ribbon and star of the Order
of the Garter. After this the oath-taking ceremony took place in the
Knights' Hall of the Schloss.

Here the Royal Family was assembled, together with the Knights
of the Black Eagle, General Field Marshal Count Wrangel and
Count Moltke, besides the Army Chiefs, Steinmetz, Herwarth von
Bittenfeld, Manteuffel, Goeben, Kirchbach and Bose. Also with

them were the members of the so-called *maison militaire* (Military Cabinet), including its Chief, General von Albedyll, the confidant and trusty friend of the old Kaiser and almost as old as his master, a striking figure because of his parchmentlike, wrinkled face. By his side was the quiet, hard-working von Wilmowski, Chief of the Civil Cabinet, and the three Adjutants General—Count Perponcher (very well made up with all sorts of French cosmetics); Count Lehndorff, a gigantic East Prussian renowned for his ready wit; and lastly, the not-so-stately, in fact corpulent, Prince Anton Radziwill. It was this Radziwill who, seven years previously, had refused to receive the French Ambassador, Count Benedetti, at Ems, thereby ensuring that as a result of the Ems Telegram [1] the French Declaration of War should be delivered.

Accompanied by his father and his uncle, Albrecht of Prussia, Prince Wilhelm entered the hall to make the vow "before the Throne and Emperor"—"Always to be mindful of the honor of the Royal House [and, to make sure] always to maintain the Royal Privileges."

What happened next was thus described afterward by the Kaiser in Doorn: "Then I knelt down and received from my grandfather the chain of the High Order of the Black Eagle. As I was rising to my feet my grandfather kissed me and gave me the accolade."

A few days later, on February 9, the Prince was formally posted as a First Lieutenant to No. 6 Company of the 1st Guards Regiment. In front of the officers of the regiment the Supreme War Lord addressed him as follows: "In the service many things will strike you as being apparently unimportant. You must, however, learn that even these things can be of significant importance. Go now and do your duty, as it is taught you!"

The "practical" service that now began for him went back in principle to the old days of pipe clay, spit and polish. Despite the experience of three wars, the old *Drill Manual* of the eighteen-fifties was still in use. The Regimental Commander alone had authority to give orders. His staff and his captains could only repeat them and pass them on. Firing lines must always be rigidly straight, without any regard to the terrain. Everything was laid down according to the old ideas and was unchangeable. Thus it was "unworthy, and

[1] A message sent by King Wilhelm of Prussia from Ems to Bismarck in 1870. By publishing only part of this telegram, Bismarck gave the public the impression that the French were provoking war.

an offense against honor for a Prussian officer to take cover or even
to lie down." From such a position it was impossible for any officer
to control the fire of his men. In a serious situation, volley firing
was regarded as a proven panacea. But Prussian parsimony only
allowed it to be practiced on special occasions, for even the crackling
of blank cartridges cost money.

During his service with No. 6 Company in Potsdam, Prince
Wilhelm made friends with Lieutenant Helmuth von Moltke.[2] Thirty
years later, von Moltke was to be his Chief of the General Staff. On
some maneuvers the Prince was quartered with his company near
Hohenfinow. Here, at a manor house, he made the acquaintance of
the jovial owner's long and lanky son—Theobald von Bethmann-
Hollweg,[3] who afterward became his Reich's Chancellor.

14. IN BONN ON THE RHINE

IMMEDIATELY AFTER these maneuvers the Prince took part
in the unveiling of the National Memorial on the Niederwald. It
was autumn and the time when the grapes were ripening and being
harvested in the vineyards. So the Prince made the acquaintance
of the Rhine at its very best. He traveled by steamer as far as Rüdes-
heim, passing through the Assmannshausen Narrows in the midst
of happy singing and then on to Koblenz, where Grandmother
Augusta was staying at the Schloss. She gave a dinner party in honor
of her grandson, to which General von Goeben,[1] the victorious army
leader of the last two wars, was invited, To the disappointment of
the young Prince he did not look in the least like a conquering hero,
but rather like a scholarly recluse with gold-rimmed glasses.

About the end of October the Prince, at the wish of his parents,

[2] General Helmuth von Moltke (1848–1916), nephew and namesake of the
great Field Marshal. Appointed Chief of the German General Staff in 1906
but relieved of his post in October 1914, a month after the French victory at
the first Battle of the Marne.

[3] *See* Appendix, page 435.

[1] General August Karl von Goeben (1816–1880). Close friend of Field
Marshal von Moltke's and outstanding field commander in wars against Denmark, Austria, and France.

entered the University of Bonn. There he was to study jurisprudence and political science. A Major von Liebenau was appointed to attend on him, a weak sort of man, given to flattery, who was the first of the series of toadies that later became known as the *Camarilla,* and whose influence over the Kaiser was far from good. Captain von Jacoby went as his A.D.C.

The Villa Frank on the Koblenzerstrasse was assigned to this miniature Royal Household. From its terrace there was a splendid view across the Rhine as far as the Siebengebirge. The adjoining garden belonged to the villa of District Administrator von Sandt, where Prince Wilhelm was a frequent visitor. He was also a guest on many occasions in the house of Professor Loersch and in that of Prince Heinrich XIII of Reuss, who was then commanding the King's Hussars in Bonn.

The Prince stayed four semesters at Bonn and following in his father's footsteps joined the Corps of the Borussen as a *Konkneipant* (honorary member). He had, of course, to wear the white student's cap, but he was not allowed to fight duels in the fencing school. Many happy hours were spent in the clubhouse and with the friendly folk of other students' clubs.

Greatly appreciated, too, were boating trips on the Rhine under the shadow of the Siebengebirge, crowned by its ancient castles. When rowing, the Prince had to sit at the starboard end of the thwart, as even an oar specially lengthened could not be worked by his crippled arm. On outings like this, or when taking a glass of wine in the Römerbrücke at Engers, the Prince would try to remove any shyness on the part of the others by a friendly slap on the shoulder or by offering the "*Du.*" Here, however, he was dealing not with the pupils of the Cassel Gymnasium but with young gentlemen, aristocrats, who knew how to behave in the presence of the grandson of their Kaiser.

Much less respectful were those gentlemen of the Catholic nobility, who refused to take any notice of "the Protestant Prince" or to invite him to their shooting parties.

In this, the consequences of the *Kulturkampf* [2] (which still raged) were apparent. The hostility which the Prussian Prince encountered led him to question whether these people could still be relied upon as "pillars of the Throne." Perhaps some fellow students in Bonn were

[2] *See* Bismarck in Appendix, page 435.

right when they asserted that the "Münster Cuirassiers" and the "Pope's Hussars" in Paderborn looked not only to the German Kaiser but also to the Holy Father in Rome as their Master.

15. BALMORAL

AT EASTER IN 1878 Prince Wilhelm left Bonn on a visit to the World Exhibition in Paris, where he met President MacMahon, whose army had surrendered to his grandfather. There were also other impressive meetings and experiences, such as a visit to the Gallery of Mirrors at Versailles where seven years before the Proclamation of the Emperor of Germany had been issued. However, the French capital, strangely enough, proved so little to his liking that he declared "he had no desire ever again to visit Paris." And in fact this was the one and only time he did so.

He liked Brussels just as little, when he looked in there to represent his father on the occasion of the Silver Wedding of King Leopold II. His dislike of the Belgian capital may be explained by the fact that this Court made little appeal to him, while the "Silver Bridegroom"—whose scandalous private life excited great indignation—made no appeal at all. It was also due to the King's displaying a not-very-desirable side of his character to his young guest, in making cynical remarks about the young Prince's relatives, which further repulsed him.

In that same year the Prince paid a visit to Balmoral, at the invitation of his grandmother, Queen Victoria.

Ever since his earliest childhood he had shown a particular affection for this grandmother. Seven years before he had been with the Queen for the first time on a visit to Osborne. At that time she had petted and spoiled her eldest grandchild and granted every wish that she could read in his childish eyes. Those young days in Osborne had proved unforgettable. The Prince still saw himself at his grandmother's feet or playing on the beach near the Bastion with its old iron guns from which he could watch the ships tacking out of the Solent on their way to the open sea.

At the end of this visit to Osborne his parents joined him for a further trip in the paddle steamer *Alberta* to Plymouth and Portsmouth, in which latter harbor they inspected the famous old *Victory*, Nelson's flagship, from which he directed the battle of Trafalgar until mortally wounded by a bullet.

From Portsmouth they went on to Windsor, again as guests of the Queen, for a brief stay. In Windsor the Queen had let her grandson have the use of the Steward's Cottage in Frogmore Park as a playground. It was a dairy farm in miniature and had been installed by Prince Albert with his own hands. When she was a little girl, "Vicky," the mother of Prince Wilhelm, used to make butter and cheese there. Permission to play in it came as a special treat to the grandson who by his nice character had won the heart of the lonely old lady.

"Always try, my dear child, to be good and honorable, for then you will be a happy man!" Having thus advised him, she produced a brand-new shiny golden sovereign, bearing the impress of her own head, and presented it to her grandchild.

He treasured it as a relic for forty years until it was lost in the turmoil of war and revolution.

Very different from Windsor was Balmoral, the Queen's residence in the Scottish Highlands. It was then approachable only by narrow tracks and in small vehicles. The castle itself had been reconstructed in accordance with the wishes of Prince Albert and had been extended by a great gatehouse which was surmounted by a square tower. In the interior everything had been done to maintain a distinctive Scottish character, thus wallpapers were eschewed in favor of hand-woven Scottish shawls. The Great Hall at Balmoral could serve as the stage setting for a Walter Scott romance.

The surroundings of the castle could not be described as in any way attractive. They consisted of bare, wild hill country, with low-lying dark-green lakes. There were a few primitive dwelling houses which the Queen, while the Prince Consort was still living, used to visit and there take tea. After the death of her husband they became for her consecrated places.

At the crossings of tracks and at special viewpoints she had memorial plaques fixed, and obelisks or cairns erected, with inscriptions to remind her that there the dear departed had rested, or had shot a rabbit, or had received some important news. Everything at Balmoral revolved around the dead Prince Consort. Although he had been dead and buried for twenty years his old manservant Brown had still to lay out his shooting kit or his Hunting Stewart on the accustomed armchair and put fresh water in the washbasin every morning as though his master might return at any moment.

Everything had to remain just as beloved Albert had arranged it.

Each day the Queen, leaning on Brown's arm, visited his bedroom, often to stand still, look around, and ask: "How was *this*, Brown, when His Royal Highness was still alive?" And in the evening, if some news came in and a decision had to be taken, she would ask: "Brown, what do you think His Royal Highness would have done in this case?"

So the lonely old lady mourned "the loss that had rent her life and made her a half-dead miserable creature." She carried her mourning so far as to refuse to see anyone except her nearest family relations and would never take part in any of the customary Court ceremonies. More than once members of both houses of Parliament went to her endeavoring to bring about a change in this stubborn attitude of reclusion. The Queen would receive them, listen to what they had to say, and even give some assurances of taking a greater part in public life, only to revert to her sorrowful isolation and make no change at all.

In order to do honor to the beloved dead, the Queen, who by her marriage had become Duchess of Saxony, had the lozenge-shaped Saxon coat of arms quartered with her own. Although she was related to the Coburgs through her mother, she had never before stressed this ancestry.

She had such a fluent command of the German language that not only did she speak it without accent, but she often used expressions that showed her knowledge of German dialects.

She spoke in short sentences, almost unintelligible when uttered in low tones, and she frequently punctuated them with haughty, rapid movements of her head. Her mouth could readily assume a mocking or sarcastic expression that was also characteristic of her eldest daughter, Princess Victoria.

It was not merely a sense of reverence but mute anguish that affected her children and grandchildren when they heard the approaching rustle of her silk skirts. Even the Prince of Wales once had to hide behind a pillar, fiddling nervously with his necktie, before he ventured to appear before his mother.

Prince Wilhelm was generally admitted to be the old Queen's favorite grandchild. Proof of this was given when immediately after his arrival at Balmoral she presented him with the outfit of a royal clansman, consisting of the green Hunting Stewart, red tartan kilt with plaid to match, silver-mounted belt and sporran, buckled shoes, a sword belt adorned with a topaz as large as a hen's egg, a sturdy claymore with its basket hilt padded with red velvet, the dagger and the knife (*skeen-dhu*). Whether or not such an attire is suitable for a wild mountainous country need not be decided here. In any case, Prince Wilhelm thought this Scottish magnificence splendid and had his photograph taken in it.

"Uncle Bertie" could not forbear talking about the masquerade that "the Berliner" had indulged in at Balmoral.

Throughout his stay there the old Queen endeavored to make up to her grandson for all that he had lacked at home in motherly love and kindness. Grandmothers are instinctively conscious of such sins of omission, especially when they are committed by their own daughters. She admonished him to take Prince Albert as his model. When saying good-by, she entreated him to do so in these words: "Never, never forget him, my dear young man! He was your good, kind grandfather. He was the most noble man in the world! Try as best you can to be like him. Go now with God, and may He bless you!"

16. THE OLD KAISER

WHILE STILL IN BONN, Prince Wilhelm had expressed the wish to be allowed to visit the East after completing his studies at the university. This application was decisively rejected by the old Kaiser: "You will be posted to duty in Potsdam, and what is more, to the Life Guard Company, to train recruits. That is far more important than traveling about."

Uncompromising decrees of this kind by Wilhelm I were by no means rare, despite his great age. He had become hard of hearing of late, but that did not prevent him from being remarkably *clairaudiant* in a matter of any consequence. If, as he approached his ninetieth year, he looked back on his life, he could only conclude that existence on earth is full of change and variety.

Thirty years before he had had to flee from the fury of the mob. His palace had been declared the property of the people. There had been nothing left for him to do except to seek a hiding place and remain hidden, on the remote Pfaueninsel (Isle of Peacocks) near Potsdam. Then, peace being to some extent restored, "Lehmann," as the people of Berlin called him in scorn and mockery, decided to fly to England under cover of darkness. After a long absence he returned to Prussia, first becoming Regent and then King. Three wars were waged victoriously, the last having one result for himself that never brought him comfort—from being King of Prussia he became Emperor of Germany, a Kaiser *nolens volens*!

Within twenty-five years he had won over the popular sentiment from aversion to adoration. The ex-Lehmann had become the Heroic Kaiser, acclaimed everywhere, when driving down Unter den Linden or in the Tiergarten, but especially when the Guard marched past the historic corner window. Here crowds used to gather to stare in astonishment at the old gentleman in general's uniform, but with a white civilian waistcoat and black bow tie.

Such fancy-dress uniform as this, which the Kaiser (and Bismarck too by the way) used to affect, was a sore affliction for old Moltke, who groaned as he put this rhetorical question to his A.D.C.: "In the name of God, what are we coming to when the highest ranking on our list of generals tolerate such a travesty?"

From past experience of a long life the nonagenarian knew well what to think of popular opinion—the older he became the more clearly he understood that one can rely only on oneself and must not throw away any God-given rights. Nobody contradicted him on that. As a keen sportsman he would never tolerate anyone's shooting across him to kill a buck (*his* buck) before his eyes, so now he would not permit anyone to trespass on his authority. When in 1882 attempts were made to question his rights as King and Kaiser, he proclaimed: "It is my unalterable will that alike in Prussia and in the legislative body of the Reich no doubt shall remain as to the constitutional right of myself and my successors to the personal direction of the policy of my Government . . ." and so on.

The "graybeard" drafted this edict out of his own head and forwarded it to his Reich's Chancellor, who took exception to any such wording as also (according to a statement by Wilhelm II) did the heir to the Throne, in that it presumed too much on the authority of the monarch and had the appearance of being provocative.

Two attempts on his life shattered his health. After the attack made on him by Karl Nobiling, Prince Wilhelm went to see him and found him wrapped in thick bandages, stoutly defying death. While the Kaiser was in the doctors' hands the Crown Prince acted as his deputy. For the first time, and for a few weeks, he could reign—to the great content of the Princess Royal, who declared with complacent irony—"Well! After all, we are of *some* use!"

So long as this interim reign lasted Prince Wilhelm tried to assist his father. In Doorn he spoke of these activities. "After the reports by the Chiefs of the Military and Civil Cabinets, there were masses of orders and commissions that my father had to sign. It fell to me to sprinkle them with sand, lay them out to dry and afterward restore them into proper order. It often happened that all the tables and pieces of furniture, even the floor, were covered with documents, so that it was difficult for visitors to find a way to the door."

17. 'TWIXT BISMARCK AND THE FRONDE

THE OLDER Wilhelm I grew, the more frequent became the fits of annoyance that occurred in his intercourse with Prince Bismarck. The old Kaiser declared that he had to handle his Chancellor "like a raw egg" if he wanted to get on with him and avoid discord, for the intolerant Prince would listen to no arguments and always wanted to have his own way. But he himself was no better disposed toward his old master. In a letter to Robert Lucius, dated January 12, 1877, he complained that "the Kaiser is cold and as hard as stone. He shows no gratitude to me at all. He only keeps me on because he thinks I may still be of some use to him." So each complained about the other, and there were mutual recriminations between the two, each being seriously concerned about the rift that had opened between them and now threatened to become wider. The trouble was in connection with Russia, toward whom Bismarck wished to alter his attitude. Shuvalov believed that he had been cheated by Bismarck, first because of the Chancellor's behavior at the Berlin Congress,[1] and then again over the the terms of peace conceded at San Stefano [2] under which the Russian troops had to retire from before the gates of Constantinople. That could not and would not ever be forgotten of the "Honest Broker"—Bismarck. Gone like a dream was the Russian hope of substituting the Orthodox Cross for the Crescent on the cupola of Hagia Sophia. Just as France sought revenge for Sedan, so now the Czar's Empire demanded revenge for San Stefano! This was the genesis of Russian hostility toward Germany, and hence of her friendship with France, out of which eventually grew the *Entente Cordiale*.[3]

Bismarck accepted this defection by Russia calmly enough, but not so the Kaiser. He followed the new development with the utmost apprehension. For him friendship with Russia represented a "noble legacy" sealed on oath between his parents and the Czar, Alexander I, over the coffin of Frederick the Great and afterward reinforced by the Holy Alliance.[4]

Striving "not to allow the thread [of good relations] with Russia" to snap, and concerned also with the idea of nipping in the bud a threatened crisis arising from a frontier demarcation in the Balkans, Wilhelm I decided to adopt the Czar's suggestion and to agree to a meeting in Alexandrowo.

Bismarck, who was taking the waters in Gastein, would have nothing to do with this projected journey. He grumbled and talked about "a summons from the Czar" and "another Olmütz." [5] Exceptionally for him the Crown Prince agreed with Bismarck's views in this case.

But Bismarck knew that this agreement would be only an isolated

[1] *See* Bismarck in Appendix, page 435.

[2] Preliminary peace treaty signed by Russia and Turkey in 1878, later considerably modified in Turkey's favor at Berlin Congress. *See* Bismarck in Appendix, page 435.

[3] The Anglo-French Treaty of 1903. *See* Bülow in Appendix, page 437.

[4] Between Russia, Austria and Prussia in 1815, effected by Metternich with the aim of ensuring the maintenance of the treaties of that year and checking any separatist or nationalistic movements in territories belonging to or controlled by those allied powers. (*Trans.*)

[5] Austrian town and site of historic meeting between Prussian and Austrian statesmen in 1850, when Austria regained positions in Germany previously lost to Prussia.

case. Moreover, he did not forget to take into account his arch-enemy, the Princess Royal. In view of the Kaiser's great age he had to reckon with an early change in the occupancy of the Throne, and the coming into power of "the Friedrichs." This suggested that he should seek reassurance. He saw it in the person of Prince Wihelm.

This *rapprochement* between their eldest son and Bismarck was followed with misgiving by the Prince's parents and the Bismarck Fronde. In order to detach the Prince from the orbit of "that malignant man" attempts were made to prejudice him against "the aging Chancellor." There were hints about his supposed dipsomania, "which was a cause of his failures and disappointments." How incompetent he could be was evidenced by the "unequaled foolish-ness" of the Berlin Congress and his permission of the *Kulturkampf,* "undoubtedly the worst blunder that any Prussian statesman had ever perpetrated."

Prince Wilhelm had seen for himself the results of *Kulturkampf* in Bonn, nevertheless he was not to be diverted from siding with the Chancellor, in whom he saw the founder of the Reich and the archi-tect of German unification. His opponents never even gave him credit for that.

Then it was insinuated that everything accomplished by Bismarck was directed toward one aim only—his advancement from the po-sition of Reich's Chancellor to that of "major-domo of the Hohen-zollerns." Even his Uncle Friedrich, Grank Duke of Baden, took part in this baiting, endeavoring to bewilder his nephew by insidious questions and taunts: "Just make this clear to me! Which is now reigning in Prussia—the Bismarck dynasty, or yours?"

Even Hinzpeter, from Bielefeld, took a hand and intervened in this distressing strife, apparently at the instigation of the Crown Prince and his wife. After long-winded dissertations on Prussian history and the deductions to be drawn from it, he went on to speak of "that almighty Reich's Chancellor, against whom the Royal powers should be used energetically."

Advice like this, wherever it emanated from, the Prince received in silence, but without changing his relations with Bismarck. As before, he frequented No. 76 Wilhelmstrasse, where the Chancellor lived on the first floor of the Foreign Office building. There his ac-commodation was modestly equipped, only the Yellow Drawing Room and the Chinese Room being comfortably furnished, but there was nothing in it to compare with the beautiful contents of the nearby mansion of Count Alexander von Schleinitz, the Minister of the Royal Household.

In these private visits Bismarck got to know Prince Wilhelm better, and was delighted with his youthful vigor and unaffectedness, which he would like to see him retain as long as possible.

"We need new young minds in our Ministries, and the fresh air of candid criticism. Our constitutional life depends upon it!"

For all that, however, the Chancellor himself clung to certain old Prussian habits of mind, such as—"The Army must always be given first priority; Progressives and Liberals must not be insolent; the anemic British Kingdom must not be taken for a model."

As one evening in Princess Johanna's drawing room the conversation turned on Prince Wilhelm, who was not present, Bismarck lowered his newspaper and said: "Latterly I have been talking almost every day with Prince Wilhelm and have got to know him quite well. So I cherish the hope that one day he will combine the Reich's Kaiser and Chancellor in one person. This Prince Wilhelm has in him something of Frederick the Great, but he also has tendencies that could make a despot of him. It's a real blessing that we have parliamentary government!"

18. BETROTHAL

IN THE YEAR 1868 Prince Wilhelm, then nine years old, met at Reinhardsbrunn, Auguste Viktoria, some three months older than himself. She was the daughter of the Herzog (Duke) Friedrich von Schleswig-Holstein-Sonderburg-Augustenburg. The Duchy was not a large one, but was of such importance because of the town and harbor of Kiel that after the Danish War Bismarck "appropriated it for the benefit of Prussia" and so excluded the Duke from mounting his throne. Thus maltreated, the Duke laid his complaint before several courts of justice without gaining any success against Prussia. Greatly embittered, he withdrew to Gotha, where the Duke of Saxe-Coburg-Gotha assigned to him a modest dwelling house. What

Nietzsche had said about "weak Princes" happened in this case: "History concerns itself only with strong personalities. The weak ones it blots out altogether."

With the intention of bringing the Duke to a more conciliatory frame of mind a project was considered in the old Kaiser's palace for a matrimonial alliance between the two Houses, and the names of the Duke's eldest daughter, Auguste Viktoria, and Prince Wilhelm, were mentioned.

Although the chosen bride was a little older than the Prince, she had the great advantage of being a German Princess who, later on as Kaiserin, would present no such problem as did the Princess Royal. It was this factor that caused Bismarck to favor the proposed marriage.

In August 1878 the Duke of Augustenburg came with his daughter on a visit to Potsdam. It did not, however, appear that a deep mutual affection was immediately established between the two parties, as the Court circulars liked to call it. But the link was established; they would correspond, and meet again. The sorely tried Duke of Augustenburg was not destined to live long enough to have the satisfaction of knowing that his daughter would one day become the German Kaiserin. On January 14, 1880, he died. Auguste Viktoria and Prince Wilhelm clasped hands over his coffin and a month later became secretly engaged. The engagement was officially announced on June second, after the expiration of Court mourning.

This reconciliation and the repair of an undoubted wrong was hailed with joy throughout the Reich. Court circles were not altogether pleased, however. They admitted indeed that the House of Holstein was of equal birth, but regretted that "the Augustenburger should have been so unimportant and so poor." They could find some consolation in the fact that the bride was, on her mother's side, a niece of Queen Victoria, and a granddaughter of that Queen's mother, so that she was related to several reigning Houses.

At the death of Duke Friedrich of Schleswig-Holstein-Sonderburg-Augustenburg that reigning House ceased to exist, for his only son, the young Ernst Günther, voluntarily renounced all claims to its sovereignty in favor of Prussia.

On February 27, 1881, the wedding took place in the Berlin Schloss. In accordance with old tradition the bride drove in a golden coach from Schloss Bellevue to the Berlin Schloss, where Prince Wilhelm awaited her in the double capacity of bridegroom and Captain Commanding the Guard of Honor.

Thus did the Augustenburger's daughter, Auguste Viktoria Friederike Luise Feodora Jenny, enter the Schloss of the Hohenzollern as predestined Kaiserin of Germany. Of her names as given above she used only the two first, both being already represented there in the persons of the Kaiserin Augusta and the Crown Princess Victoria, her mother-in-law.

19. A JOURNEY TO ST. PETERSBURG

THE PROCESS OF pushing the young Prince into the foreground, instituted by Wilhelm I and Bismarck, marked an important advance in the year 1884 owing to the Kaiser's decision to send his grandson to St. Petersburg for the occasion of proclaiming the attainment of his majority by the Czarevitch, the future Czar Nicholas II.[1] Although it was obviously right, when choosing a prince to represent the Kaiser's House, to select one as nearly as possible of the same age as the Czarevitch, this fresh favor shown to their eldest son was not at all to the liking of the Crown Prince and his wife, who felt that they were slighted.

"We are passed over on every possible occasion, and with hostile deliberation!" So the Crown Princess wrote to her mother at Windsor, and in her letter she mentioned other grievances against the Chancellor. But the old Queen, who with majestic impartiality sat in judgment over all her children and grandchildren, showed little sympathy with the grumbles and lamentations of her "Vicky." She advised her daughter to keep on good terms, despite all her difficulties, with "that important man who has rendered such undeniable service to Prussia."

Shortly before he was due to start on his journey, the Prince was sent for by the Kaiser to receive his final instructions. When saying good-by, the Kaiser recommended him above all to be tactful and obliging, for "in Russia, like everywhere else, people prefer praise to blame."

[1] See Appendix, page 443.

But it was from Prince Bismarck that he received the most valuable hints, drawn from his own varied experiences during his time as Ambassador in St. Petersburg. He made it clear to the Prince that once he passed the frontier station at Eydtkuhnen, conditions would be totally different from those in Germany. He ended his explanations with these words: "In Russia all the people who wear their shirts *outside* their breeches are decent folk—but as soon as they tuck them *inside* and wear an Order round their necks, they are . . . *Schweinehunde!*"

He was to be acccompanied to St. Petersburg by General Count von Waldersee [2] and the Lord Chamberlain von Liebenau. Their departure was fixed for May fifteenth (1884). The German Ambassador in St. Petersburg, and Count Herbert Bismarck, Embassy Counselor, would travel from St. Petersburg to meet the Prince's party.

On arriving at St. Petersburg the Grand Duke Vladimir, representing the Czar, did the honors of their reception. From the railway station they drove to the Winter Palace, where Alexander III was awaiting the Prince. The Czar was a giant who towered over a suite of giants. After handing over his credentials the Prince was conducted to his apartments, from which there was a fine view over the park and the Neva quays.

Before the festivities began, the Prince had an opportunity of visiting the fortress of St. Peter and St. Paul, and of laying a wreath on the tomb of the murdered Czar Alexander II.[3] Near the tomb stands a little fisherman's hut, brought from Zaandam, in which Peter the Great, the founder of the Russian Navy, used to live as Czarshipwright.

In Doorn, as a septuagenarian looking back on the ceremony in the chapel of the Winter Palace, Wilhelm II still had the scene vividly before his eyes:

"It is difficult to convey any idea of the splendors of the Czar's palace. When I think of how the attainment of my own majority was celebrated, the simple ceremony in the Knights' Hall of the old

[2] Count Alfred Waldersee (1832–1904), Prussian Field Marshal, veteran of the Austrian and Franco-Prussian wars. Appointed chief of the German General Staff on the retirement of Moltke in 1888. In 1900 he commanded all the European troops that marched on Peking to quell the Boxer uprising.

[3] Czar Alexander II (1818–1881), grandfather of Czar Nicholas II, assassinated by Nihilists in 1881.

Schlüter-Schloss [4] seems to me a very poor affair. It was especially the vestments of the Orthodox Greek clergy and the Court robes of the Grand Duchesses, with their picturesque headdresses and their costly jewelry, that gave life to the sublime spectacle. The only things to remind one of Berlin were some of the uniforms of the Russian Guards Regiments, such as the Garde du Corps, who wore almost the same tunics, cuirasses and eagle-topped helmets as our own in Potsdam.

"Then the fourteen-year-old Czarevitch came in, in a light blue uniform, and stood before the altar, where he read aloud the formula of the oath binding him to remain ever faithful to the Czar and to Russia, and to preserve the established order of succession to the throne. After this came prayers, intoned in chorus by the high dignitaries of the Church, and the *Te Deum*, while the bells began to ring and hundreds of guns thundered in salute.

"The members of the Holy Synod then offered their Majesties and the Czarevitch their congratulations and good wishes, after which everyone proceeded in procession to the Hall of St. George. Here a deputation of bearded Life Guard Cossacks handed over to the heir to the throne, now their new *Hetman*,[5] their ancient, richly embroidered standard."

On the following day Prince Wilhelm had an opportunity of talking with the Czar without others being present.

"The Czar, suspicious and reticent by nature, showed that he trusted me and in our conversation treated me in an uncommonly frank and friendly manner. I profited by this and tried to win him over to the idea of prolonging the *entente à trois*—with Austria-Hungary. But he proved to be prejudiced in the highest degree against the 'Danube Monarchy' and it required a great effort to find reasons that would convince him of the necessity of the 'alliance of the three emperors.' In accordance with my instructions I worked especially on the basis of the Czar's known mentality—insisting that the three empires must join together in fighting anarchy, or as I put it in an analogy used by Prince Bismarck, must hold together in presenting a three-sided bastion against the onrushing waves of anarchy."

This was the right course to take, for, as the Prince noticed, every-

---

[4] Andreas Schlüter (1664–1714), sculptor and architect.
[5] *Hetman*: Chief (of the Cossacks).

one in the Winter Palace was obsessed by fear of anarchy and anarchists. At a gala banquet a Grand Duchess confessed to him: "All of us here are sitting on a powder barrel. The revolution may break out any day!"

At the Czar's invitation the Prince visited Moscow which, steeped in its ancient orthodox, almost Byzantine, splendor of gold and mosaic, in "Asia's red dusk," made a profound impression on him. It was the Kremlin that interested him most, with its gigantic walls of hewn stone, its palaces, cathedrals, monasteries and barracks. He traversed the Halls of the Orders, each hung with damask of the color of its order, the most beautiful being the light blue of the Order of St. Andrew.

In the Hall of St. George he found a marble slab inscribed with the names of all the dead knights of that order, among them being Friedrich Wilhelm III, Blücher and Gneisenau.

He visited the Coronation Church, with its tombs of the Czars, and "Sparrow Hills" from which Napoleon had watched the burning of Moscow. Not until May 28 did he start on his return journey to Berlin. There was general praise for his conduct—even Herbert Bismarck, always ready and glad to find fault, had to admit that "in St. Petersburg the Prince has done well in solving the by-no-means easy problem of the precarious relations between Germany and Russia."

The Russian Court too was well satisfied with this first visit of the Prussian Prince. Giers, the Russian Foreign Minister, expressed it thus: "Whoever had the idea of sending the Prince to us is to be congratulated." On reading this praise of his grandson with much relish, the old Kaiser jestingly appropriated the congratulations, saying, *"Il faut que j'accepte le compliment!"*

20. THE LIFE OF A HUSSAR

THE KAISER had placed the Marmor Palais, standing in Potsdam by the Heiligensee, at the disposal of the young married couple. It was a little castle, really quite unsuitable for a dwelling house, for its so-called halls, poky and many-angled, were only connected with one another by narrow dingy passages. To make up for this, the view from the windows over the Havel lakes to the Isle of Peacocks (*Pfaueninsel*) was unique in its beauty. The park, with its mysterious cavelike buildings of the time of Friedrich Wilhelm II that were said to have been used for spiritualistic meetings, was equally beautiful.

Here the honeymoon was spent, the happiest and least disturbed time of their lives. This marriage, which—though based on mutual affection—had been dictated by considerations of politics, developed in the course of time into a model union which defied and brought to naught all attempts, made then or later, to breach it by insinuations or misrepresentations.

On October 20, 1884, the old Kaiser entrusted the Prince with the command of the 1st Battalion of the 1st Regiment of Foot Guards, the "First Battalion of Christendom" as people used to dub this body of picked men.

Soon after taking over this command the Prince applied for a period of leave—he wanted to accompany his father on a return visit to Madrid. But the Supreme War Lord refused this request of his travel-loving grandson, not without expressing his displeasure that "the Major, immediately after taking over the command, should wish to indulge in a pleasure trip."

In autumn he took part in the Imperial Maneuvers, on the staff of General Field Marshal von Blumenthal; he also had an opportunity of studying the other arms of the service, for instance by holding a command in the Guards Field Artillery.

After piecing together his experiences in the several arms, the young Prince wrote several military memoranda, among them one on the value (or uselessness) of ceremonial parades.

The Prince had worn Hussar uniform since 1881, as a Major in the Life Guards Hussars, and in Potsdam he had had cavalry training under a good instructor, Colonel von Krosigk. During that time he found a fatherly friend in the little, but dashing, General von Versen. Like all slim men, this pock-marked little General looked very well in his Hussar uniform. In the basement of his villa in Potsdam, generally known as "the tunnel," he used to organize Beer Evenings, in which Prince Wilhelm often took part. Here, too, he met the celebrated American humorist, Mark Twain, whom, however, he found boring and not at all witty.

The Prince kept up his connection with the Life Guards Hussars. In 1885 the Kaiser appointed him to the command of the regiment. In this capacity he was determined to apply the rigorous principles in matters of morality that he had already displayed in early youth. He felt that he was responsible for the well-being of his officers and their families. He forbade the younger ones to contract debts, and above all to gamble, especially at baccarat, which was greatly in favor with the Guards Cavalry.

He knew that they were playing for high stakes in the Union Club in the Schadowstrasse in Berlin, and that several excellent young officers had been ruined there and had shot themselves. To avert this danger the young commanding officer forbade those under his command to set foot in the club.

This ban enraged the club members. There was talk of "inadmissible tutelage," "unauthorized interference" and "unbelievable arrogance." So strong did feelings run that they dispatched their President, the Duke of Ratibor, to see the old Kaiser and try to get Prince Wihelm's order canceled. But the drastic action of his young grandson appealed to that old soldier. In order to gain time he deferred his decision.

When a few weeks later General von Albedyll, deputed by the club, ventured to remind the Kaiser that the matter was still unsettled, the latter referred to General von Pape, who had declared that the order was right and absolutely necessary.

It is true that Prince Wilhelm still had difficulties over his undeveloped arm. But he could hardly be called a cripple. From a little blubbering child on a small pony he had become a dashing Hussar who, with his exceptionally powerful right arm, could control any horse and who presented an elegant appearance in front of his five squadrons when he led them at a gallop across the Bornstedter Feld. Nor was there much sign of a cripple in the fact that four sons—Friedrich Wilhelm, Eitel-Friedrich, Adalbert and August Wilhelm—had already been born to him and his wife. And, with Prussian precision, three more healthy children were to follow —in 1888, 1890 and 1892.

Even Prince Karl Anton von Hohenzollern, who at first had not been at all sanguine regarding the prospects of the Prince's physical development, acknowledged frankly, after a visit to Potsdam, that "Prince Wilhelm is a character, a man of thoroughly high principles and much ability. He is the most intelligent of the Royal princes. He is courageous, enterprising and ambitious, a bit of a hothead, but with a heart of gold. His character and mentality are full of verve, vivacity and versatility. In conversation he is quick in repartee, so that one might almost think he was not a German. He adores the Army, which worships him in return. Despite his youth he has known how to make himself liked in all classes of society. He is well educated, very well read, full of plans for the future prosperity of his country, and he possesses a remarkably keen sense of all political affairs. He is becoming a prominent figure and will probably make a great ruler. Prussia may perhaps find in him her second Frederick the Great—minus the skepticism. He is very cheery and good-natured, which mitigates those little traits of austerity that, as a true Hohenzollern, he may display. He will be essentially a 'personal' monarch, who will not permit being dictated to. He has prompt and sound judgment, the ability to make quick decisions, energy, and a strong will. When he comes to the Throne, he will continue the work of his grandfather—and will assuredly destroy that of his father, of whatever kind it may be. The enemies of Germany will find in him a formidable adversary. He can be the Henri Quatre of his country!"

21. NO. 76 WILHELMSTRASSE

ON JANUARY 27, 1888, Prince Wilhelm was relieved of the command of the Life Guards Hussar Regiment, and on the same day, his twenty-ninth birthday, he was promoted to Major General and appointed to the command of the 2nd Guards Infantry Brigade. "I could hand over my Hussars to my successor with a good conscience," he said afterward in Doorn, "for even a severe and impartial superior as General Field Marshal Count Haeseler gave an appreciative report of my regiment."

Already, in the winter of 1882–1883 the Prince had for a time been employed in Potsdam in the *Oberpräsidium* [1] of the Province of Brandenburg, with a view to getting an insight into State admin-

[1] Office of highest civil official in a Prussian province.

istration under the then Lieutenant Governor, Heinrich von Achenbach. It was therefore a logical decision of the Kaiser's to give him an opportunity of becoming acquainted with the conduct of foreign affairs. No one seemed more suited to initiate him than the great statesman, the Reich's Chancellor himself. So from September 1886 onward the Prince also worked at No. 76 Wilhelmstrasse, mostly under the eye of State Secretary Count Herbert Bismarck. Here the Prince was able to note the extent to which the Chancellor's son— who had no powers of initiative—was dependent upon his father.

In this anteroom to the Holy of Holies of the Foreign Office the Prince learned how to answer telegrams, deal with documents and draft decrees. Of how important decisions were arrived at he learned nothing. "Foreign policy," said Wilhelm II afterward, "was conducted singlehanded by Prince Bismarck, who used to consult with nobody except his son Herbert. The Foreign Office was nothing more than the great Chancellor's private office."

This fact, established by his own personal experience, may well have aroused in the coming heir to the throne his first doubts as to the desirability of leaving so much power and responsibility in the hands of one official. Added to this was his discovery, in the course of his apprenticeship, of how often the obstinate and self-opinionated Chancellor had made wrong dispositions in consequence of drawing incorrect inferences. It was not hidden from his acutely observant pupil that the continental policy of the Chancellor was determined by mistaken ideas of Great Britain. "If the English tried to land on our soil I'd have them arrested!" And there were similar utterances. The Prince received confirmation of the correctness of his opinion from Privy Councilor Raschdau, who stated in reports that he made to him "that the young German Reich was pursuing a colorless and uncertain policy toward England."

Apart from this, the disdainful "marginal notes" uttered by the Chancellor on the subject of England had already roused the Crown Princess to take the field in defense of her motherland. She trusted her eldest son as little as she trusted "that malignant man." "It was an unheard-of thing," she declared, "that William should so rashly be brought into foreign affairs!"

At her instigation the Crown Prince called on the Chancellor, full of complaints in which he did not hesitate to disparage his own son, saying that "in view of his immaturity and inexperience combined with his tendencies to presumption and conceit, it is dangerous to bring him so young into touch with foreign affairs."

The Crown Princess was also shocked to find that "Henry" supported and defended his elder brother. The distracted mother called him a "stubborn ass," who, like "William," would embitter her whole life. Then, in tears, she mentioned her two dead children, Sigismund and Waldemar, "the two darlings that had all too soon been taken from her," and who had been for her like "unclouded sunshine."

The old Kaiser heard of these outbursts of his daughter-in-law and also about his son's exasperation, and as before he strove to compensate and reconcile, and to avoid everything that could possibly convey the impression that the legitimate heir to the throne was to be passed over.

As the Crown Princess could not approach either the Kaiser, her father-in-law, or Bismarck directly, she vented her feelings all the more bitterly on "William." She even went so far as to say to an Austrian diplomat who had only just taken up his appointment in Berlin, "You cannot think how I admire your good-looking, witty and elegant Crown Prince Rudolph,[2] when I compare him with my clumsy, loutish son Wilhelm!"

22. THE FRAGILE THREAD

DESPITE RENEWED EFFORTS by Bismarck to pave the way for better relations with Russia, the situation as between the two empires remained strained. In St. Petersburg the memory of the Berlin Congress was not to be easily effaced, any more than that of the two-faced attitude of Bismarck himself. The Czar would no longer trust him.

Moreover, events in Bulgaria were scarcely calculated to improve the humor in the Russian capital. On April 22, 1879, the Bulgarian National Assembly at Tirnovo, at the instigation of the Czar Alexander II, had chosen Prince Alexander of Battenberg, the son of

[2] Crown Prince Rudolf of Austria-Hungary (1857–1889), only son of Emperor Franz Joseph, was killed in the Mayerling tragedy, 1889.

Prince Alexander of Hesse, as Prince of Bulgaria. This twenty-two-year-old Prince, known in Berlin as the "Beau," had received his call to the Bulgarian Throne while serving as a Lieutenant in the Body Guard at Potsdam. Russia had confirmed his selection in the belief that in the Battenberger they had found one willing to act as the tool of the Czar. All the greater was their disappointment when, in September 1885, Prince Alexander incorporated Eastern Rumelia in Bulgaria, without having been authorized to do so by the Czar.

Thereupon, incited by Russia, the Serbs declared war on Bulgaria, but were defeated at the Battle of Slivnitza. After this Bulgarian success no further fighting had taken place, but the danger of war between Russia and Austria-Hungary was not on that account removed.

Very soon, however, a Russian-inspired agitation against the Prince met with success. His own troops mutinied, pulled him out of bed one night and conveyed him over the frontier. From Vienna, ignoring all warnings, he ventured to return to Sofia. His reappearance there excited strong indignation in the Czar's Court and this was increased by the news that Prince Alexander intended to seek the hand of Princess Viktoria, daughter of the German Crown Prince and Princess.

Prince Alexander's suit was gladly welcomed by Princess Viktoria. It was supported by the Crown Princess her mother, by Queen Victoria, and by the Prince of Wales, and had gone so far as an exchange of betrothal rings. Then, however, the opposition party showed its hand. Recalling the importance of good relations with Russia, it fostered doubts about this "English scheme" and so endeavored to prevent the marriage.

The old Kaiser, concerned again to stand fast by his sacred legacy of friendship with Russia, and not to permit any whittling away of the connecting link, shared these doubts, which the Kaiserin Augusta, too, regarded as well founded.

Prince Wilhelm now found himself confronted by the problem of deciding with which party he ought to side, whether he should accede to the heart's desire of his sister or reject it. After mature reflection he decided against the marriage, however painful his action might be for her. To comfort her he reminded her that their grandfather, the old Kaiser Wilhelm, had been obliged as a young man to renounce the choice of his own heart in a similar predicament.

If the young Princess Viktoria realized that no other course was open to her but to sacrifice her love to "those horrible politics," her mother could not be moved to yield or to abandon the project of the marriage. Since she could not venture to range herself in opposition to either the Kaiser or the Chancellor, she put all the blame on her eldest son and held him to be responsible should "Vicky" be unhappy all her life. But Prince Wilhelm would not change his mind, and on political grounds adhered to the decision he had already reached.

By decree of the old Kaiser, as head of the Royal House, it was ordained that the Princess Viktoria must forthwith renounce the marriage. Like her, Prince Alexander accepted that decision.

After this gesture of renunciation by the Hohenzollerns, feeling in the House of Romanov became more amicable. Soon there was talk of Prince Wilhelm's being sent once more on a mission to St. Petersburg, but he fell ill from his old ear trouble in the summer of 1886. All sorts of absurd stories circulated in public, to the effect that such a complaint, with a discharge from the ear, might betoken a "slight suppuration of the brain," with paralysis to follow. These fears, warmly welcomed by the interested parties, were removed by the treatment at Reichenhall. From there the Prince proceeded to Bad Gastein at the invitation of his grandfather. Besides the Kaiser, Bismarck and Princess Johanna, Count Herbert Bismarck, Perponcher and Lehndorff were also staying there.

A lasting impression was made on the Prince by his meeting with the beautiful and elegant Empress Elisabeth [1] of Austria. A few days later the Emperor Franz Joseph [2] arrived, and invited the Prince to a great shooting party. For his guest, shooting deer in the Tauern with only one effective arm was often extremely fatiguing, while the Emperor clambered about like a chamois in that Alpine game reserve. After one climb the Emperor cheerily remarked: "That was fine! But it seems to have made you a bit warm!"

[1] Empress of Austria-Hungary (1837–1898), wife of Emperor Franz Joseph and a member of the gifted and unstable Wittelsbach dynasty, rulers of Bavaria. She spent much of her life in travel abroad and was stabbed to death by an Italian anarchist in Switzerland.

[2] *See* Appendix, page 440.

In regard to politics there was little or no change as a result of this meeting in Gastein. The Dual Monarchy remained on such strained terms with Russia that the Reich could not attempt a closer union with the former. "Russia must not be upset!" From that leitmotiv the Kaiser would not budge. The departure of the Kaiser and the Emperor from Gastein was destined to be a final parting. On his way home the Kaiser's strength gave out and he had a fainting spell. He was carried back to Berlin as quickly as possible.

In order to show the Czar that the desire for friendship with Russia was sincere, the project of sending Prince Wilhelm to St. Petersburg was again revived. No sooner did the Crown Princess hear of this proposal than she staked everything in an endeavor to ensure that not "William," but "the much-more-suitable Crown Prince," should go there. Bismarck held a different opinion; he considered the heir to the Throne, who had become so fond of England, and who showed an anti-Russian attitude, most unsuitable to represent the Reich. Urged by the Crown Princess, the Kaiserin made a final attempt to get her son sent to Russia. Unwisely, she made a direct approach to Bismarck, who politely but firmly told her that he would not suffer any interference in affairs of State. As she still held her ground and demanded at least an interview for discussion, Bismarck felt obliged to go and see her himself. After that audience he noted: "Never have I seen the Kaiserin look so beautiful as at the moment of my refusal. She drew herself up to her full height, her eyes flashed fire in a way I have never seen before or since. She broke off the interview and left me standing there." Afterward the Kaiserin is reported to have remarked indignantly, "Our most gracious Herr Reich's Chancellor was most ungracious to me today!"

While this dispute was going on in Berlin, Prince Wilhelm went off to Bayreuth with Count Philipp zu Eulenburg,[3] to hear *Parsifal*. The suggestion had come from Eulenburg himself. That year he had been attached to the staff of the Prussian Minister in Munich, Count Werthern-Beichlingen. The Minister thought highly of Eulenburg and shared the opinion of Bismarck, who valued and meant to further this young diplomat with such a special flair for politics. Princess Johanna, too, had taken a great liking to that "Nordic Bard Phili," largely because "he could improvise so wonderfully on the piano." It was Eulenburg's musical talent, which Prince Wilhelm

[3] *See* Appendix, page 439.

also appreciated, that first drew him to that amateur artist and was the cause of his forming a close friendship with the Count.

This year 1886 marks the beginning of the influence that Eulenburg acquired over the Prince, an influence not always beneficial for the latter, and one that was later to prove definitely detrimental. Prince Wilhelm, however, took his newly found friend entirely into his confidence; he talked to him about family matters and about his difficulties with his mother.

Eulenburg for his part had no high opinion of the Crown Princess. To others he described her as "a mixture of outstanding intelligence with Coburg cunning, of high culture with a will of iron, but avaricious!"

This new journey to Russia of Prince Wilhelm, now decided upon, brought further discord. His mother declared that she had forebodings of evil, of all kinds of awful things that were going to happen but which would be obviated if only the Crown Prince could go instead.

For the meeting with Prince Wilhelm the Czar selected the fortress of Brest Litovsk, the powerful fucrum of the fortified triangle completed by Warsaw and Ivangorod. On September tenth the Prince arrived in Brest and received a friendly welcome from the Czar and Czarevich. Afterward he had a long private interview with the Czar in the Citadel. "The Czar informed me," he said in Doorn, "that he wished to hold fast to the Triple Alliance in order to safeguard peace in Europe. He charged me to convey his cordial greetings to my grandfather and generally showed himself to be personally most well disposed. Only once did he speak in an angry tone —when I reminded him of Germany's having sacrificed her own interests in Constantinople. Then he exclaimed abruptly—'Tell Prince Bismarck that I shall take Constantinople whenever I wish to . . . and I have no need to ask his permission!' "

After his return, the Prince thought over the impressions he had received in Brest Litovsk—at that distance they stood out more clearly before his eyes: beyond a doubt the relations between Russia and the Reich had taken a serious turn for the worse, even though polite conversations had been kept up at the Citadel. The good relations that had prevailed in St. Petersburg even in 1884 no longer existed. The link was indeed not yet severed, but it now depended on a silken thread.

23. JUBILEE IN WESTMINSTER

IN JANUARY 1887 the Crown Prince fell ill. He called it a chill. As the hoarseness did not clear up, and pallor and difficulty in breathing supervened, the Court physicians called in specialists who diagnosed a disease of the larynx. The patient was recommended to take the greatest care and on that account to give up the idea of traveling to London for the Jubilee festivities.

The Crown Princess would not hear of such a thing. The thought that "William" might once again supplant them made her forget all consideration of her sick husband. She insisted on the journey so that she and the Crown Prince should represent the German Reich at the Jubilee celebrating the fifty years of her mother's reign. But as the Crown Prince could speak only in a whisper, his eldest son was deputed to go as his assistant. This arrangement was scarcely conducive to smoothing the relations between the Prince and his parents.

Prince Wilhelm was accompanied by Lieutenant Colonel von Kessel, a favorite of the Crown Princess, who had nursed him after he had received a wound at St. Privat. Later, Kessel and the Prince had both served in the 6th Company of the First Guards Regiment (1877); after that Kessel became adjutant to the Crown Prince and Princess. The Crown Prince had shown great confidence in Kessel; he trusted him with the administration of his money and—more important still—used him as a link with Bismarck, who was a cousin of Kessel's. Now he had been chosen to go to London in order to keep the balance between the Crown Prince and Princess and their eldest son.

On a radiant June day the royal party on board the German destroyer *Blitz*, with a flotilla of torpedo boats as escort, under the command of Prince Heinrich, entered the Thames. Preparations for the festivities and for the reception of the German representatives were in confusion owing to unforeseen incidents. Amendments and misunderstandings had deranged the settled program and brought about disorder. In consequence of the strict seclusion of the widowed Queen and the lack of all festival occasions for many years past, the procedures for entertaining guests had almost been forgotten.

The early morning of Jubilee Day found half of London on foot. At last the Queen was going to show herself to her people. And it was going to be done with all the pomp of former times. From the palace gates the Queen's carriage was escorted by Household and Indian Cavalry, and followed by her sons, grandsons and sons-in-law on horseback. The German Crown Prince was a striking figure in his Pasewalk Cuirassier's uniform. Few people knew that this upright, heroic man was already doomed to death. His pale face betrayed no sign of pain, gave no hint of the agonies he had to endure. He did all in his power to avoid distressing the anxious woman at his side. It was only when the endlessly long ceremonies in Westminster Abbey and at the Court were over that he could withdraw to divest himself of his cramping uniform.

At the banquet in Windsor Prince Wilhelm found himself sitting next to a lady on his right who decidedly was not an everyday type of fellow guest. She was the sister of King Kalakaua of Hawaii.

On the homeward run, when abreast of Heligoland, an active movement of shipping could be seen heading for the mouth of the Elbe. And there were freight barges and dredgers making for Brunsbüttel, where work on the Kaiser Wilhelm Canal was just beginning.

At the ceremony of laying the foundation stone for the great shipway, to link the North and the Baltic Seas, Prince Wilhelm stood with his brother Heinrich beside the old Kaiser. The Crown Prince was not present on that day—he was "excused on account of his hoarseness."

Now, as the little *Blitz* entered the Elbe, Prince Wilhelm sent for her Commander to thank him for the happy ending and smooth progress of the mission. Later, as Kaiser, he had many occasions to repeat this, for the captain's name was Alfred Tirpitz.[1]

[1] Admiral Alfred von Tirpitz (1849–1930) held the rank of Grand Admiral from 1911 until his retirement in 1916. He was a political admiral who wielded considerable influence in the Reichstag before the war and hoped to be appointed Chancellor. He was the spearhead of the Big Navy group in Germany, opposed an accommodation with Britain, and criticized Chancellor von Bethmann-Hollweg for his indecision.

24. THE REINSURANCE TREATY

IN BERLIN relations with Russia were once again figuring in the foreground, being endangered this time by falsified news transmitted to St. Petersburg and purporting to show that Bismarck had favored the candidature of Ferdinand of Coburg as Prince of Bulgaria.

Alexander III, always suspicious, and especially suspicious of Bismarck, spoke of "an insult" and in his embittered indignation issued regulations aimed at the German Reich, among them a ukase which made it impossible for Germans to acquire landed property in Russia.

Bismarck retorted by forbidding the Reichsbank to make any loan transactions against Russian securities. This counterstroke got home. Unfortunately, one result was a heated agitation against the Reich and bellicose feelings found open expression in St. Petersburg. To restrain this and so avoid war the Czar decided with a heavy heart to go to Berlin and, as he said, obtain a definite clarification as to what the German Government really wanted and in what direction it was moving.

The prospect of being able to speak face to face with the Czar delighted the old Kaiser. In that case it was only a question of seeing that nothing happened that was likely to upset the Russian. His dread of some untoward event occurring assumed in the mind of the old gentleman—as Philipp Eulenburg declared—the character of "chimerical illusions and nightmares." Thus the old Kaiser imagined "the Czar, received by no one, standing alone on the platform of the Lehrter Railway Station in Berlin."

In view of the obscurity of the situation and the unsettled relations to the Berlin Court, the Czar declined to accept the hospitality of the Royal Schloss—he preferred to put up at the Russian Embassy, Unter den Linden. This was an unequivocal and almost provocative gesture which clearly showed that this was not, as before, a friendly visit, but an official one to collect information.

Both the Kaiser and Bismarck were anxious to bring Prince Wilhelm into the discussions with the Czar, since he had already shown in two previous meetings that he knew the right tone to adopt in dealing with that difficult individual. So, as a young man of twenty-eight, the Prince found himself acting as an intermediary between two great monarchs, and displayed so much prudence and dexterity in the task that both his grandfather and the Chancellor were highly pleased with him. The Czar, too, and the Czarina, who had come with him, showed themselves agreeably impressed by his skillful discharge of his duty.

This *rapprochement* led to the conclusion of the so-called Treaty of Reinsurance, regarding which Bismarck explained that it was his wish to remain closely allied with both the Eastern Empires, adding, as a proviso, that the realization of that wish might not be easy in view of the ill feeling between Russia and Austria-Hungary.

"Should we not succeed," he continued, "in having both Russia and the Dual Monarchy for lasting friends, as stipulated, then we must at least hold fast to the one we have!"

The pact constituted a formal Treaty of Neutrality, with paragraphs containing many clauses and reservations. Even before it was signed Bismarck had declared that as an agreement "it was as slippery as an eel." Count Shuvalov [1] called it "double-tongued." Even in the Berlin Foreign Office voices were heard to express openly the opinion that its provisions were ill-considered and pregnant with possible difficulties. All this was put down as "the third mistake of the aging Chancellor."

Nevertheless it was thanks to this Treaty of Reinsurance that the acute danger of war was averted and that the snapping of the "connecting thread" was prevented. Moreover, for the time being the menacing fear that Russia, disappointed with the Reich, might turn to France, was dispelled. The ardent chauvinist Déroulède, who had already scored some success in St. Petersburg with his agitation

[1] Count Peter Andreivich Shuvalov (1827–1889) was the member of an aristocratic Russian family who served as Ambassador to Britain from 1873 to 1879. He maintained good relations with the British during the difficult period of the Russo-Turkish war of 1877–1878 but was regarded by many Russians as too much influenced by Bismarck. Shuvalov's approval of the Berlin Congress, which modified the Treaty of San Stefano, caused him to be withdrawn from London in 1879, and he spent the remaining ten years of his life in retirement.

against Germany, found himself obliged to break off his campaign and abandon projects as yet unperformed. In June 1887 the Treaty came into force. It was one of the old Kaiser's last efforts, undertaken in great haste, as though he sought, in the short time left to him, to provide a support for the house that he had himself erected.

25. CRITICAL DAYS IN BAVENO

THE FIRST SPECIALIST called in to the ailing Crown Prince was the Household Physician, Professor Gerhardt, then living in Berlin. After the treatment in Bad Ems had been taken without results Gerhardt found no other way (with the scope of professional knowledge at that time) than to remove the thickened vocal membranes by means of forceps and a wire heated to incandescence by an electric current. Then, in March 1887, began the prolonged and agonizing ordeal of the unfortunate heir to the Throne.

In spite of this treatment the tumor continued to increase in size until Gerhardt declined to accept the sole responsibility any longer. He went to consult the Crown Prince's Physician-in-Ordinary, Dr. Wegner, with a view to choosing a surgeon. Both of them suspected cancer of the larynx. Their choice fell on Privy Councilor von Bergmann, who had the highest reputation. After an examination of the tumor, Bergmann shared the opinion of his two colleagues and proposed a surgical intervention from the outside, which he would himself carry out. But in order to be on the safe side he asked that a laryngologist should be called in to confirm his diagnosis and the necessity of the intervention proposed.

After a good deal of discussion it was decided, out of consideration for the distressed Crown Princess, to call Dr. Morell Mackenzie from London. Before the English specialist arrived the condition of the patient had changed visibly for the worse, so much so that the old Kaiser ordered further German doctors to be consulted. Unanimously they recommended an immediate partial operation on the larynx, with removal of the suppurating vocal membranes. When the patient inquired what the probable aftereffects of such an operation would be, Bergmann gave him the reassuring answer that "only a chronic hoarseness would remain."

Upon this, both the Crown Prince and the Princess agreed to the operation. The soothing effect of the verdict of the assembled doctors acted as a restorative, especially for the Princess, who had already given up all hope of a recovery. Everything had been got ready for the operation when, on the eve of the appointed day, Dr. Mackenzie arrived in Potsdam.

He too made an examination of the larynx and then explained that only he, as a laryngologist, was qualified to give an accurate diagnosis, and his opinion must be "No cancer! Only an affection of a polypous nature with thickening of the vocal membranes! Therefore, no occasion to operate!" By his method of treatment the tumor should be absorbed in about six or eight weeks. He further assured the Princess that he would restore the patient's voice so that "His Royal Highness will be able to command a whole Army Corps!"

Triumphantly the Crown Princess declared that it only needed an English doctor to come and show the German nitwits what ought to be done. But this insult gave the German doctors no reason for altering their diagnosis. They saw that they would be compelled to stand passively by and watch how this Englishman was going to carry out his miraculous treatment which, they anticipated, would never effect a cure.

The skepticism of the German doctors, and the self-assurance of the English laryngologist divided the Crown Prince's family into two camps—the Mackenzie party and the Bergmann party. So Prince Wilhelm found himself once more obliged to decide for one or the other. He ranged himself against Mackenzie, whose optimism, after talking it over with the German doctors, he could not share.

As an old man in Doorn, he endeavored to make this clear and to defend his action. "Can one blame my mother for having, in the face of so decided an opinion given by a distinguished specialist, believed in him and trusted him and elected for a treatment that presented no immediate danger? She was given to believe that this would give a better result than the operation, and might even remove the hoarseness altogether!"

In accordance with Mackenzie's prescription there now began a

series of fitful removals from one place to another—first of all to the
Isle of Wight, from there to Toblach in the Southern Tyrol, where
the Crown Prince frequently suffered from fits of depression, speaking of presentiments of death. After a visit to Innichen he decided
that the little church that stood there should be taken as the model
for his own tomb in Potsdam. And so it was.

From Toblach they went on to Venice, and finally to Baveno on
the Lago Maggiore, where they rented the Villa Henfrey. If the old
English style of the villa pleased the Crown Princess by reminding
her of home, so also did the thought that her mother had stayed
there eight years before and had planted two trees in the garden as a
memorial of her sojourn. In this house the Crown Prince spent his
last birthday. Prince Wilhelm, coming with congratulations, found
his father's condition in no way bettered, which rendered him more
opposed than ever to Mackenzie. He also found that there was
truth in the reports circulating in Berlin, to the effect that "the
Englishman, Mackenzie, was behaving like a Prussian Minister, lec-
turing everybody everywhere and making himself a nuisance by his
arrogant attitude." The representatives of the press, too, were complaining bitterly, because he would give them instructions as to what
they were to report, which was, of course, to include a good deal
about himself and the success already achieved by his treatment.

While this treatment went on, Mackenzie did not forget to collect
substantial fees in advance, and through the mediation of the Crown
Princess he procured a knighthood for himself.

Despite his dubious behavior the Crown Princess continued to
place her confidence in the English doctor. Her love for her stricken
husband made her blind. Her zeal and devotion in nursing him were
tireless and admirable. Thirty years before this her mother had just
in the same way tended Prince Albert and done all in her power to
prolong his life. All this care and self-sacrifice Prince Wilhelm was
glad to see. But he became all the more bitter against Mackenzie,
whom in private he called a charlatan.

Speaking afterward in Doorn, he said: "When one thinks that,
but for the interference of that English doctor, my father's life might,
so far as any human being can tell, have been saved, it can be understood why, from then on, I felt compelled to combat the ostrichlike
policy of my mother. The fact that she was unable to free herself

from the domination of that Englishman, even when events had made things perfectly clear to everyone else, prejudiced my feelings toward her to the very worst degree."

26. PREPARATIONS OF ALL KINDS

THE WINTER OF 1887–1888 found Bismarck confronted with the difficult task of practicing and carrying out a clear and positive policy in circumstances that were far from clear. Every day he had to reckon on the possibility of his gray-haired master leaving him, and of the Crown Prince, a dying man, coming into his heritage. What would happen then remained obscure and could scarcely be foreseen. Overhasty steps would be taken, all sorts of innovations must be expected . . . until the young Prince Wilhelm should come to upset everything once again.

In his sleepless nights the old Kaiser saw phantoms and dark clouds arising to obstruct his view of the future. His thoughts often turned to his dying son in Baveno and to his young grandson Wilhelm, on whom such a heavy burden of responsibility must soon fall. He, the son of Queen Luise, thought also of Alexander I.[1] What would happen should Russia turn her back, or even prefer war? Who would then lead the Prussian Army? He, the graybeard, could no longer do it. His son, the victor of Wörth, lay mortally ill. Moltke was nearly ninety. There remained only his grandson Wilhelm, who had only recently been made a Brigade Commander and who had had no experience for leadership in war.

In this situation, so perplexing both at home and abroad, Bismarck decided to publish in the *Reichsanzeiger,* on February third, the text of a treaty of alliance concluded two years previously with

[1] Czar Alexander I of Russia (1777–1825) made a pact with Napoleon in 1802, and then after Napoleon's invasion of Russia in 1812 and the Congress of Vienna in 1815, joined the Holy Alliance in the hope of working toward a European confederation. But during the last five years of his life he adopted increasingly repressive measures inside Russia and in foreign affairs dropped his original policy of European confederation in favor of dictatorship of the four great powers—Russia, France, Austria, and Prussia.

Austria-Hungary. Three days later he explained this measure in the Reichstag. Though he had often expressed his doubts about the value of parliaments he considered the Reichstag as the guarantor of existing arrangements, an automatic brake in the event of the two successors to Wilhelm I and the new governments being inclined to precipitate overhasty measures. Two years before he had declared in the Reichstag: "I look on it as desirable and necessary that the policy of the Government should be openly ·deliberated and discussed by a great assembly that represents the people—that without its consent laws should not be made or taxes levied—in short, that the Government should be guarded against acts of folly and partisanship by the veto of a representative body."

At the sitting of the Reichstag on February sixth, at which both Prince Wilhelm and the Princess Auguste Viktoria were present, the Chancellor openly alluded for the first time to the possibility of a war on two fronts—against Russia and France. Addressing the Deputies, he declared: "We have the wish for peace, but we shall not shirk any armed decision that may be forced upon us." Then he ended with these words, which have since become celebrated and were (as he himself confessed afterward) impromptu: "We Germans fear God, but nothing else on earth!"

The Chancellor's conjecture that arrangements had been made to suit all possibilities by the "Friedrichs" in Baveno and by Prince Wilhelm was duly confirmed. The reports he received indicated that the Crown Princess was living with only one thought in her mind—that her husband must be sufficiently restored to health to take over the Government at the death of the old Kaiser. Decrees of all kinds had been drafted, amended and were held in readiness. They were not going to let themselves be caught unprepared!

Prince Wilhelm too had not been inactive. Like his mother he was making out orders and drafting decrees. One proclamation he even submitted to the Reich's Chancellor for his opinion, with this covering letter:

"Your Serene Highness—I beg to enclose herewith a document that I have composed in view of the not-impossible eventuality of the early or sudden decease of both the Kaiser and my father. It is a brief address to my future colleagues, the Princes of the German Reich. . . ." In it the Prince went on to say that the Federal princes might perhaps have doubts about recognizing one so young as he as

Kaiser. In regard to that, he continued, it might be well to confront his aforesaid colleagues with a *fait accompli* by the prompt issue of a proclamation. He considered it desirable to have a sealed copy of that proclamation deposited in each embassy or legation. With the proclamation itself he included an outline sketch dealing with his proposals for action in the social sphere. He announced that he wished to effect these reforms immediately after his accession to the Throne.

Bismarck considered both these documents to be amateurish and also unnecessary, so he let them lie for six weeks in a drawer of his writing table. During all that time the Prince waited in vain for the approval of his tutor, who finally gave a short considered reply in which "he respectfully suggested to the writer to burn both the papers without delay."

27. THE VILLA ZIRIO

FROM BAVENO, where it could be cold in November, the Crown Prince was moved to San Remo, where the Villa Zirio was rented. It was a two-story house with tiled floors and fireplaces, but no stove and no bathroom. The Princess at once arranged for these to be installed.

The garden, not a very large one, was planted with tall palms and ran up by little terraces to an artificial grotto where, on a sunny little plateau, the patient's deck chair was set up daily.

The improvements to the house had not yet been completed when the condition of the Crown Prince took such an alarming turn for the worse that Mackenzie became uneasy and would not assume sole responsibility any longer. Hitherto he had ignored the German doctors. Now he saw himself obliged to beg the assistance of "those swindlers"—the words by which the Crown Princess, in her agitation and excitement, had designated the German practitioners.

At this critical turning point Prince Wilhelm decided to make an end of this constant shilly-shallying in the treatment of his father. His grandfather agreeing, he set out for San Remo, taking with him Dr. Schmidt from Frankfort, a throat specialist of repute. Meantime

Mackenzie had recommended to the Crown Prince and Princess two doctors with whose assistance he would be willing to continue the further treatment. These were Professor Schröter in Vienna, a specialist in this field, and the Berlin doctor, Krause, a university lecturer.

Speaking about this in Doorn, the Kaiser said: "When I reached the Villa Zirio on the evening of November ninth, my arrival caused my mother little pleasure. On the doorstep I had to submit to her remonstrances and listen to her determined refusals to allow me to see my father. She wanted me to proceed to Rome at once, as there was nothing in my father's condition to cause apprehension. The stony look on her face, quite different from what it had been at Baveno, showed me that she was not telling me the truth. Suddenly I heard a noise at the door and caught a glimpse of my father. I hastened to him and greeted him. In a whisper he expressed his pleasure at my visit. During the days that followed we drew quite near together."

Before very long, however, this reconciliation of father and son was suddenly interrupted. It was a step taken by Prince Bismarck that provoked a fresh estrangement. The Chancellor had indeed written to the Crown Prince to acquaint him with this measure that was being taken, but the Crown Princess, fearing that its contents might upset her husband, had kept the letter back. So it was from a newspaper that the unsuspecting invalid learned of an order of the Kaiser's, dated November 17, 1887, countersigned by Prince Bismarck, and addressed to Prince Wilhelm. It ran as follows: "In view of the changeability in my state of health, which may temporarily compel me to forgo the conduct of affairs, and in view of the illness of my son, the Crown Prince, I charge your Royal Highness to represent me in all cases where I shall think it necessary to be represented by a deputy in the current affairs of government; this applies in particular to the signing of orders. It will not be necessary to issue special orders authorizing you to act on each individual occasion."

Indignant at being thus excluded from governmental affairs, the Crown Prince spoke of "unheard-of tactlessness," of "Bismarck's bullet, which could have no other aim than that of hastening his death." Already made irritable by his malady, he seized his notebook and pencil and wrote, repeating the words several times, *"but I'm not an imbecile!"*

It was shortly after this that Prince Wilhelm wrote to his former tutor, Georg Hinzpeter, a letter which was characteristic of him and of his frame of mind at the time:

Dear Doctor,

Sentence has been passed by the medical attendants. The awful fate that for the few who knew the truth has for long stood in the background like a menacing ghost has not been fulfilled!

According to the definite verdict of the doctors given this day, my father is suffering from an incurable cancer and no power of mortal man can save him. It has gone so far that even the serious operation contemplated by Bergmann in the spring could no longer be of any use. This morning the doctors, assembled together, informed him of this. Standing erect, and looking the spokesman straight in the face, he heard his sentence. Without a tremor and without betraying even a trace of emotion, he thanked them for their efforts and for their care, and then dismissed them.

Silent and astonished, they left the hero, filled with admiration for his character, which designated him as a true Hohenzollern and a great soldier.

When we were with him afterward, it was he who consoled us with a calm smiling face, while we could no longer control our tears. What a man! May God send that he suffers as little pain as possible in this dreadful and shocking ending of his life!

I should never have believed that tears could come as a relief, for till now I never knew what they were. Today I found how they can mitigate a fearful pain.

A blow, a bullet, anything would be better than this most atrocious of all maladies. I can scarcely grasp it, even now!

It can be discerned that two incompatible lines of thought occupied the Prince's mind, which oscillated between the triumphant and the sentimental. The only explanation is that they ran parallel with the perpetual clash of his own feelings, for or against his parents. While for the first time he signed state papers his father had to stand by powerless and inactive as his son, passing him over, began to rule the Reich.

On February 9, 1888, it was decided, because the patient was experiencing increased difficulty in breathing, to carry out the long-planned surgical intervention. This was performed by Dr. Bramann, assistant to Professor Bergmann. He also inserted a silver canule. During this difficult operation Mackenzie, more dead than alive, waited in an adjoining room to hear of its success. His reputation as a doctor was shattered and it only remained for him to take his departure. Before he left San Remo, however, he published an explanation in which he attempted to justify his wrong diagnosis by the amazing excuse that he had only announced "no cancer" because he did not wish to attest the incapacity of the Crown Prince to govern.

What the Crown Princess had to undergo in the Villa Zirio represented an unequaled martyrdom. Her life was one of never-ending care and anguish for her beloved dying husband. The hope of being able to reign by the side of "that noble man," a hope that she had cherished for three decades, now offered no prospect of fulfillment. Should he be taken from her she had no wish to go on living. Count Waldersee described her state as "bordering on insanity." Bismarck, who heard the same report from other sources, feared that in her condition "she might be capable of any rash act."

Anyone who happened to see her at the villa found himself face to face with a desperate woman who, with difficulty, controlled her feelings. With her lips tightly closed and her features convulsed, her face resembled a mask of stone. Stony and heartless, too, was the short note she wrote to her eldest son at Christmas, in which scorn and triumph mingled as though to hide her own bitterness. "We were very gay, and had no reason to be sad, for your father is getting on well. The only sad thing is that your grandparents are so old!"

28. THE PASSING
OF THE OLD KAISER

THE OLD KAISER spent the last days of his life lying on his narrow camp bed beside which the Kaiserin Augusta sat huddled in a wheelchair. In that bedroom they awaited news, the bulletins of the doctors at San Remo. The expected improvement in the Crown

Prince's condition as the result of Bergmann's operation never took place. In Berlin no one any longer believed in a recovery. Rumors were already circulating that the heir to the throne was dying, and that in any case he would never see his native land again.

At the request of his grandfather, Prince Wilhelm returned again to San Remo, arriving at the Villa Zirio on March second. He found his father in a heart-rending state. But only three days later he was recalled by telegram to Berlin. The Kaiser was dying.

In Doorn he afterward declared: "When I reached Berlin on March seventh the doctors gave my beloved grandfather only a few hours to live. Time and again his pulse had failed. Indescribable was my emotion as I approached this deathbed, so soon after leaving another!"

Patiently the old man lay there awaiting the end, wearing a white jacket with a woolen Scottish shawl round his neck. By the camp bed were assembled the nearest relatives, his personal A.D.C.s and Bismarck, to whom the dying man made a sign. Only semiconscious, he mistook the old paladin for Prince Wilhelm, and in feeble voice spoke these touching words: "I have been very satisfied with you. You have done everything very well."

As Prince Wilhelm in his turn came to his bedside the Kaiser, still confused, thought he was the Crown Prince. With his last strength he exhorted him to go on governing on the lines he had himself laid down, and never to abandon the alliance with Russia. Then his head fell slightly to one side and he gradually passed into everlasting sleep.

The first Kaiser of the new German Reich was dead and with him an epoch came to an end. A different and restless age was to follow. Bismarck knew it would be so. Leaning his head against the frame of the door he sobbed aloud, weeping for the old master at whose side he had fought for, and won, the successes of a lifetime.

On the following morning there came a telegram from San Remo addressed by the new Kaiser to his son Wilhelm, now Crown Prince: "Deeply grieved by the death of my father, at which not I, but you, had the privilege of being present. I express my firm confidence that you, in loyalty and obedience, will be an example to all."

Scarcely had this unmistakable and pointed warning been received, when another telegram arrived, instructing Bismarck to have everything made ready for the Kaiser's enthronement. As Kaiser he wished to be known as Friedrich IV.

Bismarck, who had little time for romantic imperial niceties, opposed the idea that the new head of the State should have himself proclaimed as the successor of the medieval Staufen Emperors.[1] He replied that, in consideration of the Federal princes, the only possible name was Friedrich III; this was also in accordance with the Prussian tradition, "for the King of Prussia was at the same time the German Emperor." While the stricken Sovereign was on his way home to his own country, the Army was being sworn to allegiance to the Kaiser, Friedrich III. The Charlottenburg Schloss was allotted to him as his residence, for here, owing to its extensive park and its proximity to the River Havel, the air was fairly free from dust.

Bismarck traveled as far as Leipzig to meet the new Kaiser and Kaiserin, in order to put before them and explain a proclamation drafted by himself. But Kaiser Friedrich had brought one of his own with him, composed by the jurist Friedrich Geffcken, which was to be published at once.

The funeral of Wilhelm I took place on March sixteenth. It was an icily cold day, so Bismarck and several old Generals, mindful of their health, had to stay at home. The Crown Prince Wilhelm walked immediately behind the coffin, followed by Field Marshal von Moltke, who, despite his great age, insisted on escorting his dead master for the last time. Count Perponcher, representing the Maison Militaire, found the cold particularly unpleasant because, having to carry the cushion on which were laid out the orders and decorations of the deceased Monarch, he could not keep his hands in his pockets as the others did.

As the cortege passed by the Charlottenburg Schloss and into the park toward the mausoleum, Kaiser Friedrich stepped to a window to take leave of his father. Standing erect in full uniform, he could be seen by the troops lining the roadway. As the coffin disappeared into the Tannenallee the Kaiser was suddenly overcome by a fit of trembling. The curtains were quickly drawn and behind them the new Kaiser collapsed into the arms of his A.D.C.s.

[1] Of the line of Hohenstaufen.

29. FRIEDRICHSKRON

ALL THOSE whose duties brought them into contact with the second Kaiser were shocked at his appearance. Suffering and shrunken, his face the color of yellow wax, he was scarcely capable of making himself understood even by whispering. He wrote what he wanted to say on little slips of paper; questions he answered by nodding or shaking his head. When the Finance Minister, Scholz, came to report on the proposed issue of new gold and silver coins bearing his effigy, for the minting of which several more months would be required, the Kaiser wearily declined to discuss it, saying, "I shall not live to see it."

The Kaiserin Friedrich, as she was generally called, had now achieved, if only for a short while, that to which she had so long aspired—the supreme authority belonging now to her husband and herself—"William" was relegated to his proper place and would now have to wait and go through the same experience that she had had to endure for thirty long years. The assurance that her husband would live on varied, however, with her moods. Often she sank into fits of the deepest depression when she realized that this period of reigning must always be a losing battle against death. In such moments of despair she longed to have her mother from England beside her. In lengthy letters to her she complained of her own terrible suffering, and with impetuous entreaties implored her not to forsake her "Vicky" now. In reply to these cries for help, Queen Victoria decided to go to Berlin. To accompany her she chose Prince and Princess Henry of Battenberg. Immediately on reaching Charlottenburg the Queen, with her solid and calm common sense, realized that this son-in-law of hers—"who could only just breathe"—was doomed. She saw that her "Vicky" was living in a state of hoping against hope, and that sooner or later she would have to face the stubborn facts. They were the same facts that, twenty-seven years before, had left the Queen a solitary figure after the death of Prince Albert.

From the high hopes aroused by a temporary improvement in the patient's condition the Kaiserin was plunged into disconsolate despair when the doctors shrugged their shoulders and had to confess that human aid could now only mitigate, but never cure.

On May 24, 1888, the marriage of Prince Heinrich of Prussia with the Princess Irene of Hesse-Darmstadt was celebrated in the chapel of the Charlottenburg Schloss. It took place in an atmosphere of gloom, for the Kaiser's worn-out appearance resembled that of a man already dead. Recalling the occasion in Doorn, Wilhelm II declared, "Never have I attended such a wedding as that!"

It did, however, provide the Crown Prince with an opportunity of meeting his "Uncle Bertie" again, and of renewing the relations established between them eight years before in Marlborough House. The nephew showed himself so obliging and modest that the Prince, when leaving, could only confess to sister "Vicky" that nothing had pleased him so much as "William's" friendly attitude toward himself!

One morning the Kaiserin found a note on her breakfast table which read: "Where I was born, there too will I die." She knew then that the sick man was convinced that his end was near. Further notes gave instructions for a move to the Neues Palais at Potsdam, which by his desire was to be given the name of Friedrichskron.

On the evening of May 31, 1888, the Kaiser drove to the mausoleum in the Charlottenburg Park to see the tombs of his father and grandparents, and to take his leave of them. The next day the journey to Potsdam was made in the yacht *Alexandra*. The waterway was chosen on the advice of the doctors, since to travel by smoky railway or dusty road would be harmful.

From the window of the saloon the Kaiser could enjoy the views over the Wannsee, the Isle of Peacocks and Heilandskirche (Church of the Saviour), which recalled many memories of the sunny days of his youth. Thence the route lay under the bridges from Potsdam into the Templiner See, where the *Alexandra* was moored close to the shore of the Wildpark.

To everyone's astonishment, in the ninety-nine days of his reign the Kaiser had not made any fundamental changes, or even sought to pay off old scores. He had indeed dismissed the old gentlemen of his father's suite, with honors, had appointed new A.D.C.s and made Prince Radolin Lord Chamberlain, but the most important change of all, which people both at Court and at large had regarded as imminent, the dismissal of Reich's Chancellor Prince Bismarck, had not been effected.

Immediately after his accession Kaiser Friedrich had assured the Chancellor of his absolute confidence, and Bismarck himself, impressed by this generous gesture, had grasped the outstretched hand and held it fast. He even attempted to establish tolerable relations with the Kaiserin and was to some extent successful, as appears from the droll humor of the words he used in writing to Lucius: "I am now associating with the Kaiserin Friedrich as if I was an old man in love!"

This inexplicable shift of the Imperial couple toward amity with Bismarck, their old adversary, was interpreted in Court circles as meaning that this conciliatory attitude had only one object—to remove the Crown Prince from his influence.

In point of fact everything was aimed at keeping the Crown Prince out of State affairs. The attitude of the parents toward their eldest son remained cool, not to say aloof. When he called on his father and mother at Friedrichskron he would be met on the doorstep by footmen who, like so many trained parrots, blocked the way with assurances that "His Majesty is sleeping," and "Her Majesty has visitors."

There was no lack of visitors to Friedrichskron. Among them was Sir Morell Mackenzie who, in spite of all that had happened, regained his *entrée*. To demonstrate his influence in the palais he received journalists there and even took them into the bedroom of the dying man, who was powerless to stop them.

As a precaution the courtiers and ministers began now to "cultivate" the Crown Prince. Heinrich von Friedberg, Minister of Justice, in the course of a stroll together, informed him that as minister he was obliged to put before him, immediately on the death of the Kaiser, a document which had been drawn up by King Friedrich Wilhelm IV. The document was an appeal to his successors to restore the Constitution to its pre-1848 form, since only an authoritarian monarchy could succeed in Prussia. Every king of Prussia should be answerable to God alone, in accordance with the formula, "My Throne I hold from God alone. To Him alone am I accountable for every day and every hour of my reign."

The cover of this document showed two records of having been "seen," one by Wilhelm I, the other by Friedrich III. Both had read it, and returned it to the State archives. After his accession, Wilhelm II returned only *the cover* to the archives, with the endorsement "Contents perused and destroyed."

Only once did a foreign ruler appear at Friedrichskron. He was King Oscar of Sweden, who came on a visit on June 13, 1888. The Kaiser received him in the uniform of the Pasewalker Cuirassiers. When he attempted to take a few steps to meet his guest, his strength failed him.

The seat of the malady lay hidden under the white collar of the uniform. The tissues of the throat were already decomposed. The silver tube no longer served to admit liquid nourishment, which flowed away with the blood and pus by its side. The windows of the sickroom had to be kept wide open to make the atmosphere bearable.

On the evening of June fourteenth Surgeon General Professor Bardeleben and Dr. Schrader reported that artificial feeding was no longer possible, that there was a progressive failure of strength and that the end must soon come.

Before the final agony began Prince Bismarck was admitted to the sickroom to see the Kaiser for the last time. The dying man recognized him, took his hand and laid it in that of the Kaiserin, pressing them together with an appealing glance at Bismarck.

During the following night the heir to the Throne slept in a guest room at Friedrichskron, not far from his father. On the morning of the fifteenth he was awakened by his sister Viktoria and brought to his father's bedside, where the Kaiserin and the other children were already waiting. Once again the Kaiser's trembling hand guided his pencil across a slip of paper. He wrote, "Victoria, myself and the children." They were his last words. The second German Kaiser had passed away.

The previous evening Prince Wilhelm had arranged for his new Marshal of the Household, Major von Natzmer, with a picked group of devoted officers, to be accommodated in Friedrichskron. These were given instructions that "nobody, not even the doctor," should be allowed to communicate with anyone outside the Schloss, and that nobody should leave it. Anyone who made difficulties—no matter who it was—was to be arrested at once.

"Scarcely had Friedrich III closed his eyes," said Robert Dohme, a close friend, "when detachments of the Training Battalion arrived at the palace at the double. Systematically, guards with loaded rifles were placed around the terrace. Major von Natzmer chased round the Schlóss issuing orders and checking the sentry posts. Then suddenly the Guards Hussars appeared at the trot and posted groups at each of the entrances to the park. The Schloss was closed hermetically by military posts."

In the course of the morning more orders followed. No telegrams were to be sent from the palace without the consent of the new Kaiser. Even the telegram composed by the board of doctors to summon Dr. Virchow for the dissection had to be submitted for a visa.

The Kaiserin Friedrich was now, as she complained, a prisoner in the hands of her son. Now she turned to her daughter-in-law, Auguste Viktoria, with the request that her liberty should not be curtailed at that difficult moment when her dearly loved husband had not even been buried. As this appeal fell on deaf ears she addressed herself to the Kaiserin Augusta, "Fritz is dead and I am desperate. She who was so proud and happy to be his wife weeps for your only son, weeps with you, his poor mother! No mother ever had such a son! Only this very morning, early, he sent his greeting to you!"

As Wilhelm II explained afterward in Doorn, "The measures taken were severe, but necessary. The object of isolating the palais was to prevent State or secret documents being conveyed to England by my mother, a possibility of which Bismarck had warned me. That even those measures were insufficient is shown by the fact that important State papers did reach England and were made public there, to the detriment of the German Reich."

Among ordinary people in general no one could understand these precautionary proceedings, and in any case could not comprehend a mother's being treated like that, especially immediately after she had suffered so grievous a bereavement.

The ordering of the funeral ceremonies was undertaken by Wilhelm II in person, for so he was styled in succession from his grandfather, Wilhelm I. The preparations in the Jaspis Gallery for placing the body on the bier have been dsecribed in detail by Philipp zu Eulenburg: "The dead man was very hastily dressed in his uniform. Just as hurriedly the gallery was emptied of its contents, while the coffin, surrounded by workmen plying their hammers and by flowers and fabrics, stood on the floor like a tool chest. No heads of foreign States were invited. The whole route as far as the Friedenskirche (Church of Peace) was lined by a cordon of troops."

While Eulenburg noted the dignified bearing of both officers and men, he was all the more severe as regards the clergy, who, he said, "stood around laughing and chattering." He had some unfavorable comment to make, too, about Field Marshal von Blumenthal, who, with the Royal Standard hanging down his back, was reeling this way and that, showing little sorrow for his deceased Kaiser.

Immediately after the interment a number of new orders were given out which showed that the young Kaiser meant to go his own way, just as Bismarck had foretold. These were written on sheets of paper which still bore the heading "Friedrichskron." This was struck out and the original designation of Neues Palais substituted in a way that underlined the significance of the act.

30. NEUES PALAIS

WITH THE ACCESSION of Wilhelm II two epochs came to an end. Scarcely had he become Crown Prince when, at the age of twenty-nine, he received the scepter that had shortly before fallen from the hand of one aged ninety-two. As Kaiser, he was warmly welcomed by, above all, the young and progressive generation. Great hopes and expectations had been entertained for him, though nobody knew whether or no they were to be fulfilled. Little was known of the new ruler except that he had a will of his own and for that reason had not got on particularly well with his parents.

The older generation sincerely mourned the two dead Kaisers. Under them they had felt secure. What would happen now remained obscure. People were afraid of reforms and changes, which were already appearing at the Court. The former General Aides-de-Camp had been dismissed and in place of the old-fashioned Maison Militaire there had come into being the Great Headquarters.

Alike at Court and in the Civil Service there was apprehension regarding the "change of course" and fear of the possibly menacing "blue letter." [1] For that reason many were mourning in earnest and wore their black clothes for a disproportionately long time.

The new Kaiser elected to model himself on his grandfather. The grandson would now only speak of him as "Wilhelm the Great," an epithet not at all to the liking of the old gentleman, who would have always strenuously rejected that designation of himself. Later on he would allude to him in even more extravagant terms: "If that great leader had lived in the Middle Ages he would have been canonized and pilgrimages would have been made from all parts of the country to say prayers over his bones." And again: "When the dawn of the new German Reich rose radiant then he, a grown man, was permitted to realize the dreams of his youth. With the German sword in his fist, the son won on the bloody battlefield the Imperial German Crown for the father. It is thanks to his hammer blows that the Emperor's armor was solidly forged."

These extravagant and bombastic words are untrue both in form and substance, for Wilhelm I had always found the title of Emperor repugnant and had even refused to act as President of an assembly composed of the German princely aristocracy because he was strongly of the opinion that it would detract from the Prussian idea of kingship. Only the pressure of those about him had persuaded the old gentleman, who would much have preferred to remain King of Prussia. The young Kaiser overlooked these facts. Even more than his father he allowed himself to be dominated by his bent for the romantic, a bent encouraged by a soon constituted clique at Court, which acquiescently and uncritically approved of everything that their young master did or wanted to do.

To figure as "the enlarger of the Reich" represented for Wilhelm II the most lofty of aims and meant the fulfilling of that "Divine Grace and Favor" of which both his father and his grandfather had wisely been chary of speaking.

There was no one there who had the power to exercise any restraining influence on him. His mother was cut off from him. So, too, was old Hinzpeter, who no longer ventured to give his former pupil advice, or to remind him of what he had himself set down, fourteen years before, as his confession of faith. "I know that great and difficult tasks await me in the coming years of my life and I am conscious that God will one day demand of me an account of whether and

[1] Blue envelopes were used to enclose letters of dismissal.

how I have performed my Christian duty; the thought of this will never make me discouraged, but I shall make it serve me as a protection against all pride."

Wilhelm II preferred not to be crowned in Königsberg as his grandfather had been on October 18, 1861. Nine days after his father's death he came to Berlin for the opening of the Reichstag on the following day, June twenty-fifth, in the White Hall of the Berlin Schloss. Those present included, besides the Deputies, the members of the Imperial House with their ladies, all in deep Court mourning, all the Federal princes, the high State officials and the Knights of the Order of the Black Eagle. By special command the knights were to appear in red cloaks, but Bismarck refused to do so. It was really a trivial matter, yet it was a significant one, in that it was the first instance of the young Kaiser's being confronted with opposition by the Reich's Chancellor.

31. BISMARCK AND SOCIAL DEMOCRACY

AFTER THE OPENING of the Reichstag and the Landtag, with speeches from the Throne, preparations were begun for the "accession visits" to friendly foreign Courts, and first of all for the visit to St. Petersburg. This made the Kaiserin Friedrich highly indignant. She, and Queen Victoria also, as mother and grandmother, respectively, of the young Kaiser, claimed that his first visit should be to the Court of St. James.

When Bismarck heard of these demands of the two Victorias, he spoke of their interfering "like governesses" and rejected their claim. He could imagine what meddling in German affairs would have come from Windsor had "the Friedrichs" reigned for longer.

As the young Kaiser knew he could never convince his mother of the correctness of his decision, he wrote to his grandmother explaining how necessary it was for political reasons to give this priority to the Court of the Czar. There could be no question of any personal slight to his grandmother!

The old Queen showed herself surprisingly rational, agreed with her grandson and expressed the hope that his visit to Windsor would be paid immediately after that to St. Petersburg.

Matters of internal policy now claimed the Kaiser's attention, owing to the miners' strike that began in the Ruhr district in May 1889. Some hundred thousand men were involved, and in order to secure an increase of pay they had adopted a menacing attitude. When their emphatic demands were refused, disturbances increased, and at the request of the mineowners troops were sent to the troubled areas.

Bismarck not only agreed to this but asked for the proclamation of a State of Emergency. The Kaiser would not hear of it. In order to satisfy himself that the situation was really serious he sent a telegram to the officer commanding the troops on the spot. The latter's reply was classically laconic: *"All quiet except for the authorities."* From that moment the Kaiser decided to take the part of the workers. "Employers and shareholders must give way—the workers are my subjects and I have to look after them. Yesterday I warned the Governor of the Rhine Province that if the industry does not at once concede the wage demand I shall withdraw my troops. Then, when the villas of the wealthy owners and directors are in flames and their gardens are all trampled over, they will soon come down a peg or two!"

This telegram the Kaiser showed to the Chancellor, who at first felt unable to make any comment. Then he remarked in his high-pitched and rather tired voice: "I rather think that the owners are also subjects of your Majesty!"

There was, also, a larger project of the Kaiser's with which Bismarck had little sympathy. It was for the calling of a conference in Berlin, in which both industrialists and the workers should take part. In this assembly the Kaiser proposed to hear both sides and to ascertain their wishes and demands in order to have them examined by experts in attendance.

In the middle of this conference the Chancellor unexpectedly came in, sat down at the table and even took part in the discussions, very vexed that anything should be done without his consent. As he saw that all the questions and answers were addressed to the Kaiser, he interjected ironical remarks designed to divert attention to himself. As these proved a failure he rose to his feet in a provocative manner, declaring that he would assume no responsibility for any decisions that might be taken there, and walked out of the room.

Bismarck's prescription for managing his third Kaiser was already proving of no avail. He had intended, he said, to steer a middle course between sovereign and grandson. But the headstrong young man had proclaimed his independence and no longer listened to his hitherto all-powerful Chancellor but to others whom Bismarck despised. Among these latter was Dr. Hinzpeter, who from Bielefeld, that is, from the vicinity of the strike area, had sent in reports with which Bismarck was none too pleased. Perhaps it was for this reason that the Kaiser made Hinzpeter a member of the Prussian State Council in 1890, got him to deal there with school reforms and in the end promoted him to membership of the Herrenhaus (Upper Chamber).

His other tutor—Bismarck—found himself being more and more neglected. In the spirit of one whose feelings had been hurt and whose fatherly friendship was not being well received, but who at the same time tried to show that he was not wholly inappreciative, he remarked: "I'm not angry with my young master. He is ardent and keen. He wants to make everyone happy. At his age it is only natural."

The questions of settling the mining strike and of dealing with the workers and social democracy generally had come to a trial of strength between Kaiser and Chancellor. Bismarck consistently rejected all attempts to conclude agreements with "those unpatriotic fellows." He considered the Kaiser's toeing of the line to be, as he expressed it, "wrong and dangerous from the standpoint of public expediency." Every such concession would only be interpreted as weakness on the part of the Monarchy. In his opinion no concessions should be made to a party that put itself forward as being the authorized mouthpiece of "rebels." And he referred to the fact that he had himself been the promoter of the first measure of social reform in Prussia—the Right of the Disinherited. To him, also, was due the idea of public assistance. Now, however, he protested against showing further compliance and was not inclined to countersign the Workers' Protection Acts brought forward by the Kaiser.

On February fourth there appeared a new decree concerning workers, without the Chancellor's countersignature but edited by him. What he had to say about it was this:

"Decrees had for long been a favorite idea of the Kaiser's. Hinz-peter, Hugh Sholto Douglas and others, in short, people who held no position in any service, had been busy consulting with the Kaiser what he should do. By these decrees the Kaiser hoped to gain success in the elections. A draft was shown to me that went further than the one that has appeared. I was in principle opposed to any decree, but if it had to be published—and the Kaiser insisted on this—then I wanted that at any rate it should follow my draft, which would have the effect of toning down the original. I therefore undertook the editing and I wrote the decree in its present form, as a servant of the Kaiser. I also inserted a mention of the International Conference (to summon one was also a favorite idea of the Kaiser's at the time). I thought it would act like a sieve and be to some extent a check on the humane 'be-kind-to-the-workers' plans of our Ruler."

Bismarck's fear that the law might turn to the disadvantage of the one who made it was soon proved to be justified. In the elections for the Reichstag the Social Democrats gained twenty-four new seats, giving them thirty-five in all and making them the fourth strongest party there.

The older generation viewed this development with alarm. Having grown up in an age which bore the stamp of strong personalities, it was witnessing a new upsurge and a new display of power. Now it was to watch how the young master, with his sudden impulses, rash meas-ures and risky experiments, was checking and endangering a pros-perous evolution. This apprehension caused the humorous weekly *Kladderadatsch* to publish a cartoon showing King Gunther in the act of breaking away from Hagen and stepping into a boat, to travel alone on the rapidly rushing flood. Just as Hagen in the *Götterdäm-merung* sat on watch all alone in the dark night, so did Bismarck. Sadly and silently he did his duty. He never failed to show respect for his King, but many a time he must have had to restrain himself lest something should burst out as it did with Hagen. Those who were able to observe Bismarck when in consultation with the Kaiser noticed how often his lips would move though he did not speak, how his bushy eyebrows drew together in a menacing frown from under which shot lightning flashes that portended no good.

The experienced old Chancellor was standing silently before his young master presenting sheet after sheet and muttering to himself now and then, until the other looked up at him in astonishment. For some moments he stood fumbling in his dispatch case as though looking for something.

"Anything else?" inquired the Kaiser.

"Oh, yes! Your Majesty . . . a letter from London!"

The Kaiser was impatient to know what news might have come from there, but he waited in vain for the Chancellor to hand it to him.

"Well, then! Read it out!"

(*As though greatly shocked*) "I cannot do that, Your Majesty!"

The Kaiser snatched the paper and read what Prince von Hatzfeld, his Ambassador in London, had to say in his report. . . . According to this the Czar had been criticizing the Kaiser in extremely derogatory language, ending with this remark: "*Il est fou! C'est un garçon mal élevé!*"

The Kaiser turned pale and without a word handed the paper back to the old gentleman, who bowed and silently left the room.

Once at home the Chancellor contentedly opened a bottle of champagne. He had had his triumph, but knew that the young Kaiser would never forgive him for that lesson. In his fight against superficiality and amateurism he fought alone. Roon, with whom he had not been on good terms at the last, was dead. Moltke was in retirement and moreover was incensed against him because of some supposed lack of consideration. He was now seventy-five years of age. "To remain long at such a height is not given to mortal man, and the descent is accomplished much more rapidly than the ascent." So wrote the historian Johannes Scherr.

There were plenty of forces at work in the Court to accelerate the downfall of the Reich's Chancellor. Even members of the German princely houses were taking part in this, being, like the Grand Duchess Luise of Baden, unable to overlook his little weaknesses, and too narrow-minded to appreciate his greatness. Both she and her husband the Grand Duke asserted that the Chancellor was a confirmed drunkard and no longer "right in his head." Their nephew, the Kaiser, only kept him on because he needed him for the new Army Bill. The German Governor of Alsace-Lorraine, Prince Chlodwig zu Hohenlohe-Schillingsfürst, said that many times Bismarck had given the impression of being "not quite a sound man."

No doubt Wilhelm II found it not at all easy to get on with the aging and often ill-humored Chancellor. At a Court ball in Brunswick he complained to Eulenburg about the "intolerable behavior of the Prince, with whom I am having fearful difficulties."

Once more the thunderclouds seemed to divide, on New Year's Day of 1890, when, after the ceremony of giving out the password at the arsenal, the hearty good wishes of the Kaiser, addressed to his principal State official, were made known. "I know very well how great a part of our successes in recent years has been due to your self-sacrificing and creative energy and I pray to God that in my arduous and responsible business of leadership I may enjoy for many years yet the benefits of your faithful and proven counsel."

32. THE CHARACTER OF THE YOUNG KAISER

THE SMALL PRINCELY HOUSEHOLD of the Marmor Palais had now become the great Court at Frederick the Great's Grand Palais. Built just after the Seven Years' War, ostensibly to show Prussia's foes that she still had some money in the State coffers, this "New Palace" comprised rooms and halls of imposing dimensions, several galleries, a theater and magnificent staircases. The Great King seldom had lived in it; the residence of his choice had been the little Schloss Sans-Souci.

On the first floor the young Kaiser had his own private apartments —the Green Damask room, with its wide outlook over the park as far as the Great Fountain, became his workroom. Pictures by Watteau and Poussin adorned walls hung with pale green damask. The costly furniture of rosewood and ebony included one especially valuable commode with inlay of the time of the Great Frederick. Here the Kaiser used to receive his A.D.C.s, and here the red document folders with their golden crests were placed for his signature. Occasionally, too, less important audiences were given here.

Anyone granted an audience found himself in the presence of a man of middle height, which by reason of his erect bearing seemed more than five feet ten inches. His hair was light brown, shading into fair, and still very full. The mustache was twisted up at the points so that it looked almost like the letter W. The mouth appeared wide and energetic. The chin was somewhat too short and receding. There was something strange about the pale-blue eyes, friendly enough, but liable to turn gray and hard in anger. From long practice in concealing the withered arm that defect was scarcely noticeable by one who saw him for the first time; for that some credit was due to the tailor who made the uniform. If, however, one could observe the Kaiser at mealtimes, one could see how handicapped he was by that arm, although he used a special appliance that combined knife and fork. His hands, carefully attended to, were striking by their whiteness and also because of several rings set with diamonds and blue sapphires . . . a practice which guests coming from England especially disapproved.

His manner of receiving visitors could be very friendly; sometimes it could be captivating. He approached his guests in a natural, informal manner, which might be considered a little too "free and easy" for an Emperor. In any case, his attitude was artless and candid.

"Germans in general need more time for their development than Englishmen," was the opinion of the Kaiserin Friedrich, and it may be correct. Hitherto Prussian heirs to the Throne had had ample time to prepare themselves for reigning. Wilhelm II had not had that preparatory schooling. Skipping a whole generation he became Emperor of a people numbering some fifty million subjects.

Just as the Kaiserin Friedrich often showed herself to be unbalanced and disputatious, so, too, the character of her eldest son was fundamentally unstable. Many pedagogues maintain that upbringing may modify a person's character but cannot materially change his basic nature. That applied to Wilhelm II, who might by self-discipline modify his propensities to impulsiveness, hastiness, zeal for novelty, brusqueness and capriciousness, but he could never eradicate them.

Control over oneself is the key to control over others, but mastery over himself was a thing that the Kaiser never really learned. He always found it difficult to curb his tendency to sudden changes of mind, and in the conduct of affairs in attaining that kind of consistency recommended to the Duke Karl of Württemberg by Frederick the Great, "Weigh beforehand the pros and cons, but once you have made up your mind never swerve from it for anything on earth!"

A fundamental feature of the Kaiser's character was his facile acquiescence. Eulenburg spoke of his "fatalistic optimism," and the Kaiser once confessed—"I am an out-and-out optimist!" This was also the reason why he tended so rashly to put his trust in others. He would do so at once if a person seemed agreeable to him.

Remarkable also was the spirit of playful levity with which he approached all sorts of things, showing a tendency of shallowness. Coupled with this was the lightheartedness, not to say frivolity, which, together with an unusual capacity for rapid adaptation, backed by his knowledge of foreign languages, allowed him to behave at foreign courts with surprising assurance.

In contradiction to all this was his almost complete inability to enter into the world of thought of others. He never could bring himself to do it and took no trouble to learn the art. Usually he took little account of other people's opinions. They served only to make his own ideas seem to him all the more valid. Though he might often lack both knowledge and experience in a certain matter, he still felt entitled to pass judgment and give decisions.

Another disadvantage was that the Kaiser could not listen to others; not even later at Doorn. Seldom did a Minister manage to conclude a report without interruption, and once the Kaiser began to speak he would carry on with the subject in his own way to the bitter end, generally ending with conclusions that were the direct opposite of those to which the Minister had been trying to lead.

The Kaiser was himself aware of this weakness of his for snatching at a subject under discussion, monopolizing it and deciding the issue in his own way without giving anyone else the chance of getting a word in. Only rarely did he come across so intrepid a visitor as a Budapest newspaper editor, of whom he afterward remarked laughingly, "The fellow wouldn't wait for me to speak to him. He rattled on so that I never got an opportunity; and that is a thing that doesn't often happen to me!"

Like his mother he had a quite remarkable memory and a skill amounting to virtuosity in using striking comparisons, both in speaking and writing. Added to this came his propensity for exaggeration, for reveling in superlatives—especially in letter-writing, where bombast and sentimentality were often mingled together.

These extravagances of Wilhelm II probably sprang from an inferiority complex, which became apparent very early, on account of his withered arm. The infirmity had to be glossed over by noisy fanfaronades. Just as the firm grip of his strongly developed right hand would prove when greeting anyone that it was not the hand of a weakling.

Indeed the Kaiser gave almost daily proof of his sound physical health, not always to the content of his long-suffering personal staff. Field service exercises, parades and inspections followed one another in seemingly endless sequence. For hours on end he would be in the saddle on the Döberitzer Feld, riding hither and thither without the slightest sign of fatigue. After that he would walk for miles up and down lines of troops, inspecting and saluting, and winding up with an address to the regiments.

In speaking personally with others his desire to dominate was even more clearly evident. He tried to gain the upper hand from the start, beginning by putting some question to a visitor which the latter could not have expected. It usually related to some weak point in the visitor's armor and was calculated to confuse and embarrass him at once. It might happen to anyone bidden to an audience that having thus been thrown on the defensive he was never able to bring out the points which he had been at great pains to prepare. As the Kaiser was always careful to inform himself beforehand about any visitor he had not already met and about the subject that might be brought up, there was always the possibility of his taking that visitor unaware and putting him in a quandary. Those whose duty it was to converse daily with him became in time immunized against his interruptions and deliberately laid snares. The best thing to do was to let him run on until some pause occurred and then to carry on firmly with what one wanted to say. Bülow, Eulenburg, Waldersee and also Tirpitz used to employ those tactics and thus gained their ends.

It would, however, be wrong to suppose that the Kaiser's desire to dominate was synonymous with an intention of accepting nobody's advice at all. Those who were entitled to do so often found opportunities of speaking their minds freely, of giving counsel and achieving their object. There were, of course, two presupposed conditions *sine qua non*—to choose the right moment, and to have no one else present as a witness but to speak tête-à-tête. Tirpitz confirmed this, also Ballin,[1] who states in his memoirs that "when alone

[1] Albert Ballin (1857–1918), Director General of the Hamburg-Amerika Line, under whose management its capital value was increased ten times over. The Kaiser relied heavily on his advice in matters of trade and shipping, and

with the Kaiser one could freely tell him the truth, even if it were not always agreeable to him." On the other hand there were cases where a well-meaning adviser, forgetful of those conditions and expressing an opinion or venturing a criticism in the presence of, for instance, an A.D.C., found himself simply ignored and treated like empty air.

In fine weather Kaiser Wilhelm liked to go for a ride before his audiences began. For choice it was in the Tiergarten and he was accompanied by only two A.D.C.s. He rejected all the appeals of the Police President to let himself be attended by mounted, plainclothes men.

He had perfect control of his horse. By daily exercise on a rowing appliance in his dressing room he had so developed his right arm that he could ride a thoroughbred mare, or drive four-in-hand from the box. In the early years of his reign he more than once drove his brake, with a team of stallions, from the Neues Palais in Potsdam to the Berlin Schloss, covering the seventeen miles in an hour and a half (an average of just twelve miles per hour).

As all his life went at this tempo, he had little time to spare for his family. He confined himself to making a careful choice of his sons' tutors, and later on to superintending the education of his only daughter, Viktoria Luise. Each teacher was required to give individual treatment to each of his children according to their respective qualities of character and to preserve their particular individualities and talents.

For the most part the children saw their father only in the evening; then he would read to them or tell them something about Scotland, or Russia, meantime drinking a small glass of beer, for as far as alcohol was concerned he was, and always remained, most abstemious.

The gentlemen of the Horse Guards had a poor opinion of him, laughed at the austere married life of the Kaiser and his consort and cracked jokes about them. Bismarck thought otherwise; he gave great credit to his young master for his moral conduct, knowing at the same time that the young man was, as he had himself confessed in private, "endowed with a healthy sexual appetite."

The precepts so strongly impressed on the mind of his successor by Friedrich Wilhelm I—not to claim power but to crave God's

---

he died, it is said, of a broken heart on the day the Kaiser abdicated—November 9, 1918. He came of a Jewish mercantile family from Hamburg.

grace for his position and for his family—were those which Wilhelm II strove earnestly to follow. He saw himself, exactly as Friedrich Wilhelm IV had seen himself, responsible to God for his people and his House every day and every hour. He was prepared to take orders from God alone . . . for God to him represented none other than the Head of the family, set over it, but invisible.

33. THE DISMISSAL OF BISMARCK

IN JANUARY of the year 1890 the estrangement between the Kaiser and the Chancellor grew more pronounced. One might almost say that it increased day by day. What seriously annoyed the Kaiser and brought him into open conflict with the Prince was an article of Bismarck's, published in *The Times*—then anti-German. In it Bismarck declared himself opposed to the Kaiser's idea of calling for an international conference on workers' welfare, to be held in Berlin. In the same tenor he had stated to a representative of the by-no-means well-disposed *Matin* that he regarded such a conference as a grave mistake.

Criticism such as this, handed out by his own principal civil official to foreign countries, the Kaiser could not tolerate. Because of this, and for other reasons as well, he definitely decided to part from the Chancellor. He overcame any scruples in consideration of the fact that Bismarck was already over seventy and that in any case his successor should be sought. The dismissal, which he wished to effect in the early part of the year, would be carried out with the greatest possible consideration, even if the Prince should make difficulties.

Bismarck was not unprepared for what awaited him. He spent sleepless nights pondering the "fearsome question" of whether he ought to yield to the pressure of his young master or resist it. On that question he said afterward: "My love for my country told me 'You must not go—you are the only one who can still hold your own against that will.' But I knew, too, the disposition of the Kaiser's mind and it led me to expect most grievous possible developments. The drama that had been played out fairly smoothly in Bavaria with

Ludwig II might, in a military state like Prussia, assume a disastrous character."

Owing to all this pondering and fumbling on either side, decisions and their implementation were upset, amended and even changed into the reverse of their original intentions. Sobering scruples caused the Kaiser to hesitate about carrying his sentence into effect. One morning he explained to his surprised Chief of Cabinet, "Dismiss him? I've often thought of it! The cocksure manner of the Prince is really unbearable—but the country has need of him."

"The young man is really unbearable!" declared the Chancellor to his trusty friend Baron Robert Lucius. "God be praised that I have a sense of humor!" Armed with that sense of humor he was able to put up with many things that otherwise must have made him lose his temper. "The whims of a monarch are like the weather—you take an umbrella, but you get wet all the same!"

As this silent wrestling match between the young Kaiser and the old Chancellor went on, the number of whisperers and plotters increased. They maintained in the Kaiser's presence that Bismarck was no longer capable of writing a rational line without the help of his son Herbert. They revived the rumors of his addiction to drink. Von Liebenau, the wily Marshal of the Court, went even further—he declared that the Chancellor was a confirmed morphomaniac. Other flatterers pointed out to the Kaiser that Bismarck was in no way qualified to keep up with the progress of new ideas as they were evolving. He knew nothing of modern economic leadership, not to mention the recent developments and needs of German industry.

On March 15, 1890, there was another discussion between the Kaiser and the Chancellor. On this occasion Wilhelm II referred to the fact that he had first learned of important measures taken by the Chancellor after they had already been carried out. He wished to have more say in governmental affairs than hitherto.

Bismarck made a soothing reply and promised an alteration in procedure. In reality, however, he altered nothing at all! Furthermore, the ministerial heads of departments remained invisible to the Kaiser. If they did now and then appear at the Schloss with a report it was only to reflect the views of Bismarck, who seemed to be standing behind them like a phantom. The position of the ministers, compelled to respect two different opinions and to receive contradictory orders, became more and more difficult. They were in danger, to use an expression of Hatzfeld's, of being ground between the upper and the nether millstone.

As the Chancellor persisted in his obstinate attitude, so the breach became wider. The Kaiser felt he was being pinned against the wall, ignored and eliminated. Afterward, in Doorn, he spoke of it: "In the course of an interview with the Chancellor, that March, an interview that passed off quite peaceably, I asked him, almost humbly, to let me take a greater part in Government affairs, saying that in point of fact I was being entirely by-passed by him, though that was an offense against the Constitution. I saw nothing of my ministers—they were the ministers of Prince Bismarck, and they rendered their reports to him. From what they did tell me I learned only what the Prince thought fit to let me know. They were serving the Chancellor, not the Kaiser. I was young and wanted to act for the best. Above all, I wanted to bear in mind the dawn of a new era which would never be understood by the older generation. The outmoded and the outworn had to disappear. Anyone who did not fit into that new era had to go!"

Apart from all this there was another matter that had annoyed the Kaiser. It concerned some alarming news from the German Consul in Kiev which, so far as he could see, had been laid before him six weeks after it had been received. As he was complaining about this and requesting that such reports should be submitted to him without delay in future, the Chancellor inquired in a plaintive voice, "Am I standing in Your Majesty's way?"

When the protests of the young Kaiser against his exclusion were renewed the Chancellor suddenly bethought him of an old Cabinet Instruction of King Friedrich Wilhelm IV, dated September 8, 1852. By this antiquated decree it was forbidden that a Prussian Minister should ask for an audience with the King without the knowledge of the Minister President, and on every occasion of such an audience the Minister President had, if he so wished, to be present. The Kaiser, as well as his advisers, saw in this exhumation of an obsolete Cabinet Instruction only another example of the Prince's malice.

Afterward Bismarck rejected this imputation on the following grounds: "Since its first appearance this decree has remained decisive as regards the status of the Presiding Minister in relation to the States Ministry. It alone gives to the Presiding Minister the authority that enables him to assume that measure of responsibility for ministerial policy as a whole which is expected of him by the Diet and by public opinion. If every Minister were able, without having come to an understanding with his colleagues, to snatch orders from the highest authority of all, no uniform policy, for which someone should be responsible, would be feasible. This feature of collective responsibility was lacking under the Absolute Monarchy and would be lacking again today if we return to Absolutism."

However, the final shock, that led to an open breach between the two came from an unimportant call paid on the Chancellor by Ludwig Windthorst, leader of the Center party. Windthorst had gone to see the Chancellor to discuss with him some questions then pending in regard to parliamentary procedure. He had not had any success, and Bismarck had rejected his request.

Early the following morning there had appeared in the Center party press an account of this discussion with the Chancellor, and it could only have been written by Windthorst himself. The Kaiser read it, and being already in a bad humor, lost his temper. What then happened has been the subject of a statement by the Kaiser.

Though it was so early he had a carriage ordered by the Marshal to take him to the Wilhelmstrasse. Bismarck was still in bed. He wanted to get up, but the Kaiser forestalled him, went to his room, greeted him quite pleasantly, and, as he laid his cap and gloves on the table, inquired, "Tell me now, Your Serene Highness, how are things really going with Windthorst?"

Bismarck was taken aback. He had never anticipated that Windthorst would be so quick with his publication. He drew the counterpane tighter around him. "I regret, Your Majesty, that I cannot give any information about negotiations which, even if conducted with party leaders, lead to no settlement and have no results."

There was a pause. The Kaiser remained for a moment or so in thought. Then he went to the window and looked out. Without turning round he said, "And these negotiations with Windthorst took place here, in your house, Your Serene Highness?"

Bismarck propped himself up in bed as if he was about to repeat the words just spoken and thought he might have misunderstood them. Then, however, he sat up and in his quiet ironical tone of voice said, "It is a great honor for me, Your Majesty, that you should interest yourself in what goes on in my house. I must, however, most humbly announce that I cannot submit to any such supervision in my own house. The authority behind a Royal command ends at the threshold of my wife's drawing room!"

The Kaiser: "Even when your King gives the order?"

Bismarck: "Even then!"

The Kaiser, who had already picked up his cap and gloves, turned again to the Prince: "I shall await a written account of that interview from Your Serene Highness!"

No doubt the Kaiser was responsible for starting the quarrel that morning. Bismarck might perhaps have been able to defer the final breach had he spoken with less scorn and irony, but the breach was now inevitable.

Two days passed without any line from Bismarck. In the end the Kaiser found himself obliged to take steps. He deputed the Privy Councilor Lucanus to go and fetch the report that he had demanded of the Chancellor. When Lucanus was admitted and asked for the document the Chancellor glared at him: "I am not in a position to make any written report on this business of His Majesty's that you refer to."

When the Kaiser received this reply he was highly indignant and at once dispatched a senior A.D.C. to the Wilhelmstrasse, with a peremptory demand that the Chancellor should immediately tender his resignation.

Although Bismarck had expected this, it came as a surprise. After enumerating his reasons for doing so he declared in writing that he would stay on, being firmly convinced that he could still work in the best interests of the Kaiser and of the Reich.

The Kaiser would not accept his arguments. He was now determined not to yield again but to free himself from Bismarck's tutelage. "There can only be one Leader in the land—and I am that! Anyone who sets himself against me I shall crush!"

Once again Lucanus was sent to the Chancellor—with explicit marching orders. "His Majesty can only expect that Your Serene Highness will forthwith tender your resignation. Your Serene Highness will kindly attend at the Schloss at 2 P.M. to hand it in."

Bismarck, who did not much like the bearer of this order, answered curtly, "I am not well enough to go to the Schloss. I shall write!"

The Chancellor's attitude showed that he meant to leave the initiative and the responsibility to the Kaiser. "The Kaiser can of course dismiss me if he wishes. I have no objections to raise against that. I am quite ready to give validity to my dismissal by countersigning it, but I cannot relieve His Majesty of the responsibility for it—that he must bear himself. It is my duty to vindicate myself before history, and for that I need time!"

The vindication ran to six pages in print. He laid all the blame for the trouble on the Kaiser. When he had put his signature to the request for acceptance of his resignation, he made his way, pale and excited, to Princess Johanna's salon, to wait there for the reply.

The Kaiser, too, was uneasy and nervous during those dramatic hours. He had made sure that Philipp zu Eulenburg should be there to support him on that critical afternoon. To divert him, Eulenburg played some of his own compositions. As he was doing so the General A.D.C. von Hahnke entered the room. At a sign from the Kaiser he went over to the piano and whispered, as he produced the hoped-for message, "Your Majesty, the resignation is here!" This was on March 18, 1890.

34. THE DRIVE TO THE LEHRTER STATION

BISMARCK SAID AFTERWARD (in Chapter 32 of his *Thoughts and Memories*): "Our relations and my attachment to the Kaiser were, in principle, based on the fact that I was by conviction a royalist, but the special form which it took is only possible by the exercise of a certain reciprocity of good will between master and servant, just as our feudal law assumed 'loyalty' on both sides.

"Relations such as those in which I stood to Kaiser Wilhelm are not exclusively of a political or feudal nature; they are personal and they must be won by the master as well as the servant if they are to be effective."

In another passage he touches again on the subject of his relations with the Kaiser: "When I was young I followed my King wherever he led. Now that I was old I could no longer accompany my Master when he went so far afield. Hence it was inevitable that advisers who stood nearer to him should win his confidence at my expense.

He was very easily influenced when plied with ideas that he took for granted must turn out to be for the good of the people, indeed he could scarcely rest until he could put those ideas into practice. He wanted to win renown for himself—I have my own to think of, and I am defending it. I sacrificed myself for it and I will no longer have it called in question."

The first vague official news about Prince Bismarck's dismissal caused great excitement among the public—most people spoke of it as a catastrophe. The *Hamburger Nachrichten* had a leading article headed *Dietrich von Bern und Hadubrand*—a well-chosen analogy. The *Frankfurter Zeitung,* however, thought it must not join in the general expressions of regret at the disappearance of the great statesman. In imitation of the donkey that aimed a kick at the dying lion its kick appeared in its issue of March 21, 1890. "May the saying, that nothing returns, once it has departed, also apply to Bismarck. The nation will soon add March eighteenth to its list of red-letter days!"

The leave-taking ceremony at the Schloss was conducted quite conventionally, though the Kaiser was obviously at pains to make the parting as little painful as possible. But in reply to his first inquiry as to the Prince's health, he received the disdainful answer, "That is good, Your Majesty!" When Bismarck heard of his elevation to the Dukedom of Lauenburg—a title he would never use and a coat of arms that he would never display—he would have none of it. Afterward he stated bluntly the reasons why he "bristled up" at the idea of having to spend the last years of his life as "a poverty-stricken Duke." But he added, "If I were to get two million talers I'd let them make me a Pope!"

A further and more tangible honor from the Kaiser was his promotion to the rank of Colonel General in the Prussian Army—given more for its publicity value than as a solace to the departing Reich's Chancellor. Still without the three stars on his shoulder straps and in the overcoat of the Halberstadt Cuirassiers, Bismarck paid the one and only leave-taking call that his heart bade him pay. He drove to the mausoleum in Charlottenburg and laid roses on the sarcophagus of his old master.

In the afternoon furniture vans drove up to 76 Wilhelmstrasse. The business of removal had to be hastened, for in the Chancellor's apartment decorators and upholsterers were already busy taking measurements for new furniture and trying samples of wallpaper. An escort of the Cuirassier Guards was in readiness outside. The Prince came out, arm in arm with the Princess. "A first-class funeral!" he whispered in her ear. Then began the drive to the Lehrter Railway Station over the Königsplatz and past awe-stricken crowds who saluted silently.

At the station only a few old friends were gathered—it was known that the names of those attending would be reported to the Kaiser, and a special service of information had been arranged to note the progress of the departure.

As he bowed his farewell at the window of the saloon carriage he said, *"Le roi me reverra!"* firmly convinced that "the young gentleman" would one of these days need him, and recall him. He expressed this conviction, too, to Prince Max of Baden, the only German Prince who put in an appearance at the station. Twenty-eight years afterward this Prince Max was destined to play a part in a similar setting . . . when Wilhelm II was himself dismissed.

35. THE PILOT LEAVES THE SHIP

"THE DUKE OF LAUENBURG seems to be still angry with me because I brought about and accepted his resignation as Reich's Chancellor. I confess it was exceedingly painful for me to break finally with that old and proven servant of my grandfather and my father, but what else could I do?"

In terms such as this, designed to set his own mind at rest, the Kaiser sought to make intelligible the step he had taken. They met, however, with little approval. The dismissal of Bismarck was regarded as rash and ungrateful. The Army generals also shared that opinion. When the news of the Chancellor's departure reached the ears of the aged Moltke the comment that fell from his thin lips was, "Not at all a nice story! That young man will set us many puzzles yet!"

A speech that the Kaiser made immediately after Bismarck's departure left no doubt at all that he was now determined to undertake the management of State affairs himself. "The duty of watch-keeping officer in the ship of state has now devolved upon me! The course remains as it was! Full steam ahead!"

Punch adopted this analogy and published a cartoon showing Pilot Bismarck leaving the ship by a rope ladder, while Skipper Kaiser, leaning over the rails, looked down on him with every sign of contentment. Princess Johanna hung a copy of it over her bed in Friedrichsruh.

Several attempts to smooth over the break with Bismarck in the eyes of others came to nothing. Thus, when he proposed to retain Herbert Bismarck in office and asked the ex-Chancellor for his approval he received the curt reply, "My son is of full age!"

Herbert Bismack, however, declined to take advantage of that fact. His reply was, "I am accustomed to serve under my father and I could not appear before any other Chancellor with a portfolio under my arm!" To this he added in his own often high-flown language and not without betraying the Nordic-romantic influence of his friend Eulenburg, "I am so bound up with my father by every fiber of my existence that my one and only joy is to live and work for him with all the strength that remains at my command. I can scarcely imagine a life without him. It would be like the conditions depicted in our old northern sagas where, should the wolf Fenris ever manage to swallow the sun, there would be cold darkness, confusion and despair everywhere! I should greatly prefer not to live to see that; it would be too great a contrast after our country has for so long stood upon the heights of fame and world history!"

The Kaiser also sought to vindicate himself in the eyes of his grandmother Queen Victoria and the Emperor Franz Joseph by giving them the reasons that had caused him to separate from "that obstinate man." The letter to Franz Joseph ended, after bitter recriminations, with this piece of overacted sentimentality: "The man that I had idolized all my life, for whom I had endured hellish tortures of moral persecution in my parents' house, the man in support of whom I alone threw myself into the breach after my grandfather's death and thereby drew upon myself the wrath of my dying father and the inextinguishable hatred of my mother, that man paid no heed to all this but strode arrogantly across my path, because I would not comply with his wishes! What a dagger thrust to my heart!"

Despite all the fears and apprehensions, the parting with Bis-

marck involved no great commotion either at home or abroad. The
young Kaiser did not want to impair his success by any imprudence.
The old gentleman in the Sachsenwald was bound to make some
mistakes—embittered old people are prone to make them, especially
when they have nothing to occupy their minds. One such mistake
was his giving to foreign journalists, as early as in April 1890, information about internal affairs of the Reich. This was published
throughout Europe and caused a damaging sensation, so that the
German diplomatic representatives plied the Wilhelmstrasse with
urgent inquiries.

It was then that the Kaiser intervened, and this time really skillfully. "His Majesty is convinced that either a calmer mood will su-
pervene of itself, or that what has been reprinted in the press will,
even in foreign lands, be correctly assessed at its real value. . . . His
Majesty marks a distinction between the Prince Bismarck of the past
and he of the present and would like to see anything avoided that
could contribute to dimming, for the German people, the picture of
their greatest statesman."

36. LEO VON CAPRIVI

IT was generally expected in the Reich that General von
Waldersee would be Bismarck's successor, as he had himself hoped.
But the young Kaiser decided otherwise. His choice fell on General
von Caprivi,[1] who had already been recommended to him by the old
Kaiser and even by Bismarck. Sometime before the latter's dismissal
the Kaiser had summoned Caprivi to the Schloss to hear of the plans
he had in mind. "I have asked you to come here, Your Excellency, in
order to tell you that you should hold yourself in readiness for all
eventualities. Sooner or later the office of Reich's Chancellor will

[1] Count Georg Leo von Caprivi (1831–1899) was a professional soldier
whose administrative ability led Bismarck to refer to him as his possible successor. The public knew little of him when he took office as Chancellor. His
most important achievement was reaching agreements with Britain in Africa,
especially his acquisition of the island of Heligoland in the North Sea in exchange for withdrawing German claims in Zanzibar. He always regarded himself as a nonpolitical soldier and the servant of his Emperor.

fall vacant. I have designated you as successor to Prince Bismarck. My grandfather pointed you out to me as such, in case of Bismarck's death. But it appears that I shall have to part with him before that. He is so ill-disposed toward my actions in the question of the workers, and is so reluctant to accept them, that our ways cannot but diverge before very long."

In the Army opinions were divided as to the qualifications of the new Chancellor-designate. Some rated him as a good soldier, who knew little or nothing about politics. To that Caprivi himself had confessed, stating it was likely to prejudice his chances of being selected. Others, who disliked him, took him for a job-hunter, a typical courtier-general, seeking to satisfy his ambitions by intrigues. These opponents of his asserted that he had a masterly knowledge of how to hide those ambitions behind the airs of an honorable general.

In outward appearance Caprivi resembled the old Prussian type of officer. The most striking thing about him was his round head, which had earned him the nickname of "the Seal."

His worst enemies were those in Pomerania, West and East Prussia, who feared to find in the General a complaisant tool of the Kaiser for bringing the working-class legislation into force. Moreover, the people living east of the Elbe were not at all in sympathy with the policy for the eastern provinces favored by Caprivi. They had chalked up a heavy score against him because, on the occasion of the Kaiser's visit to Marienburg, he had given all the best seats to the Poles, whereas the nobility of East and West Prussia had to stand just anywhere, without being offered seats. He did not earn much gratitude from the Poles for favoring them in Marienburg. When the Kaiser had made his entry into Posen only the houses of the German residents were beflagged; the Polish ones stared blankly onto the street with shuttered windows, as though they were deserted.

It proved very difficult for Reich's Chancellor Caprivi, who as an old soldier was accustomed to thinking and acting methodically, to work with the impulsive, capricious and changeable Kaiser. What astonished him most—and it astonished other ministers too—was the unshakable belief of the young Kaiser in the efficacy and persuasive power of his own personality. By his personal charm, he thought, he could influence the leaders and the peoples of all Europe and unite them, in solidarity, under his own leadership. But the crowned heads would have nothing to do with such propositions and their mistrust only grew until it led to their wishing to have nothing to do with Wilhelm II.

If there could as yet be no talk of an encirclement of Germany by her enemies, the danger of it had come a good deal closer. The repeated protestations of friendship between France and Russia proved this most distinctly. But before the two countries decided finally to enter into an alliance, the Russian Government made a last attempt—shortly before Bismarck's retirement—to renew the so-called Treaty of Reinsurance.[2] In January 1890 Count Shuvalov had proposed to the Prince-Chancellor an extension of this treaty to six years. Originally it had been for three years only. Bismarck had been in favor of it, and so had the Kaiser—despite the Czar's insulting references to himself as "*fou*" and "*mal élevé*." It was after Bismarck's sudden fall that the matter came up for deliberation. But Caprivi and the other responsible people in the Foreign Office were doubtful whether the complicated treaty should remain as it was, especially as its continuance might, in the long run, disturb the good relations existing with Austria-Hungary and Rumania. There was a hard tussle between fors and againsts until the disapproving attitude of Holstein,[3] Marschall,[4] Kiderlen,[5] Berchem, Raschdau, Hammann, and even of von Schweinitz, the German Ambassador in St. Petersburg, decided the issue in favor of *not* renewing the Reinsurance Treaty.

When the ex-Chancellor in Friedrichsruh heard of this, he raised his hands in dismay and called the nonrenewal "a fateful event, an unparalleled mistake," although he had himself cast doubts on the value of that agreement if a long view were taken. In the *Hamburger Nachrichten* he spoke of "a rash decision" and of its being made "at an unpropitious moment." In Berlin, he said, people had forgotten how to bide their time. "A statesman can never accomplish much

[2] *See* Bismarck in Appendix, page 435.
[3] *See* Appendix, page 442.
[4] Baron Marschall von Bieberstein, Foreign Minister under Caprivi and during the first two years of Hohenlohe's chancellorship.
[5] Alfred von Kiderlen-Wächter (1852–1912), German diplomat, originally the protégé of Holstein, later Foreign Minister under Bethmann-Hollweg until his death in 1912. A forceful yet realistic man who might have avoided the errors of his successor, von Jagow, had he lived.

by himself. He can only wait and listen until he hears the sound of God's footsteps through the march of events . . . then he can spring forward and catch hold of the tails of his cloak—that is all!"

Other political measures, too, of the new Chancellor did not meet with Bismarck's approval. The ex-Chancellor was greatly amused by the "laurels in advance" that were showered on Caprivi, and he often laughed when he read in the papers such eulogies as "this simple General, with his wide political outlook, always knows how, at the right moment, to protect the Fatherland against grave dangers."

While a clean sweep was being made of relations with Russia, the attitude toward France remained irresolute under Caprivi. This undecided posture operated all the more detrimentally because in France General Boulanger, with his chauvinistic speechifying, had kindled afresh the already dwindling hopes of revenge. The *rapprochement* with Russia also served to revive those hopes.

When the French fleet entered the Russian naval base of Kronstadt, its visit was made the occasion for a significant ovation. It was received with shouts of *Vive la France!* and *Vive l'Alsace-Lorraine!* Those going ashore could scarcely escape from the tumultuous demonstrations of the people. A return visit of the Russian fleet to Toulon evoked a similar storm of enthusiasm.

The Kaiser endeavored to overlook these events and to treat them as of minor importance, rather than to regard them as any kind of unfriendly action against the Reich or himself. He tried to awaken some sympathies in France by little acts of amiability. On several occasions he had wreaths laid in his name and he sent messages of condolence, with a contribution of money for the relief fund, after the disastrous fire at a charity bazaar in the Rue Jean Goujon. In Paris these well-intentioned gestures were viewed in no friendly spirit. With embittered scorn came the reply, "Is this the first installment of the repayment of the five milliards extorted from us?"

In spite of all the renewed fanfaronades of Boulanger and the call for revenge, the French people did not venture to take any serious action against the Reich. First of all, leadership was lacking. Nor was it sure what form of constitution they aspired to in Paris. The Monarchists lacked a suitable Pretender to the Throne, nor could the Republicans produce an eligible President. No one of the caliber of Léon Gambetta was at hand.

Caprivi desired to establish good relations with Great Britain, and therefore would have nothing to do with the Kaiser's widely advertised naval policy. If Caprivi's policy in this matter had been followed, there might have been different constellations in Europe later on. "By our naval policy we are merely weakening our military power on land and bringing ourselves into conflict with England, our one natural ally. For Germany today and in the immediate future it can only be a matter of deciding *how small* our fleet can be . . . not *how large!*"

A breakaway *pas seul* of that kind by his Chancellor was a thing that the Kaiser could not tolerate. He was compelled to recognize that this man was disappointing him seriously, because "he lacked the breadth of view to carry out any large-scale policy."

Thus, owing to the Kaiser's attitude, it was easy for Caprivi's enemies to work for his downfall. Their leader was the shrewd but scheming Minister of Finance, Johannes von Miquel, who caused malicious and damaging accusations to be spread about against the Chancellor. Caprivi was not very successful in defending himself. Against only one of the falsehoods circulated by the League of Agriculturists did he inveigh effectively, namely, the assertion that he had lost a fortune in exchange speculation. His reply was, "I have never had a fortune. Since the time when I was a captain I have lived on my pay and I am proud of it, for it means that I fought my own way as an officer in the proper manner."

He had now risen to the rank of Count, but was forced to recognize that he could not win through against the Kaiser and the ever-increasing evidence of hostile elements. He handed in his resignation, which was at once accepted by Wilhelm II. It was usual to employ in the formal letter of acceptance of such a resignation, the formula: "Permission to retire is *graciously* granted." In this case the word *graciously* was omitted.

This sudden downfall of Caprivi was followed in an equally rapid sequence by others. Among them were those of the Minister von Heyden; also the Minister of Justice, von Schelling, who was called out of a conference by Lucanus, not to return to it again.

In his self-sought solitude the second Reich's Chancellor had leisure when pensioned to reflect on how difficult it is to be the successor to a great man and at the same time to be the servant of a young master. In contrast to other chancellors who came after him,

Caprivi left no memoirs. His adversaries maintained that there was little or nothing to write about, for his chancellorship showed little of such importance as to be worth recalling.

37. THE KAISERIN AUGUSTE VIKTORIA

IN THE POMP and ceremony of the Neues Palais, where the Kaiserin now resided with her children, she must often have looked back on her quiet life at Schloss Dolzig. A great change had come over her since her marriage. Many a time, as she herself admitted, she felt out of place in her new surroundings.

On the first floor she had her own apartments—the Blue Drawing Room opened off a reception room (also used as a music room) in yellow and silver. Next to this was the *Jagdkammer* or hunting chamber (used as a resting room) and the writing room in white and gold with its walls hung with brocade.

In these rooms the third Kaiserin lived, and from there she ruled over what was called at Court her "three K's"—*Kinder, Kirche und Küche* (children, church and kitchen).

As Wilhelm II had little time to devote to his offspring it was she who saw to their education, played with them on the garden terrace laid out by the Kaiser or pushed the pram through the park. She planned the birthday parties, made all the preparations for Christmas, which, under her motherly care, became a real family festival. On each Christmas Eve every member of the family was given his or her special Christmas tree, Princess Viktoria Luise, being the youngest, getting the smallest tree of all.

Christmas, however, meant for the Kaiserin more than merely a family gathering. On such occasions she always put the religious aspect in the foreground, and wherever possible sought to play a part in Christian activities. Soon there was no charitable organization and no charity bazaar of major importance on whose management she did not figure in the chair.

As the Kaiser was patron of all the Evangelical Church congregations she endeavored for her part to animate his duties by a practical adherence to Christian principles. She had the welfare of the Evangelical Church throughout the Reich very much at heart, and all its activities had claims on her attention.

Among the common people she was known as "*die Kirchengustl*" (the Church Gustl [1]). It was, however, no bigotry that prompted her, rather was it that "pious simplicity" that Martin Luther had intended. Supported by the Chief Steward of her household, Baron von Mirbach, she was intent on building churches everywhere in the Reich. Since there was not sufficient money forthcoming for such an object, she searched for charitably disposed people and it was all one to her whether they were Berlin speculators, dollar millionaires, Catholic Princes or Jewish bankers. To be received in audience by Her Majesty was enough for most of these people to make a contribution for her building plans. Those who supplied the bigger contributions proved to be pretentious, expecting the award of a decoration, the title of Commercial Councilor or even the ennobling "*von*" . . . and they received it, too, if their contribution was sufficiently large.

The Kaiserin only concerned herself with the kitchen at the Schloss on special occasions—for instance, if a member of the family was ill and had to have a prescribed diet. The menus for the day were submitted to the Kaiserin by the Chamberlain on duty, who brought them from the royal kitchen. She seldom made any alteration to them, unless the chef had forgotten the favorite dish for a child's birthday, or the like. The menus for large dinner parties she left to the head chef, whose suggestions she nearly always approved.

When the Kaiser was at home he liked to read aloud to his wife and children in the evenings. Though she took little interest in literature, art or science, the Kaiserin was a patient listener. Knowing that the Kaiser hated scenes and that they only drove him away, she avoided complaints, entreaties and tears.

Though she regretted her husband's many absences while on his travels, she accepted anything that he declared to be necessary. It could, however, happen that she showed what she felt, as when in 1896 she complained to Count Waldersee: "Ah, Your Excellency, this eternal traveling about! The Kaiser must have some proper rest and sleep, he's just a bundle of nerves!"

When the Kaiser came back from one of his tours he would often be exhausted, run-down and in a bad humor. The surroundings to

[1] Gustl=short for Auguste.

which he returned made him feel "cribbed, cabined and confined," even petty. They were, in any case, less stimulating than visits to foreign lands and meetings with interesting people. If, in a fit of temper, he spoke angrily to a servant, or if nothing was to his liking, the Kaiserin could do nothing but patiently set about appeasing her excitable husband and trying to get him into a conciliatory mood.

In Court circles she was regarded as proud. Those who said it would add that it was her one real failing. Because of her inaccessibility people were rather afraid of "Dona," as she was called. Little episodes, which show her from a different side, did not change people's opinion; they may possibly have taken place prior to her elevation to her exalted position.

Pride and dignity may be coupled together, and in the case of the Kaiserin Auguste Viktoria they were blended harmoniously. She was a handsome woman; this was especially evident when she appeared on horseback in her long, white riding habit with a wide, white-feathered hat and the orange ribbon of the Black Eagle across her breast. That the Pasewalker Cuirassiers should look up with pride to the Colonel of their "Queen's Regiment" was only natural.

After ceremonial parades, excursions and visits she returned with renewed zeal to her favorite business of forwarding the interests of the Evangelical Church. Her religious attitude made her averse to everything that seemed to her inconsistent with Christian doctrine. She would never receive people whose mode of life was not irreproachable. Moral failings stood for her on the same footing as the idea of Satan. Possible evidence of the Kaiser's adultery would have thrown her into despair, because, apart from personal feelings, it would have meant that he had offended against the main article of the Lutheran Catechism. Although the Kaiser never made a slip in regard to his marriage vows, the Kaiserin never ceased to be jealous. She mistrusted his friends, fearing that they might give him bad advice or lead him astray. If ever she had a suspicion, she did not rest until she had ascertained the truth. Her aversion to the guilty party was then unrestrained and amounted to hatred. That accounted for her dislike of Count Herbert Bismarck, of whom she had heard it said that on some occasion in the past he had offered to procure a mistress for Prince Wilhelm. When she was obliged to mention his name she sometimes spoke of him as "that drunkard," or "that roué."

As a sound and healthy woman she instinctively fought shy of Eulenburg, Holstein and Bülow. She greatly resented the increasing influence of Count Philipp zu Eulenburg over the Kaiser. It could happen that in answer to her question where the Kaiser was, a footman would reply: "His Majesty is in the music room with the Herr Graf zu Eulenburg and does not wish to be disturbed."

Eulenburg had also become the constant companion of the Kaiser on his travels. One autumn he did not break off a tour although the Kaiserin would be celebrating her birthday on October twenty-second. She had to spend her birthday without her husband and was furious with Eulenburg, whom she blamed for her disappointment. What did hundreds of white lilies (her favorite flower) mean for her if the Kaiser only sent them and was not there to present them himself?

She used to pour out her woes to her one intimate friend, the widowed Countess Brockdorff, whom she had brought with her to Berlin from her own country. The Countess, who was a great-grand-daughter of Wilhelm von Humboldt, remained all her life a faithful companion to her mistress, both of them sharing their joys and sorrows to the end.

Even among the splendors of Potsdam the Kaiserin could never forget her own land. The Kaiser was aware of this attachment to, and love for, Schleswig-Holstein, and once, when on a visit to the town of Schleswig, he used the following words in proposing a toast:

"The link that binds me to your province is this jewel that shines by my side, Her Majesty, the Kaiserin! Sprung from your soil, she is the ideal German woman! It is thanks to her that I can bear the heavy responsibilities of my office with a cheerful heart!"

38. THE OLD MAN OF THE SACHSENWALD

THE NEWS of Bismarck's dismissal was received in silence by the people at large. Even the Reichstag cut a sorry figure—it would not agree to vote an address of thanks to the departing founder of the Reich.

Only the Conservatives ventured to demand the recall of the Chancellor and to speak openly of "the longing for the Cuirassier's boot": "The Bismarckian Age, in which people felt glad to be Germans, is, alas, past and gone! Troublous times lie ahead. It will take many years to bridge the gulf that has been opened between the people and the Government. Today we might well cry 'a kingdom for a Bismarck.' "

Later on, too, on the eightieth birthday of the ex-Chancellor, the Reichstag did not deem the occasion worthy of notice, and did not even send a written message of congratulation. When Paul de Cassagnac, the energetic head of the French Imperialist party, heard of this he remarked resignedly, "No, the Germans are not nice people. We Frenchmen would not think the Pantheon, or even the firmament, too big to do honor to a Bismarck."

If Wilhelm II seized on every possible occasion to speak about "Colonel General Prince Bismarck" he did so with the naïve desire that the politician Bismarck should be forgotten. The danger that Bismarck might take his seat in the Reichstag was always threatening. The Kaiser's fears sprang from his own sense of insecurity and from his anxiety lest he be criticized in open session of the House by the irate old gentleman. For Bismarck at the head of an Opposition could have effected a great deal of good and prevented much.

With his usual persistence and despite all rebuffs from Friedrichsruh the Kaiser sought to establish tolerable relations between himself and the ex-Chancellor. For a few weeks it seemed that these attempts might succeed. Then, however, Bismarck's embitterment and exasperation broke loose. Using his gift of sarcasm he tried to expose the Kaiser as begging his pardon and make him a laughingstock.

It was feared that the Kaiser would not tolerate such outright rejection, but he acted in such a manner as to show that he himself held the whip hand. "If people imagine that I am going to send Bismarck to Spandau [1] they are mistaken. I have no intention of making a martyr of the Prince and having people going on pilgrimage to him!" When he heard of some caustic comments by Bismarck he remarked tersely, "Shouldn't be made public! It only discredits the name of Bismarck!" On the other hand the young Kaiser was quite ready to belittle Bismarck's merits. When someone sent him a document in which Bismarck was designated as "the Founder of the

[1] Fortress used as a prison.

Reich," he wrote in the margin—"That is not true! Grandpapa was that!"

Utterances of that kind did not escape the ears of the old gentleman in Friedrichsruh. He continued to take an active interest in all the political events in the Reich, greatly to the Kaiser's annoyance. When Wilhelm II demanded blind obedience from his ministers, as in the time of Frederick the Great, Bismarck thought it well to apply a corrective. "Earlier rulers looked for ability rather than obedience in their advisers. If obedience alone be the criterion, the universal talents of the Monarch would be taxed to an extent which even Frederick the Great would not have been able to satisfy, although in his day the framing of policies for war and peace was less difficult than it is today."

Relations between Berlin and Friedrichsruh became strained again in the summer of 1892, when Count Herbert Bismarck was married in Vienna to the Countess Marguerite Hoyos. Wilhelm II straightway turned to Schönbrunn to express his hope that the Hapsburg Court would ignore this wedding. He charged his Ambassador in Vienna, Prince Reuss, to refuse all participation in the ceremony and to decline all invitations sent to members of the Embassy staff. When the Bismarcks found that they were to be disowned in Vienna, they decided that the marriage should be celebrated in the strictest privacy, and attended only by members of the two families. When the Prince and his wife touched Berlin on their return journey members of the Court remained invisible.

After this display of hostilities carred on *coram publico* the Kaiser began to reflect that it might be better after all to make another attempt at a *rapprochement*. Perhaps he was thinking of the warning given him by Prince Albrecht, who said, "If Bismarck were to die without your being reconciled with him, what would posterity say about it?"

An illness of Prince Bismarck furnished him with an excuse for sending a telegram (on September 19, 1893) to Varzin, where Bismarck was staying, worded thus: "To my sorrow I have just learned that Your Serene Highness is suffering from a somewhat serious illness. As, thanks be to God, news has also reached me of a steady improvement, I wish to express my warm satisfaction at hearing of this at the same time. Wishing to ensure that your convalescence may be complete, I beg Your Serene Highness to exchange your quarters in the climatically less suitable places of Varzin or Friedrichsruh for one of my castles in Central Germany, and there to pass the winter months. After speaking to my House Marshal I shall inform you of the castle selected."

The thought of having to live in a castle of the Kaiser's—and as his guest at that—seemed so awful to Princess Johanna that she was anxious for the proposal to be rejected out of hand.

Speaking of this afterward (to the author) the Kaiser confessed that he was bound to say that it was to the credit of the Princess that, although she had become his bitter enemy in all personal matters, she had never intervened in political affairs.

Bismarck's reply to the Imperial invitation began quite conventionally: "Highly honored by Your All-Highest's gracious expression of sympathy . . . ," but it ended with the assurance that "the desired recovery would in all probability be brought about soonest in long-accustomed domestic surroundings."

Despite this rebuff the Kaiser ventured on yet another attempt to bring the Prince to a more mellow frame of mind. He sent him, by once of his A.D.C.s, a bottle of old Steinberger-Kabinett, which he knew the old gentleman would appreciate. In fact, Bismarck was so impressed by this ingenious attention that he declared he was prepared to pay a visit to the Kaiser in Berlin. In Court circles the prospect of meeting the once all-powerful figure in the Schloss started a panic. In the Foreign Office, too, everyone was terrified. Holstein could already foresee a reconciliation, the return of the Prince as Reich's Chancellor and his own dismissal. How this would be brought about he depicted to himself in the most gloomy colors. He could see himself before the High Court, figuring as the principal accused over whom the irate man from the Sachsenwald would let loose his flashing thunderbolts.

On January 26, 1894, Bismarck arrived in Berlin accompanied by his son Count Herbert. It was the eve of the Kaiser's thirty-fifth birthday. For four full years the old Chancellor had not been in the capital, and had only once traveled through it.

The Kaiser later related that when the Prince, supported by his son, reached the top of the flight of steps at the entrance to the Schloss, he found awaiting him there the Kaiser, who embraced him, kissed him, and then led him away to his study, leaving Count Herbert and the Court officials outside to speculate on what was happening.

At the luncheon that followed the Prince endeavored to introduce political subjects, but each time the Kaiser evaded the issue and brought the conversation round to military matters. There was no longer a Reich's Chancellor sitting at the table, only a Colonel General.

When the Kaiser drove out afterward with Bismarck the enthusiasm of the populace was ecstatic, especially Unter den Linden, where people were standing shoulder to shoulder.

Mindful of the unpredictable character of Wilhelm II, the high officials, the generals and the personnel of the Court restricted themselves to an attitude of reserve in regard to the Bismarcks. They confined themselves to leaving cards, while avoiding personal calls.

To the astonishment of Court circles the Kaiser decided to take yet another step on the road to reconciliation. On March 26, 1895, he paid his return call at Friedrichsruh. Motley indeed was the suite he took with him—Cuirassiers, Uhlans, Hussars, Guards, Infantrymen accompanied him to the Sachsenwald. Once again the emphasis was on the military side, and it was strengthened when the Kaiser presented the Prince with a sword of honor, on the scabbard of which was engraved (from the Kaiser's own design) the arms of the Dukes of Lauenburg crossed with those of Alsace-Lorraine.

Already much annoyed at having to accept this gift, the Prince had to endure a toast proposed by the Supreme War Lord which further enraged him. For this he had to return thanks. His speech was brief: "Your Majesty will permit me to lay my most humble thanks at your feet. My military rank vis-à-vis Your Majesty will not allow of my expressing my feelings further. I thank Your Majesty most dutifully."

The Kaiser did not allow himself to be upset by this snub. In the event of any of his other devices going amiss, he had reserved one more surprise for Bismarck. He produced it suddenly—it was a small box. When he presented it to Bismarck, the latter made as though to receive it unopened, thinking it must contain the insignia of some order. On this the Kaiser suggested that he should first take a look at what was in it. Bismarck pressed the spring—and before him lay the seal he had known so well, the seal of the old

Kaiser, which he had used daily when appending his signature to documents.

Lost in contemplation, the aged ex-Chancellor gazed at this witness of many momentous decisions. Then he caressingly passed his trembling hand over the familiar object, with a grateful glance at the one who had given him that great pleasure.

Scarcely had Wilhelm II returned to Berlin when he thought it fitting to ascribe the successful outcome of the reconciliation entirely to his own cleverness.

With the scene-shifting propensity which the Hohenzollerns had brought with them from Swabia, he looked with keen satisfaction at the balance of advantage he had gained by that visit to Friedrichsruh. "Good! Now let them put up triumphal arches for him in Vienna and Munich. . . I'm always a nose ahead of him!"

The Kaiserin Friedrich, clad in her widow's weeds, wandered like the ghost of some ancestress about the Reich—the Reich over which her son now reigned in place of "that great man, his father." She was kept well informed of all that her son did, and she heard of his visit to Friedrichsruh. With closed eyes and a despairing shaking of her head she sighed, "For the love of heaven, how will it all end? The monarchy will be put to a severe test by that young man! I tremble to think of the future!"

39. HOHENLOHE

It was during Caprivi's time as Chancellor that the British island of Heligoland was bartered for the German-protected island of Zanzibar and a strip of land, Witu, in Uganda—"a trouser button for a whole suit of clothes." The credit for getting possession of this North Sea islet the Kaiser claimed for himself. It was owing to his initiative, he maintained, that this island, important from the naval standpoint, as well as for reasons of prestige, was incorporated in the Reich. In Germany there were loud protests against the deal, for it was claimed that the surrender of the African territories was too high a price to pay for "that bare and barren rock," as Bismarck used to call it, all the more as the island could strategically be controlled from the mainland. When the Kaiser heard of this criticism from Friedrichsruh he laughed. "I am not going to start a model farm on the 'bare and barren rock'!"

A successor had now to be found to Caprivi, who had been so unceremoniously removed from the political scene. It was not easy to hit upon the right man for the office, which had now become so strenuous a task. The Kaiser's choice fell eventually on the Governor of Alsace-Lorraine, Prince Chlodwig zu Hohenlohe-Schillingsfürst.[1]

Bismarck had to take his discharge at the age of seventy-five, because he was too old—and Hohenlohe took over his office as Reich's Chancellor at that same age. Strange as that choice may appear, it was a very well-considered one, for the Kaiser thought that by appointing an elderly man who was also a Prince he could all the sooner make people forget the elderly man in the Sachsenwald. Again, he hoped by using Hohenlohe as an intermediary to be able to effect a relaxation in the tension of his relations with the Bismarcks.

It was only after some hesitation that Hohenlohe answered the call, and it was against the wishes of his strongly Russophile Princess, who shuddered at the idea of establishing her salon in "Prussian Berlin."

Hohenlohe brought with him excellent experience. In 1870 he had been a Minister of the Kingdom of Bavaria. Later, as Councilor to the Bavarian Throne, he influenced King Ludwig II to take a favorable view of the unification of Germany. Finally he had been successful in asserting himself in the most difficult position of Governor in Strasbourg. Even the French had praised his patience and tact, two qualities that especially distinguished him.

Hohenlohe was a man of the world, a man of rank, a well-read *grand seigneur*, who, in contradiction to Bismarck, did not like abrupt language, spoke little himself and would often express agreement by a mere nod of the head, or refusal by a wave of a delicate white hand interlaced with blue veins. Whatever he said was well considered, well formulated and unaffected by any emotion. Coolly observant, he could be ironical when he had to deliver a judgment. Despite his age he knew very well what he wanted and how to carry his intentions into effect. In the Reichstag he avoided conflicts; his strength lay in his art of working by compromise and conciliation.

[1] *See* Appendix, page 442.

The Kaiserin called him "Uncle Chlodwig," for on her mother's side she was related to him, and the Kaiser became accustomed to do so too . . . but he used that familiar form only when he was in agreement with "Uncle Chlodwig." If that were not the case he quickly altered it to "Your Serene Highness."

Uncle Chlodwig was not only related to the Kaiserin, he was also a cousin of Queen Victoria's, who, having long known him as a shrewd and sensible man, esteemed him highly. When the old Queen spoke of him she never did so without some laudatory attribute such as "My much-cherished cousin . . ." or "My clever relative, the German Chancellor."

Despite all his tolerance, Hohenlohe found that in his association with the Kaiser things happened that "drove him mad." It was especially little acts or words that showed the Kaiser's lack of consideration that vexed him and made him angry. Eventually, however, he, like Bismarck, cultivated a hide like that of a rhinoceros —"I was firmly determined never again to take offense at anything. If I had done otherwise I should have had to send in my resignation at least once a week!"

40. THE KOTZE CASE

WHEN THE KAISERIN FRIEDRICH complained about the increasing corruption of morals in Court society, and declared that "much reminded her of the times of Roman decadence," her complaint seems not to have been unfounded. What the Dowager-Kaiserin especially condemned were the intrigues that went on. "For vulgarity they cannot be surpassed. They send one another anonymous letters, with warnings, and threats. It is disgraceful!" She made complaints like this to Frau von Schrader, with whom she was well acquainted, and who was soon to be involved in a Court scandal herself.

Ever since the autumn of 1892 several members of Court society had been receiving anonymous letters, some of them even directed to the Kaiserin Auguste Viktoria, accompanied by pornographic photographs in which the original faces had been taken out and been replaced by those of members of the Kaiser's House or of the Court. About two hundred such letters were received in two years. Many of these photographs, which were made in Paris, and "in respect of erotic imagination left nothing to be desired," had the head of von Schrader, the Marshal of the Court, stuck on them. As von Schrader had a deadly enemy at Court, in the person of his colleague von Kotze, suspicion was obviously bound to fall on the latter. Kotze, always a cheery fellow and much liked by the Kaiser, was now kept quietly under observation by detectives, until at last a piece of blotting paper was found in his office, which showed in a mirror handwriting like that of the anonymous letters. Everyone was at once ready to conclude that he was the guilty party and the sender of the photographs, although he himself had not been immune from receiving some. When the Kaiser was shown the blotting paper he was quickly convinced that Kotze had written the letters. Without any further investigation, or hearing the accused Marshal, the Kaiser ordered his arrest. He was taken away to the Military Detention Barracks in the Lehrterstrasse.

Kotze being now behind bars, his adversaries were exultant. For one thing they had put the *enfant gâté* of the Kaiser "in the bag" and cleared the path for their own careers, and secondly they thought they were now to be free from those highly unpleasant references to their various vices.

However, despite the fact of the Court Marshal being under lock and key, the infamous letters were again lying on the desks one morning. There was a general panic! The President of the Military Court, who after the first hearing was of the opinion that von Kotze was not guilty, now called in a graphologist to compare the handwriting of the accused with that of the anonymous letters. This graphologist declared that the letters had not been written by the person in custody. Thereupon the President annulled the order for his arrest.

What then followed was a series of law suits dragging on for years between Kotze and Schrader with interludes of duels between the principal parties, and after them more complaints of injuries and insults until at last a full declaration in favor of Kotze, with an apology, put an end to the matter.

It was Eastertide. So the Kaiser bethought him of writing a full stop after the Kotze case. He sent the deserving, gravely maligned and blameless Court Marshal a present—a large chocolate Easter egg! No chronicler tells us what the recipient said when he received it, but in any case the general public took the view that a rehabilitation of that kind was hardly satisfactory or tactful. After all, the innocent man had spent a whole week in prison.

But the most astonishing thing about the Kotze case was the fact that after the release of the wrongfully accused man no further steps were taken to discover the real culprit. Perhaps Count Waldersee was right when he declared that the anonymous letter-writer was none other than a near relative of the Kaiser, so that, when this was proven, he had to be allowed to go free.

The faithful Kotze had the rest of his life to ruminate on just how capricious the benevolence and gratitude of a monarch can be. Similar lawsuits were to follow in great numbers. The denunciations went on and claimed fresh victims. And in any society where the practice of denunciation takes root, there begins the process of decline and decomposition.

41. THE KRUGER TELEGRAM

In 1894 Queen Victoria appointed her grandson, Wilhelm II, to the Honorary Colonelcy of the "Royals" (the Royal Dragoons), and at a later date—yielding to his further demands—made him an Admiral of the British Navy. On donning his new Admiral's uniform the Kaiser, in proposing a toast, declared that it was his most ardent wish that in the future the British fleet and the German Army should become the joint guarantors of peace. Friendly as those words sounded, nobody in England supposed that they were spoken in earnest. The British public had not forgotten certain utterances of the Kaiser's though they dated back to ten years previously. At that time (1884), when anti-English riots broke out in the Sudan, Prince Wilhelm had remarked: "Let us hope the Mahdi will drown all the Englishmen in the Nile!"

Even now the old Queen was little edified by the vacillating and doubtful attitude of her grandson toward England. She reproached him with a lack of family feeling and requested that he should at last begin to show a friendly attitude toward his mother's country.

A fresh cause of disagreeable dissension between them came in the shape of Dr. Jameson's incursion into the Boer Republics of South Africa. "Doctor Jim," as he soon came to be known in England, had put himself at the head of a band of mounted Volunteers, crossed the Transvaal border and attacked the Boers, with the tacit approval of Cecil Rhodes. After a first encounter which ended in favor of Jameson, the Volunteers resumed their advance.

In Germany the English invasion of peaceful Boer territories was viewed very unfavorably, as the Reich had considerable financial interests in the Transvaal and the Orange Free State. Thus it was thought necessary in Berlin to make a protest to the Foreign Office in London. As, however, the news of Jameson's failure arrived soon after, it was decided to withdraw the protest through the German Ambassador in London. He succeeded in getting it back unopened, which meant unread, because it was a Sunday and there was nobody in Downing Street to receive it.

Meanwhile the reasons for Jameson's defeat became known to all the world: the preparations for his incursion into the Transvaal had been betrayed to the Boers, who had had sufficient time to entrench near Krugersdorp; on January second they made an attack, surrounded the Volunteers and forced them to surrender.

Sympathy with the Boers was world-wide. Under Piet Cronje they had fought like heroes. The German press openly voiced its sympathy and also concern for the Germans living in Pretoria. These appealed to the German Government, calling attention to their dangerous position and asking for help in the event of fresh disturbances. This appeal reached the Berlin Foreign Office quite opportunely. Holstein saw in it a chance of letting England know "that we—the Germans—were still there." His Gray Eminence took into his hand all the threads of the drama that was now being staged, and so became stage manager of the swiftly changing scenes that were to follow. On his advice the Secretary of State, Baron von Marschall, informed the German Consul in Johannesburg that it had been decided to send the cruiser *Seeadler* to Delagoa Bay "for the protection of the German colony." In certain circumstances sailors would be landed, should this be necessary for the protection of German interests. At the same time the Lisbon Foreign Office was asked whether the Portuguese Government would permit German Marines to cross the territory of Mozambique from Delagoa Bay to the Transvaal border. These proceedings evoked a storm of indignation in England, so much so that the Government decided to take prompt measures of defense.

On New Year's Day (1896) the customary drive of the Diplomatic Corps to the reception in the Berlin Schloss was taking place. As the Reich's Chancellor Prince Hohenlohe was about to offer his good wishes, the Kaiser drew him aside and demanded that "the most severe measures be taken against England." Hohenlohe, who for some time had been following with apprehension the pro-Boer pronouncements of the Kaiser, endeavored to appease him and to divert his thoughts from taking any such action. He made no concealment of his argument that interference by the Reich in South African affairs, which if closely examined were only of secondary importance, could mean war with England.

On the day after the New Year's reception Hohenlohe went to see Privy Councilor von Holstein, to tell him of the Kaiser's frame of mind. Holstein, the proper authority in matters of foreign policy, took fright when he heard of the Kaiser's interference in what was his own special province. He insisted that the Chancellor should see to it that His Majesty did not interfere in matters of such grave importance.

As, however, the Kaiser persisted in some action against England being taken, Hohenlohe proposed a conference at which, besides the Kaiser and himself, the Secretary of State Baron von Marschall; the Embassy Councilor von Kayser, head of the Colonial Section of the Foreign Office; Admiral Hollmann, Secretary of State for the Navy; and Admiral Knorr of the Admiralty Staff, should take part.

At the meeting Hohenlohe reiterated his opinion that any intervention in the Transvaal constituted a challenge to England which he personally considered out of place and unnecessary. When, however, he found that unless he made some sacrifice he had no prospect of getting the Kaiser to abandon his demand for "action against England," he proposed a course which might satisfy the Kaiser and ensure a happy issue of the conference.

He suggested making a declaration warning England against taking any further measures against the Boers. The Kaiser gladly acceded to this idea and demanded that to put the proposal into action a telegram should be sent to the Boer President, Kruger, making it clear that the German Reich would stand behind Kruger and the Boers, and that "no attack on their freedom would be tolerated without a counterstroke."

Marschall and Kayser sat down to compose the text of the telegram. They wanted to consult Holstein, but he was not to be found either in the office or at home. As so often happened at a moment of crisis, he had disappeared off the face of the earth, an artifice for which Bismarck had already envied him. While they were racking their brains over the wording of the telegram in the Foreign Office, His Gray Eminence was sitting quietly in his regular place at Borchard's in the Französiche Strasse, sipping his claret in the private room always reserved for him. In perfect peace he was free to imagine what extraordinary effects that telegram would produce in London. Without his having assumed any responsibility for it, that telegram to President Kruger would once more enable him to "swat several flies at one stroke." England, as was quite to his liking, would get a sound snubbing; Marschall's position, which threatened to become dangerous for himself, would be shaken severely; and— what delighted him most of all—the Kaiser would figure as the principal culprit. To safeguard himself against any attack from the rear, he wrote a few lines to his friend Eulenburg in Vienna, worded so as to induce Eulenburg to send the letter on to the Kaiser in Berlin. This was done.

After the explosion in London the Kaiser received and read the letter in which it was made clear that he (Holstein) had wanted to have nothing at all to do with the telegram to Kruger, and that Marschall and Kayser alone were responsible for it. It was a mystery to him that a man like Marschall could commit so stupid a mistake as letting that telegram go, when it was certain to act as a bombshell in London. . . . "The Kaiser was much too shrewd and farseeing to suggest anything of the sort . . . but alas! alas! he does not get good advice!"

The wording of the telegram that caused the explosion was, as published in the *Reichsanzeiger*: "I offer you my most sincere congratulations on having been successful, with your own people, without appealing for the help of friendly nations, and by your own energetic measures, against the armed bands that invaded your country as disturbers of the peace, also on your restoring peace and preserving the independence of your country against outsiders."

Although all mention of "the support of the Reich," asked for by the Kaiser, had been omitted by Marschall, the telegram at once excited boundless indignation in England. It could be said that with the exception of the "Ems telegram" (of 1870) no message of its kind before the turn of the century had ever caused such a sensation.

In Germany, as a manifestation of sympathy with the Boers, it met with assent. Even Bismarck was satisfied with it and considered its dispatch to have been right, as he maintained in two articles in the *Hamburger Nachrichten*.

In Britain the excitement, far from abating, assumed proportions that exceeded even Holstein's expectations. The press spoke of "a gross lack of tact," and "unheard-of interference in British affairs that were no concern of the Kaiser's." The bitter feeling was such that German seamen in Dover and German businessmen in London were assaulted. Some German business premises in Liverpool were demolished, and German workmen beaten up in the docks. German associations all over England were compelled to close their doors and barricade their windows.

All these attacks and demonstrations were, however, directed specifically "against the Kaiser," who was regarded as being responsible. Speeches against him were delivered in the theaters before the performances began. In the officers' mess of the Royal Dragoons the portrait of their Honorary Colonel was torn from the wall, cut in pieces and thrown into the fire.

Afterward, in Doorn, the Kaiser declared that "English society ladies wrote insulting letters to me, notifying me that they would never again receive a German, or set foot on German soil."

Official Britain spoke through its representative Sir Michael Hicks Beach, giving an unmistakable declaration that the United Kingdom was now "ready for anything . . . even to meet the world in arms."

The English newspapers were unanimous in demanding the sharpest retorts to the "German provocation." The *Morning Post* demanded "as the one proper reply to Germany" the concentration of the English fleet in the North Sea and concluded its wrathful article saying that England would never forget this German tactlessness, but would bear it in mind in the future orientation of her policy.

In London, too, the French diplomat Marcel Laurent expressed his opinion of the Kruger telegram in most violent terms: "This provocation of an England friendly to us is also an insult to France. So long as Alsace-Lorraine remains German, the German Reich will remain our most bitter enemy."

The chorus of indignation and antipathy to the person of the Kaiser upset him and made him nervous. Those who met him noticed his drawn features and the embarrassed smile with which he endeavored to preserve appearances before others.

Everyone in England expected that the Kaiser would make some kind of apology to his grandmother. This was not forthcoming; he did, however, carefully avoid doing anything that might cause further ill-feeling.

On January sixth Marschall called upon the British Ambassador in Berlin and declared that "the relations between the two countries have not for a moment been disturbed." That was not true, but it sounded well and had some calming effect.

A week later, on January thirteenth, Marschall repeated from the tribune of the Reichstag that relations with England "are once more untroubled and friendly." To this asseveration he added that an unhappily worded telegram should not be regarded as an official pronouncement.

Although he, as Secretary of State, had weighed the text of that telegram word by word, he made it appear that he took no responsibility for it. The Kaiser felt that he was being shown up by this conduct, and that he was being pilloried as the sole author of all the turmoil.

One reckless act often leads to another, and so it was in this case. With the idea of showing how he, the Kaiser, aspired to unclouded relations with England, he instructed Colonel Schele, who had originally been charged with giving military advice to President Kruger, to prepare a plan of campaign for use by England against the Boers! Greatly astonished, Schele made out a plan and handed it to the Kaiser, who proposed that it should be handed to the British Military Attaché in Berlin and forwarded to the British General Staff in London . . . as a present! Only at the last moment was this prevented.

All these dramatic events had occurred within only fourteen days. Privy Councilor Fritz von Holstein emerged from them as the only well-satisfied participant. His Majesty was compromised on the facts of the case; the position of Secretary of State Baron von Marschall had been severely shaken, as Holstein had hoped; the Ambassador in London, Prince Hatzfeld, very nearly handed in his resignation. His counselor at the Embassy, Baron Hermann von Eckardstein, declared that "because of the incomprehensible insanity that has afflicted the Kaiser and the Wilhelmstrasse I no longer wish to remain at a post whose utility has disappeared."

The soothing spirit in this grave crisis was the Reich's Chancellor, Prince Hohenlohe. When calm returned once more, Count Clemens Schönborn, the Chancellor's nephew and A.D.C., remarked to his chief that a good deal had been gained. Whereupon old Hohenlohe drew himself up from his stooping posture, looked his nephew straight in the face and in his quiet voice replied: "Nothing at all has been gained, but much has been prevented!"

42. THE BUILDING OF THE GERMAN FLEET

EVERY HOHENZOLLERN since the crowning of the first kings had issued a proclamation to his army on the occasion of his accession. It was Wilhelm II who, for the first time, coupled his proclamation with a special message to his navy. "The Navy knows that it fills me with great joy to belong to you through the external link [of my position as War Lord], and also knows that since my earliest youth, in fullest accord with my beloved brother Prince Heinrich of Prussia, a lively and warm interest binds me to you."

In Mahan's great work—*The Influence of Sea Power on History* —which, as a pupil of the Cassel Gymnasium, the Kaiser had even then chosen as his favorite reading, there appears this sentence: "In the history of the world sea power has always decided the destiny of nations."

By his visits to the Isle of Wight and by his glimpse of the English fleet in Kiel harbor in 1881, Prince Wilhelm may have been reminded of those words. It was then that he had set himself the aim of remedying one day the German lack of maritime strength.

At the time of his accession the only war vessels lying in Kiel were a few old crates with high wooden superstructures, partly under sail, such as the English-built armored frigates *König Wilhelm, Kronprinz* and *Friedrich Karl.* There were no large shipyards, only small privately owned yards, which at best could turn out corvettes or gunboats. In summer these vessels performed coastal duties; when the ice began to form they were taken out of action and were hauled up on land.

It was the Hanse towns especially that supported the Kaiser's efforts to provide a modern German war fleet. But there were also difficulties and objections that hampered those efforts. There was a lack of trained officers, of training ships and of a rising generation with the desire and aptitude for service at sea. Moreover, funds for the task amounted to next to nothing, for the budgets of the Ministry of War were all earmarked for the Army. Once more did old Field Marshal von Moltke open his tight lips to warn against the danger of starving the Army estimates for the sake of the Navy. And in the messes of Army officers the building of a fleet met with little favor. The conviction was firmly held that since the Army had hitherto done all the work, it must be wrong to embark on a costly gamble in a navy. The East-of-the-Elbers also aimed their blows at this when in the Reichstag they voted to allot all the available money for the requirements of the Army and would have nothing to do with the "awful fleet."

A year after his accession the Kaiser had for the first time appointed a marine specialist, Count Monts, to be head of the Admiralty, a post hitherto held by a general. His successor was to be Admiral Hollmann, "one of the most trusty of those I trust," as the Kaiser afterward described him. Then came Alfred Tirpitz, who, with his flowing beard, most appropriately resembled an image of the sea god Neptune.

The real business of building a German war fleet was first begun under Tirpitz, who also developed the organization of its administrative services, the Admiralty staff and the Navy departments. The two last were at first placed under the immediate orders of the Supreme War Lord, to cut out interim offices.

Popular interest in the Navy was gradually aroused as the "tinkers' workshops" (as Tirpitz called the old shipyards) disappeared and were replaced by modern yards in which the first ships of the line were built. Some early martyrs of the young Navy also helped to focus attention on the service. The brave young Duke of Mecklenburg went to the bottom with his torpedo boat off the coast of Africa; the *Iltis* was wrecked after a terrible struggle against a typhoon off the coast of China, and the training ship *Gneisenau* fell a victim to a gale in the Bay of Malaga.

It was a hard school through which the young German Navy had to pass as it was built up from its foundations. When, at the beginning of the Boer War, two German merchant vessels were captured by an English warship, the German Government did not let it pass but retaliated with a similar action. Tirpitz rubbed his hands in delight. "Now at last, and thanks to the English, we are sure of getting the support we need for the Reichstag to pass the new Navy Bill." And he declared in jest that he was prepared to recommend the English captain for a German decoration in acknowledgment of his assistance!

In June 1895 the important Kaiser Wilhelm Canal was opened in the presence of naval delegations from all the European Powers and with the participation of French warships. What a poor figure did the four old representatives of the Brandenburg class cut beside the big armored vessels! Soon afterward they were broken up for scrap.

In April 1897 there was as yet no sign forthcoming of the new German fleet, so on the occasion of his grandmother's Diamond Jubilee the Kaiser was unable to send any really representative ship with his brother Prince Heinrich, to whom he sent the following telegram: "I deeply regret that for the festivities I cannot place at your disposal any ship better than *König Wilhelm*, while other nations, with their stately warships, will make a glittering display. This is the sad result of the conduct of those unpatriotic people who seek to prevent the provision of the necessary vessels. However, I shall not rest until I have brought my Navy to the same high level at which the Army stands." This telegram was intended less for Prince Heinrich than for German public opinion, which needed awakening, as was slowly being done, especially by the German Navy League that was formally founded shortly afterward.

In contrast to his predecessor Caprivi, Hohenlohe was all in favor of the naval program. He, a South German, seconded the Kaiser once he had recognized the correctness of his (the Kaiser's) aims: "I am all for a battle fleet; nothing can be accomplished without one!"

And in the Reichstag he declared: "It is not merely a question of giving protection to individual ships, or even of backing any demands we may have to make on other countries, but it is a matter of safeguarding our existence as a mercantile World Power."

Some detractors of Wilhelm II declared at the time that he had made a wrong estimate of the British Navy, otherwise he would not have ventured to think of a German fleet and of building bigger warships. Against this was quoted the declaration made by the Kaiser in 1896, to the effect that "the German fleet never could or should attain parity with the English fleet, and was at the moment far from it."

In spite of reassuring statements such as this, the determination with which naval construction was pressed forward, once it had begun, created difficulties in foreign policy, primarily vis-à-vis England.

The fleet was the Kaiser's hobby. Only if war with England were looked upon as inevitable should a fleet which formed a direct challenge to England be built. In such circumstances the policy which had been indicated by the approaches to France and Russia in 1894, and by German colonial politicians, should have been pursued with absolute consistency. Then, too, the promotion of France's colonial expansion, even at the expense of England, would have been necessary. It would also have been essential to aid Russia in her Asian struggles, and to make use of the Boer War and existing differences between France and England, and between Russia and England to create a Continental front against Britain. This was not what was wanted by Berlin, least of all by the Kaiser. The Kaiser's policy was for friendship, not war, with England, despite the Kruger telegram and the program of naval reconstruction.

From then on what the Kaiser called his "New Course" remained enigmatic and illogical. The destination of the voyage was lost in the fog of the German future, which, as the Kaiser had declared, "lay upon the water."

43. THE LEASE OF KIAOCHOW

AS ALL NAVAL QUESTIONS were given priority by the Kaiser, a report by the Commander of the Cruiser Squadron in East Asia was promptly submitted to him, together with the expert opinion of the geographer Baron von Richthofen, from which it appeared that the Bay of Kiaochow, hitherto overlooked by the other Great Powers, was well suited to serve as a coaling station for the German fleet. It was emphasized in the report that the bay provided good anchorage, was free of ice in winter and had good communications with the hinterland.

The Reich's Chancellor, Prince Hohenlohe, thought it well to seize this lucky opportunity and to occupy Kiaochow. But St. Petersburg, having got wind of the German designs, intervened to claim the bay for itself, on the ground of "the right of first anchorage."

As the German jurists declared that they had never heard of that right, the Kaiser called in the Admiralty Privy Councilor Perels, an expert on international sea law, to inquire into the facts and the basis of the Russian claim. Perels came to the conclusion that this law of "right of first anchorage" did not exist, or else had been fabricated by the Russians.

During a visit to Peterhof in 1897 the Kaiser had an opportunity of touching on the subject of Kiaochow and informing his cousin the Czar that the Russian claim was unfounded. Then, thanks to his persuasive arts, he succeeded in extracting from "Cousin Nicky" a declaration of Russian disinterestedness in the Chinese bay.

Scarcely had he arrived back in Berlin when news came of the murder of two German Catholic missionaries in Shantung. The Catholic Center party was expostulating at the Foreign Office, calling for stern measures to be taken against China and for protection to be afforded to the German missionary stations in that country.

The Kaiser and the Chancellor found this appeal most opportune. As the Kaiser was staying in Letzlingen for winter shooting, Hohenlohe went there himself, and a conference, which Prince Heinrich attended, was held in one of the towers of the Schloss. It was decided to entrust Prince Heinrich with the command of a squadron which should start at once for East Asia and occupy Kiaochow.

This was accomplished without incident in December 1897, though neither England nor France was at all well-disposed toward the idea of Germany's getting a foothold in the Far East. On March 6, 1898, a lease by China was signed, placing the territory of Kiaochow at the disposal of the Reich for the term of ninety-nine years.

44. THE DEATH OF BISMARCK

THE EIGHTY-THREE-YEAR-OLD Bismarck in Friedrichsruh was still watching with undiminished interest all that was happening or was being decided within the Reich. There was much that he no longer understood. It was "a new and a different age," as he found and had to admit when on a visit to the port of Hamburg he saw the rapid development of its commerce. In order to keep in touch with him the Kaiser commissioned General Count von Waldersee to act as his liaison officer, and for that purpose appointed him to the command of the IXth Army Corps in Altona.

Bismarck was not at all pleased with this arrangement and was still less appreciative of Waldersee's frequent visits. "I always have the feeling, when he pays me a visit, that he either wants or has been told to find out whether it is time to be ordering a decent wreath!"

Waldersee's position was by no means an enviable one. When he thought he had created a favorable atmosphere and might be able to persuade the Prince to abandon his stubborn attitude, the old gentleman would burst out with this sort of thing: "I've been shown the door, and cannot ask for admission but must wait for an invitation."

"I can see," Bismarck complained to Waldersee, "that all my work will be brought to ruin by clumsy and shortsighted people." He disclaimed resolutely all responsibility for the policy then being pursued in Berlin. He would have nothing whatever to do with it. When a Liberal Deputy reproached him as being the one to blame for allowing the link with Russia to be broken, he waxed indignant against that mendacious perversion of the truth. "Until the year 1890 the two empires were in complete agreement on the point that should either of them be attacked the other would remain benevolently neutral. After my elimination this agreement was not renewed." What may have happened after his departure was the concern of Count Caprivi, for whose mistake he (Bismarck) could not and would not be answerable.

When the Kaiser saw that he could not better his relations with the Prince through any mediation by Waldersee, he arranged for an invitation to be sent him through Admiral Tirpitz to appear, as the ship's godfather, at the launching of the armored cruiser *Bismarck*. But, thus honored, the old gentleman replied with a curt and definite refusal "on account of his great age." Upon this, Tirpitz wrote again asking whether he might come and talk about this matter to Bismarck, but his letter came back unopened, with a note on the back to say that "letters that do not bear on the envelope the name of the sender are not accepted." After a third attempt Tirpitz was allowed to come to Friedrichsruh, where he had no more success than Waldersee, for as soon as the Admiral made a flattering remark the old gentleman interrupted him rudely with, "I'm not a cat, that gives off sparks when you stroke him!"

After being thus rebuffed the Kaiser lost all desire to venture on further advances to his former tutor and Chancellor. He could not conceal his disappointment and vexation. In his peculiar, impulsive way he used the occasion of the swearing-in of recruits to deliver a speech in which he complained about "highly placed persons" who frustrate all efforts to procure their co-operation and do not shrink from being traitors to their country and Kaiser.

The old Prince did not let these assertions pass in silence. When some students organized a torchlight procession in his honor he spoke bitterly as follows: "In the past all my endeavors were directed toward inculcating monarchical sentiments upon the minds of the common people. In the world of officialdom I was feted, but the people wanted to stone me. Now the common people greet me with shouts of joy, while the others carefully shun me. I suppose that is what is called the irony of fate!"

In expectation of his death, of which he often spoke, he warned the Kaiser against "letting good things, acquired by great toil, fall into decay." And he went on: "I should be glad to depart this life without any gloomy visions of the future of my country. I am sorrowful as one standing at the bedside of a beloved sufferer for whom there is no hope, and whom I am powerless to help, were I the most able of doctors."

Paying his last visit to Friedrichsruh the Kaiser felt the atmosphere to be icy and his hosts aloof. To distract the Prince he assumed a free-and-easy manner and cracked jokes which seemed to amuse himself immensely. Bismarck was as one turned to stone. It looked as though it was going to be impossible for him to carry out his intention of giving the "young gentleman," as a legacy, one last piece of advice. But as the Kaiser began to chat gaily about his Army and his officers, Bismarck's bushy eyebrows lifted. His words of farewell were bitterly sarcastic: "So long as Your Majesty has that corps of officers with you, anything at all is permissible. But should this once cease to be the case . . . it would be an entirely different matter!"

It was while on his Scandinavian cruise in 1898 that the Kaiser reecived the news of Bismarck's death. He at once set course for Kiel and from there proceeded to Friedrichsruh. In a well-worded obituary notice—published as an Army order immediately after arriving in Kiel—he honored the memory of the great statesman, his grandfather's friend.

It was proposed to organize funeral ceremonies for the first Reich's Chancellor on a grand scale. The sarcophagus was to be deposited in the Berlin Cathedral and the Royal Stalls were to be made over to the Bismarck family for the service. But Bismarck's will ruled out the Royal burial and Royal Stalls—even as a dead man he was obdurate and could signify his obduracy to the young Kaiser.

45. A BREACH WITH ENGLAND

WITHIN THE FIRST YEAR following Bismarck's death there appeared the first two volumes of his *Gedanken und Erinnerungen* (*Thoughts and Memories*). They found a ready sale in Germany, where everyone was anxious to familiarize himself with the recent past and the lifework of the great statesman. However, on closer examination these *Memories*, despite their convincing and gripping portions, were found to contain errors which could be traced to the fact that the writer's own memory had often failed him. Moreover, in these records it is only the voice of the Chancellor himself that speaks, who did not trouble much about the opinions of his contemporaries. Even while the books were being written, Lothar Bucher had drawn the attention of the Prince to the danger of such a subjective presentation, but he had been unable to bring about any change in Bismarck's views.

Although Wilhelm II strove to escape from the shadow of the dead giant, he altered nothing in his own views of foreign policy. In order "to see things with his own eyes" he did much traveling. In the autumn of 1898 he went to Palestine, this time accompanied by the Kaiserin. They reached Jerusalem on October twenty-ninth, in time to attend the consecration of the newly built Church of the Redeemer. The Imperial couple were disagreeably surprised at the uncared-for condition of the holy places, and the whole trip might perhaps have been one continuous disappointment had not this crusade concluded with some profitable transactions in the field of commerce. There was first of all the concession for the construction of a harbor at Haidar-Pasha, and then for the laying of a German cable from Constantinople to Constanza. Other economic advantages were also secured, which the *Commis voyageur impérial* was able to bring home from his Eastern tour.

Before the Kaiser left Turkey he sent the Sultan a message of thanks and an assurance of his friendship. "May your Imperial Majesty and the three hundred millions of Mohammedans always be assured that at all times the German Kaiser will be your friend!"

After his journey to Palestine the Kaiser's attention was once more directed to England by a number of speeches made by Joseph Chamberlain,[1] Secretary of State for the Colonies. Ostensibly Chamberlain was concerned to bring about a better understanding with the

[1] Joseph Chamberlain (1846–1914), British statesman, father of Sir Austen and Neville Chamberlain. Although he never rose to the position of Prime Minister, he played a leading political role as an exponent of Empire tariffs and closer bonds with both the United States and Germany. As Colonial Secretary he made two approaches to the Germans in 1897 and 1898, but the Kaiser and Bülow rebuffed him and from then on Chamberlain supported the Anglo-French *Entente Cordiale*.

Reich, which Tirpitz interpreted as meaning that he wanted to ascertain whether the political moves of the Reich meant risking a bid for true sea power, or whether the whole thing was to be regarded as a piece of bluff.

As before, the Kaiser once again began to vacillate, undecided as to whether he hated England or loved her, honored her or despised her. "Poor Grandmamma!"; "Wonderful Boers!"; "Ungrateful Kruger!"; "Brave Roberts!" [2] So his mind kept on changing, swinging this way and that, influenced by every passing mood.

It was obvious that a Reich founded only twenty-five years before, but now grown to be a powerful and rich State, should wish to show that it was strong. Every word that came across from England was subjected to a suspicious examination seeking to find whether the new Great Power was being ignored, laughed at or derided over there.

Wilhelm might scent aversion and hostility everywhere, but what he dreaded above all was not being taken seriously on the other side of the Channel. This fear of being belittled accounted for those "over the borderline" speeches that aroused fresh astonishment and wrath in the country of his mother and grandmother. He talked about "the breakers of the ocean that are knocking at the doors of the German people." And again he declared that "the ocean knows that on it and far beyond it no great decisions will ever again be reached without the participation of Germany and of the German Kaiser. I have no intention of allowing our German people, who thirty years ago conquered and bled under the leadership of their princes, to be thrust aside when great and important questions of foreign policy come to be decided. Should that occur it would be my duty and my highest privilege to take fitting steps, and if necessary to employ the most severe measures, regardless of consequences!"

On another occasion—in a telegram to the Czar Nicholas II—he took up this idea of "ruling the waves": "the Grand Admiral of the Western Ocean sends his comradely greetings to the Grand Admiral of the Eastern Ocean!"

On this the Admiralty staff in London made no observation save that "so far as it is aware, Lord Fisher is still the Admiral of the Western Ocean."

[2] Lord Frederick Roberts (1832–1914), British commander in the Boer War.

Wilhelm's "eccentricity," as "Uncle Bertie" called his way of openly offending the English, now led to an open breach with his grandmother, who hitherto had always been disposed to extend her protection to her favorite grandson. Now, however, she was so irate that she let "Willie" know that he would not be expected to visit Windsor on the occasion of her eightieth birthday.

The Kaiser thereupon addressed a long complaint to her, trying to show that he could not suffer such a slight without protest. He and his Reich must not be treated like Portugal, Chile or Patagonia. As for the conflict that had arisen over Samoa, he complained of the injustice with which Britain sought to pursue her claims without regard to himself . . . "and all this about a stupid little island that can never be worth a hairpin to England in comparison with the thousands of square miles that she annexes right and left every year without anyone's objecting."

When going closely into the subject of his attitude toward Britain, as he did afterward in Doorn, the Kaiser said that he had come to the conclusion that it would not have been a good thing at that time to have been allied to her. "In memoirs I often find the opinion expressed that in the situation then existing in Europe, the combination of the strongest sea power in the world with the strongest land power on the Continent had already become a rational necessity. But that argument rests on a wrong basis. All the renunciations and disadvantages would then have had to be on the German side. Our naval preparedness was so primitive that in world politics we had to be content with the crumbs that England grudgingly threw to us, while we, as a continental Power, would have had to shoulder all the risks inherent in the function of acting as England's vassal."

46. THE CAMARILLA

THE KAISER once said about Bismarck's entourage that "the Prince lay like a mighty block of granite in a meadow—if you rolled it over you found only worms and half-dead roots." It is true that the Reich's Chancellor left behind him no successors, no one with wide schooling in politics, but only a lot of "worms," subordinate servile souls in ill-fitting frock coats who trembled before the all-powerful presence.

In general, the German does not care for cringing, slavish servility. "Camarilla," too, is a foreign word, unknown in Prussia until it reached there in the time of Friedrich Wilhelm IV. It means a clique of servile courtiers who speak only to echo what the monarch has said, in the humble hope of winning his favor and thereby gaining some advantage. Heinrich von Treitschke says in his historical treatise on events after the accession of Friedrich Wilhelm IV: "Thus it happened in Berlin that owing to the powerful upsurge of genuine loyalty to the King, there was also a stirring-up of that servile mentality never wholly lacking even in noble monarchies, which used to show itself in all its ignominy when a new king mounted the throne."

So again at the accession of Wilhelm II the same type of servile mind was soon in evidence, and with it a degree of abasement exceeding that of sixty years before. When Ballin, depressed by what he had seen at Court, expressed the hope that one day the Kaiser would see through those flatterers and send them all to the devil, Waldersee replied, "I don't think so at all! There can never be too much flattery for the Kaiser!"

To give some idea of the extent to which adulation by the Camarilla was rife, let us reproduce a speech by Count Franz von Ballestrem, a man bearing the high dignity of President of the Reichstag, who said these words in an address to a plenary meeting of the House:

"When the Kaiser takes the field with his troops . . . when the Kaiser . . . stays at a Schloss, the Imperial Standard is hoisted. And that is right, for the people must always know where the Kaiser is. And if it be right as an outward and visible sign, how much more right must it be in the spiritual field. Our greatly revered Kaiser is aware of that! As soon as any question arises to trouble the minds of the people he takes some opportunity of expressing in public his opinion thereon and his attitude thereto, he hoists an intellectual standard that can be viewed from afar! Gentlemen, as I see it, he does not hoist it with the aim of compelling the people to stand by, mute and inactive, but he hoists it so that the question may be examined, weighed and discussed by all those whom it concerns and, above all, by the representatives of the German people.

"The Hohenzollern princes have always been men with a sound understanding of their own times. In the Middle Ages they were knights in armor. In the New Era they have been great leaders in war, like Frederick the Great and Wilhelm the Great!"

Then the speaker went on to indulge in praise of "the glorious Kaiser": "Gentlemen, all that the Kaiser does must fill us with admiration and we may thank Providence for giving us, in such a time as this, such a Kaiser!"

If a representative of the Prussian nobility could strike such a note, what could one of the smaller fry say, if he wanted to bring himself to the notice of the Kaiser? A certain Bavarian professor tried to solve that problem with the following effusion: "When the Kaiser begins to speak his face reflects a range of impressions that are interesting to study. His features, immovable and even rigid at first, light up as soon as he opens his mouth, lightning flashes over his energetic countenance, his eyes gleam with a fascinating luster and the finely designed upper lip often displays two rows of dazzlingly white teeth."

As the press was most closely associated with the Camarilla and was always careful to see that every word uttered by His Majesty was commented upon with gasping superlatives of admiration, everything he said sounded to the good citizens like a revelation. People paid no attention to the blasphemy contained in a notice in the Berlin *Kreuz-Zeitung* which published the news that "the All-Highest Sovereigns betook themselves to the cathedral to return thanks to the Highest."

And what was the plain citizen of Berlin to make of it when he read in the *Vossische Zeitung* of January 27, 1899, a supposedly democratic paper: "He who today is forty years of age is an Emperor, a Caesar, more than a Napoleon, and that is true not only for us but for the whole world! In Europe today all eyes are turned toward the banks of the Spree, toward our old and lovely royal Schloss, in which the Idol, the God of the Day, does us the honor to reside!"

The center of gravity of the Camarilla lay, of course, within the Berlin Schloss, and to it belonged not only the Court officials but also generals like Keim and Deimling, whose later capacity for turning their coats was proof of their astonishing versatility.

On the other hand, how could a young man, called upon to rule, develop naturally or acquire sensible opinions when before him he saw only people with cringing, bowing backs, not disdaining even to kiss his hands to the accompaniment of awe-stricken stammerings of honorifics such as "Most mighty Kaiser . . . !"; "Most Serene Highness . . . !"; "Most Gracious Master . . . !"

By comparison with this sultry, suffocating atmosphere of the Court the old German form of address "*Herr König* . . . !" (Sir King!) comes like a fresh breeze of spring.

Everything had to be pressed into the service of perfuming the person of the Kaiser with incense, even his marriage. Thus a few years after his accession a journalist had the impudence to write that "Kaiser Wilhelm II, whose world-mastering, piercing glance is so truly Frederician, has through his happy marriage become acquainted with the tenderness of that affection which first constituted the subsoil of the real patriarchal way of life."

It is sad to say that the nobility—even the old Prussian nobility—participated in these extravagances. Amid reiterated assurances of his "unchangeable fidelity" and his "inextinguishable gratitude" Prince Dohna-Schlobitten, the representative of East Prussia, went so far, on the occasion of a shooting party in the Rominter Heide, as to ask the Kaiser if he would permit that his cows at Schlobitten could carry bells like those of the Kaiser at Cadinen. The Kaiser cannot be blamed for answering, "It's all the same to me what sort of cowbells your cattle wear!" Count Eberhard Dohna was no exception. Eulenburg has told how the Count used to scatter "thunderbolts" on the beach, knowing that the Kaiser would go looking for them when taking a walk. In doing this, Dohna acted as some archaeologists did on another occasion when they planted a find and covered it lightly with earth, so that by a lucky chance the discovery of the treasure might take place before the Kaiser's own eyes.

So it came about that the Court toadies, as they were called in the officers' messes, gradually drew a tightly closed circle about Wilhelm II, hiding from the All-Highest Master everything that he might find vexatious—"His Majesty must have *sunshine*!"

In time this chorus had so perfected its technique that a word from the Kaiser sufficed for it to exclaim in unison, "That's pure Frederick the Great!" or "Your Majesty has now deigned to create something that will be eternal!"

Very soon the Kaiser had no honest adviser at all—only this mendacious clique and claque that automatically and indiscriminately applauded and approved all he did. Even his dachshunds would be enticed by surreptitious offers of chocolates, though they would never touch them. Yawning, they showed that they were bored with such acts of homage.

In the end the Kaiser became bored too. The long-drawn spell of time-serving became too much for him.

When a pamphlet entitled *Guillaume II en vue de France* ("Wilhelm II from the French Standpoint") was put before him, and he found in it an expression of the hope that he, like Lohengrin, would free Alsace-Lorraine "from distress and disgrace," he remarked disdainfully, "Mere twaddle!"

On the other hand, the Kaiser, by his own conduct, did much to encourage the irresponsible activities of the Camarilla.

Whereas Frederick the Great recognized flatterers as "enemies of the Throne" in that they concealed the truth and sought only to conceal the fact by their frothy talk, Wilhelm II, on the contrary, chose his friends from among them.

The old Kaiser had never tolerated flatterers about him. As Bismarck tells us in his *Thoughts and Memories*, no one would have dared to address a commonplace piece of flattery to that old gentleman. With his kingly dignity he would have thought that "if anyone has the right to praise me to my face, he would also have the right to criticize me to my face!" And he would permit neither the one nor the other.

The more a person is praised the more sensitive he is to criticism. So there ensued a whole series of trials for *lèse-majesté*. In one of these the judge defined the idea of respect for Kaiser and Throne as follows: "Respect for a monarch is not shown by lying at his feet in Byzantine fashion and by flattering him. Real respect consists rather in holding high before him the truth."

When Wilhelm von Liebenau, the Marshal of the Court, showed him this opinion and inquired anxiously whether there was any occasion for taking proceedings against the judge, the Kaiser answered angrily, "No occasion at all! The man is quite right!"

Niccolò Machiavelli, speaking of flattering princes, observed: "Princes have but one good means of protecting themselves against flatterers, namely, to leave no one in doubt as to this: no one can displease them by telling them the truth. A prince who proceeds otherwise will either be ruined by the flatterers, or else will find himself forced, by the diversity of the advice given him, to be constantly vacillating."

The pernicious effects of a Camarilla had been long before appreciated by a contemporary of the Great King, the great German philosopher Immanuel Kant, who wrote and left behind him "a warning to all whom it may concern: Flattery is the real destroyer of those who are great and powerful."

47. RELATIONS WITH THE FEDERAL PRINCES

In 1898 there occurred for the first time a dispute with a Federal prince. Until then Wilhelm II had succeeded in maintaining good relations with these princes, although not all of them—not, for instance, the Grand Duke Ernst Ludwig of Hesse—were well-disposed toward the Kaiser.

Many of them suffered from *Reichsverdrossenheit*—a feeling of resentment against the Reich, its institutions and its ways, a distaste that had especially affected the old rulers of Bavaria and Baden and was expressed by the desire not to be interfered with, but to be allowed to live in peace. The minor Federal princes did not venture to break ranks, though they might have wanted to do so, if only to take revenge for the overbearing attitude of the Kaiser.

They took it amiss when he wrote to them in pencil, and scolded them at powwows on maneuvers, or facetiously dealt them *coram publico* a smack on the behind. The young Grand Duke Adolf Friedrich of Mecklenburg-Strelitz rebelled against such familiarities after receiving a smack of this kind in the officers' mess of the Guard Uhlans, and made a bitter speech about such antics of the Kaiser.

A prince who often fell foul of Wilhelm II was the Count Regent of Lippe-Detmold. In the summer of 1898 he protested energetically against any interference by the Kaiser in his affairs and demanded from him recognition of the Count's line then governing, the title of Illustrious for himself and military honors. The Kaiser was of the opinion—which was shared by the professors of public law—that such an elevation and such a claim were quite out of place as long as the fight for the Lippe succession had not definitely been settled in the courts of law.

The Kaiser's reply to the requests of Regent Ernst was this: "Your letter received. High Command instructions issued with my approval. To the Regent, what is due to the Regent, and no more. For the rest, I must once and for all forbid you to use such a tone as that in which you have seen fit to write to me."

The Count would not put up with such treatment without retaliating. He appealed to the Federal princes, who took his part, for none of them knew whether one day they might next themselves be treated in a like manner. His colleagues of Bavaria, Württemberg, Saxony and Hesse encouraged him to take a firm stand against the Kaiser, who had shortly before spoken in one of his orations about "One master in the land."

Supported by these princes and by his own belief in the justice of his case, the Count Regent of Lippe-Detmold laid his plaint before the Federal Council, which, after further hearing, decided to remit it to the supreme court in Leipzig. This court in the end returned a verdict in favor of the plaintiff.

The Kaiser's interference in the affairs of a Federal prince, which was repeated seven years later in Lippe, aroused suspicions and ill-feeling, more especially among the South German princes. The matter was taken up by the *Kölnische Zeitung*, and in a leading article it was summed up thus: "A gradually swelling wave of discontent has been spreading over South Germany, extending beyond the circle of the Particularists to involve politicians who gave an enthusiastic welcome to the formation of the German Reich, to the rule of Kaiser Wilhelm I and his paladins. People loyal to the Reich, and now finally the Federal princes, are beginning to look with mistrust and apprehension toward Berlin."

Even one so little vocal as King Wilhelm II of Württemberg ranged himself against the Kaiser and gave him a warning, reminding him, on the occasion of a festival in Friedrichshafen, of Bismarck's speech of March 26, 1886, in which the Chancellor had declared that the greatest danger that threatened the Reich was the possibility of the King of Prussia, or of Bavaria or of Saxony, repenting of the sacrifices involved by being brought together into one common fold.

The Prince Regent Luitpold of Bavaria, too, complained in May 1900, in these words: "I cannot understand why we, forming part of the German Reich, are not accorded exactly the same rights and privileges that are given to North Germany. Above all, let Bavaria protest against the reproach that she ought to consider it a favor to be allowed to belong to the Reich, for the Reich is welded together just as much by Bavarian blood as by the blood of any other breed, and for that reason we wish to be regarded, not as minors, but as brothers of full age."

Even though the Kaiser might lose his temper on receiving reprimands like this, he knew that he must give way and have due regard to maintaining good humor. When Count Schack bequeathed to him his celebrated gallery of pictures in Munich, he took the opportunity of paying his compliments to both Munich and Bavaria in a most conciliatory manner. He built a stately new mansion, combining it with a Prussian Embassy in the Prinzregentenstrasse, and hung the pictures in it, "being happy to possess a house in which every friend of art will always be welcome."

It was not possible, however, to exorcise apprehensions and misgivings by such charming and easy gestures. Waldersee, that great listener, who had ears in each of the twenty courts of the Federal princes, confided his anxiety to his diary. "Will the Kaiser lead the Reich onward by an uphill road, or will he bring it to ruin? Blessed with so many talents, filled with the very best intentions, he has initiated too much, but, alas, has carried nothing through to an end. He has brought about confusion from which no escape is yet in sight, and it clouds the future with forebodings of trouble which are felt by most of the Federal princes."

Bismarck had left all sorts of prescriptions for the treatment of the Reich of his own creation, and how to rule it with success. For dealing with the Federal princes he had passed on to his "young master" special directions to remind him, the King of Prussia, that he was only *par inter pares*. "It is not difference of stock but dynastic relations upon which centrifugal elements repose. It is not attachment to Swabian, Lower Saxon or Thuringian or other particular stock that counts for most, but the dynastic incorporation with the people of some severed portion of a ruling princely family as in the case of the Brunswick, Brabant and Wittelsbach dynasties."

48. THE BOXER REBELLION

ON JUNE 12, 1900, the Second Fleet Bill came before the Reichstag. On the basis of this addition to the previous bill the German fleet was to have thirty-eight warships by the year 1917.

Shortly afterward the revolt of the Boxers broke out in China, directed against the white population, their settlements and representatives. The German Minister, Baron von Ketteler, and other Europeans were murdered in Peking. The Emperor of China offered to organize processions of burned offerings to atone for the murders, but the Kaiser rejected this as insufficient. He sent the following personal telegram to Tsai-tien, "I, the German Emperor, have received the telegram of His Majesty the Emperor of China. I have noted with satisfaction that Your Majesty is endeavoring to atone, according to the usage and practice of your religion, for the murder of my Minister, a shameful act done in defiance of all civilized culture, but as German Emperor, and as a Christian, I am unable to regard this horrible crime as one to be atoned for by burned offerings. Besides my murdered Minister a large number of Brothers of the Christian Faith, bishops, missionaries, women and children, who for their faith, which is also my faith, died under torture, have appeared before the Throne of God and will be your accusers. Can burned offerings ordered by Your Majesty suffice to atone for the deaths of all these innocent people? I do not hold Your Majesty personally responsible for this wrong committed against the unimpeachable principles of diplomatic representation, accepted by all peoples, nor yet for the grievous injuries done to many nations and religious persuasions. The advisers of Your Majesty's Throne, the officials, on whose heads lies the blood guilt of a crime that has filled all nations with horror, must expiate their infamous acts."

On July twenty-seventh the East Asian Expeditionary Force embarked at Bremerhaven. Before it sailed, the Kaiser gave an address from which some sentences are worth recalling: "A hard task lies before you! You will have to avenge the most grievous wrong ever known! The Chinese have violated the law of nations. In one of the most unheard-of ways recorded in world history they have scorned the sanctity of embassies and their obligations under the laws of hospitality. You know well you will have to fight against a cunning, brave, well-armed and cruel enemy. When you meet him—remember!—no quarter will be given—no prisoners will be taken! Use your weapons so that for a thousand years no Chinese will dare to look askance at a German!"

The wording of this address became a subject of great reproach for the Kaiser. A Zürich paper gave its opinion thus: "The firebrand character of this speech, the order to take no prisoners, can scarcely be designated as Christian, when in the communication to the Emperor of China there was so much talk of real Christianity. The speech, if it can at all be justified, may perhaps be explained by the excitement that has gripped all Germany."

From the military point of view the expedition constituted a hazardous undertaking in view of the great distance of the theater of operations, which was not linked with the homeland by any kind of line of communications offering intermediate bases.

Field Marshal Count von Waldersee was entrusted with the command. The choice fell on him because, apart from the fact that this traveled and amusing society man had been acquainted with the Kaiser since 1883 when the latter was heir to the Throne, he was recognized as having a good knowledge of foreign armies; he was a quartermaster general trained in the school of old Moltke.

In Guards circles a whole garland of good stories hung around Waldersee. It was known that he never carried an ordnance survey map with him during Army exercises or at maneuvers. He used to tell young officers: "You should not keep your head in your maps, but keep the maps in your head!" At maneuvers he used to astonish everyone by being able to recognize and name every railway signal box and trigonometrical point in an area without a glance at the map.

Another thing that made him talked about was his tame raven. While its master was at work in the Red House on the Königsplatz, the bird would sit on a stone in the courtyard of the building and wait there until Waldersee reappeared. Then it would perch on one of its master's gold shoulder straps. So they would leave the courtyard together, with the sentry presenting arms to both. This raven would never allow itself to be touched by anyone, not even by the Kaiser, who tried his best, but in vain.

To these peculiarities of Waldersee may be added his inclination to bigotry, for one could scarcely call it piety. His wife, an American, had introduced him into some religious sect which in the end dominated his whole outlook on life. She also tried to convert the Kaiser.

In Berlin the Countess, who suffered from "apparitions and inspirations," was generally held to be mad. Waldersee later wrote his memoirs under her influence, and in the original text they sound as if they had been dictated to him by God Himself. In them one finds lamentations such as this one: "Would to God that I were able to record any good thing coming from, or concerning, the Kaiser."

As Commander in Chief of the composite force made up of several contingents from different nations, Waldersee soon came to be known as the *Welt-Marschall* (World Marshal). He actually arrived in China when the military operations were almost concluded and preparations had already been made for the signing of peaceful agreements with the Imperial Chinese Government, so that he had to hurry in order to qualify for the "laurels in advance"—which he had already received—before the door closed.

The results of the expedition proved to be paltry. The Emperor of China was to dispatch Prince Chun to Germany as an Atoning Prince charged with expressing to the Kaiser, in the name of the Chinese Emperor, regret for the murder of the Minister.

The ceremony of atonement was degraded to the level of a theatrical scene by the extravagant fitting-out of the hall in the New Palace, where it was performed.

Hohenlohe, Chancellor of the Reich, had now become tired of office. Looking back on the six years of his activity, he could see disappointments all along the line. He could register as successes the compilation of the Code of Civil Law, reform of the methods of military punishment, the settlement of the dispute over Samoa, the occupation of Kiaochow, the Yangtse Agreement, and the Fleet Law.

The aged Prince Chlodwig Hohenlohe handed in his resignation, which was accepted without demur. Like his two predecessors he had to leave the Wilhelmstrasse in haste, for his successor, Bernhard von Bülow, hitherto Secretary of State, was waiting impatiently to move in.

49. PRINCE PHILIPP ZU EULENBURG

IF THE KAISERIN AUGUSTE VIKTORIA was afraid of the Bülow-Holstein-Eulenburg confederacy, it was Eulenburg who appeared to her to be the most sinister of the three. In this year of Hohenlohe's resignation the Kaiser elevated him to the dignity of Hereditary Prince. It was a thank offering to the only real friend the Kaiser possessed, as he himself admitted.

The new Prince came of an old East Prussian family that had given eminent statesmen to Prussia. He had first known the Kaiser as Prince Wilhelm and had remained in touch with him ever since. Then the Princess Auguste Viktoria had been captivated by the young Count's charm and his talent as a raconteur. The Kaiser, recalling that happy year in Potsdam, said, "When Eulenburg entered our home, it was always like a flood of sunshine falling on our everyday affairs."

Before the Kaiser's accession Eulenburg had made a hesitant attempt to draw further apart from his friend who was "soon to be so highly placed," because as he explained, "everything is going to be quite different."

At the New Year of 1888 he had written to the heir to the throne, "How I am tortured by the thought that the gulf which divides us socially, a gulf that our friendship has bridged, must grow ever wider, ever deeper, by reason of the Imperial Crown."

But the young Kaiser held fast to the friendship. He even used the "*Du*" in addressing Eulenburg, but that of course was on his side only, for Eulenburg himself had never, even before then, addressed his master otherwise than in the third person.

After his accession the Kaiser used him as a liaison officer between himself and the dismissed Chancellor. Even in Friedrichsruh, Eulenburg soon succeeded in making himself well liked, especially by Princess Johanna, who delighted in listening to him playing the piano and singing. He was on equally good terms at first with Herbert Bismarck, but that was not to be for long.

His popularity in Friedrichsruh, however, decreased as his friendship with the Kaiser increased. Bismarck thought he could detect insincerity in him, and called him "a slippery eel that one cannot get hold of." Afterward he expressed himself more strongly. He declared that Eulenburg's eyes would spoil the best of luncheons for him! Hohenlohe had said something of the same sort, calling "Phili" "the man with the cold eye of a snake." This pet name, by the way, was given him, not by the Kaiser, but by Bismarck.

Eulenburg once confessed to using the "*Du*" to people who were his own worst enemies. A witticism to the same effect was current in the Court, "If you were to bring Eulenburg and his friends together there would be a terrific row!" Nor could these enemy friends come to any clear decision about Eulenburg—they felt as much attracted to him as repelled by him. In their opinion he showed off too much—showing himself to be shifty, vain, self-satisfied, overbearing, malicious, superficial and amateurish. Then again they would call him likable, good-natured, well-informed, even discreet. His habit of speaking in superlatives, in order to dazzle people and make a sensation, was repulsive to many on meeting him for the first time.

The Kaiser appeared not to notice these diverse attributes. For him his friend was only the brilliant entertainer who could crack pointed jokes, cite quotations, and mimic to perfection personalities whom he had only seen once. Moreover, he looked on him as a gifted composer, whose *Untergang von Atlantis* (*Destruction of Atlantis*) he never tired of hearing him play. More praiseworthy than this and other ballads such as the *Sang an Aegir* (*Hymn to Aegir*) —of which the Kaiser claimed to be the author—are Eulenburg's *Rosenlieder* (*Rose Songs*), which in the delicacy of their melodies— though these are rather similar in form among themselves—are almost reminiscent of Schubert's works.

Afterward, in Doorn, the Kaiser admitted that he had overestimated Eulenburg. "But that cannot alter the fact that he was one of the most charming men I have ever known. In music he may have been a dilettante, but everyone who loves folk songs will soon discover the *Rosenlieder*. As an entertaining companion he was sublime; he could seize on any little trivial incident of a journey, make a fascinating story out of it, and tell it in such an interesting way that one had to listen to it, and the time passed as though on

wings. He was also well versed in the history of art. As a cicerone
he was indispensable to me. He was like an encyclopedia, except
that that may make a slip and he never did. Eulenburg's biographer,
the otherwise excellent Professor Johannes Haller of Tübingen, falls
into the same errors that I did forty years before: he tries to over-
value Eulenburg. But Haller's hero was neither really a hero nor a
genius. That must not be taken as meaning that I am seeking to disparage him. He was my friend and as such he will remain in my
memory."

Although Eulenburg could rely on the friendship of the Kaiser,
that was not the case with either Privy Councilor von Holstein or
the new Reich's Chancellor von Bülow. All his life Eulenburg stood
in awe of the Gray Eminence, because Holstein knew too much
about his private life. So there was never any honest association between them. Equally precarious were "Phili's" relations with
Bülow. Neither of them trusted the other. Each dreaded betrayal
and defamation by the other and tried to cover it by the exchange of
excessively friendly letters. Protestations of "eternal fidelity," larded
with superlatives and sultry sentimentalities, alternated with inflated
assurances of friendship, so that even the extravagant expressions
commonly used about the *fin de siècle* provided no excuse for the
unnatural style adopted. Thus, Bülow writing to Eulenburg: "It is
not only because we share so many beautiful and painful memories,
but because in the depths of our natures we think alike and find that
in daily life we supplement each other; that is why we have become
such good friends. . . . Sisterlike, our souls ascended from the mysterious spring of all existence; only different coverings and wings of
different colors were given us."

Holstein, who was given the letter by Eulenburg to read, seized
on the word "sisterlike." [1] He carefully noted this sentence in his
dossier marked "Bülow." He knew well that one day he would produce this entry from his desk and use it as a weapon.

Eulenburg expressed himself in his letters just as Bülow did; perhaps he even surpassed him in sentimentality. Even the most simple
ideas, such as anxiety about Bülow's health, were worded in extravagant terms. Thus (in the second person) to Bülow: "Apart from

[1] "Sisterlike" in German is not as peculiar as it sounds in English. Since
"soul" in German is of the female gender, he could not have used "*brüderlich*."

the fact that you, dearest, must not entirely abstain from your work, your health is far more important for the Kaiser, the Country, and your Service."

Eulenburg's enemies maintained that he had made make-believe his normal behavior so that, in the end, he could not act any differently. From morning till night, they said, he lied to his friends, including the Kaiser, and deceived them, his adoring eyes directed at them all the time. As far as the Kaiser was concerned, this could not have been the case.

If, too, Eulenburg must be counted a member of the Camarilla, his was an exceptional case, for he was almost the only person at Court who, on many occasions, showed that he had the courage to tell the Kaiser the truth. When raised to the dignity of Prince, he felt it was more than ever incumbent upon him to speak his mind freely when it was urgently necessary to do so.

"Your Majesty's personal standing in the Reich has not been improved by the way personal rule has been so strongly emphasized on various occasions!"

"The narrow-minded elements in Germany are finding it difficult to understand Your Majesty's restless ways of living!"

"There is a great deal of ill-feeling against Your Majesty in the country!"

During the Kaiser's Scandinavian cruise of 1899 Eulenburg even ventured to speak of "threats of enforcing abdication or of placing under restraint." "Cardinal Hohenlohe, whom Your Majesty reveres, impressed on me with his last words before he died: 'I know that you are absolutely devoted to the Kaiser and also that you are in a position to give him advice quite openly. The Kaiser should be very much on his guard. I know for certain that the idea of declaring him mentally unsound has occurred to many people and that very many, even highly placed persons, would gladly lend their hands to instituting proceedings. Warn His Majesty!' "

The Kaiser received such warnings of Eulenburg's in silence. Afterward Eulenburg declared that the Kaiser never resented plain speaking once he recognized the justice of a remonstrance. Once, when he was protesting against the number of speeches the Kaiser was making and told him that they only made people unsettled and angry, the Kaiser replied: "I like your frankness. I am most grateful to you for it. If you won't speak frankly with me, who else should do it? For the future I shall keep my mouth shut and use it only for eating, drinking and smoking!"

Often, however, it might happen that he only laughed at the Prince: "Philipp, don't be taken in by that nonsense!" or telegraphed back: "Quite unnecessary excitement on your part!"

The fact that he only summoned up courage to make protests or to give advice to the Kaiser when he felt sure of being successful tells against Eulenburg. Things that might annoy the Kaiser he often passed over as unsuited to his mediation. "I cannot tell His Majesty anything so unpleasant!"

On the other hand, when he took exception to the "un-Prussian fiddle-faddle" of the new Court dress for hunting and shooting—which the Kaiser had devised—he did not mince his words but said straight out what he thought of it, though he knew that his derogatory comments would be at once repeated to the Kaiser. "When His Majesty pays me a visit I have to strut about in disguise, make a report to him in my peaceable room, and to cap it all, sit down to my piano in high yellow riding boots and silver spurs to sing folk songs to him. And all this in my old Liebenberg!"

Soon after being appointed German Ambassador in Vienna, Eulenburg was able to say: "At this moment the entire Triple Alliance depends on Goluchowski, the Schratt [2] and myself!" And that was perfectly true. Not only had he very quickly acclimatized himself with the Viennese, but he had also ensured for himself, as representing the Reich, a position in the Metternichgasse to which no ambassador before him had attained.

Everything that he saw and heard in Vienna he placed at the disposal of his friend Bülow in the form of reports and papers: "Out of the gradually increasing hoards in my storeroom I can pass on to you much material that will enable you to proceed, with a lighter and therefore a more assured touch, with the erection of that edifice which, against your real inclinations but for the good of our Kaiser and country, you have in hand."

In March 1897 Eulenburg again had occasion to warn his imperial friend, when differences of opinion had arisen between the Kaiser and the German Foreign Office. These differences became so

---

[2] Agenor Goluchowski (1849–1921), Austrian statesman. Minister for Foreign Affairs, 1895–1906; Katharina Schratt, Baroness Kiss von Ittebe, friend of Franz Joseph.

serious that—as Eulenburg maintained—the Foreign Office quite unreservedly considered the Kaiser mad. "It may happen," Eulenburg declared, "that by Your Majesty's personal intervention the functioning of the machine is interrupted. I might repeat that unity between you and your Foreign Office is the paramount necessity."

Eulenburg might easily have been successful, with his magic powers, in influencing the Kaiser and getting many things altered or stopped altogether. But to accomplish all that, consistency, patience, constancy and also logic would have been necessary, and these Eulenburg did not possess.

Looking back on Prince Philipp zu Eulenburg the Kaiser summarized his own opinion of him—after an interval of thiry years— thus: "I am indebted to him for much that was fine and beautiful in art, science and literature. For decades he was loyal to me as a good friend. Whether there is truth in certain allegations made against him, I cannot decide. In any case I shall always cherish a grateful memory of him."

50. THE KAISER'S SPEECHES

UNTIL THE ACCESSION of Wilhelm II it had never occurred to any reigning Hohenzollern to address himself often, or at great length, to the people, telling them of what was being thought and intended, or explaining who was to be feared . . . and threatened. Neither the Great Elector nor Frederick the Great delivered many orations; but if they did speak, like Frederick the Great before the battle of Leuthen, it was necessary to do so and was done in finished style at a time of very great peril when the very existence of the State was at stake.

By the year 1900 there were already four bulky volumes of speeches by Wilhelm II, and after that it was scarcely possible to keep count of them. What is striking about these speeches is the overlarding of simple facts by high-flown expressions and their conjunction with false analogies. The almost torrential eloquence of the virtuoso cannot gloss over the ill-considered and the overhasty, the contradictions and slips that as often as not were the result of free improvisation. Carried away by his impetuous nature the Kaiser would often discard the text that he had himself prepared and go on to speak "beyond his brief" of matters to which he had not given any consideration. Promises were made, mystical-romantic embroidery followed—superfluous matter crept in—so that the unity of the speech was impaired. Once again the superfluous proved to be the enemy of the essential.

Whereas political orators carefully weigh their words in the scales to provide themselves with a mask so as not to betray their real intentions, the Kaiser rejected that idea because he could never bring himself to dissemble. He spoke as he thought, let himself be guided by his temperament, and followed up every issue that occurred to him, regardless of its being acceptable or offensive, or of its having any logical connection with what had gone before. He honestly believed that by this kind of frankness he could bewitch not only his own subjects but also the general public of Europe that listened to him.

Much speaking is generally a sign of weakness, especially when it is done to an accompaniment of saber rattling. Among the ancestors of Wilhelm II the weak and peevish King Friedrich Wilhelm III had tried saber rattling when he declared to Napoleon: "My plans are unshakable. I fear nobody. I await events with my weapon at my side!" Because he proved to be neither unshakable nor fearless he lost half his country. For the rest of his reign he remained silent.

It is surprising that the Kaiser never understood how gravely these speeches harmed both himself and the Reich. A very significant caricature depicted him as a man strolling about among barrels of gunpowder with a lighted cigarette.

It was difficult for the Chancellor and ministers to keep up constitutional appearances before outsiders and to assume responsibility for speeches of the Kaiser that they had neither suggested, composed nor edited. Quite ingenuously the Kaiser put the matter in a distorted form, upside down: "Thinking and acting on constitutional lines is often a tough job for a prince, who always has to shoulder the responsibility in the end!"

The Kaiser's technique of making speeches soon had many imitators. First of all the gentlemen of the Camarilla took to aping him in word and manner. It was not long before every commanding officer and every district president was making addresses in the style of the All-Highest and being careful to ascribe the reign of "H.M." and the Hohenzollern dynasty to the work and will of God. The future was always painted in rosy colors on the Kaiser's birthday, for "His Majesty would not tolerate prophets of gloom" (1906).

Kladderadatsch represented the Kaiser as Mark Antony in a toga, addressing the people in the Forum; in another issue he is shown at his doctor's. In reply to the patient's inquiry as to what illness he is suffering from, the doctor replies, "Only speechitis, Your Majesty!"

In 1905, when President Loubet declared that he was ready to receive the Kaiser in Paris, which was a most courageous offer in face of the popular feeling in the French capital, the Kaiser answered by a speech from Cassel, compared with which a fanfaronade of General Boulanger's would have sounded like a murmur of the breeze: "The Order of the Day is: keep your powder dry—keep your sword sharp—and keep your fist on the hilt!" On that, of course, the journey to Paris fell through; the Kaiser went to Kiel.

Such bellicose utterances, as the "mailed fist" answer to France's offer of reconciliation, gave the impression that the Kaiser wanted war. Moltke had already warned against threatening with weapons which one did not seriously intend to use. Frivolous conduct like that meant playing a dangerous game.

The constantly reiterated assertion that he, the Kaiser, alone knew what was the right thing to do, had a terrifying effect. As early as February 24, 1892, he had declared: "My course is the right one, and it will be followed!" A year later, in addressing recruits, he laid it down that "there is only one law, and that is my law!"

Soon after that he thought it necessary to emphasize again his idea of personal rule, and in a variant on the theme declared before the Diet of the Rhine provinces that "one man is master in the Reich! I tolerate none other!"

He also liked putting provocative expressions of this kind into print or writing, as when he decided on the motto *Sic volo, sic jubeo* for the subject of a painting to be hung in the Conference Hall of the Ministry of Education.

When a District President of Arnsberg declined to let one of the Kaiser's statements pass without contradiction, the Kaiser had him transferred. Later on, in a more gracious frame of mind, he sent him a signed photograph of himself with the admonition *"Nemo me impune lacessit!"*

Many of his reprimands and judgments were imprudent, rash or inconsiderate. Thus in 1908 he called Count Ferdinand von Zeppelin, the designer of airships, "the greatest German of the twentieth century"—a century that had only just begun.

What is generally accepted as an example of a *good* speech by the Kaiser is his address on the occasion of the unveiling of a monument in Bremen on March 22, 1905. "I have vowed, because of what I have learned from history, never to aspire to a barren world dominion, for what became of the so-called great world empires? Alexander, Napoleon, and all the great heroes of war, have swum in blood and left behind them subjugated peoples who rose in revolt at the first opportunity and brought their empires to ruin. The world empire that I have dreamed of for myself must consist in this —before all else the newly created German Reich must enjoy absolute confidence on all sides as a quiet, peaceful neighbor, and that if in the future anyone should speak about a German world power, or a Hohenzollern world dominion in history, this reputation shall not have been won by conquests of the sword but by the reciprocal trust of nations pursuing similar aims."

But, alas! the concluding sentences of this pacific oration relapse into the old style. "The Lord God would never have taken such pains about our people had He not reserved for us yet further greatness! *We are the salt of the earth!"*

Similar in the main to this speech at Bremen was one delivered in Düsseldorf on May 7, 1891, and expressing peaceful sentiments: "I wish that European peace lay in my hands alone. I should see to it that it was never disturbed!"

As regards the Army, the speeches addressed to it by the Supreme War Lord were concerned wholly with the eventuality of such disturbance being initiated by outside parties. "Uncle Bertie" in Sandringham called the tone adopted in these speeches "that of a trumpet major." There were too many speeches, and too much about glory, and far too much about Wilhelm II's becoming, as he had himself vowed to become, an "expander of the Reich." His aim was always to make his people strong and happy—"I lead you on toward glorious days!"

Painfully often he reminded the Army, and the Guards Corps in particular, that it was their duty to protect him in case of need. He must have been thinking of 1848 and the possibility that Berlin might rise in revolt against the hereditary ruling House. Addressing the Guards Grenadiers on the barrack square by the Weidendamm Bridge, he declared, "My Alexander Regiment (as he named it) is called upon to be ready by day and by night to act as a bodyguard to the King and his House, and if necessary to risk their lives and their blood. And if the City of Berlin were to rise again in revolt against the King, impudent and insubordinate as in the year 1848, then it would be for you, Grenadiers, to run those insolent and unruly people down at the point of your bayonets!"

It might be pleaded as an excuse for the Kaiser that many of his speeches were not intended for the public ear. Nevertheless, they found their way into the newspapers and caused much harm. Events might have taken a different turn, if only Wilhelm II had not spoken so much, and if he had left out the many jingling words about fists, swords and glory. Schopenhauer remarks about glory that "it is nothing else but a precious morsel of our self-esteem." If that dictum of a German fits the Kaiser, a quotation from Shakespeare applies to King Edward VII, who might have said, "In silence, Nephew, pursue thy politics!"

51. ENEMIES

THE KAISER'S speeches and his toleration of the Camarilla made him bitter enemies. He had only reigned for twelve years and the number of these enemies had grown so great that they threatened to become dangerous. When Eulenburg called his attention to this menace the Kaiser only laughed at him, "Philipp, you're seeing ghosts!"

It was particularly people of the intelligentsia who began to bestir themselves. Among them was Professor Ludwig Quidde, a pacifist and a member of the Democratic party in the Reichstag. In a brochure entitled *Caligula, A Study of Roman Caesarian Insanity*, he depicted Wilhelm II as a second Caligula, though he disguised his attack by making ancient Rome the setting for his satire.

Like Caligula, Wilhelm II had come to the throne by missing out one generation. Caligula was hated by his mother—in Quidde's eyes she resembled the Kaiserin Friedrich. And the figure of old Bismarck was not lacking, appearing as Marco, the Prefect of the Praetorian Guards. Like the gray-haired Chancellor, Marco had been badly treated and in the end dismissed by his young master. After the removal of the disagreeable counselor, Caesar could reign untrammeled. Since his sycophants all praised whatever he did Caligula felt himself raised and exalted above his subjects. At that point Quidde put into the mouth of his Caligula the words of Virgil already used by Wilhelm II: "Let one be Ruler, only one be King!" linked with which was the celebrated aphorism *Oderint, dum metuant!* (Let them hate me, provided they fear me!). Caligula was as happy as a child once he felt that he held the power. He exulted at the thought of being able to throw out his ministers at any moment. . . . Thus the parallel continued.

With the idea of safeguarding his commentary against confiscation Quidde then wrote a postscript for it, which, despite the disguise adopted, hit once more at the Kaiser: "This story charms us whether we look on it as a scarcely credible work of imagination, or as an exaggerated satire by some Roman writer on contemporary Caesarism, while so far as our researches have gone up to the present day it is in all its essential features the plain historical truth."

Though Professor Quidde dealt so severely with the Kaiser in passing judgment on him, he himself was, throughout, the well-bred man who knew how to wrap his antipathy in the pleated toga of the philologist. Very different was the lampoon by Richard Balls, a former secretary in the German Foreign Office. This was an unsuccessful act of revenge on the part of a pompous little nobody. Only at the very end of his brochure was he right in saying, "I know that my notes will please even the highest circles, but that they will bring angry wrinkles to the brow of the Kaiser!"

The hope that the intangible Kaiser would read these missives of revenge or hatred kept his enemies up to the mark. Thus, ten years later, Princess Daisy of Pless, once a friend of the Kaiser's, fondly indulged in the expectation that he would read her two volumes of memoirs—"I am sure he will seize on my books and read them!"

On a somewhat higher level stood the treatise of a psychiatrist—Dr. Paul Tesdorpf—which was published by a reputable Munich firm. Prejudice and animosity, accuracy and misrepresentation, followed one after the other. A great deal appears to be unverified and quoted after reference to parties who are not named. Some things that are entirely untrue are also included in this pamphlet, as for instance Tesdorpf's statement that Kaiser Friedrich had intended to declare his eldest son Wilhelm a minor [1] and that the only reason why that intention was not carried out was the severe illness and early death of Kaiser Friedrich.

This statement can easily be refuted, since long before the commencement of his illness the Prince's father declared him of age; he had ten full years at his disposal if he had really wanted to place the Prince under tutelage. Tesdorpf ended his medical study thus: "For the experienced physican and psychiatrist there can be no doubt that from his early youth Wilhelm II was mentally defective."

It is astonishing what the Kaiser had to put up with in the way of malicious jokes and witticisms, despite all the enactments against *lèse-majesté*. The *Fliegende Blätter* gave him "a piece of good advice"—to have chin straps attached to his crown, to make sure he did not lose it in his continual galloping about.

Since the Kaiser would only allow proceedings to be taken in special cases—such as that of *Simplicissimus* when it turned personally aggressive—his silence was taken to be that of one who was powerless and had given up all idea of defending himself.

There were also others who vented their aversion to Wilhelm II in milder forms. Thus the citizens of the Free Hanse City of Hamburg proved to be stone cold when the Kaiser demanded that the dedication "Wilhelm der Grosse" (Wilhelm the Great) should be inscribed on the equestrian statue of Wilhelm I on the square in front of the town hall. The aristocrats of the Alster would not hear of it, nor yet of the history lesson the Kaiser gave them on the occasion of the unveiling. They adhered to their choice of "Wilhelm I" for the inscription.

Even in Conservative circles movements hostile to the Kaiser were beginning to take shape. People objected to his personal interference in matters of everyday life and to the superficial way in which he thought to settle such matters. Count Reventlow summarized his own objections on the Kaiser's mania for criticism thus:

"Let us ask ourselves quite objectively, how is one to account for

[1] Under age, i.e., not capable of accession to the throne.

this many-sided knowledge of the Kaiser? For all his acuteness of intellect it is not possible for the Kaiser, particularly in the course of his governmental activities as King of Prussia and German Emperor, to force his way deep into all the territories with which he is concerned and to master them. The quick-acting and agile mind of the Kaiser is not to be denied, but it would be sheer flattery to infer from that either profundity or thoroughness."

Even in the friendly Dual Monarchy the feeling was gaining ground that if things went on like that "the Reich would very soon be nearing an abyss." As long ago as 1888, a few weeks after the accession of Wilhelm II, the Crown Prince Rudolf wrote (on August twenty-fourth) to a political friend of his—the journalist Moritz Szeps: "The Kaiser is bound to bring about a vast turmoil in Europe before very long . . . he is just the one to do it . . . energetic and capricious, taking himself for a consummate genius. . . . In a few years' time he will land Hohenzollern Germany into the situation she deserves!"

At a luncheon party attended by people of high social standing, Count Adalbert Sternberg declaimed loudly against the way the German Kaiser "treats us Austrians like idiots."

"If Friedrich II (for Sternberg the name *Friedrich der Grosse* did not exist at all) showed some respect for our great Emperor and Empress, it seems that this successor of his has lost all regard for our Hereditary Imperial House. He thinks he can treat the Hapsburgs as people who are quite distinguished but pretty hard up!"

In France, too, opinion hardened against the Kaiser. If, at the turn of the century, there were some who accepted *Guillaume Deux* and even admired him, that had all changed, and not least of all because of the speeches of that *fameux poltron* whose sergeant-majorlike politics found little favor in Paris.

After visiting Germany the young King Alfonso XIII of Spain returned to Madrid disappointed. He complained that he had heard nothing there but "the big drum" (of the Kaiser's speeches), which had ruined any pleasure he might have found in Berlin and Potsdam.

Some anonymous person—a "prophet of woe," as he called himself—attempted in 1906 to come to terms with the Kaiser's opponents; later he gave the Kaiser a stern warning, in his essay *Deutsche Sorgen* ("German Anxieties"), to turn back on his perilous path. "A modern monarch cannot arbitrarily or for long ride roughshod over public opinion. One day Wilhelm II will be compelled to recognize this."

52. BERNHARD VON BÜLOW

WITH THE NOMINATION of Secretary of State Bernhard von Bülow as Reich's Chancellor the era of "grandfatherly advisers" came to an end. As a contrast to Bismarck, Caprivi and Hohenlohe, "any of whom might have been my grandfather," as the Kaiser himself said, there now came Bülow, who, though getting on, was at any rate more nearly his own age. He had already proclaimed in 1895 that "Bülow shall be my Bismarck!" not without admiration for the supple and clever diplomat who, like himself, had been a pupil of the great Chancellor. After serving as Minister in Bucharest, Bülow became Ambassador to the Quirinal and then Secretary of State, already designated to follow Prince Hohenlohe as Reich's Chancellor.

Bülow had to thank Philipp Eulenburg for becoming personally acquainted with the Kaiser, shortly after his accession. The Kaiser, like so many others, had succumbed and paid forfeit to the elegant Mephisto and his arts. By the mere force of his outward personality, by his engaging and rather jovial manners—which had something of the play actor in them—Bülow was bound to make a strong and lasting impression on the young man. In addition, he was a brilliant conversationalist.

Stresemann, who knew half of *Faust* by heart, and Bülow used to let loose on each other their stocks of quotations during the beer evenings in the Chancellor's palace, where Bülow could declaim from memory pages from Horace, Camoëns, Villon or Platen. He mastered a number of languages and could converse fluently with foreigners, to the great astonishment of his interlocutors and the silent embarrassment of his own class, the Agrarians, who looked on him as a bit uncanny, like a cow that gave whipped cream.

He was an opportunist of the first water, a dazzling dissembler who could swerve gracefully aside from anything disagreeable, always trimming his sails to the wind. As a charmer and a man of the world he was sure of his entree to the highest society. He was a stickler for all questions of ceremonial or etiquette, and while adept in the pliant language of flattery he could nevertheless be cutting, malicious, ironical or cynical as soon as he felt he was in command of a situation.

He had a way of making a speech that was all his own. Rolling each word, he would begin by speaking in short concise sentences. Then his voice would rise crescendo to the culminating point, where there would be a most impressive pause. From that the tone would drop sharply, becoming softer and softer, until it ended in what was almost a whisper. It was a pleasure to listen to him. He spoke German, but afterward one thought that never before had one heard so seductive a language.

What was repellent about Bülow was, as with Eulenburg, a first impression—*unecht*! (not genuine). His enemies used a stronger word—*verlogen*! (mendacious). His declamations really represented nothing but a screen behind which he sought to hide. Apposite quotations he borrowed from others, being incapable of developing or enunciating any great thoughts of his own. His most bitter opponents declared that "the fourth German Reich's Chancellor only existed and subsisted on a legacy from the first Chancellor."

In Bülow's favor it must be said that when he took over the office of Chancellor he found its frontiers already determined so that he had to do what he could in the field left open to him, such as it was, with good and bad commitments. If to these handicaps he added shortcomings of his own, and thereby aggravated the already precarious situation of the Reich, it must be reckoned to his credit that, despite the dangerous crisis over Morocco, he preserved peace for Germany.

Again, the way in which he handled the Deputies in the Reichstag was worthy of admiration. His addresses there were, to speak like the Kaiser, "star performances." The institution of Election Syndicates was also Bülow's work. By this he succeeded, for the first time since the Reichstag was constituted, in dealing a severe blow at the Social Democrats.

To this day Bernhard von Bülow has been given no monument in marble or bronze. Should anyone wish to erect a memorial to him, he should be represented in his black frockcoat with the white cravat, the fingers of his right hand thrust between the buttons of his coat—he hid them because they were short and ugly—and under the arm the black flexible portfolio containing the *Decree for Dissolution of the Reichstag*, an instrument useful to him for keeping the House in order.

In his handling of Wilhelm II, Bülow followed the approved practice of the Court—he took the Kaiser as the Kaiser wished to be taken. If he wanted to get anything particular done, he always chose, like Holstein and Eulenburg, a devious path, knowing that a direct approach would be the longest way to his objective. Only later, when his indispensability was firmly established, did he take a different course with his master; but even then it was never with frankness, but with veiled threats, glib deceitfulness and unparalleled inconsistency.

With the progressive strengthening of his position, Bülow would speak of the Kaiser in the tone of an indulgent patron:

"I can see I'll have to go to the Kaiser's help again!"

"There's nothing left for me to do, except to pull him out of his difficulties once more!"

He said things like that when among intimate friends in the Chancellor's palace, which he succeeded in making the center of social life in the capital. It was especially the Princess Maria von Bülow,[1] the divorced wife of Count Dönhoff and now the wife of the Chancellor, who gave their house its particular cachet. By birth she was Italian, a Beccadelli di Bologna, of the House of the Princes Camporeale, and had grown up under the care of her famous stepfather Marco Minghetti and of her mother, the spirited Donna Laura, who because of her elegance and cleverness was so highly esteemed by the Kaiser.

Contrary to what one so often reads about her, Princess Maria was by no means a beautiful woman, but she had charm, was vivacious, and could carry all before her in conversation, thanks to her temperament, with which she captivated and won over every visitor. As a former pupil of Franz Liszt she was an outstanding pianist, especially in the works of her teacher, but also in the old Italian classics. What was lacking in the Chancellor, the ability to be unaffected, frank and natural, was possessed by Princess Maria in com-

[1] *See* Bülow in Appendix, page 437.

pensatory measure. Thus it might happen that in the course of a dinner party some cynical remark from Bülow might provoke an awkward pause in the conversation which would be smoothed over by her amiable tact.

The Kaiser possessed a key of his own to the grounds of the Chancellor's palace, and after a ride in the Tiergarten would go there to discuss questions of the day with the Chancellor. Under the old trees, planted by Radziwill and nursed and tended by Bismarck, many an important decision was taken. After a stroll such as this the Kaiser would often stay to lunch at the palace, where at all events he was certain of finding interesting company at table. The wily Bülow well knew how to place his guests according to the attitude and mood of his master.

In many political matters it turned out afterward that the Kaiser's insight had been more accurate than that of his Chancellor. Nevertheless, at least until the *Daily Telegraph* affair, he overrated Bülow. He once told Eulenburg, "I am happy to leave Bülow to deal with things. Now that I have him I can sleep in peace!"

Bülow's position as Reich's Chancellor, after being raised in quick succession to the dignities of Count and Prince, might indeed have been an enviable one, were it not that in the German Foreign Office sat a man who constituted to him a permanent danger—Fritz von Holstein. The two men had known each other for many years, and knew too much about each other not to try to use their respective knowledge of each other now and again. In this struggle for hegemony it was the Gray Eminence who prevailed. His material against Bülow was better. The Chancellor would only have been too happy to be free from "that vampire," but he dared not take any action himself, for fear of his own position. But by a cunningly devised maneuver he did succeed in ridding himself of his dangerous assistant and in wresting from that intriguing Privy Councilor the power he had held for so long.

Pensioned off, Holstein was lying on his deathbed when he learned for the first time from Maximilian Harden who it was that had really been the cause of his undoing—it was Bülow, the same Bülow whom Holstein himself had hoisted into the saddle.

As he lay dying, Privy Councilor Fritz von Holstein declared: "Now that I see it all clearly I know that since Cesare Borgia there has never existed such a liar as Bernhard Bülow!"

53. HOLSTEIN AND HIS
FOREIGN OFFICE

WHILE MOLTKE, in the Red House on the Königsplatz, had carefully taken his pick of the rising generation and trained it for military leadership, no such precautions in regard to the recruitment of the Foreign Service had been taken by Bismarck. It was enough for him that he and his son Herbert should be there, with the son designated by himself as his successor in the business of the State. Those who now were serving in the Foreign Office were the old Privy Councilors of Bismarck's day, described and disposed of by the Kaiser as "leathery bureaucrats" or "tedious bores." They were leftover right- (or left-) hand men of ministers long since dead, hard-working no doubt, experienced and thorough, but also, as Knights of the Red Eagle or the Crown, haughty, and proud of having served the State for decades and passed through all the various grades. Grown gray in the service, they had become pedantic and prone to pettifogging. They did their work ceremoniously, without making allowances or being able to take a more general view. Their predilection for taking notes of everything, even the unnecessary, meant that most tasks were needlessly delayed. Everything about them was old-fashioned, even the outmoded formal German of official documents that had come down from the time of Friedrich Wilhelm III.

From those functionaries there evolved a kind of Guild of Councilors which Bismarck used as "books of reference" but never called on for the framing of decisions.

It was no wonder that the foreign diplomats accredited to Berlin used to laugh at the German Foreign Office. The American Ambassador once remarked to a journalist, and Tirpitz reported it, that "the German people are quite unaware that their most dangerous enemy is their own Foreign Office!"

In this Foreign Office resided and presided Fritz von Holstein, generally known in Berlin as *l'Eminence grise*, or as "the Reich's

Jesuit," an official like the rest but one with great knowledge and the ambition to rule the roost there. He passed for being vain, shifty and one who avoided difficulties (*"Surtout pas d'histoires!"* [Above all, let us have no awkward repercussions!]), also for being "an odd person" and a woman-hater. Inaccessible to his subordinates, he was feared by everyone, even by Bismarck, who had brought him into the service "without any inquiry into his moral worth," and had himself given him employment. When Bismarck had mentioned the name Holstein, it had always been like threatening thunder, like a warning against "the dangerous passenger who, if one wanted to kick him out of the coach, would probably start telling tales abroad!— Holstein knows a great deal, perhaps too much . . . it's better that he should stay in Berlin!"

Holstein had no intention of leaving his room on the first floor of No. 76 Wilhelmstrasse, of "giving up his stable," as Eulenburg expressed it. "The proper place for Holstein is in the loose box for nags that bite and kick!" Thus would Eulenburg write maliciously to Bülow about Holstein, always behind the back of the last, who thereby became firmly convinced that he was better at deception than the other two, without their noticing it. These three "friends" assiduously and carefully collected material for use against one another. Anything that was wanting was procured by hired sleuths.

Without Holstein, Eulenburg was powerless, suspended in midair, and Bülow only a façade. It was Holstein's work that provided the Chancellor with the substructure for his speeches, exposés, telegrams and reports to the Kaiser. But he also made use of the other two, for it was only by doing so that he could himself remain in the background, which he preferred to do. Since he had for years past been well acquainted with all the German diplomats, knew what languages they had mastered, what private means they and their wives possessed and many other things besides, Caprivi and Hohenlohe had left it to him to select the ambassadors and ministers of legations. Anyone he did not like was flatly turned down as being "Russophile" or "Anglophile" or "too much of a pacifist" or as being "an advocate of a nice new joyous war," just as he thought fit. If needs were, he would invent some story that would provide him with a pretext for rejecting candidates he did not favor as "unsuitable for the posts in question."

The suspicious old Holstein might remind one of Molière's characters, of Tartuffe and Harpagon, or of *le Malade Imaginaire*. But if this Tartuffe was called into action, he surpassed his prototype in intrigue. No one dared to enter Holstein's office without being summoned. Councilors of legations and messengers, when they had documents to put before him, used to wait uneasily by the padded door before venturing to approach the writing table of *Son Eminence grise*.

If he took offense at anything that happened in the course of his duties he sent in his resignation. He had done this so many times before that nobody any longer took it seriously. When in the end this threat lost all effectiveness and produced no results, he cleared his desk, by way of emphasizing his intentions. But he moved his things back when Bülow assured Holstein on oath that in the future nothing should happen to annoy him.

As an old bachelor Holstein found his only consolation in good food and noble wines. At Borchardt's—where he was a regular client —he used to give the chef directions as precise and strict as those he gave to envoys in the Wilhelmstrasse, and these latter could often guess from his letters what the all-powerful Councilor had been eating and drinking.

"Look after Deputy Chabrier as though he was a precious bottle of *Moulin à Vent!*" . . . "By all means give them an English omelet. But don't use Russian eggs . . . they're not suitable, and are no use once they are broken!"

Holstein's power reached its zenith under Chancellor Bülow, who was not a free agent. In all foreign affairs Holstein overrode the chief official of the State. Foreign ambassadors negotiated and concluded agreements with him, so that once the Kaiser had to hear the French Ambassador, Jules Cambon, say: "Many thanks, Your Majesty, but I do not need any recommendation to His Excellency the Herr Reich's Chancellor. I shall talk it over with Privy Councilor von Holstein!"

Holstein, who never even possessed evening dress, only once came into personal contact with Wilhelm II, at a luncheon in the Chancellor's palace. The Councilor had hoped to be able to take the opportunity of putting to the Kaiser some important—and probably very insidious—questions about policy, but the chance never came. Presumably the Kaiser had guessed the intention and so did not let the dangerous questioner get a word in. "Well, Your Excellency, I know you come from the Oder fen country . . . you have excellent ducks there!" And with that he turned away to engage other guests of Bülow's in conversation.

Even before this episode, Holstein had become a bitter enemy of the Kaiser—he hated him. After the Kaiser's accession he likened him to the weak and frivolous Emperor in Part II of *Faust*, and when the aging Hohenlohe was appointed Reich's Chancellor, he wrote to Eulenburg: "The Kaiser is his own Chancellor! And this . . . for an impulsive and alas! wholly superficial man who hasn't the least idea of statecraft, of political precedents, of diplomatic history or of handling men." More than once he advocated placing the Kaiser under tutelage, on the ground of insanity. He called him "a serious psychopathic case," whereas it was an open question whether he were not one himself, as his enemies strongly maintained.

As Holstein quite openly commented in contemptuous terms on the Kaiser, even when speaking to foreign diplomats, he did much harm not only to Wilhelm II but also to the Reich. He advised Sir Edward Goschen, the British Ambassador, to treat the Kaiser as either a child or a fool.

He did not even shrink from putting to a Dutch Crown Jurist the question "whether an allegation of intermittent irresponsibility in the conduct of business would carry enough weight and suffice to support an indictment of Wilhelm II for interference in the handling of State affairs?"

The entire malignity of the Councilor was concentrated on this question and involved not only the suggestion of tutelage because of of the Kaiser's carrying on a comic-opera policy, but also the framing of a charge against him of violating the Constitution.

In his hatred Holstein assumed the leadership of the *Drachenblut* (blood of dragons) composed of Bülow, Eulenburg and himself, and was ever ready to plan a "political Jena" for the Kaiser, or to "let him fall into a wolf trap."

At that time Wilhelm II had not realized how dangerous Holstein was. Afterward, in Doorn, striving to do justice to the embittered Councilor, he said: "Holstein's memoranda were certainly ingenious and dazzling, but often were as guarded and ambiguous as Pythia's oracular pronouncements. It could happen that after I had made a decision based on one of those many memoranda, Herr von Holstein let me know, in very sharp language, that he had intended the exact opposite of my interpretation. In the Foreign Office he was the last representative of a dying century, one who would have been well placed as an intriguer and plotter in the Renaissance. Later on he joined forces with Maximilian Harden to ruin Eulenburg with the help of Harden's periodical *Zukunft* (*Future*). And he wanted to ruin me too! I broke many lances for Privy Councilor von Holstein, although he made the Wilhelmstrasse even more crazy than it was already!"

Very few people succeeded in asserting the force of their own personalities against *Son Eminence grise*. The first to do so was Baron von Marschall, a colossus à la Bismarck, but with a stentorian voice, a State Attorney to begin with, then Undersecretary of State, and Ambassador in Constantinople, where he was greatly in demand because of his all-round competence, until finally he was selected by the Kaiser for the important post of Ambassador in London. There he occupied a commanding position, unfortunately only for a short time.

Secretary of State von Kiderlen-Wächter was another who managed to hold his own against the difficult old Councilor. Holstein rated him as "a clever but crafty Swabian, too much of a *Korpsstudent* [1] and too addicted to heavy wines, fat cigars and, above all, to Frau Hauptmann Kypke [his housekeeper]."

Holstein declared that Kiderlen himself had promoted her to Frau Hauptmann in order to facilitate her entry into society. Holstein was not at all pleased with this intention of Kiderlen's as there had already been complaints from Bucharest about this Frau Hauptmann, because Kiderlen had wanted to introduce his mistress into the Rumanian Court, greatly to the annoyance of King Carol.

Apart from this, the Councilor and the "overrated Kiderlen" were on bad terms because Kiderlen could not accommodate himself to working with him. So, to damage Kiderlen, Holstein proceeded to have a number of cards with witticisms of double meaning, referring to the Kaiserin Auguste Viktoria, and composed and circulated by Kiderlen, passed to Her Majesty.

Speaking about this in Doorn, the Kaiser said: "The Kaiserin came to me to complain about Kiderlen." Then, seizing a book, "just read these passages in the notes of the Rumanian Minister,

[1] Student belonging to a club where drinking and dueling were encouraged.

Beldimann: 'The time of Herr von Kiderlen-Wächter's tenure of the office of Secretary of State marks the period in which German diplomacy reached its lowest depths. If Kiderlen were still alive he would have to appear before the State Court; for he sent secret documents to his lady friend Kypke, who made it her business to show them in the original to the parties interested.' "

Another who fell foul of Holstein for a time but was later rehabilitated was von Eckardstein, Secretary to the Embassy in London, who afterward became known for his *Reminiscences of my Life*, though these are not always reliable. Holstein said of him what Napoleon once said about an Anglophile envoy he had installed in London: "The man I have in London, as my Ambassador, is no more than a dupe of the English Government!"

A German diplomat of a very different stamp was Prince Karl von Wedel, general and politician, a dignified, unpretentious and efficient man, who succeeded Prince Hohenlohe-Langenburg as Governor of Alsace-Lorraine. Wedel won respect in Strasbourg by his amiable ways and at the time of the Saverne (Zabern) crisis, when there was grave danger of conflict between the population and the occupying German forces, he succeeded by his skill and resolution in avoiding the development of a menacing situation.

Resembling Prince Wedel, and coming from the same school, but with a weaker and less decided personality, was Baron von Schön, afterward Ambassador in Paris for many years. Holstein looked on him as clever and businesslike, a good speaker, but without much ambition. As an Undersecretary of State, Schön had been much liked for his friendly manners, even by the Kaiser, though Schön had several times had occasion to speak his mind freely to him. In the Reichstag, too, Schön knew how to get on well with the Deputies. On the outbreak of war in 1914 "le Baron de Schön," as he was called in Parisian society, disappeared from the political scene to pass the remainder of his days in the privacy of Berchtesgaden.

As a diplomat, Baron von Tschirschky und Bögendorff proved to be not unlike von Schön, and was about his age, but he lacked Schön's gift of eloquence. In the Reichstag he did not always figure to advantage and even in ordinary conversation he showed a certain stiffness. Because of his hesitant way of speaking he gave the impression of being a scholar, and this was strengthened by a pair of gold-rimmed spectacles.

Being subject to fits of depression, he was a regular visitor at Dapper's Sanatorium in Kissingen. His friends could foresee a pessimistic mood from the look on his face; this could give rise to apprehension, since his decisions depended on such little fits, and resolutions might thereby be deferred although prompt action was called for. All the more surprising was his sudden leaping at the chance, when he was Secretary of State and a favorable opportunity occurred, of turning Holstein out of the Foreign Office.

54. THE TREATY OF BJÖRKÖ

RELATIONS WITH RUSSIA WERE, as usual, bad. In St. Petersburg there was no disposition to abandon the attitude of mistrust once that attitude had been adopted, so there could be no talk of any betterment coming from either side. To this must be added the fact that the Franco-Russian Alliance stood in the way of any German efforts toward renewing the "frayed thread." Nevertheless, Wilhelm II had provided support and brought Russia some advantages at the time of the Sino-Japanese peace negotiations in Shimonoseki, and had afterward facilitated the voyage of the Russian Baltic fleet by delivering coal. When people accused the Kaiser of having intentionally let the Czar slide into the Russo-Japanese War, they wronged him by such unfounded statements. Rather was the contrary correct, for Wilhelm II knew well that a strong Russia would be the best defensive screen for the German Eastern frontiers against the "Yellow Peril."

Despite all the Kaiser's endeavors, Czar Nicholas remained suspicious. He was not going to let himself be wrapped up, or taken in tow by "Willy." As the Russian saw it, that would be an absurdity, turning the world upside down, for only fifty years before Prussia had been merely "an outpost of the Czar's Empire and a vassal of the House of Romanov."

Bismarck himself said in his *Thoughts and Memories* that "under the government of Alexander I we lived as vassals of Russia until 1831, when Russia could scarcely have settled matters with the Poles without us; and again in all the European combinations from

1831 to 1850, when we always accepted and honored Russian bills, until after 1848 the young Austrian Emperor seemed to suit the purposes of the Russians better than the King of Prussia. So the Russian arbitrators coolly decided against Prussia, preparatory to inflicting upon us, as a reward for our friendly aid in 1831, the humiliation of Olmütz."

Despite such unfortunate experiences in the past, Wilhelm II had striven hard to win over the Czar and his anti-German Czarina ("Alix"—of the House of Hesse-Darmstadt). For a while he had some success. When, in Doorn, he gave his recollections of Nicholas II he said, "People have tried to criticize me about my correspondence with my cousin, the Czar. To that end they have seized on sentences out of their context and rushed them into print. But this is not the way to proceed, if you wish to obtain a true picture of our relations. What I used to write to the Czar was well thought out and entirely attuned to his mentality. Only those who knew him as well as I did could understand why I employed certain particular expressions. For the Czar was a ruler with an almost Godlike prestige—on the whole enjoying the standing of a semi-Asiatic despot."

On another occasion the Kaiser spoke of "the presumption of certain people in my Foreign Office, who took it upon themselves to edit my letters to the Czar. I would never tolerate their making corrections in my private correspondence with him; that would have made my letters more and more like notes or memoranda, which I especially wished to avoid. It would have made the Czar more suspicious than ever if he were to discover that it was some councilor who wrote my letters."

In these letters every possible subject was touched upon—family affairs, political questions and economic problems. Thus, after the fall of Port Arthur, the Kaiser sent "Cousin Nicky" no letter of condolence but a plain business proposition: "I hope you will not forget to remind your authorities of our great firms in Stettin and Kiel. They will be able, I am sure, to supply you with the finest types of warships."

When the Czar seemed to be delighted with such good advice, and referred to the necessity of their holding together against a world of republicans and anarchists, the elder "Willy," feeling superior, answered that such pronouncements were mere phrases and had little real value.

So the thread of his relations with the Czar and Czarina was not yet broken. On the other hand, there were no relations at all worth mentioning with the Russian grand dukes. Wilhelm II considered them to be, as a whole, "unscrupulous, extravagant, devoid of moral sense, and always trying to bring about war," because in this way only—as the Russian Minister-President, Count Witte,[1] had declared—would they be able to pay their many debts. Nor did the Kaiser think much of the Czar's advisers, neither of his "ambitious, self-seeking and dishonest ministers," nor yet of Rasputin. Before Rasputin false prophets of the same kind had already figured at the Russian Court—the mystic Kondrati Schivanov, Juliane von Krüdener, the monk Photius and Katharina Tatarinov.

Being at pains to keep himself well informed about the Czar and the latter's views on current events, the Kaiser left no stone unturned to secure intelligence of this kind. When the Prussian Major von Runckel, on his way home from the Russian headquarters in East Asia, presented himself at the Schloss to make his report, His Majesty asked him what impressions he had gathered about the Czar. When Runckel spoke out plainly and described Nicholas II as weak, vacillating and entirely dependent on the party of the grand dukes and the anti-German generals holding commands, the Kaiser broke off the interview and left the Major standing there alone in the room. An example of imperial affability!

In July 1905 the Czar and the Kaiser decided to meet. As Wilhelm had already set out on his northern cruise, the Czar proposed a rendezvous in Russian waters, off Björkö. When the *Hohenzollern* anchored off the appointed shore her crew looked out on a flat and desolate spit of land without a tree or a bush, silent in its solitude.

Immediately the Czar's yacht *Polar Star* appeared the Czar sent over an invitation to luncheon for the Kaiser and his suite. General von Moltke, nephew of the "Great Silent One," has described this first meeting as follows: "The longer we sat at table the more the Czar thawed. In the end he became quite cheerful, laughing and conversing vivaciously. It was obvious that he felt at his ease, because in those surroundings he felt safe. He and the members of his

[1] Count Sergei Julievich Witte (1849–1915), Russian Premier and Foreign Minister, largely responsible for the construction of the Trans-Siberian Railway and head of Russian delegation to Portsmouth Peace Conference in 1905.

suite were markedly amiable, they all even spoke German, and appeared altogether changed."

Wilhelm II also was clearly delighted that the necessary good humor had set in so quickly. Seeking to seize the favorable opportunity, he produced a treaty which had been drawn up in Berlin by Tschirschky and of which a copy had already been sent to St. Petersburg for inspection. It was a Treaty of Friendship, which aimed at so binding Russia that the German Reich should be freed from the menace of "a war on two fronts." Bülow had advised that it should be treated ostensibly as of minor importance, and that no attempt should be made to rush its signature. For that reason he had not traveled to Björkö himself but had sent only Tschirschky with the Kaiser, who had accepted the advice.

The Czar, with almost exaggerated politeness, apologized for not having brought with him the draft copy sent him. "But I remember . . . yes, certainly I remember it quite well! But the *details* I cannot recall! What a shame!"

The Kaiser has himself described the subsequent course of the conference on board the *Polar Star*. "The Czar took me by the arm and led me out of the dining saloon into his father's cabin and at once closed all the doors. 'Please show me the treaty!' His usually dreamy eyes were sparkling brightly.

"I took the envelope out of my pocket, unfolded the sheet on the writing desk of Alexander III, in front of a picture of the Empress Mother that stood between photographs of Fredensborg and Copenhagen, and laid it out before the Czar. He read it through—once—twice—thrice. I ejaculated a little prayer to the good God that He should now stand by us and guide the young ruler. Everything was still as death, except for the murmur of the sea—the sun shone gaily and serenely into the cosy cabin, and right in front of me lay, gleaming white, the *Hohenzollern*, the Imperial Standard fluttering in the air high above her."

In Doorn, later on, casting his mind back to Björkö, the Kaiser endeavored to reconstruct the subsequent conversation:

The Czar: "This is quite excellent!"

Kaiser: "Should you like to sign it?" [*sic*]

The Czar: "Yes! I will!"

"Without further ado he seized a pen and signed *Nicolaus*. Then I signed in my turn. This was on July 24, 1905.

"When we had exchanged mutual good wishes for the outcome of the treaty, we called in Admiral Birilev and Tschirschky as counter-signatories. They each read it through once more, suggested some minor alterations, and then signed their names."

On returning to the *Hohenzollern* the Kaiser showed how delighted he was and how he hoped that this Treaty of Björkö would renew the old friendship with Russia, remove "the peril in the rear," and above all shatter the dangerous *Entente à Trois*. Only later was it found that reservations on two points, which the Kaiser in his first transports of joy had failed to notice, were entered by Birilev—namely, that the treaty was valid only *en Europe*, and that it was to come into force only after the conclusion of the Russo-Japanese War.

When Reich's Chancellor Prince Bülow (he had been made Prince a month before, in June 1905) saw the addition of the words *en Europe*, he declared that the treaty was worthless. He was so furious over this "amateurish behavior" in first signing a State treaty and not taking into account clauses added afterward, that he sent in his resignation. He did not seriously intend to resign but rather to make it clear to the Kaiser that if he, Bülow, were not consulted nothing would be done properly.

In this dispute Eulenburg sided with the Kaiser. He saw in the treaty "a great measure of pacification between the two peoples," in spite of what he called "the prima-donna-like vagaries of the piqued Bernhard." And he asked, "What are we coming to now, if the Reich's Chancellor starts following Holstein's example and clears his desk?"

For the Kaiser, who looked on the conclusion of the treaty as a personal success for himself, it meant a bitter disappointment on his arrival in Kiel when he had to listen to the disapproving criticism of his Chancellor, instead of the approval and praise he had expected. He refused to accept Bülow's resignation. "No, my friend, you will remain in office and with me. We shall go on working together *ad majorem Germaniae gloriam*! You cannot and must not let me down. It would mean that all your own policy would be disavowed by you yourself, and that I should be made to look a fool forever, a thing I could not survive. Let me have a couple of days for rest and composure before you come, for the nervous shock of your letters has been too great. At the moment I am in no condition to discuss things quietly. Your true friend, Wilhelm I. R."

After he had sent off this pitiful appeal, the Kaiser sent another: "I appeal to your friendship for me. Let me hear no more of your retiring, telegraph me the words *'all right'* [2] after receiving this letter, then I shall know that you are staying on, for the morning after your resignation would find the Kaiser no longer living. Think of my poor wife and children!—W."

This letter, sounding so insincere with its exaltation and sentimentality and threatening with a widowed Kaiserin, can only be accounted for by disappointment, overwhelming excitement and above all by dread of public censure.

Bülow, for whom the occasion had afforded convincing proof of his high value in the eyes of His Majesty, might well be content. He did *not* telegraph the "all right" awaited by the Kaiser, who had to be made to feel his dependence on his Reich's Chancellor.

The Czar, too, on his return from Björkö, had many unpleasant things to listen to in St. Petersburg. On closer examination it transpired that the Treaty of Björkö embodied terms that ran counter to those of treaties already concluded with France . . . and to accept them might cost France's friendship.

Overhasty as the conclusion of this treaty had been it vanished into oblivion just as quickly. In fact, it never came into force. After this, so far as German politics were concerned, Russia receded into "impenetrable darkness," back to the immeasurable spaces so well described by General Count York von Wartenburg: "For Prussia, the Czar is almost within reach at Moscow; he is dangerous at Kasan, and he is invincible in Tobolsk!"

55. PROTECTOR OF THE EVANGELICAL CHURCH

JUST AS THE CZAR of Russia regarded himself as the head of the Orthodox Greek Church, so Wilhelm II looked on himself as the Supreme Bishop and Protector of the German Evangelical Church.

[2] In English in the original.

Everything pertaining to the Church was regarded by the Kaiser as important. This was due largely to the enduring influence of the Kaiserin Auguste Viktoria. In Berlin alone she had caused no less than thirty-two new churches to be built.

Besides the Berlin Cathedral which, with its wealth of internal fittings—disposed as directed by the Kaiser—its statues, splendid candelabra and tapestries, almost suggested a Roman Catholic church, the Imperial couple had a special preference for the Potsdam Garrison Church, where on Sundays they attended the Divine Service for the troops.

From early in the morning detachments of the Guards infantry, of the bodyguard, of Hussars, Uhlans and field artillery marched through quiet Potsdam, which was so old-worldly that it would not have been in the least surprising if the "Old Fritz," on his charger, had suddenly appeared trotting down the roadway. In contradistinction to the Berlin Cathedral, the interior of the Garrison Church was equipped in simple and soldierlike fashion: the woodwork was largely of pine, the pillars of plain stone with iron bands, to which were fixed old regimental colors and standards. Illuminated texts hung from above on the walls, between carvings of coats of arms and Prussian eagles. Before the altar and the vault behind it, in which lay the sarcophagi of the two Prussian kings, Friedrich Wilhelm I and Frederick the Great, stood the royal pews.

As the Kaiser entered the church the organ would begin to play in honor of the head of the Evangelical Church. In point of fact, it was not clear to which of the Evangelical churches the Kaiser properly belonged. He never liked to be pressed for an answer, even in later years.

From the historical standpoint, the Elector Joachim II (Hektor) of Brandenburg had, in 1539, professed the evangelical doctrine. Afterward, in 1614, the Elector Siegmund changed over to the Reformed Church and proved his adherence to Calvinism by his *Confessio Marchica*, which he wrote himself. None of his successors made any formal change, though the last Hohenzollerns should probably be accounted Lutheran. That would apply to Wilhelm II, though he never avowed it. Since he sought to tack to and fro between the two Protestant doctrines, one could assume that he favored the association of the two churches brought about by Friedrich Wilhelm III.

The German Protestants had every reason to be satisfied with their Protector. New churches were built at every opportunity—one at Holtenau on the occasion of the opening of the Kaiser Wilhelm Canal, and fifteen garrison churches on occasions of great reviews of troops.

Church windows and altar furnishings were provided, often at great cost . . . if not always beautiful. Even in foreign lands churches sprang up, such as the Church of the Redeemer in Jerusalem, already mentioned, which was inaugurated on October 13, 1898, by the Imperial couple, when the Kaiser made a speech "in the place where once the Redeemer walked." He said, "Out of Jerusalem came the Light of the World . . . in its brightness our German people became great and glorious. . . . For what the German people have become they are indebted to their standing under the banner of the Cross of Golgotha!"

At Jerusalem the Kaiser had already given expression, not exactly judiciously, to his abhorrence to "the Powers of Darkness," meaning thereby Islam and Buddhism. And after the battle of Tsushima he gave a warning, putting it very naïvely, against concluding, from the Japanese victory, that Buddha might be superior to Christ.

Belief in the divine power of Christ had been a vivid trait of the Kaiser's character from his early youth. To the end of his days he remained firm in his belief. His opponents used to laugh at him for it, and even called him hypocritical. In that they certainly did him wrong, for Wilhelm II needed his belief in God to provide him with support. For him that belief was a private and highly personal affair, a household medicine, to give him a rest from the turmoil of the day's work. He never boasted of his belief or made a display of it to others. He went to Communion services twice a year, on New Year's Eve and on Maundy Thursday.

From his own implicit belief in God he deduced that man can only believe if God Himself has made him qualified to do so. Apropos of a lecture by Friedrich Delitzsch, the Assyriologist, on the subject of Babylon and the Bible, he wrote to Admiral Hollmann: "I have never had the least doubt that God always reveals Himself in the human race that He has created. He breathed His own breath into man, that is, He has given him a portion of Himself, a soul. . . ." He went on to speak of those "chosen by God" and named the following: Hammurabi, Moses, Abraham, Homer,

Charlemagne, Luther, Shakespeare, Goethe, Kant . . . and Kaiser Wilhelm I.

"These men He sought out and empowered with His grace to accomplish, in accordance with His will, glorious and everlasting things for their own peoples." He concluded by saying: "Religion was never the outcome of science, it is an effluence from the heart and life of man, resulting from his communion with God."

In Doorn he once said, "I'm glad to be a believer! One who believes in God can always bear things better than one who denies Him!" As to belief and unbelief, Wilhelm II agreed with Goethe, who, however, would have liked to see all that was merely confessional eliminated: "The main theme of world history is the struggle between Belief and Unbelief." "All periods of Unbelief can be shown to have been decadent." "Man only remains creative for so long as he is religious."

Wilhelm II was on friendly terms with a number of theologians. One was Adolf Harnack, whom the Kaiser called to Berlin against the wishes of the Orthodox churchmen, and another was Ernst Dryander, the "practical Christian," soon appointed Court Chaplain and afterward Superintendent General.[1]

Even as Supreme Bishop of the National Church the Kaiser tended to drop into that unpleasant loud tone that so often made him disliked. He would forget that he had parsons in front of him instead of a batch of recruits.

"Preach no sermons if you have no marching orders specifying the direction!"

"Political parsons are an absurdity!"

He once sent the following telegram to Hinzpeter: "Anyone who is a Christian is also 'social.' Christian-Social is all nonsense. It leads to people's overvaluing themselves, and to intolerance, both of which are diametrically opposed to Christianity." He continued: "Pastors should concern themselves with spiritual welfare and foster charity, but should leave politics alone because it is no business of theirs!"

Unfortunately there were a few clergymen ill-advised enough to emulate the language of the Camarilla. Expressions as servile and sycophantic as those that were uttered by some of these pastors were seldom to be matched even in the circle of the Court toadies. One

---

[1] Highest evangelical clergyman in some provinces.

cathedral preacher uttered this effusion from the pulpit in Schwerin:
"When the French windows closed behind the trim figure of the
Kaiser and the curtains again veiled the gleaming helmet . . . then
was the Kaiser alone, as a spouse with his wife, as a man with his
God. At last, for a moment unobserved, he could put away constraint, tension and constriction and doff the burdensome purple . . .
and the Kaiser's countenance, as though chiseled from marble,
could relax into the simple, trembling, human face which, like a
child's, would like to cry over a broken toy, over its shattered
world."

The preacher then went on to liken the Kaiser to King David,
"who played the harp as magnificently as Kaiser Wilhelm II." This,
however, was not a very felicitous comparison, for the Kaiser could
never even play the piano properly, and for the rest had little in
common with that adulterous monarch, King David.

After this, for the Kaiser's special delectation, he inveighed against
England, claiming that Shakespeare's Richard III represented the
real type of Englishman.

At the head of those who sang loudest in praise of the "Almighty
Ruler"—who, in this case, was not God—stood the Königsberg
Superintendent General. In 1911 he spoke in the cathedral, where
Immanuel Kant lies buried, as follows: ". . . confronted by such
great talent, by so many diverse abilities, we must recognize that
compared to the Kaiser we are—excuse the word, gentlemen—we
are nitwits!"

Self-depreciation and extravagant laudation of this kind were repugnant even to the Kaiser. In fact, it could happen that he did not
listen to such rubbish, and ignored the sweetly smiling cringers. If
in welcoming him to any assembly of clergymen too many texts
from the Bible were employed, it might happen that he would seize
on one of them and give it a twist in his own fashion.

The emphasis on religion prevalent at the Court had the result
that ministers and generals spoke a great deal in their addresses
about heaven and heavenly hosts, so much so that the young officers
expected that the three cheers called for at the end of an oration
would be given, not for H.M., but for God.

To turn this state of affairs to advantage Bible societies sprang up
everywhere, also commercial enterprises such as that of a Berlin

concern specializing in the sale of Genuine Jordan Water, with which Biblical liquid every ordinary citizen could have his offspring baptized like those of the royalties.

Serious warnings were given against such excrescences, most of which were tinged with hypocrisy.

Even during the reign of Friedrich Wilhelm IV the Court clergy had confirmed the Divine Right of the Kings of Prussia, and had described him as "God's chosen instrument on earth." Thus Friedrich Wilhelm believed himself to have been appointed by God and looked on his reign not only as foreordained but as a mission. His Privy Councilors were men who, because of their servility, could never give him proper advice, which he probably would never have followed in any case, for to the very end he maintained that God was his best and only adviser.

Unfortunately, Wilhelm II adopted this and made his own these ideas of his great-uncle, though in an attenuated form. Here again there operated that propensity to mysticism that he inherited from his father. A few sentences from a speech made by him at Königsberg may enable us to grasp his conception of *Dei Gratia*. "Inasmuch as I regard myself as an instrument of Heaven, I go my way without regard to the events or the opinions of the day."

Again, referring to the words of St. Paul in the Epistle to the Romans: "For there is no authority but from God, but where there is authority so it was decreed by God. . . . *By God's Grace I am what I am!*"

This latter dictum had, during the time of the Roman Emperors, been claimed by the Pope for himself, as the successor of the apostle Peter. Thus one might describe him as the inventor of the theory of Divine Right of Kings. It was only some two thousand years later— for not even *le Roi Soleil* went quite so far as to claim divine protection for himself—that this conception was adopted by the Prussian kings and made to figure as the motto of a monarchy. How firmly Wilhelm II was convinced of the correctness of the idea is shown by the fact that he was always careful to write both Sein (His) with reference to God, and Mein (my) concerning himself, with a capital letter.

This insistence on *Dei Gratia* gave rise to heated controversies, wrong inferences and even awkward situations. For instance, it suggested the question why, if the Grace of God did really apply to kings, a monarchy like that of the Guelphs, far older than that of the Hohenzollern, should have been blotted out by another monarch (Wilhelm I). Heinrich von Treitschke referred to this question and drew from it the conclusion that "on the precedent of the case of the Guelphs, a popular government could even depose the Hohenzollern without committing any breach of legality."

Every man exists by God's grace and therefore is answerable to divine authority. It is indisputable that this sense of responsibility was shared by Wilhelm II. It was real, it weighed upon him and obsessed him. It made him shrink from leading his country into a war repugnant to the ideas of the Christian religion. Despite several occasions on which the danger of war seemed imminent Wilhelm II succeeded in giving his people a full quarter of a century of peace.

56. THE VOYAGE TO TANGIER

IN ORDER TO COMBAT the policy pursued by France of eliminating Germany from Morocco, where the Reich had economic interests to safeguard, Bülow demanded a demonstration—a visit by the Kaiser to Tangier. There he was to make a speech expressing his sympathy with the Sultan and to give an assurance that he, the German Kaiser, would use his influence in favor of the "open door" in Morocco and would never tolerate that door's being closed against the Reich.

The Kaiser was little enamored of so risky an act of provocation, for such the proposed visit certainly was. Apart from the fact that a miscarriage might have effects directly opposite to those intended by Bülow, he saw also what would be the result of such a challenge to France—a renewed outburst of chauvinism.

In the end, however, he consented, although Eulenburg described the venture as sheer lunacy. Apart altogether from the political considerations, Eulenburg knew that the Kaiser would have to disembark in the open roadstead off Tangier, and he realized that this must be a perilous undertaking, owing to his crippled arm, especially in a rough sea. Then again the detectives who were to accompany him raised objections, saying that they could not accept responsibility if His Majesty had to ride through the narrow streets of the town on a strange horse. It would be a direct invitation to chauvinists and anarchists to make an attempt on his life.

The voyage to Tangier was made in the Hamburg-America liner *Deutschland*. On the way fresh thoughts occurred to Wilhelm. He had a talk with von Schön, Undersecretary of State, who was on board, and who also regarded the objections raised as valid. A telegram was sent to Bülow to this effect and brought the reply that "in the interests of the Reich the landing at Tangier should be carried out and the program already arranged should be adhered to."

When the anchor was dropped in the roads off Tangier the difficulties envisaged by Eulenburg began, for a heavy sea was running. Soaking wet in his Uhlan uniform, the German Consul, Richard von Kühlmann, managed to clamber on board. The Kaiser, too, got soused by breaking seas as he got into the pinnace. The rest of the passage to Tangier was uneventful. What happened after he came ashore has been described by the Kaiser himself. "On a little open space was a crowd of Spaniards with flags and much shouting. According to the security official who accompanied us these were all the Spanish anarchists assembled together. As I rode through the narrow streets the yelling continued to the accompaniment of shots from the guns of Kabyles and the dull booming of the military band. My horse became nervous and uneasy, shying many times at the things waved and brandished by the motley crowd of spectators, whose appearance was not one to inspire much confidence. It was a marvel that I got to the Sultan's palace without any incident."

The Kaiser then took it upon himself to alter the program arranged by Bülow, dropping the speech he was intended to make; he restricted himself to assuring the Sultan in the course of a conversation that the independence of Morocco must remain unimpaired and that the German Reich would use its influence to that end.

After his visit to Tangier, which had, as expected, raised storms of indignation in France, the Kaiser crossed to Gibraltar. He was anxious to ascertain, while standing on English soil, what the reaction of the British Empire had been to his trip to Tangier. In accordance with telegraphic orders from London, his reception at Gibraltar was "respectfully icy." What people in England thought of his "unconscionable exploit at Tangier" was best expressed in the words of Sir

Eyre Crowe, who after this Moroccan provocation compared the relations between England and the Reich to those depicted in the celebrated picture of "Dignity and Impudence."

57. WILHELM II AND EDWARD VII

DURING THE LAST YEARS of her life, relations between the old Queen Victoria and her eldest grandson had been tolerably good, this being made possible by indulgence and forgiveness on her side and on the part of the Kaiser by the awe and respect that he felt and displayed toward her. Wilhelm II had always been more attached to the old Queen than to his own mother, who never received loving letters from him like those which he wrote to his aged grandmother.

On January 17, 1901, the first news of Queen Victoria's being seriously ill reached Berlin. On that very day Prussia had made ready to celebrate the two-hundredth year of its existence as a kingdom. The Knights of the High Order of the Black Eagle had assembled in the capital of the Reich that same evening, many members of the House of Hohenzollern had already arrived for the festival, when the Kaiser decided to cancel the arrangements and to leave for England.

A telegram from London said he need not come, as the Queen's condition had taken a turn for the better. But the Kaiser was not to be deterred. The thought that he might never more see his grandmother alive impelled him to start at once. He reached Osborne just in time to see her before the death agony began, and the eighty-two-year-old Queen of England and Empress of India breathed her last in the arms of Kaiser Wilhelm II.

It was rumored in diplomatic circles in Berlin, after the Kaiser's return, that he had profited by his visit to seek on his own account a new *rapprochement* with England. A question was promptly asked in the Reichstag as to the truth of the rumor. To this the Reich's Chancellor replied in person, stating that "this visit to England is merely a private one, and no political deductions can be drawn from it."

Within the space of four years England had three times made attempts to reach an understanding with the Reich, without eliciting any favorable response from either Kaiser or Chancellor. Today that holding-back by Germany is accounted as one of the greatest blunders of Williamite policy.

Referring to this afterward in Doorn, the Kaiser pointed out that such solicitations by England could only have been dictated—as Bismarck had predicted—by the desire to ensure the aid of Germany in the event of England's being obliged by external complications to seek it.

As early as 1897 a first feeler for such a *rapprochement* had been put out. Wilhelm II had then written to the Czar to say: "So far as I can ascertain the English are eagerly seeking to find a Continental army to fight for their own interests. I fancy they will not find one so easily—in any case they will not get mine."

The question put by Sir Frank Lascelles, British Ambassador in Berlin, as to whether England might not in fact be a valuable ally for Germany, was answered in the negative by Wilhelm II, who reasoned thus: "The whole of England's armored fleet could not safeguard a single village on the long-drawn Russo-German frontier!"

Whenever matters concerning England were being dealt with the Kaiser looked on every question that arose as being his own exclusive and personal concern, without being able to exclude his hatred of England, or his regard for the country of his grandmother, from the factors that influenced him. Because he regarded himself as one who knew England well, he rejected advice from others and adhered to his own views. When he happened to be in a rage against "Perfidious Albion" he declared that one must always deal harshly with the English, and if necessary handle them with their own particular brutality. "Englishmen do not let themselves be intimidated," he maintained when he was over seventy years of age. "You must always confront Englishmen with inexorable facts."

Many prominent English people have spoken with appreciation of the Kaiser despite his often hostile attitude. They were agreed among themselves that he was gifted in many ways and often saw things more clearly than his advisers. No one could quarrel with him for trying to make the German Reich great and powerful after the model of the British Empire.

Sir Edward Goschen, who in 1887, at the time of the Jubilee celebrations, had met the young Prince Wilhelm in London, praised him for his intelligence and modesty. Later he became British Ambassador in Berlin.

Joseph Chamberlain, too, expressed the following favorable opinion to Eckardstein, "I have had two long conversations with the Kaiser, which confirmed my earlier impression of his extraordinary capacity and his understanding of European politics."

In the same year Arthur James Balfour assured Prince Hatzfeld, then Ambassador in London, that he thought the Kaiser admirable, and that he had formed an excellent impression of him.

Wilhelm II never underrated English statesmen—rather was he inclined to do the reverse. He was impressed by the English coolness of judgment, by English self-control and the habit of approaching all problems calmly. These good qualities he often found lacking in his own advisers. The old Emperor Franz Joseph of Austria once remarked that "the English are indeed the most reasonable and most capable politicians—they always know how to bring off a good compromise!"

With the accession to the throne of King Edward VII, the attitude of Great Britain toward the German Reich changed. Three times they had offered their services as a partner, and three times their offer had been rejected. That was enough! For the successor of the Great Queen it meant the task of restoring a balance of power in Europe and forging those links which were to lead to the *Entente Cordiale* of 1904.

"When England is no longer committed to Germany, and the Government of H.M. King Edward VII succeeds in coming to an understanding with France and Russia, then the situation of Germany in Europe will become critical." Such was the view of the Foreign Office in London. To achieve it was the aim of Edward VII.

Count von der Schulenburg, the German Military Attaché in London, gave warning in his reports: "King Edward's program provides for an agreement and reconciliation with Russia. . . . If that plan succeeds Germany is isolated. I do not believe that the King, or the English Government, harbors any intention of attacking Germany . . . nevertheless Germany must bear in mind the possibility of war. I must emphatically deny that there is any prospect that within a foreseeable time friendly relations between Germany and England can be restored."

Confronted by such a prognosis as this, Bülow had to admit (in 1902) that there was no one who could mend the impaired relations with England—unless indeed it be the Kaiser himself. In a letter to the Ambassador Count Wolff-Metternich he confirmed this, saying: "His Majesty [the Kaiser] is far and away the best card we hold against England!"

The Kaiser had no objection to being played by his Chancellor, but unfortunately the latter frequently played him wrongly, and the English people took note of it. Mistrust and malignancy reigned on both sides. When some English newspaper reporters were once allowed to interview the Kaiser in Berlin, they maliciously misrepresented what they were really told, so that the Kaiser wished to deny it. But Bülow advised against this, since what had occurred would not thereby be made any better.

These experiences made Wilhelm II cautious in dealing with England. When the Boer generals came to Europe and received a rousing welcome on the Continent, he declared that he was only prepared to receive the Boers in audience if King Edward VII, whose subjects they were, had no objection to his doing so.

Again, when it was proposed to start a fund for the benefit of the Boers, the Kaiser stopped this.

Bismarck had always been apprehensive about the "English Uncle business" and had given warnings against it. However, his fears proved to be unfounded as there could be no talk of any influence on German policy being exerted by "Uncle Bertie." Whereas Wilhelm and the Prince of Wales had been able to meet amicably on the occasion of Queen Victoria's funeral, this relationship had changed after the accession of "Uncle Bertie" to the throne.

The Kaiser, influenced by his entourage, became prejudiced and soon came to believe that he was being belittled, slighted and even turned into a laughingstock by his mother's brother. This suspicion was fostered by talebearing from certain circles of the Camarilla, until the Kaiser took revenge by making derogatory statements about his uncle. These were promptly communicated to King Edward, who, equally astonished and annoyed, retaliated in kind.

Edward VII, like his great-uncle Leopold I of Belgium, was a scion of the House of Coburg, and both shared the business capacity of that House. To do profitable business good connections are essential, and King Edward had these through his family relationships. Through his wife Queen Alexandra he was son-in-law to King Christian IX of Denmark and brother-in-law of Princess Dagmar, who was now the widow of Alexander III, Czar of Russia, also of the Duchess Thyra of Cumberland and of King George of Greece. Again, he was father-in-law to King Haakon VII of Norway, uncle of the Crown Prince of Sweden . . . and last, but not least, uncle of the German Kaiser. Over and above all this, King Edward had relations of cousinship with the Royal Houses of Saxony, Belgium, Hanover, Portugal, Bulgaria and Spain, as well as with the House of Hesse-Darmstadt. The "Royal businessman" knew how to approach all these relatives of his adroitly, to use them, and even to entrust them to act as his representatives.

The things that his relations most admired in "Uncle Bertie" were, apart from his subtlety and dexterity, his sagacity and his infallible knowledge of men, all concealed behind a superficially charming frivolity. The Kaiserin Augusta, always quick to pass judgment on people, had put him down as a *bon vivant*, an arbiter in all questions of fashion, and an elegant man of the world.

It was known that he used to frequent the salons of Notre Dame de Lorette in Paris and that he was a confirmed gambler. He played high in the *cercles privés* of the casinos in Cannes and Biarritz, and also on the green table of high politics. His visits to Paris and the Côte d'Azur had brought him, at an early age, into contact with French life. He was "France's friend." When only fourteen years old, making his first acquaintance with Paris, he expressed his admiration to Napoleon III, telling him that his was the most beautiful country in the world.

King Edward was not without enemies. He had been called, quite unwarrantably, "the bloodthirsty butcher of the Boers," "a warmonger," or, as the Belgian Ambassador in Berlin expressed it, "a disturber of the peace." ("The peace of Europe is never more endangered than when the King of England concerns himself with maintaining it.") Other attacks made on him were more difficult to counter. His mother, the old Queen, had sighed, with despairing eyes, when a list of the people who were received at Sandringham was shown to her. Among them were members of the Parisian demi-monde, and also adventurers and gamblers.

When, in August 1901, the lonely Kaiserin Friedrich succumbed to cancer, it seemed as if her brother Edward and her eldest son wished to establish once more, on a more amicable basis, the weakening relations of kinship. Generously overlooking the past, King Edward wrote to his nephew.

A year later, in 1902, he wrote again saying that he had the utmost confidence in the sincerity of Wilhelm's feelings and in his loyal friendship for England. He added that he fully appreciated the difficulties Wilhelm had to contend with in Germany, where he was regarded as an Anglophile.

King Edward was soon to learn that his nephew was no longer Anglophile but something very different. His eyes were first opened when he accepted an invitation of the Kaiser to Kiel. The Kaiser himself had arranged the *mise en scène* for this dramatic occasion. The Marshal of the Court, von Zedlitz-Trützschler, has reported how "the Kaiser superintended down to the smallest details the embellishment of the *Hohenzollern*. A huge awning was stretched over the promenade deck, wonderful floral decorations with little fountains and splashing waterfalls rejoiced the eye. A dinner party for 108 persons and a tea party for 220, were given in the King's honor. The Kaiser saw to everything with such assiduity that he was dressed and up three-quarters of an hour before the festivities were due to begin, pacing the deck nervously, unable to wait patiently for the time to pass."

Then, when "Uncle Bertie" appeared on deck and saw lying before him in the bay the German fleet, he understood the meaning of his invitation—a triumph for the German Kaiser: another and larger program of naval construction completed in secrecy, and the English, including their King, deceived.

Not so long before the King had remarked complacently, "Let him play with his fleet!" These German squadrons lying off Kiel were no longer toys. Now he was confronted with a new situation, one with which no one in England had reckoned. It was bitter earnest from now on! One must act now, but in silence! To show his feelings was not King Edward's way. The English people had not dubbed him "the perfect gentleman" for nothing. But that did not prevent him, when seriously angry with his nephew, from calling him "the most brilliant failure in history." The nephew replied in similar style, so the King soon found himself obliged to protest at the

German Embassy against various insults. He complained to the Councilor von Eckardstein about a letter from the Kaiser in which he called the English ministers "unmitigated noodles." "What do you think your Kaiser would say if I were to provide his ministers in Berlin with similar titles?"

The King was especially touchy about the Kaiser's upsetting his sporting pleasures in Cowes. Since 1890 the Kaiser had frequently been a guest at Osborne for the regatta, and even then it was little to the liking of his uncle, who had scornfully remarked, "It's all very well his being interested in boats, but when one finds him careening about on deck with his paralyzed arm there must be some anxiety lest he should do himself some injury!"

He is recorded as saying that "My whole pleasure in the regatta is spoiled for me, every time, by his coming here!" His spirits did not revive until the Kaiser departed, or (as it was expressed in private) "when the Boss of Cowes sailed away."

Wilhelm II for his part was not backward in returning, in appropriate fashion, any derogatory epithets coming from "Uncle Bertie." He called him "an old peacock." And he took a diabolical delight in annoying "the old peacock." On one occasion, when the race for the Queen's Cup was about to start, the Kaiser put in an appearance in the *Meteor*, but swung round immediately after the starting shot and left the uncle to complete the course by himself.

At the end of that Cowes Week the Kaiser nominated "Uncle Bertie" to the Colonelcy of the Stolp Hussars. Their jacket was rose pink and the Kaiser figured that it would look absolutely comical on the stout form of Edward VII.

That so vexed and ridiculed an uncle should come to entertain hostile feelings for his nephew is understandable. And the Kaiser himself said to his biographer in Doorn, "I had three bitter enemies during my reign. They were old Bismarck, August Bebel, the Socialist, and Edward VII."

Speaking (on March 19, 1907) with his House Marshal, Count Robert Zedlitz-Trützschler, he summarized his opinion of his uncle in these bitter words, "He's a devil! You wouldn't believe what a devil he is!"

58. THE TRAVELING KAISER

IF KING EDWARD VII was fond of traveling, so also was his nephew, Wilhelm II. The German periodical *Simplicissimus* produced a cartoon showing the two monarchs acting as "travelers" for their respective firms. The King was depicted as the dignified representative of his House—the Kaiser as a crafty *commis voyageur*. *Kladderadatsch* also took an interest in this "perpetual tourist" and gave Wilhelm II the name of Reise-Kaiser. His numerous gaddings-about—in the one year, 1894, he put in nearly two hundred days of travel—aroused apprehension in many circles. It became a question of how affairs of State were to be carried on consistently and how decisions were to be taken, when the one man who held the reins of government in his hands had to be sought for each time his signature was required, or had to be consulted either by telegram or (later on) by telephone. Moreover, this traveling about was largely unnecessary, the reason for it being mostly attendance at reviews, the laying of foundation stones, unveiling of statues, consecrations of churches, naming of ships or swearing-in of recruits.

Count Waldersee pronounced a severe judgment on these journeyings, which he confided to his diary: "The worst misgivings that afflict all those who have to deal with him arise from the fact that the Kaiser himself has no longer the slightest desire to work. Dissipations, playing about with the Army and Navy, traveling and shooting, come before everything else. So, in fact, he has scarcely time for work."

If ever the Kaiser heard of such talk as this he would dismiss it offhand. "How shortsighted! Why, we're living under the Sign of Travel!" Later on, in 1906, he spoke—perhaps a little prematurely, though he proved to be right—of "the sign of the motor." So it came about that the Berliners seldom got a glimpse of their Kaiser.

The Kaiser's travels involved great expense and a vast amount of trouble. The mere preparations for a journey involved an amount of forethought and planning that few could suspect. A commission had to go in advance to survey and arrange officially the accommodation that the Kaiser was to occupy. Often enough those who offered hospitality, such as Prince Dohna at Schlobitten, had to reconstruct their entire Schloss in order to satisfy the demands made on them. The Kaiser was seldom told of these self-sacrificing performances. Thus it was that in the case of Schlobitten the Kaiser, when taking leave of Princess Dohna, informed her that he had been particularly pleased at "her having made so little ceremony on his account!"

Apart from the arrangements with the railways, the royal stables, the police and the wardrobe attendants, all had to receive special orders. The royal uniforms, with their full-dress accessories, cloaks and overcoats; undress uniforms, sabers, swords, sashes, epaulets, helmets, caps, spurs and the insignia of orders, all had to be selected and packed.

Besides Prussian regiments, the Kaiser was Colonel of units in Baden, Saxony, Württemberg and Bavaria. He had the right to wear the uniform of an English field marshal, and that of a commander in chief in the Austro-Hungarian Army, besides those of a British admiral, and of an admiral in the fleets of Russia, Sweden, Norway and Denmark. Then there were the uniforms of Austrian infantry units, of Hungarian Hussars, English Dragoons, the Russian Life Guards, the Russian Wiborg Regiment and a Russian Narva Dragoon Regiment, and those of the Fourth Portuguese Cavalry Regiment.

All the uniforms required for the particular occasion had to be got ready and packed, with the different regulations regarding the wearing of each, for orders and decorations, sashes and aiguillettes. The Kaiser himself attached great importance to being correctly turned out according to regulations, and that of course applied to his officers as well. Once when Alfonso XIII, the young King of Spain, came on deck in the *Hohenzollern* in the uniform of a Prussian colonel about which something was amiss, the Kaiser told him, before his whole suite, to go back to his cabin and have it put right.

To all these many uniforms were added various costumes for fetes and so on, including one of the Grand Elector of Brandenburg, in which the Kaiser had his photograph taken, to give to Bülow with a dedication. The Prince thought fit to show it to a newspaper editor, who published it and made the Kaiser look ridiculous.

Then there were civilian clothes, shooting costumes, tall hats, yachting and tennis kits, with all their paraphernalia. And there were cases for orders and decorations, caskets for rings and tiepins, tobacco boxes, cigarette cases, watches and silver- or gold-framed photographs of the Kaiser, to be given as presents on the way. Often the getting ready of all the uniforms and accessories had to be completed within a few hours, for it frequently happened that the route was suddenly changed, making havoc of everything already arranged. The Kaiser's hurried decisions to pack up and start away were the result of his unbridled capriciousness, which earned him the popular and facetious nickname of "Wilhelm the Sudden," pointing to the arbitrariness and lack of consideration for others shown in his proceedings.

On a par with his unnecessary travels were other instances of impulsiveness, such as the "Kruger telegram," the bestowing on Lord Roberts of the Order of the Black Eagle, the futile visit to America of Prince Heinrich, the painful and pointless journey of the Kaiserin Friedrich to Paris, and the hasty bestowal of the *Pour le Mérite* on the Russian General Stössel. Then there were his receptions of Cecil Rhodes in Berlin and of the Russian Minister Witte at Rominten, his telegram to Goluchowski ("the brilliant second" [1]), all to be accounted wrong because such "policies of hasty decisions and telegrams" must inevitably have unfortunate consequences.

Before starting on a journey the Kaiser would dictate an endless series of telegrams: "Inform Her Majesty the Kaiserin of my departure." "Inform Prince Fürstenberg of the time of my arrival." "Inform the Foreign Office of my address." "Tell the Wildpark Station to have the royal train standing ready."

Then, when all the many preparations had got so far that the actual start came in sight—always supposing that it was not canceled at the last minute—the luggage had to be loaded under the supervision of the valet Schulz, who was responsible that nothing was forgotten. When helping the Kaiser to dress, Schulz had to see to it that the bandolier crossed from right to left, or from left to right, as the case might be; that the sword knot was fastened on the hilt in the correct regulation manner, and so on. Of this valet Schulz, who remained at his master's side to the day of his death, the Kaiser always retained an affectionate memory.

[1] *See* page 248.

The royal train was made up of dark-blue coaches with ivory surrounds, and usually comprised a drawing-room car, a sleeping car and a dining car for the Kaiser himself. Then there was a sleeping car for the suite, the cook's galley and a luggage van. It was generally hauled by two locomotives, and on special occasions engineers in frockcoats and top hats stood on the footplates and were responsible for the driving.

If shooting was to be included in the program a special personnel with the guns, cartridges and other equipment needed was also carried. The Kaiser was very fond of shooting on the Rominten Moors. On the way there he would visit the royal model farm of Cadinen, near the Baltic Sea, and the well-known Majolica pottery factory, also the Trakehnen stud farm. Then, from the little railway station of Rominten he would drive by coach with a team of fast-trotting Hungarian coach horses across the wide moor to the isolated little Schloss that was his shooting box. Here was a game preserve of some 100,000 *Morgen*,[2] with uncleared forest interspersed with little lakes disposed checker-wise so as to provide broad rides and facilitate the work of the gamekeepers. About a hundred forestry employees did duty there. They were charged not only with the care of the game in their own areas, but also had to see that the original character of the natural preserve was disturbed as little as possible and that the footpaths and stands were always kept in good order, so that His Majesty could, whenever he liked, follow the noble sport of shooting.

The Kaiser's way of shooting was not at all liked by the foresters. They had to mark out a figure eight with fences, and the Kaiser, with his loaders and guests, would post himself at the intersection of the two loops and shoot down the game, driven toward them down the loops, with sustained gunfire.

He himself used only his one useful hand, with which he held his gun high up to his shoulder, lowering it to fire.

He now rarely visited the Russian game preserves where formerly he used to hunt bears. This was not always conducive to complete peace of mind for his host, who used to take the precaution of posting a few good shots around the distinguished guest—a wounded Russian bear is a different proposition from a Rominten hare!

[2] "Morgen," old German measurement equivalent to an acre.

However, above all his other travels, those which gave him the greatest pleasure were, as he stated himself, his Scandinavian cruises in the *Hohenzollern*. The building of this ship, for service as a dispatch vessel with heavy armored squadrons, had duly been authorized by the Reichstag. Parliamentary circles were therefore astonished to hear that the Kaiser proposed to appropriate her for the use of himself and his family. But they were even more astonished when he announced his intention of doing so on the occasion of her launching. Before naming her he addressed the ship as follows: "Your slim build, your light structure, that exhibits no menacing gun ports, no heavy turrets like those carried by the warships of my Navy for battle against an enemy, prove to us that you are designed for the work of peace, to skim lightly over the seas from land to land, to provide rest for one who works hard, to bring joy and happiness to the Imperial children and to the noble mother of our country. Let that be your destiny! May you wear your light artillery for adornment rather than for fighting! So . . . I baptize you by the name of . . . the Imperial yacht *Hohenzollern*!"

After the general amazement had died down the *Hohenzollern* traveled the seas of Europe. Her logbook recorded visits to Björkö, Corfu, the Peiraeus, the Golden Horn, and Acre in Palestine. "On board her one lived as though on an island; nobody bothered you, but you could send your orders by telegram wherever and whenever you wished!"

The Kaiser felt particularly at home when in Norwegian waters. "Standing on the bridge, with only the stars above one, communing with oneself"—thus he enjoyed the strange magic of the white nights and the sublime unfolding of mountain panoramas when steaming into the fiords.

He seldom went ashore in Norway, but he did undertake a few short trips into the interior, driving one of those little two-wheeled traps that can negotiate the narrowest mountain tracks. That these trips were not always devoid of incident is shown by an entry in General von Moltke's diary after one of the expeditions:

"I had palpitations of the heart when we met carts coming from the opposite direction. The Kaiser drove close alongside a precipice below which the water was boiling over the rocks, holding the reins with his crippled left hand while he took off his hat to acknowledge the greetings of people that he passed. The natives gathered on the inland side of the track to greet the visitor with '*Du*' and they addressed him as *Herr Kaiser*."

Though Wilhelm II was treated in Norway with all due respect, he never had any real contact with the people. The fact was that the Kaiser was never liked in Norway, even when he presented them with the Fridthjof statue—or perhaps it was because of his doing so.

But he was never really at ease until he was back again on board the *Hohenzollern*. There in his cabin he was surrounded by pictures and photographs of his family and his relatives. On the stairway hung a present from Grandmamma, an engraving done in 1887 from the picture showing the scene in Westminster Abbey on the occasion of the celebration of Queen Victoria's Jubilee. The comfort of the accommodation created a particularly homely atmosphere and made life on board, in the midst of friends, officers and crew, resemble a patriarchal community with Wilhelm II as head of the house. He tasted the seamen's food in the galley, preached on deck on Sundays and carved the joints at table. After dinner he would indulge himself with his long cigarette, comforted by the thought that he no longer had much to suffer from seasickness. The Kaiserin was a good sailor, but not the Czar (Nicholas II), for whom every journey by sea meant torture.

Anyone who received an invitation to the *Hohenzollern* could consider himself highly honored, for it was seldom that guests were asked to come on board during a cruise. Then they were mostly experts who could give lectures about the coasts and harbors to be visited. The marine painter Willy Stöwer was one of the privileged people, and he was often to be found on deck at his easel.

Among the other favored guests were the "Bard" Prince Philipp zu Eulenburg and General von Chelius of the Guards Hussars, a masterly pianist and an enthusiastic admirer of Richard Wagner, whose influence on his own compositions was undeniable. The Kaiser was attracted to him, not only because of his musical talent but also because he was esteemed as a highly cultivated and well-informed man. Moreover, he was an excellent officer and a remarkable lecturer. "Steadfast as a rock was that rare man," said the Kaiser speaking of him in Doorn; "he was my friend and remained my friend throughout all the vicissitudes of the times to the day of his death in 1923."

Then there was the Kaiser's Aide-de-Camp, General von Hahnke, rather older than von Chelius, who to the end enjoyed the unabated confidence of his master. Tall, with sharp features, he was more like a Southerner in appearance.

General von Kessel, too, was included in the select circle. Although he had been a confidant of the Friedrichs during the ninety-nine days of that reign, he had been taken over by the Kaiser. "All his life he has been a true friend and adviser to me," said the Kaiser.

On board the *Hohenzollern* the various roles were well distributed —Kessel was the quiet listener, Löwenfeld told funny stories, while Hahnke confined himself to discussion of the pleasures of the table, especially wines. Eulenburg sang his *Rosenlieder* and Chelius played Viennese airs or Parisian *chansons*.

But there were also other attractions on board—there were Count Wedel and the A.D.C. von Senden, indefatigable in inventing all kinds of funny games; Count Görz, imitator of animal noises; Hülsen, skilled in all the arts of magic; and lastly Danckelmann, who shot gulls and could have appeared as a trick shot in any circus.

Serious-minded people who stayed on board the *Hohenzollern* for any length of time left the yacht with the uneasy feeling that the distractions offered there might be very nice just to pass a gay evening, but that it was really surprising to find that an emperor could take pleasure in them as a continual and continuous form of entertainment. Even Eulenburg, usually prepared to fall in with and say "Yes!" and "Amen!" to anything at all in such matters, found that "the atmosphere, charged with jests and trivialities, was simply unbearable."

Added to this was the fact that responsible people who knew Wilhelm II well regarded this sort of life as most unsuitable for him because, as a creature of moods, isolated for long periods in a confined space, there was danger of his being unduly influenced and used by clever officials such as Lucanus and Müller.

In Doorn, when the Kaiser came across the book by Professor Johannes Haller of Tübingen in which life on board the *Hohenzollern* during the Scandinavian cruises was subjected to severe criticism, on the strength of information given by Eulenburg, he exclaimed angrily: "That was not so! Lectures by learned men were often given on board, many serious talks and debates were organized. It seems that the worries he had at the last must have dulled the good Eulenburg's memories of what really happened!"

After the Kaiser's acquisition of the little castle of Achilleion in Corfu the cruises of the *Hohenzollern* extended to the Adriatic, when she was generally accompanied by two small cruisers as escort.

The Achilleion was reached by a three-hour journey by road from the little town and harbor of Corfu. It was a bad road, leading past the old citadel between hedges of agave and cactus, through olive groves to the vineyards about San Rocco, and then on to the castle. This provided so little room that only the Imperial couple, with the Marshal of the Court and a few menservants and maids could be accommodated there. The rest of the company had to be primitively housed in a building on the old road. There was little need for kitchen staff, for everything required for the more important meals was prepared on the *Hohenzollern*, moored in the harbor, and sent up to the Achilleion, where it only needed to be warmed up. The very capable steward, Hoppe, saw to all the service.

Marble terraces overgrown with climbing roses, shrubs, springs and antique statuary—among which was the *Dying Achilles* (bought by the Kaiser)—a little shrine with a bust of the Empress Elisabeth of Austria, led to the garden proper, with its many orange trees, whose fruit, by the Kaiser's order, was not to be picked until after his departure.

There was a wonderful view from the bastion in the garden, ranging over the rocky slopes and the shimmering Adriatic as far as the blue mountains of Albania, with the dimly discernible islands of Leucas and Ithaca on the horizon.

During the Kaiser's stay the little castle was constantly guarded by Greek soldiers and German plain-clothes police. There was no great danger, for the inhabitants worshiped the Kaiser, who brought them all kinds of amenities—donations for the poor of the island, a doctor, medicines and the ship's band, which now and again gave concerts on the esplanade in the town.

Nowhere save here could Wilhelm II have led so idyllic and undisturbed an existence. He wore no uniform, save on special occasions. He was a civilian, and enjoyed being one. In the daytime he was seen in suits of raw silk, in the evening in yachting kit. The Kaiserin, too, was in her element, for everything was simple and unconstrained—a condition to which by now she had almost become unaccustomed, but which well suited her real temperament.

It was only because it reminded him of the charming island of the Odyssey that Corfu so delighted the Kaiser. He was greatly interested in the excavations by Wilhelm Dörpfeld, and every afternoon would go over to Garitza to see the progress made. Then, one day, the waiting was rewarded . . . Professor Dörpfeld managed to unearth a find in the presence of the Kaiser! It was the head of a Gorgon, in high relief. Thirty years later, in Doorn, Wilhelm II wrote and published an almost scholarly paper about that Gorgon.

59. THE LEFT ARM

THE TRIPS TO CORFU and Norway served not only to calm his nervous restlessness and appease his pursuit of pleasure, as the critics of the Constant Tourist averred, but also as a convalescence after an illness.

In the autumn of 1903 the Kaiser's doctors had recommended a sea voyage as being urgently necessary because serious symptoms had developed in his throat. For some time he was only able to speak in a hoarse whisper. Both his father and his mother had died of cancer and a hereditary tendency was to be feared, though this is not proven to exist in the case of cancer. His complaint was at first kept secret, until on November 7, 1903, a surgical intervention had to be undertaken. A polypus growth was removed from the throat, which was ascertained to be nonmalignant, and by Christmas the Kaiser was able to speak in his normal voice.

Even more serious seemed a recurrence of the old ear trouble, with a purulent discharge, which was watched anxiously by the Court physicians, who feared it might affect the brain. Waldersee, too, was afraid lest an extension of the disease should entail "severe mental disturbance."

But the Kaiser overcame the ear trouble without any marked ill effects remaining. He bore the severe pain with the same fortitude that he displayed in his fight against his physical disability. Just as he had asked his American dentist not to worry about hurting him because he never felt pain, so he began again, with the same disregard for his sufferings, to try to strengthen his stunted left arm and bring it into use by physical exercises and rowing practice on a special apparatus. This was not successful, but it did result in the arm's being not entirely useless.

Much has been written about this arm and its effects on the development of his character. Foreign biographers of the Kaiser have regarded it as being of decisive importance in this connection. For them, all possible and impossible psychoanalytical investigations lead to the final diagnosis that in this disability lay the main cause of many of the weaknesses of character shown by Wilhelm II.

The now fifty-year-old *Imperator Rex* certainly did not look like a cripple. There was a photograph taken of him near Aalesund (but never shown in public) in which he displays a fine martial beard. He resembled a hefty old salt whom one would gladly trust to weather any storm at sea and to hold his own with anyone. The beard must have been renounced at the urgent request of the Court photographer, who saw himself being ruined and left with thousands of old pictures of the Kaiser on his hands.

The upturned mustaches of Wilhelm II won him enormous popularity. He became the most caricatured sovereign in Europe. In the waxworks in Berlin nobody, neither Queen Victoria, Boulanger nor Oom (Uncle) Paul Kruger, excited as much interest as he did. If he had any competitor it was his old adversary Bismarck who, while unable to boast of anything so fine in the way of a mustache, did proffer his bald pate of yellow wax with its three celebrated hairs.

60. THE KAISER AND THE PARTIES IN THE REICHSTAG

ALTHOUGH BISMARCK had declared the Reichstag "a necessary institution," he saw in that Parliament no ideal solution of the problems of government. All too soon it appeared that this newly created popular assembly was in danger of losing whatever esteem attached to it, owing to the wrangling and bargaining between the various parties. Through seeking to protect their own special interests, through cleavages and factious opposition, more especially in regard to questions involving the religious Confessions, the several groups were reduced to powerlessness and were no longer capable of pursuing any positive course.

Bismarck had in particular complained of the Social Democracy which advocated open rebellion and already felt certain that no one other party could ever again oppose it with any prospect of success. According to Bismarck's ideas, the Liberals "shot only at disappearing targets," the Center party "had nothing in their heads except the Holy Father," while the Conservatives "clung to an egoism that left everything else behind." "It is this schismatic party spirit that I shall accuse before God and history if all the noble work done in 1866 and 1870 is allowed to fall into decay and if everything is to be ruined by the pen that was created by the sword."

It was in just such a fit of pessimism as this that the old Reich's Chancellor declared, shortly before his dismissal, that "an enlightened Absolutism is the best kind of rule for the German Reich." His last efforts had been "to keep the members of the Reichstag so busy at work that they would drown in their files." Then at least one would avoid further mischief caused by their foolish speeches. After his dismissal Bismarck had followed with increasing apprehension the further developments in the Reichstag, especially the events of January 1893, when the Government only succeeded in carrying their Trade Agreement Bill with the help of Social Democrats, Progressives and Poles.

Soon after Bismarck's death it was clear that it was becoming increasingly difficult for the Government to work harmoniously with the Reichstag. Caprivi, Hohenlohe, and even more so Bülow, had this experience. When Bülow (in 1906) demanded a supplementary credit on account of the war in German Southwest Africa, where the Herrero Rebellion had broken out, the Black-Red bloc (of the Center and the Social Democrats) proved so refractory that he proceeded to dissolve the Reichstag and called for new elections—the so-called Hottentot Elections.

Wilhelm II fully agreed with this dissolution of the old Reichstag, the "Gossip Shop." If it had rested with him all the querulous obstructionists would have been hanged. His declaration, "I mean to have peace in the ship!" applied also to members of the Reichstag. He followed with intense interest the preparations for the polling; he even saw every valet and footman in the Schloss to impress upon them how important it was to vote against the "enemies of the Reich

—the Red-and-Blacks." Since the floating vote was mobilized, polling was heavy. On the night following polling day, the Kaiser did not sleep at all. The incoming telegrams giving the results were more important than sleep. By early morning the victory of the Government and of Reich's Chancellor Bülow was assured. This result was a personal success for the Kaiser—the monarchical sentiment that had already begun to lose its grip had been rallied and had asserted itself victoriously.

For the Social Democrats the result of this defeat was to cause them to close their ranks and discourage everything that might tend to split the party. Although the party was no older than the Kaiser himself, it had managed in those fifty years, despite this last setback, and by following the precepts of Marx and Lassalle, to constitute itself the articulate representative of the German working class. This class provided the majority of Social Democrat voters, reinforced by voters from the middle classes, who felt repelled by the idea of personal rule, by the strident speeches and unintelligible measures of the Kaiser.

Immediately after his accession the Kaiser had endeavored to placate the Social Democrats by showing sympathetic understanding and willingness to listen, and above all he tried to gain the confidence of their leaders. Regarding the difficulties that he experienced at that time, he confessed afterward that "it makes a great difference whether a Government be guided by a man of ninety, with a lifetime of activity and success behind him, like my late grandfather, who was the senior of all his colleagues and whose advice was sought for, or whether it be a young man of thirty, whom nobody knew, and who was only beginning his reign. I had first of all to win people's good will and trust!"

At that time (1890) when the Kaiser was anxious to have Sunday labor and the employment of women and children in factories restricted, with a view to checking exploitation and physical overwork, it had been Bismarck who was unwilling to support such measures on the ground that "the workers would always be demanding more." In the Kaiser's entourage all making of compacts with the Sozis [1] was opposed; they would much prefer to see them rooted out lock, stock and barrel.

"But I cannot reply to the demands of my subjects with quick-

[1] Sozis was the name given to the Social Democrats (Sozialdemokraten).

firing guns!" protested the young Kaiser to Bismarck. "I don't want to be called a Grapeshot Prince like my grandfather!" These remarks were accorded a cool reception by Bismarck, who declared, "I consider all hesitation in dealing with Social Democracy to be a mistake. . . . Sooner or later the Social Democrats will have to be shot dead!"

When the Kaiser referred to the first decade of his reign and his endeavors to come to some reasonable understanding with this party that had become so powerful, he said to Major Niemann, "I have by nature a strong social sense. It was my genuine intention to be a *roi des gueux*. It is my conviction that to think socially and to act socially is the quintessence of practical Christianity."

But when, about the turn of the century, the real aims of Social Democracy proved to be the abolition of capitalism and the founding of a workers' state on the lines of communistic teaching—incidentally, of course, making away with the monarchy—the Kaiser's attitude changed, having been affected also by "the mean and underhand action of the Social Democrats" in connection with renewed demands made by the workers in Krupp's. He now had to acknowledge that his hope of "Social Democracy's sowing its wild oats and being only a passing phenomenon" had been a delusion. His antagonism to the Sozis was increased by whisperings that exaggerated the immediate danger of the Red Specter and represented it as being maliciously disposed toward himself.

Baron von Stumm-Halberg assured the Kaiser that he held proof that August Bebel wanted to overthrow the monarchy. When President Sadi Carnot was assassinated in 1894, Wilhelm II was convinced that the Reds were trying to bring about anarchy in France also. Then in Bremen, on March 6, 1903, when a youth named Weiland threw a piece of iron at him and wounded him under the right eye, it must again have been the Sozis who had instigated that outrage. In point of fact, however, the lad was not traced in any register of members of the party, but he did figure in the list of feeble-minded persons in the care of the city authorities.

Now that the issue was fairly joined, the Kaiser knew that for the Hohenzollern dynasty it was a case of "to be, or not to be." The rival banners confronting one another in the lists were inscribed with the Hohenzollern device *Suum cuique* (To each, his own) and the Social Democratic slogan *Allen dasselbe* (The same for all).

In endeavoring to ward off the danger of Social Democracy the Kaiser often made mistakes in his choice of methods—he aimed at exercising a restraining influence on the refractory elements by intimidation and threats. Thus, when addressing some mine-workers, he declared, "For me, every Social Democrat is an enemy of the Realm and of the Fatherland. If I find that social-democratic tendencies are involved in your movement and are inciting you to unlawful resistance, then I shall intervene with unrelenting severity and I shall employ all the power at my disposal—and that power is great! That party which dares to attack the foundations of the State, which revolts against religion and does not even stop at the person of the Almighty Ruler, must be crushed! I shall be happy to shake any man's hand, be he workman, prince or plain citizen, if only he will help me in this struggle!"

He concluded by mentioning his own "patent solution" of the trouble, according to which it would be the simplest and best thing in the world if all the Sozis, as they did not wish to be Germans, would emigrate and leave the country.

Everything had been done by Bismarck to further the policy of protective duties, which, however, led directly to the strengthening of those very forces whose political influence the Chancellor wished to restrain, namely, those of the socialistically minded workers and those of the newly introduced capitalists.

If, under the purposeful leadership of August Bebel, the Social Democrats showed, beyond doubt, an important increase of stature and represented, as a whole, a convincing expression of the will of a portion of the people bound together by necessity, that could not be said of the Liberals. Infected by Americanism, the chase after money, combined with the disposition to frequent the *nouveaux riches* that had laid hold not only of the representatives of the *bourgeoisie* but also of the *bourgeoisie* itself, the liberal parties swung to and fro between the democratic and the conservative, often showing themselves to be undignified, avaricious and greedy when it was a matter of distinction and titles. Anyone who managed to become a Commercial Councilor or to receive the ennobling "von," felt that he was nearing his goal of being introduced at Court and of playing some part in the capital of the Reich. The desire to be presented at Court tended to become a mania, until the Marshals of the Court were completely at a loss how to keep the ermine-crazy ones away.

From the decay of parties it was above all the Catholic Center party that profited. It, and the Social Democrats, constituted the inheritance that Wilhelm II had to take over from Bismarck. If the Reds were working for what they thought a brighter future, the Blacks stood like something left over from the Middle Ages on the ground of the past. Nevertheless, these two parties had one object in common—to weaken the power of the Imperial Evangelical authority, if not indeed to abolish it. After the ending of the *Kulturkampf*—the prolonged struggle between the Roman Catholic and the Protestant Churches, especially in the field of education—Bismarck had declaimed bitterly about the behavior of the Ultramontanes, or "Romelings" as he called them, and had penned these scathing words: "Therapeutic treatment of the Roman Catholic Church in a secular State is made difficult by the fact that the Roman Catholic clergy have to lay claim to participation in the exercise of secular authority outside the scope of Church affairs. Disguised as a Church it is a political institution, and it gives its collaborators the definite conviction that its freedom lies in its authority, and that the Church, wherever it does not exercise that authority, is entitled to complain of a Diocletianlike persecution. The way the Center party is behaving in the new empire shows its cunning, its political refinement and its self-control. The party is letting the fruit ripen quietly, and then, at the right moment, when the others are again quarreling, the black coats will be spread out to catch the crop that falls into their laps."

The reasons for the rapidity with which the Center party had taken root and gained ground in Germany continued to preoccupy Wilhelm II even in his old age. He eventually came to the following conclusion: "The Center, originally rising from the clerical-particularist opposition to the founding of the Reich, gathered in, because of its political, social and confessional objectives, so many heterogeneous elements such as Poles, Alsatians and Protestant Guelphs that at first one could scarcely have given it a long expectation of life. It was, however, firmly consolidated by the *Kulturkampf*. The party as a confessional body in a political assembly—a thing unique in Europe—became, so to speak, an end in itself. Spiritually dependent upon a foreign power—the Pope—the leadership of the Center has never abjured its aversion to the Protestant Imperial

Realm, nor has it been able to accept without reservations the idea of the Reich."

The Kaiser had certainly displayed the same good will toward the Center party that he had shown to the other bourgeois parties in the Reichstag. He was always concerned to enlist friends in the struggle against the Left. Though some of the leaders of the Center were personally uncongenial to him, he overcame his dislikes and sought to build up tolerable relations with them. If these efforts to bring the Center into positive co-operation failed, that was not his fault alone.

Since the Social Democrats stood in openly hostile opposition to the authority of the Kaiser, the Liberals and Progressives, alternating between abuse and enthusiasm, came to occupy no clearly defined position, and the Center party was only intent on realizing its own advantages, irrespective of Kaiser and Reich, there remained (besides the National Liberals, who were also unstable) the Conservatives—often designated as the "Pillars of the Throne"—who constituted the only single important element.

The Conservatives—who were also called the "Blues," from the idea of blue blood—proved indeed the most effective counterweight to the Reds. At the bottom of their hearts they looked on all those politico-humanitarian dreams of social reform and the legislation for defense of workers as of little use. They were unwilling to abandon their old principles or renounce their rights to place and privilege. For many of them their position vis-à-vis the King of Prussia remained as it had been expressed so facetiously by the poet Chamisso: ". . . *und der König absolut, wenn er unseren Willen tut!*" (. . . and let the King be absolute, so long as he does what we want!). They did not utter a conviction like this, but gave assurance of unshakable loyalty to the Hereditary Ruling House. They boasted of the fact that their fathers, grandfathers and a long succession of ancestors had provided the Prussian monarchs with good officers and officials, who had been brave, reliable and modest in their claims and pretensions. In fact it was true that right up to the turn of the century the Prussian nobility had known scarcely anything in the way of luxury. In Prussia people generally thought like that lieutenant of the Guards who, hearing of a disdainful remark by the Crown Princess Victoria, declared: "It is quite true that we are poor, but that is only because we were loyal!"

In this time when everything was being rebuilt, Prussian simplicity threatened to lose its bearings. Old, firmly rooted and well-tried conceptions were being diverted into other channels and were disappearing slowly but perceptibly.

"Adel verpflichtet!" (*Noblesse oblige*) cried the Kaiser to the Conservatives, thinking less of them than of his project for the Kiel Canal, which was strongly opposed by the Right. He felt obliged to remind the "Pillars of the Throne" of their obligations. "As the ivy twines itself around the gnarled trunk of the oak, adorning it with its leaves and protecting it when storms rage around its crown, so clings the nobility of Prussia to my House! May it, and with it the whole nobility of the German nation, be a shining example to the portion of the people that still holds back!"

This analogy belongs to the category of *gaffes* into which the Kaiser so often slipped, for ivy does not protect, but suffocates.

As the Conservatives would not desist from their opposition to the canal, the Kaiser addressed them once again. "I have had to note with a heart deeply troubled that in the aristocratic circles standing closest to me my best intentions are misunderstood and to some extent attacked. Indeed, I have even heard the word opposition. Opposition by Prussian noblemen is an absurdity!"

This appeal was frigidly rejected. The Conservative *Kreuz-Zeitung* wrote, "If the nobility is henceforth to offer no opposition to the Crown, it must, so long as it sits in Parliament, either renounce its nobility or lay down its mandate. It should therefore not stand for election, or sit in the *Herrenhaus*" (Upper House).

A voice spoke even more plainly in the Königshalle at Königsberg: "If the nobility still has a mission, this consists, over and above its performance of military duties and its agricultural activities, in warning the Government and the head of the State against taking the wrong road on which they are already beginning to travel. Any notion of the Kaiser's own devising, that he is an autocratic ruler, does not dispense the nobility from carrying out its mission and doing this duty!"

Once before, two hundred years previously, the nobility had used similar language to the first King of Prussia, who afterward was careful of how he addressed that "rock of bronze."

Thus began the Conservative revulsion, not from the monarchy, but from Wilhelm II. They would have nothing to do with his "progressive policies," his "horrible fleet," and they cared very little about his "miserable colonies." As representatives of the extreme Right, one may cite Ernst von Heydebrand und der Lasa, and Elard von Oldenburg-Januschau, the latter a hard-bitten chip of the old block, who compared the *vox populi* to the lowing of cattle and was quite prepared, if necessary, to have the Reichstag closed by a squad of a lieutenant and nine men. Oldenburg not only inveighed against the Kaiser, he went to see him and spoke his mind freely, but without any success.

How bitterly opposed to the Kaiser individual Conservatives were can be seen from a later pronouncement by Gerhard von Bredow, a March nobleman, whose ancestor had already defended the first Hohenzollern in the March: "The Conservative party, ever loyal to its King, is, alas, tied to this mentally abnormal man and so shares in great measure the blame for the disgrace of the monarchy. . . . Had Wilhelm II been placed under tutelage twenty or thirty years ago, as was quite justifiable and recommended on medical grounds, many today would, I imagine, be thinking . . . *not* about a Republic!"

61. THE QUESTION OF COLONIES

AFTER THE READJUSTMENTS effected during 1906–1907 in the Government departments, the Colonial Section of the Foreign Office was transformed into the Colonial Office. The Hereditary Prince Ernst zu Hohenlohe-Langenburg—known as Erni in Court circles—was selected for the post of Secretary of State in the new office, but although he had for some time conducted the business of the old Colonial Section, he was not nominated, since the Center party looked on him as an adversary.

Apart from the Hanse towns the German public showed little interest in the colonial question. The feeling in the Reichstag proved to be equally indifferent. First of all it had been upset by some little scandals concerning Jesko von Puttkamer, the Governor of the Cameroons, and then there had been the disclosure of the conditions prevailing in the Colonial Section. It turned out that certain Privy Councilors in that section had been carrying on fierce feuds against one another in the press, each trying to watch his own interest with regard to those from whom he received commissions—heavy industry or various banks.

Even in the Hanse towns people were trying to reckon up the cost of developing a desert like Namaraland in German Southwest Africa, and how long it would be before the money commenced to flow back. Investments like that could only mean more taxation to come. The fear of this alone was sufficient to deter the pro-Colonial and make him adhere to the party that refused to have anything to do with throwing money away on "Hottentot Land."

As a true Conservative Bismarck had also been opposed to the acquisition of colonies. He considered it justifiable only if such territories could later on be used as bargaining counters.

However, as the evolution of Germany into a Great Power progressed, interest in colonies slowly increased. As the Kaiser said afterward, "Interest brought with it the instinctive and justified feeling that the growth of the Reich favored at the same time its widening at the base—and that implied possession of colonies. Only thus could the drifting away of the people into foreign countries—which meant abandonment of their Fatherland—be prevented."

The Norwegian writer Knut Hamsun took up, at a later stage, this question of German expansion. "Seventy million Germans are living packed closely together, and they see how Frenchmen and Englishmen enjoy a superfluity of land and soil. Is it to be wondered at that they say 'Give us some! We need it for our hunger!' " Hamsun saw in the overpopulation of Germany the main cause of the first World War.

France, even more than England, had always looked on German colonial expansion as an invasion of her own rights. Had the German Reich renounced colonies—and her fleet—a good accommodation with England would probably have become thinkable. But in that case Germany, confined entirely to the Continent, would have been compelled to look around for possibilities of expansion there. That would have been virtually synonymous with war.

In a conversation with Major Niemann, the Kaiser said afterward, "Either we went in for world politics, in which case our enterprises in East Asia and the Near East were necessary, or we did not, in which case we should have had to stay at home and export our people, as we used to do so lavishly before the foundation of the Reich. There was no middle course!"

62. BERLIN—BAGHDAD

PRUSSIA HAD HAD friendly relations with Turkey as far back as the days of Frederick the Great. In the reign of Friedrich Wilhelm III she had played the part of mediator in the Russo-Turkish War of 1829 and the Sultan was indebted to the Prussian General von Müffling for securing easy terms in the Treaty of Adrianople. Afterward, the young General Staff officer Helmuth von Moltke had been active in Constantinople as Turkey's first military adviser. After Moltke there followed Colmar von der Goltz and Liman von Sanders.

From his youth the Kaiser had been interested in Turkey, and soon after his accession he had gone to Constantinople as a guest of the Sultan. He was then accompanied by Count Herbert Bismarck, whereby it was intended to make clear from the beginning that the form of the *rapprochement* desired by the Kaiser would be acceptable to the Reich's Chancellor.

Napoleon had once called Constantinople the "Key of the World." If that was no longer true at the beginning of the twentieth century, the city represented an important starting point for communications leading to a hinterland as yet undeveloped economically.

Thanks to a concession granted by Sultan Abdul-Hamid II, and with the help of the Deutsche Bank, construction of the railway from Haidar Pasha to Eskisehir was begun in the years 1888–1891, with the intention of extending it as far as Baghdad and the Persian Gulf. Commercial circles in Germany originated the catchword "Berlin-Baghdad," a password under which a brisk trade was soon to develop between the Reich and the Near East.

Neither Russia nor England could or would tolerate such a German advance into their spheres of interest in that quarter. A Russo-British defensive agreement was concluded, by which the two signatories, hitherto keen competitors, engaged themselves to pool their resources in combating the German intrusion and excluding its extension into the territories between the Black Sea and the Persian Gulf, which they looked on as vital to themselves. But London and St. Petersburg were too late. German influence, encouraged by Abdul-Hamid, was already too strong in Anatolia and Mesopotamia to be eliminated.

This German success served to increase St. Petersburg's antipathy to Wilhelm II. When the Kaiser read the reports sent in by his Ambassador, he decided to invite the Czar to a conference at Swinemünde. Nicholas II accepted the invitation, but this time he was in a different frame of mind from that of Björkö. The Kaiser, though quite a heavy sea was running, had himself put on board the Czar's yacht, where the rails were lined with Russian officers and saluting seamen. In spite of the heavy seas, the Kaiser, in Russian uniform, managed to climb up the gangway and arrived on deck, fairly dry, to greet the Czar cheerfully.

Without having much opportunity for private conversation with him, the Czar had to stand by and watch how all the interest was centered on his cousin, how he was admired and listened to by those around him, who enjoyed his pleasant manner of talking. Cousin "Nicky" stood by, very vexed and determined to weigh anchor at the earliest possible moment.

After this interview at Swinemünde both the participants had the impression that now, finally, the linking thread between their countries was definitely worn through. Nothing ever altered this, though for another decade attempts were made to knot and tie together this torn thread.

63. THE DOWNFALL OF EULENBURG

WHENEVER THE KAISER was at home and remained settled for a while he led an exemplary family life. It was a patriarchal family life, not very different from that of a well-to-do gentleman's home in the March. The Kaiser was the sole authority in the family;

he alone decided, lectured, preached, consented or forbade. He showed solicitude regarding the matrimonial affairs of his seven children, putting political considerations on one side and personal inclinations to the fore. His children must be happy!

Crown Prince Wilhelm elected for a love match. When he married the Duchess Cecilie of Mecklenburg the union was acclaimed as being just that. It reminded people of another Mecklenburg Duchess who many years ago came to Prussia as heiress to the throne —Queen Luise. When Crown Princess Cecilie gave birth to a son (Friedrich Wilhelm) in 1906 Wilhelm II became a grandfather for the first time.

Though there was no issue of the marriage of the second son, Eitel-Friedrich, three other sons, all of them married to German princesses, saw to it that there were descendants. These were the Princes Adalbert, August Wilhelm and Joachim, of whom the two last named were, like their elder brother Eitel-Friedrich, unhappy in their married life.

While the sons of Wilhelm II and the Kaiserin Auguste Viktoria and afterward their daughter (Viktoria-Luise) all married members of princely German houses, Prince Oskar (the Kaiser's fifth son) chose his bride from the nobility of Mecklenburg. She was the Countess Ina von Bassewitz, who was first raised to the rank of Countess von Ruppin, and later to that of a Princess of Prussia. Theirs was a happy marriage.

The Kaiser's brother, Prince Heinrich of Prussia, chose Princess Irene of Hesse for his wife, and thereby renewed the link connecting the House of Brabant with the Hohenzollerns.

If many people saw in Prince Heinrich a so-called Heir-in-Reserve to the Crown, like the brother of Frederick the Great of the same name, and expected that for reasons of opportunism he might set himself up to oppose his brother the Kaiser, they were disappointed. Prince Heinrich unreservedly acknowledged the rights of his elder brother and always regarded himself as his brother's subject. Significant in this respect was his formal style of address to his "Illustrious Kaiser, Mighty King and Ruler, Glorious Brother." Entrusted with the building of the German fleet, he gave himself up to the task, without, however, especially distinguishing himself. When, at the orders of his brother, he had to fulfill a mission in London, New York and East Asia, he was personally liked for his courtesy and modesty. Many who knew him well rated him higher as a man than as an admiral. His mental capacity was not conspicuous, as he freely admitted himself. He felt at his best in the family circle, in the calm atmosphere of his Hemmelmark estate near Eckernförde, where he lived a retired and frugal life, occupying himself now and again with bookbinding, a handicraft he had learned in the school at Cassel.

The Kaiser's household has also been described as frugal. In 1888 the Civil List was raised in consideration of the allowances payable to the two widowed ex-Kaiserins, and the birth of five children. Afterward, except for entertainment allowances, there were no additions worth noting. In the estimates for the household there were no secret accounts for *maîtresses en titre* as in the time of Friedrich I (1657–1713), and nothing for paramours as with Friedrich Wilhelm II (1744–1797), instead of which there were thick volumes of accounts for many and costly journeys.

Despite the nonexistence of a *maîtresses* account there were rumors that would have it that the Kaiser had had tender spots for some of the ladies about the Court and had been on terms of intimacy with them. Included in the list were the names of the elegant Czech Princess zu Fürstenberg, the brunette Duchess of Ratibor, Princess Daisy of Pless ("pretty as a picture"), of British birth, the willful Princess Henckel von Donnersmarck, the charming Venetian Contessa Morosini, and the American-born Countess Sierstorpf, as well as the delightful singer Geraldine Farrar.

At a lucky moment it was possible to question the Kaiser at Doorn as regards the correctness of such rumors. He laughed aloud, but it was an angry laugh. "This stupid trash," he said, "can be believed by nobody, at any rate by nobody who knew me. Those stories originated with reports invented by journalists in search of something interesting during the dull season. They knew so little about the life at my Court that they were incapable of understanding what nonsense they put into their filthy publications. Let us take the good Contessa Morosini—on a visit to Venice I was alone with her in a State gondola during a moonlight Serenata—that is to say, we were alone except for gondolieri in gala dress standing one in front and one behind us, in full view. Our gondola was escorted by others, full of German and Italian secret police, who never took their eyes off us for even a moment. After the Serenata I saw her again in the Palazzo

Rezzonico, at the ball the city of Venice gave in my honor. There were about three hundred people there. Now I ask you, even if I had wanted a love affair, how could I have gone about it in those surroundings?

"And then there was another silly story, about Frau Farrar, the concert singer, coming to me in the royal box during the performance to offer me *une demi-heure du berger*. Now every Berliner knows that in the Opera House the passage from the stage to the auditorium runs on the opposite side of my box, that is to say, behind the box of the general manager. So the lady would have had to run—presumably scantily attired—round the auditorium, past the box attendants, the cloakroom attendants, the Court servants and the police on duty, to reach the anteroom of my box in the dress circle. There she would have run into her chief, Count Botho Hülsen-Haeseler, and not only into him but into my whole suite. It is really too stupid to take notice of such journalistic twaddle, or of these reporters' canards. They ought to be shot—I mean, of course, the canards!"

Undue prominence was given to these rumors, because accusations of a different kind were being made openly against the Kaiser, more especially in foreign countries. He was accused of abnormal propensities, on the strength of allegations made by certain persons of his entourage.

The Kaiser, about whose "staid Old-German married life" Kiderlen had cracked his worst jokes, was—and the fact is beyond all doubt—entirely unsuspecting when he heard of the propensities of some of his gentlemen, especially in the case of his friend Philipp Eulenburg.

In 1891 the publicist Maximilian Harden had used intermediaries to offer to the Kaiser his services against Bismarck. The offer had been rejected in a form that admitted of no misunderstanding. Thereupon Harden placed himself at Bismarck's disposal. The old Chancellor was aware of Harden's abilities as a publicist and had even made use of them on occasions. Bismarck and Harden, Harden and Bülow, but above all Holstein and Harden, were each of them alliances of a dangerous kind, dangerous for anyone against whom they chose to turn, and particularly dangerous for Wilhelm II, who had spurned Harden's offer.

So it was pique that was at the bottom of the attacks that began against Prince Philipp zu Eulenburg, the intention being to strike at the Kaiser through him, and to disgrace Wilhelm II in public.

On November 17, 1906, there appeared in the *Zukunft,* of which Harden was the editor, an article headed *Praeludium* (a Prelude). This curtain raiser began thus: "Today I point openly to Philipp Friedrich Karl Alexander Botho, Prince zu Eulenburg and Hertefeld, Count of Sandels, as being the man who with indefatigable zeal has striven, and still strives, to insinuate into the mind of the Kaiser the idea that he is called upon to reign alone, and that as sole dispenser of grace and favor, he should look for light and implore aid only from the Realm above the clouds from whose heights the Crown was bestowed upon him, and that he should feel himself answerable to that Realm only. The pernicious activities of this man shall at any rate not be carried on in the dark."

This was a declaration of war, and to do Harden justice, it was addressed, not to the man himself, but to the most influential adviser of Wilhelm II.

In the presence of the author, Harden spoke as follows to Viktor Hahn, publisher of the *National-Zeitung*, "If Eulenburg had confined himself to utilizing his artistic talents, as general manager of the Court Theater, for instance, then I should not have bothered about him and there would have been no attack on him in the columns of the *Zukunft!*"

Again, if Eulenburg had been more conciliatory toward Harden, or been brutal like Holstein, or crafty like Bülow, this prelude would not have been followed by the tragedy that occurred. But he felt so disgusted with Harden that he declined to have any dealings with him, or to try to come to any arrangement.

It was not until Act I began in the *Zukunft* with revelations of Eulenburg's private life that the Crown Prince decided to enlighten his father. He did so in the course of a walk in the garden of the Marmor Palais. The Kaiser was so shocked that he was unable to utter a word, but "with a set, despairing face," signaled for the car and drove back to the Schloss.

Having thought it over for a while, the Kaiser decided to intervene. He was determined to have the matter cleared up, so he insisted on Eulenburg's taking proceedings for libel against Harden. But it was already too late! A Munich editor stated in public that Harden had accepted hush money from Eulenburg, and Harden was now taking proceedings against that editor! Eulenburg was brought into the case as a witness and had to give evidence on oath. After that the Public Prosecutor, at Harden's instigation, laid a charge of perjury against him.

Thus exposed before the whole world, the accused was now disowned by his Imperial friend with the intimation that his presence at Court was not desired until further notice. General von Hahnke even wished to divest him of the Order of the Black Eagle.

In the course of the trial dramatic incidents followed one after another until catastrophe came with Eulenburg's arrest. The last act began with the deployment of 145 witnesses. The accused was so exhausted by excitement that he had to be removed to a hospital. No verdict was returned, for Eulenburg, stricken and infirm, was declared incapable of following the proceedings and in the end had to spend twelve solitary years in Liebenberg, awaiting death.

Together with Eulenburg fell a whole file of other personalities of the Court who were accused of the same failings. Among them were a Prussian Prince; an A.D.C., Count Hohenau; Count Kuno Moltke; Count Wedel, Master of Ceremonies; and Count Lynar.

Harden's work was done. He had no need to trouble about Bülow, for he had already had his share of worry, as another scribbler had accused him of having the same propensities as Eulenburg. In the ensuing court case Bülow was only able to clear himself, thanks to his persuasive rhetoric. Without turning a hair, and to remove the last trace of suspicion from himself, he had signed the paper which assured the downfall of his friend Eulenburg. He dared not hesitate. It might look strange and cost him his career.

In this way Bülow evaded the danger that hung over him, together with *l'Eminence grise*, who was from the outset safeguarded by being Harden's ally. The old Privy Councilor could contentedly register his new triumphs—the dangerous Eulenburg eliminated, Bülow warned, and the Kaiser's prestige damaged. The victor in the Eulenburg case was not Harden, but Fritz von Holstein.

64. THE KAISER'S ATTITUDE TO ART AND SCIENCE

HAD EULENBURG become general manager of the Royal Court Theater that post would not have been badly filled. Since the death of Count Volko Hochberg, Count Botho von Hülsen-Haeseler of the Guards Cuirassiers had been in control of the playhouse. He was not a man of genius, but he was passionately fond of the theater, an amateur producer, a courtier and an officer all in one. What made him especially suitable for the post was his capacity for coping calmly with the whims of prima donnas and the megalomania of tenors. He knew how to deal with the intrigues and jealousies of the stage, the tears, the fainting fits and hysterical outbursts. Over and above all such tantrums stood his imperturbable Excellency, with his pouchy cheeks and his remarkably soothing voice, ever ready with his gentle irony to hold the company together.

Under him, in the Court Opera, there matured artists who came to be numbered among the world's finest.

At rehearsals of plays which were ordered by the Kaiser, such as *Kerkyra* and *Sardanapal*, Count Botho was himself stage manager; the performance of the latter was billed as "With the assistance of the German Oriental Society," or even of His Majesty in person. Driven by curiosity, the Berliners went to see this artistically worthless production (at a cost of 60,000 gold marks), and facetiously expressed the opinion that *Sardanapal* was not a ballet but an opiate.

Interventions such as this by the Kaiser in the repertoire of the Court Opera did not redound to its advantage. Nor did Leoncavallo's *Der Roland von Berlin*, commissioned by the Kaiser, meet with favor, and it had to be taken off soon after the first night.

When Camille Saint-Saëns came to Berlin his *Samson and Delilah* was presented as a gala performance. But he declined the Kaiser's offer of a commission to compose a work for Berlin.

The Kaiser could not appreciate the music of Richard Strauss. After the Berlin première of *Salome* he remarked to Hülsen, "That's a nice snake I've reared in my bosom!" Still less did the Kaiserin appreciate *Salome*. Her religious sentiments made her dislike it, but she was not able to secure its removal from the arranged program. She did, however, succeed when she insisted that after the finale the symbolic Star of Bethlehem should rise on the stage sky.

It was the constant intervention of the Kaiser in artistic matters that, above all else, brought the criticism of the intelligentsia into the field. They advised him in the future to put himself into the limelight; he knew a great deal about that. It was, of course, a brilliant sight when the theater was full for a special occasion. Then the general manager would appear in the center box with his staff of office and give the three raps that were the signal for everyone to rise from their seats, on which the Kaiser entered the royal box. The wags of Berlin maintained that he wore a uniform appropriate to the particular opera being performed—that of the Guard Rifles for *Freischütz*; that of an Admiral for *The Flying Dutchman*.

At concerts in the Schloss, the Kaiser confined himself to the part of auditor. In clubs he now and again wielded the baton, in the family circle he would play the *Hymn to Aegir*, but he avoided taking part in any public musical events. Grieg, whose acquaintance he had made during his Scandinavian cruises, and the celebrated violinist Joseph Joachim, with his quartet, were often invited to give concerts in the Schloss.

Unfortunately, Wilhelm II exerted no good influence on the formative arts. The artists whom he furthered, deserved, as a rule, neither recognition nor support. Speaking in his usual inflated language he declared, "I am filled with pride and joy by the work of the artists who execute such sublime things. It shows that the Berlin School of sculptors stands so high that scarcely any finer can have been known, even in the days of the Renaissance."

Reinhold Begas, the sculptor, was at that time *persona grata* to His Majesty. To him was entrusted the Neptune Fountain (the subject of much sarcastic comment) and also the statue to be erected to "Wilhelm the Great" in front of the Schloss. Badly sited, with its wild lions and its sprawling allegorical figures, it entirely failed to express the modest character of the old monarch.

Although conscientious artists such as Eberlein and Uphues had worked on the shaping of the *Siegesallee* (which the Berliners call *Puppenallee*, or Doll's Avenue), it was still an absurdity; a monument should commemorate outstanding persons, but not a string of mediocrities who, in their time, ruled the March Brandenburg, and not always to its benefit. As it is, quite the most artistic of the individual monuments is that erected to a Margrave, the Wittelsbach Otto the Idle, who scarcely ever set foot in Brandenburg and would greatly have preferred to sell it. It often happened that for want of authentic evidence the portrait likeness could not be reproduced, and thus it comes that a medieval Margrave was given the features of . . . Philipp Eulenburg! The artistic qualities of the *Siegesallee* were grossly overrated by Wilhelm II. "The impression it makes on strangers is quite overpowering. Everywhere it inspires profound respect for German sculpture. Long may it stay at that height and may my grandchildren, and the great-grandchildren, whom I might one day have, find such masters as these at their service!"

The marble abominations that shot up like mushrooms in the Tiergarten attained the nadir of artistry in the "Marble Quarry" (provocative of many gibes) by the Brandenburger Tor. These are the monuments to the parents of Wilhelm II—the Kaiser Friedrich and the Kaiserin Victoria, together with two fountains. In the statues everything is rendered with the utmost banality—from helmet spike to spurs, from the crown on the sleek Victorian coiffure to the heels of the shoes. When the sculptor, Adolf Brütt, objected to having to represent *sitting* eagles with outstretched wings on these monuments, because that was not the way an eagle would naturally sit, he received orders "from Supreme Authority" that "Prussian eagles, even when sitting, must be represented as if they were flying."

Among other rigidly specified commissions was that for the statue of the Kaiserin Auguste Viktoria (while she was still living!). The unfortunate artist, already hampered by many restrictions, had to represent her corseted and tight-laced. On the other hand, the bronze Amazon by Louis Tuaillon, on the Museum Island, between two arms of the Spree, was regarded by the Kaiser as being an artistic masterpiece. Other talented sculptors never got such commissions and felt themselves slighted by the Art Dictator Wilhelm. Among these were Adolf Hildebrand and Max Klinger.

The Kaiser also used to interfere with the architects in their plans. Paul Wallot and his Reichstag building fared worst. Because of the Kaiser's continual objections and his insistence on alterations, the edifice when completed was pronounced to be "patchy, mutilated and disfigured."

Other buildings growing up in the capital continued to show the characteristics of the *Gründerzeit* (years of reckless building and promotion); this was particularly noticeable in the large dwelling houses in the old West Quarter, with their elaborate, high, narrow frontages, heavy ornamented gables, marble front steps and dark rooms that led like a tunnel into a back yard.

A countercurrent to the revival of the "German Renaissance" and the ornamental *Jugendstil* was first started by the architect Alfred Messel, who founded the Style of Practicality (*Stil der Sachlichkeit*) in Berlin with his Pergamon Museum and Wertheim's stores.

At an early age Wilhelm II became acquainted with painters through his mother, who herself painted. In 1871 he attended the studio of Anton von Werner, and was encouraged by him to take up painting. He had often tried his hand at sketching. The drawing named "Peoples of Europe, guard your most holy possessions," ascribed to him and intended to be presented to the Czar, is well known. It depicts the Archangel Michael gathering the peoples of Europe under the Cross, preparatory to leading them forth to combat the Yellow Peril.

The Kaiser showed special favor to the draftsman and painter Adolf Menzel. He looked on him as the right man to expound the glory of his ancestor Frederick the Great and of Prussian history in general. He loaded Menzel with honors so that the little man became an Excellency and a Knight of the Order of the Black Eagle. When he died the Kaiser insisted upon walking behind his coffin, a tribute never before paid to anyone other than a Prussian General Field Marshal such as old Moltke.

The Kaiser showed very little appreciation of Menzel's successors, or even of Max Liebermann's work. For Wilhelm II the German Modernists, and especially the Futurists, were representative of "the art of the gutter."

The Kaiser himself was often painted, one of the best portraits being that by the fashionable Hungarian artist Fülöp László. Most of these pictures were intended for impressive display and were presented to ministries, town halls, clubs and officers' messes. Waldersee deprecated this as savoring of undue self-assurance and thought it quite improper to hang a portrait of the Kaiser, in the uniform of the Bodyguard, in the reception room of the German Embassy in Paris, for only the future could show if such an apotheosis was justified. "If," he said, "Wilhelm II accomplishes great things, it will be an outstanding piece of portraiture . . . but if it be the other way about, it will simply look ludicrous."

Eckardstein in London agreed with Waldersee's views and reminded the *Welt-Marschall* of how the French General Dupont had stood examining the picture and shaking his head, only to declare, *"Pour vous dire la vérité, ce portrait-là, c'est une déclaration de guerre."*

Even as many of the buildings in the reign of Wilhelm II possessed only mediocre artistic value, the numerous restorations of old castles were unsuccessful. The Kaiser's passion for supplementing and reconstructing went so far that (within the bounds of possibility) *everything* must be restored. Thus the "enemy of ruins" had the Hohkönigsburg in the Vosges rebuilt to the plans of Bodo Ebhardt, with the result that it seemed to have been constructed from a child's box of bricks. Again, the fortified Roman camp of Salburg was reconstructed in the Taunus and dedicated to the Emperor Hadrian by Wilhelm II—as a colleague.

While the Kaiser showed interest in sculptors and painters, he neglected poets and writers. All that attracted him in literature lay in the past, such as the Bible-Babylon investigations and the new version of the medieval "Wilhalm." Gerhart Hauptmann only received a Red Eagle, IVth Class, not even a Schiller prize, which the Kaiser refused both to him and to Ludwig Fulda. He would have nothing to do with Fulda because of his play *Talisman*. On the other hand, he awarded the Schiller Trophy to Kadelburg, a writer of farces, after seeing a performance of *Familientag* (*Family Reunion*). Ernst von Wildenbruch (a descendant of Prince Louis Ferdinand of Prussia) also received the same trophy. While his "Hohenzollern" pieces were inspired by the desire to idealize their subjects, their lack of realism and their evasion of debatable matters made them unimpressive. They did not go down.

The Court poetry of Joseph Lauff was riddled with false sentimentality. His feeble verse was crammed with fulsome flattery of the Kaiser, and moreover was written in miserably bad German. As he was very quickly ennobled with the "von" for his activities, he soon encountered competition, which he strove to outbid in toadyish servility, beginning his "poems" with words such as:

"The German eagle strikes his claws in fast . . . !"

"Our Leader watches . . . !"

"Ardently beloved Kaiser . . . !"

"Indefatigably there cares for thee . . . !"

Wilhelm II cannot be spared the reproach of having tolerated this Court poetry with all its extravagances. By doing so he encouraged these people to push their sycophancy to the very limits of toleration.

If the Kaiser did not think much of the Germanists and accepted the old dictum that they were "the best enemies of true German literature," he had great regard for Professor Erich Schmidt of the Berlin University and often used to attend his lectures. Other teachers at the university, such as the incorruptible Heinrich von Sybel and the self-willed Heinrich von Treitschke, did not share that honor. On the other hand, Professor Theodor Schiemann ranked as a special favorite. In university circles this preference was not altogether understood, because as a historian he was alleged to be ill-informed, as a politician he was said to be partial and as a writer he expressed himself in clumsy language.

The Kaiser's proposal to place the technical high schools on a level with the universities had at first been keenly opposed by the latter. But the Kaiser would not give way, for he rightly saw that the new century would be lived, as he had himself declared, "under the sign of the motor," and that technology would soon be advancing with such rapid strides that study of it must be placed in the forefront. In the end he was able to get his projects adopted and he also succeeded in obtaining for heads of technical high schools the same rights of presentation to the Upper Chamber (*Herrenhaus*) as those enjoyed by rectors of universities.

The founding of the Kaiser Wilhelm Society is likewise to be ascribed to his initiative. From it have come scholars who became famous in all branches of science. Several have been awarded Nobel Prizes.

However, the Kaiser's activities, spread in so many different spheres, meant that his knowledge could be only superficial and his judgment that of an amateur. His enemies were not unjustified in declaring that during his reign art and literature degenerated into shallow sentimentality, bombastic hero worship, a virtuosity of faddists with a passion for sensationalism. "Our art," said one of the most prominent members of the academy, "is only a circus trick confined to strict limits by training."

The avowedly conservative Pastor Naumann, after making a careful survey of all these various activities of the Kaiser, came to the following conclusion: "The Kaiser presents the Friedrichshain with a design for its fountain. He is not only Supreme War Lord, Supreme Agent of foreign policy, Supreme Guardian of industry, commerce and agriculture, Supreme Bishop of the Federated Evangelical Church, but also Supreme Director of science and Supreme Judge of art. At his feet kneel Ares, Athene, Poseidon, Apollo and all the Muses. He finds time for all the affairs in these fields and reduces the leading authorities to mere assistants. Even if the Kaiser should be right, which is possible, but by no means certain, the Kaiserdom has lost much prestige owing to its authority being stretched to cover petty and questionable actions."

65. THE KAISER AND THE ROMAN CATHOLIC CHURCH

WILHELM II never relaxed his efforts to convince the twenty millions of his subjects who were of the Roman Catholic faith that the days of the *Kulturkampf* were over and that he, though professing a different creed, was ever ready to stand as defender of theirs. So energetically indeed did he take up the cause of the German Roman Catholics that the Papal Curia was unable to refuse him full recognition. Commendation such as this, coming from the Vatican, aroused suspicion in Protestant circles, where already there was talk of the Kaiser's being "a Catholic in disguise."

Discussing this afterward in Doorn, the Kaiser said, "A reconciliation with the Curia was all the more necessary because the opposing Confessions, as they affected politics, were endangering more and more, year by year, the national stability of both our eastern and western provinces."

This reconciliation presented little difficulty to the Kaiser. The medieval mysticism surviving in the Roman Catholic Church attracted him as to that time in which the dignity of kingship was, as he had expressed it in one of his speeches, "encircled by a religious nimbus." Similar lines of thought had been familiar to his father, as well as to the Kaiserin Augusta, whose leanings toward Catholicism had been no secret.

This accommodating attitude of the Kaiser's was eagerly and thankfully acknowledged by the Roman Catholic Church, though occasionally its gratitude was expressed in truly strange ways. Thus a stone effigy, poised above the portal of the cathedral in Metz, in the midst of a concourse of saints, was given the features of Wilhelm II. But such glorifications of the Kaiser were by no means exceptional in the Protestant churches of Germany. In Lüneburg there was a stained-glass window in a church depicting the Emperor Heinrich II in a kneeling posture and wearing, not his flowing red-golden beard, but the upturned mustaches of Kaiser Wilhelm II!

Like this Emperor Heinrich II, who had been canonized by the Pope as being "the father of all monks," the Kaiser was a protector of the monasteries, especially those of the Benedictines. In them he saw the prophets and diffusers of Western culture.

In 1901 the Kaiser showed himself equally well-disposed toward the Benedictine monks of Maria-Laach. When he saw that their high altar had been entirely destroyed by fire, he at once declared himself ready to provide a new and more beautiful one. "It stands to reason that the high altar is my affair! Father Desiderius shall design one, and I will have it made in marble, porphyry, gilded bronze and mosaic. It shall be a memento of my visit to Maria-Laach!" (The memento—not at all beautiful—is now stowed away in the vault of the chapel.)

This friendly attitude toward the Church of Rome attracted the attention of the aged Pope Leo XIII, who expressed the wish to make the Kaiser's acquaintance. Wilhelm II paid three visits to this exceptionally shrewd man, the last just after Leo XIII had reached the age of ninety-three. The aged pontiff was still so alert mentally that he had a most excellent conversation with his temperamental visitor. After their first meeting the Pope knew how to handle him. For the next visit all the pomp of the Vatican was displayed—with cardinals, bishops, chamberlains, in full-dress vestments and uniforms, including the Noble Guards and the Swiss Guards in their picturesque costumes.

The Vatican was especially pleased with the last visit, the *Osservatore* in its enthusiasm going so far as to congratulate those Frenchmen who in 1871 had passed, with Alsace-Lorraine, under the rule of Germany, "whose valiant and intellectual Kaiser, no more than nominally a Protestant, extends his patronage to those Catholic martyrs banished by the *sans-culottes* from the Seine!"

The German publication *Germania* took the same line when referring to the "persecution of the Church in France." "How insignificant and dwindling is the respect accorded by world opinion to that conglomeration of place hunters and political rowdies that calls itself the French Government, compared with the sovereign authority enjoyed by our Kaiser all the world over, as a monarch, as a Christian and as a man. Therefore, throughout the Catholic world—and not excluding the true Catholics of France—his visit to the Pope will serve to increase people's kindly feelings toward our Kaiser."

After leaving the Vatican the Kaiser, in a telegram to Leo XIII, expressed his satisfaction that such excellent relations had been established with the Supreme Head of the Catholic Church: "It does my heart good to show how dear to me are those religious interests of Catholics which the Divine Providence has entrusted to me. Once more I pray Your Holiness to accept the assurance of my sincere affection."

Pope Pius X, who succeeded Leo XIII, was concerned to maintain these good relations with the Protestant Kaiser. So, on the occasion of the Crown Prince's wedding in Berlin, he sent him, by the hand of Cardinal Kopp, a present of a mosaic image, which Kopp handed over with the following address: "Having regard to the millions of Catholic subjects who in true love and affection look up to Your Majesty as their ever kindly father and just ruler, and in view of the exalted position of Your Majesty, whose influence makes itself felt from pole to pole, and who with firm but gentle hand strives to re-establish intercourse between the peoples on the everlasting principles of Christian order, and looking to the personal link of trustful relations that Your Majesty, with wise appreciation of the importance and blessing of peace in the churches, has constantly maintained with the occupant of the Papal chair as with the late

Pope Leo XIII, His Holiness is impelled to participate heartily and joyfully in today's high festival!"

Such words, coming from the mouth of Germany's oldest cardinal, could not fail in their effect upon the Kaiser. He sang the praises of the Prince-Bishop, called him his friend and "a simple, shrewd, but ingenuous German soul." He expressed his opinion of the Prior of Trier in similar brief terms, calling him "a bright and energetic young fellow."

He also had a high opinion of the German Bishops Simar, Schulte, Bertram, Thiel, Faulhaber and Hartmann. Moreover, he used to converse with and behave toward these Catholic dignitaries as one authority dealing with another. This was in flagrant contrast to his dealings with their Protestant opposite numbers, whose wranglings over dogma and lack of self-respect often proved repugnant to him. So the Abbot of the Monastery of Monte Cassino, Monsignore Krug, was marked out for treatment as a Prince, and the Cardinal Secretary of State in the Vatican, Mariano Rampolla, was awarded the Order of the Black Eagle. Two years later, Prince-Bishop Kopp, in the name of His Holiness, invested the German Kaiser with the Great Cross of the Order of the Holy Sepulcher.

Apropos of this, the *Leipziger Neueste Nachrichten* wrote in May 1905, and not without good reason: "One need not be a political prophet to arrive at the conviction that this decorating of the Kaiser is only an episode in a highly significant course of action, only a psychological speculation based on the character of a monarch whose fanciful imagination makes him a willing prisoner of that romanticism which derives as much from the idea of the Holy Sepulcher as from that mighty structure called the Papacy. We have known for a long time that Kaiser Wilhelm has built up an idealistic and visionary picture of the Roman Church in order to convince himself that Rome is as ready as he is to practice complete tolerance, and even to approach Protestantism in a spirit of conciliatory charity."

If the aged Leo XIII had been prompt to see how he should deal with the Kaiser in order to get his own way, that art was soon acquired by the princes of the German Catholic Church as well. Archbishop Fischer of Cologne proved the most adept of them all, for on every possible occasion he paid homage to "the sovereign that reigns by the Grace of God," or to "the exalted, glorious Imperial Master."

When the Kaiser, speaking at Aix-la-Chapelle in 1903, used the words, "He who does not set his life on the basis of religion is lost," the Archbishop of Cologne followed this up by stating in an address, "If the Pope and the Kaiser differ in many respects, we must admit that they have much in common. . . . This co-operation between the two greatest rulers of this present time becomes all the more important as the spirit of negation, destructiveness and subversion spreads more widely in our Fatherland."

The idea of the Fatherland reappeared a few months later when he commented on it in a pastoral letter, stating categorically, "We German Catholics love Rome and the Pope, but we also love our Fatherland and our people!"

This word "also"—the openly admitted preferment given to "Rome and the Pope" and the relegation of "Fatherland" to the second place—caused a number of Protestants to spring to arms, indignant at such a statement. Nevertheless, the Curia succeeded in securing from Reich's Chancellor Bülow the long-awaited consent to the return of the Jesuits to Germany.

The *quid pro quo* that Wilhelm II demanded from the Roman Catholic Church in return for such concessions had been expressed when taking his leave of the abbot and the monks in Beuron: "What I expect of you is support in my efforts to preserve religion for the people and to increase their respect for both throne and altar, so that in these stormy times the thrones of the Christian princes may be protected through the medium of the personality of Christ!"

66. WILHELM II AND FRANZ JOSEPH

IN JUNE 1908 the Emperor Franz Joseph celebrated the Diamond Jubilee of his reign amid expressions of sympathetic interest from all over the world. A survival from the long-past days of Metternich, the Emperor stood as the one remaining pillar that bore the weight of that already decrepit and tottering edifice—the Austro-Hungarian Dual Monarchy. When President Theodore Roosevelt was taking leave of him at Schönbrunn, the aged Emperor remarked, "In me you see the last European monarch of the old school!"

Scarcely ever seen in public, and entirely withdrawn from the world without, the seventy-eight-year-old Emperor lived on in the Schloss of his ancestress, the Empress Maria Theresa. There, in Schönbrunn, each and every day passed in accordance with the inflexible rules of the Spanish Court ceremonial that dated back to the days of Philip II. Like that Hapsburg ruler, Franz Joseph sought to hide himself behind a screen of etiquette. Life could menace him with no more terrors—he had had too many of them already. Maximilian shot in Mexico, his son Rudolf dead in horrible circumstances, the Empress Elisabeth in perpetual flight from herself, from Vienna and from the Emperor, whose very name was sufficient to agitate her. "Franz Joseph? What have I to do with him; he's only a sergeant major!" And in the end this restless, wandering Empress died by the dagger thrust of the Italian anarchist Luccheni.

The only person now capable of mitigating the loneliness of the old Emperor was Katharina Schratt, the Baroness Kiss von Ittebe, the former actress of the Hofburg Theater. Franz Joseph knew he could trust her as a confidante and break away from his benumbing restrictions while chatting with her in her house on the Gloriette-gasse.

In the Schönbrunn Schloss, that endless labyrinth of rooms, galleries and stairways, the absence of sound was alarming. The furniture was all covered, the chandeliers were veiled, and only a few rooms were in use. Through these there crept the old aides-de-camp, moving on tiptoe and conversing only in whispers. Something of the Napoleonic days, and of the time of the hapless Duke of Reichstadt, still seemed to breathe there. Through the empty State rooms wandered ghostlike the shadow of Schwarzenberg, who had inflicted on Prussia the humiliation of Olmütz. What a strange historical sequence of ups and downs had been the relations between those two Germanic lands, Austria and Prussia! Leuthen and Hochkirch; Leipzig and Olmütz . . . then Königgrätz!

The son of the victor at Königgrätz was now coming to Schönbrunn accompanied by the Federal princes of the German Reich and representatives of the Hanse cities, to greet Franz Joseph on this day of an exceptional Jubilee. It was a handsome gesture on the part of the Germans, impaired only by the fact that the predominance in power had shifted more and more in the last few decades from Vienna to Berlin.

A warm summer morning ushered in the day of Jubilee. The windows of the Imperial apartments in Schönbrunn were thrown open and the green sun blinds were lowered against the glare, so that within there was semidarkness, through which flickered only stray beams, dancing hither and thither. From without came a soft humming as of bees—gathered there by the Burgomaster were thousands of Viennese school children, who filled the place in front of the Schloss to do homage to their Emperor. And then their song burst forth. Meantime from faraway Mariahilf other music could be heard. It was that of the regimental bands at the head of the great ceremonial procession.

At the Western Railway Station preparations for the reception of the German princes had begun on the morning of the preceding day. The first to arrive were the archdukes in their open landaus with gilded wheels, each drawn by six black horses, the coachman high on his box and a footman standing at the back wearing a powdered wig. Following them came the black-lacquered carriages of the various suites. When all were present the General March was played, soon followed by the National Anthem—a signal that the Emperor Franz Joseph was approaching. An outrider led the way, then came the State coach, drawn at a slow trot by eight gray horses, with General von Bolfras, Master General of the Ordnance, riding as escort by the door and two footmen in richly laced black coats standing on the back platform. Behind the coach rode guardsmen in red, white and gold tunics with silver helmets, and next the Hungarian Life Guards, with leopard skins over their shoulders and tall white aigrettes on the calpac.

With his usual light and springy step (everyone in Austria imitated that walk, unconsciously) the old Emperor alighted from the coach, turning on his hips, which, like his whole figure, seemed to belong to a young ensign rather than to an old man. It was said and believed that two years before, when attending the Teschen maneuvers, he had ridden for hours on end, to the horror of his old A.D.C.s, who were nearly rolling off their horses from exhaustion.

His white tunic fitted him like a glove, the green plumes of his general's headdress fluttering in the breeze and making a striking contrast. At every step the Ram of the Order of the Golden Fleece swung to and fro on his breast like a pendulum.

Sprightly and smiling, but with a determined look in his porcelain-blue eyes, he strode down the lane kept open for him. His whiskers were silvery with only a touch of yellow at the edges, and formed thick bushy tufts at the level of the ears. His cheeks were surprisingly pink—but that was make-up and was belied by the wrinkles engraved on them by the passage of many decades.

The Emperor then took his stand at a point on the red-carpeted platform marked by a chalk line and the archdukes ranged themselves a pace behind him on either side. Those who were entitled to do so wore German uniforms and German decorations. Behind them were the dignitaries of State and Court.

The German royal train glided into the station and stopped exactly at the point indicated by an arrow. The steps were run into position and Wilhelm II appeared at the door. He walked quickly over to the old gentleman and greeted him heartily. This marked cordiality of the younger man was always noted with approval by Franz Joseph. The German Kaiser had always sincerely endeavored "to show the best side of himself when in Vienna; one has to give him credit for that."

Nevertheless, no real friendship came of it. In the eyes of the aged Emperor, who claimed that he alone was entitled to be Emperor in the Germanic lands, Wilhelm II seemed almost an intruding stranger. He was repelled by his "undignified vagaries" and his passion for speechifying. He disliked precipitate action and impetuosity.

Yet despite their fixedly different outlooks they had something in common. Both looked upon God as their only superior—Franz Joseph in his capacity of Apostolic King of Hungary and as King of Jerusalem, and the Protestant Kaiser as being the Head and Protector of his Church. Doubtless, too, the sense of the two Empires being linked by fate in a common destiny, with the consequent necessity of making common cause together, played the decisive part in bringing about the readiness of each to search for community of interests.

If, after the fall of Bismarck—despite all his grave suspicions of that Chancellor—Franz Joseph was a mistrustful observer of what happened in Berlin, he now had to admit that the word *Nibelungentreue* (fidelity like that of the Nibelungen) as applied to the policy of Wilhelm II was no mere empty phrase, and moreover he now saw that an old dictum of Bismarck's was assuming a fresh significance. "The continued stability of Austria-Hungary as a strong and independent Great Power is indispensable for Europe's equilibrium."

Wilhelm II was aware of a certain restraint in the Emperor's attitude to him, but owing to his optimistic temperament he would only see the friendly side in the other's behavior, so that he could truthfully say that "he had been treated by the Emperor Franz Joseph almost like a son." Besides the respect that he felt for the aged ruler, there was also his great admiration for the distinguished character of the Hapsburg Court, which he declared to be the most elegant in all Europe.

He well remembered coming to Vienna in 1873 with his parents when he was aged fourteen. They came for the World Exhibition, and had stayed in the little rococo Schloss in Hetzendorf. He had a particularly clear recollection of the Archduke Albrecht, the victor at Custozza, and of the beautiful Empress Elisabeth, who even at that time was so concerned for her slender figure that she lived only on meat juices and strawberries. He had also made the acquaintance of the Crown Prince Rudolf, who was about his own age. For Rudolf's wedding in 1881 he had again been in Vienna with his young wife, and had spent unforgettable days in the imperial capital. Afterward the two royal heirs, with their wives, had met again, in Vienna and in the Prague Hradcany and at the Kiraly Palota in Ofen, on which occasion he had met the Hungarian politician Count Gyula Andrássy. Despite these ceremonial visits the Crown Princess Auguste Viktoria never made friends with the Crown Princess Stefanie, nor was there any real cordiality in the relations between their husbands.

Later on, Wilhelm changed his opinion of the Austrian Crown Prince, influenced by certain disparaging reports that Rudolf had spread about him in an offensive way. "Rudolf was a stimulating, shrewd character, captivating because of his brisk vivacity, full of bubbling humor that was not, to be sure, devoid of a considerable element of sarcasm. We were both great lovers of nature and shared a passion for game shooting. Rudolf was, moreover, a knowledgeable zoologist, specializing in ornithology. To my regret, however, as time went by I could not help noticing that he paid no serious attention to religion. It was painful for me when he used to pour out his scoffing, caustic wit over the Church, the clergy and the simple beliefs of the countryfolk.

"There were other weaknesses of character, too, which I could not overlook, and so it came about that my original faith in him diminished and we drifted further and further apart. Add to this that I gradually came to realize how little store the Crown Prince inwardly set on the new German Reich and on the alliance of our two countries. In his heart he hated the idea of Prussianism more than anything else."

What further irritated Wilhelm was Rudolf's extraordinary nervousness and his undue sensitiveness, aggravated by his unhappy marriage. Joyless married life had also changed the Crown Princess Stefanie and left her benumbed. The Viennese called her "the chilly blonde"—and someone even named her "the volcano with an ice cap." Now Rudolf was dead. In his place there figured on that day of Jubilee, as Heir to the Throne, Franz Ferdinand of Austria-Este.

All the way from the station to Schönbrunn the streets were thickly lined by eager spectators. There were many uniforms to gaze at—staff officers in dark green, infantry in dark blue, Bosnians in light blue with a red fez, no longer Turkish troops and not yet Austrian, riflemen in pale green, Polish Uhlans, braided hussars, artillery in brown, dragoons with red breeches, officers with white gauntlets calling their commands to attention. This was the army of the Emperor Franz Joseph, trim and smart, as many-colored as the lands from which its soldiers were drawn.

The Emperor was himself a remarkable polyglot. He spoke most of the tongues of his many peoples, so that at maneuvers he was often able to intervene as an interpreter and overcome the difficulties caused by the different languages.

Another thing that gave the German observers serious cause for uneasiness was the extreme age of the generals.

Franz Joseph was no friend of changes or innovations. That applied not only to his generals but also to his civil servants. For that reason the old Emperor would at first have nothing to do with the "revolutionary" Karl Lueger when he had been elected Burgomaster of Vienna. "Handsome Karl," as the Viennese called him, was for the aged Emperor a sinister oddity like motorcars and aircraft.

Lueger had been at pains to ensure that the capital should present a worthy appearance during the Jubilee festivities. In particular, the Hietzing quarter, where Schönbrunn was situated, was profusely decorated.

The reception of the German princes at Schönbrunn provided an opportunity of displaying, in majestic good taste, the splendors and the opulence of the House of Hapsburg. The gates of the forecourt opened wide, military music burst forth and the carriages rolled up the drive to stop before the great flight of steps covered with blue carpet and lit by girandoles that outshone the daylight. The walls were hung with Flemish tapestries, crystal lusters hung from the ceilings, every table and chair was a precious object with a history of its own. For Schönbrunn is history crystallized.

By the windows, thickly curtained with fabric of golden silk, stood gentlemen-at-arms, halberd in hand, and between them were giant candelabra with innumerable wax candles that diffused the sweet scent of honeycomb.

Before the billiard-room door stood the Master of Ceremonies, with his long white staff, who had the folding doors opened, thus allowing a view of the dining table, resplendent with gold plate. Behind each chair stood a footman, and behind these the servers, bodyguards and runners.

At table the Emperor and the Kaiser sat opposite each other. In their toasts they gave assurances of inviolable friendship, which was especially essential in those days, for someone was at work, endeavoring to detach the Hapsburger from the side of Wilhelm II— Edward VII.

Franz Joseph had given a courteous reception to King Edward at Ischl in 1907 and must have heard from him how fatal it would be for him to remain in alliance with the fickle and unreliable Wilhelm II. The Dual Monarchy would inevitably be led into some dangerous situation and then it would be too late to free itself from the German snare. All the King's conjurations were, however, unavailing. The Emperor made it clear that he was not prepared to alter his attitude. His personal antipathy to King Edward may have played a decisive part in this. But he extended that antipathy to England as a whole, though he had never set foot in that country in all his life.

Despite his ill-success the English King referred to the old Emperor as "most distinguished and dignified." His opinion of the leading Minister, Baron von Aehrenthal, was quite different, and he called him "a slippery man." What prejudiced the King against Aehrenthal was the latter's desire that the Dual Monarchy should annex Bosnia and Herzegovina, which was in fact accomplished in 1908. This extension of territory had indeed been provided for at the Berlin Congress. Now, however, King Edward was opposed to it, and so also was his nephew the German Kaiser. Each opposed it for a different reason. King Edward wanted no increase of the power of Austria-Hungary—Wilhelm II only regarded the moment as inopportune for proceeding with the annexation.

Wilhelm II was thinking of Russia and Izvolski,[1] who had already uttered a warning, "The annexation of Bosnia and Herzegovina will inevitably bring about a severe conflict. War may perhaps not break out for five or ten years, but it will be inevitable."

In St. Petersburg it had been decided, after the defection of Bulgaria, to make Belgrade the main Slav strong point in the Balkans. The plan was to create a "Kraljevina Jugoslavija" which should extend between the Adriatic and the Aegean as far as the Danube and the Drave. For this reason Wilhelm II considered the annexation of Bosnia and Herzegovina as "untimely and likely to be disastrous." He feared also for his good relations with Turkey. "If my ally were to offend our friends the Turks we should be unable to protect them or even to support them. Instead of that, I should have to look on while England, and not I, advised and protected Turkey, proceeding moreover according to principles of international law that are formally indisputable." So, in Wilhelm's view, his task was to exert a restraining and appeasing influence on Vienna and to defer the annexation for as long as possible.

The festivities in Schönbrunn were not overshadowed by the appearance of these clouds in the political firmament. Wilhelm II was in high spirits and well pleased with everything; so, too, was Franz Joseph, who had long conversations with the Prince Regent of Bavaria and the King of Saxony, in which he was for the most part content to be a listener and, with his head slightly bent forward, only now and then interjected a "*So—so, so!*"

The German guests left Schönbrunn that same day, not wishing

[1] Alexander Petrovich Izvolski (1856–1919), Russian Foreign Minister from 1906 to 1910, when he went to Paris as Ambassador until after the outbreak of the first World War.

to cause inconvenience to the old Emperor. The security services breathed freely once more as the train with its load of German princes passed safely over the Austrian frontier. Although some anarchists had come into Vienna, unwilling to let such an exceptional opportunity slip, not a shot had been fired, not a bomb had been thrown.

Once the days of rejoicing were over, Franz Joseph boarded his royal train to move to quiet Ischl. He took with him Count Paar and his Court physician, Councilor Kerzl. In his saloon car he had a bed, a writing table, his favorite green armchair, his usual china and his brioches for breakfast just as in Schönbrunn.

A small altar stood at one end of the compartment. There the Emperor could give thanks to his God that this Jubilee was safely over.

67. THE NOVEMBER STORM

IN THE SUMMER OF 1907 King Edward decided that when making his annual visit to Marienbad for the cure he would break his journey at Wilhelmshöhe in order to have a talk with his nephew, the Kaiser. When toasts were exchanged, the King concluded his speech with these conciliatory words, "Your Majesty knows that my dearest wish is that none but the best and most cordial relations should exist between our two countries!"

The following day he arrived in Ischl for his second visit to the Emperor Franz Joseph. He was well aware of the old Emperor's antipathy to himself. All the more circumspectly did he seek for the best line of approach, and for the best way of inducing the Emperor to oppose the German plans for increased naval armaments. Franz Joseph, however, politely rejected the suggestion that he should intervene in this or any other of the affairs of the German Reich.

A year later, on August 11, 1908, King Edward again endeavored —this time in Friedrichshof—to persuade his nephew to reduce his program of naval construction and to put a stop to the competition in armaments. But Wilhelm II would not hear of it. He declared that he saw no reason for reducing his armaments. He was responsible for the German Reich's being able to defend itself, and it was his duty to see that it was capable of doing so. Thus disappointed, "Uncle Bertie" left the Taunus to try in one last visit to Ischl to persuade the old Emperor to abandon his German ally. Despite all his astuteness he was again unsuccessful.

Before his second visit to Ischl, King Edward had already (in June 1908) had a meeting with the Czar in Reval. He was then accompanied by Sir Charles Hardinge, Undersecretary of State for Foreign Affairs, and brought with him Admiral Fisher, Sir John French and other naval and military officers. At the interview the Czar had with him the Minister-President Stolypin, and Izvolski, the Minister for Foreign Affairs. The two parties had then recognized that the political situation called imperatively for action in common by Great Britain and Russia, so as to be armed against the danger threatening from the German Reich.

Both in Paris and in Brussels the King had soundings made as to how they stood regarding the new German armaments, and if, in case of danger, an alliance with Great Britain would be desired. This was the real commencement of what was often called the "encirclement" of Germany, by which King Edward chiefly hoped to be able to bring pressure to bear on Wilhelm II and his government. But the nephew in Berlin was not to be frightened in that way. Already (on May 29, 1908) he had addressed a number of officers on the Döberitz training ground in words intended less for them than for "Uncle Bertie": "Should it be true that Germany is to be encircled, I can only reply, 'Let them come; they will find us ready!' "

But what brought English feelings to the boiling point was the announcement in April of the new German Navy Bill providing for three more dreadnoughts, which would bring it almost up to the strength of the Royal Navy in that class of ship.

Admiral Fisher gave a warning against the fresh program of modern naval construction in Germany. This, coming from such an acknowledged authority, further increased the anger and nervousness of the English public. In order to appease public opinion the Government announced that the fleet and the Army would be reorganized. In the event of a Continental war an expeditionary force of 150,000 men would be provided.

These precautionary measures, however, did not suffice to placate the irate press. There was a general demand that the German Reich should be forbidden to build any more warships. Were that summons ignored, something would have to be undertaken on the lines of what Nelson had done in 1807, when he destroyed a hostile fleet sheltering in the nominally neutral harbor of Copenhagen. In other words, the German fleet should be "copenhagened," attacked and destroyed without a declaration of war.

The Kaiser, always proud that the English public should interest itself in his fleet, and be afraid of it, met this nervousness with scorn and irony. "The simplest solution would be either an entente or an alliance with us! The English would then be free from all their anxieties. And it is well enough known that we make good allies!"

When figures of German naval construction were produced in the British Parliament, figures that in Wilhelm II's opinion were incorrect, he turned to Bülow and got him to make out "a correct statement for the British, who had gone totally crazy!" The statement was as follows: "Our law provides for a fleet of forty ships of the line for 1918–1920. This strength has been laid down by H.M. the Kaiser and Admiral Tirpitz as amply sufficient and has been confirmed and passed into law by the Reichstag. No new supplementary law for 1912 or later is contemplated."

Taking the April Supplementary Bill into account, the situation as regards ships of the line would be, according to Wilhelm II: *In 1908*—Germany 22, England 59. *In 1914*—Germany 24, England 62.

To counter the continual attacks against himself made by the English papers, Wilhelm II wrote (on February 16, 1908) to Baron Tweedmouth, First Lord of the Admiralty, as follows: "It would be quite a simple thing for England to say: 'We have a world-wide empire and the greatest volume of trade in the world. To protect this we must have battleships and cruisers, as many as necessary, to ensure our superiority at sea. They must be built and manned for that.' That is an absolute right of your country and nobody would waste words about it. Whether it be a matter of sixty ships or eighty or one hundred makes no difference. Such an augmentation of your fleet power could never be questioned. However high might be the figure which you thought to be right, everyone here would accept it. But the Germans would be grateful, too, if their country were to be left out of the discussion, as it is annoying for them to be represented continually by the press of various opposing parties as the only danger and menace to England, while at the same time other countries are building ships and even fleets still bigger than Germany's."

Before this outburst of anger in England against the new Navy Bill, Wilhelm II, in the hope of bettering his personal relations with the Court of St. James, had suggested a visit by himself and the Kaiserin to Windsor. In the late autumn they left for England. Seven days in that ancient castle passed unexpectedly in complete harmony in company with "Uncle Bertie."

After his stay at Windsor the Kaiser had (on November 18, 1907) accepted an invitation from Colonel Stuart Wortley to Highcliffe Castle, near Bournemouth. In return for this hospitality the English Colonel was invited by the Kaiser to attend the German autumn maneuvers.

In the course of these maneuvers the English Colonel proposed, in order to allay the prevailing ill-feeling in England caused by the German naval armament, that he should publish the conversations that had taken place between them, and the Anglophile feelings expressed by the Kaiser at Highcliffe. Such a publication could not fail to make a good impression in Great Britain. Both Stuart Wortley and the Kaiser were solely concerned to better the relations between their two countries, and Harold Spender, brother of the editor of the *Westminster Gazette*, offered his services to them for the editing of the article. From the first it had been agreed that publication should be made in the *Daily Telegraph*, whose proprietor was a great friend of Wortley's.

Anxious to make no mistake, the Kaiser, having received the edited article at Rominten, forwarded it to Reich's Chancellor Prince Bülow at Norderney with a note to the effect that if the Chancellor agreed to the article's being published, he (the Kaiser) had no objection to its being printed in the *Daily Telegraph*. With the article and the accompanying note of the Kaiser, Councilor von Jenisch (who was a relation of Bülow's), in attendance on the Kaiser at Rominten, enclosed a letter which expressly pointed out that in any case the article must be strictly scrutinized.

Bülow, who was not at all pleased at being thus disturbed during his holiday and greatly preferred to wander through the dunes with his poodle Mohrchen, only glanced at the article and then handed it to von Müller, an Ambassador who was staying with him at his villa. Müller advised that the article be sent to the German Foreign Office, which Bülow did, with the delphic advice "to examine the enclosed article carefully, then to have it copied on separate sheets by hand (or better still, by typewriter) and with any desired corrections, additions or omissions inserted in the margin in the same writing." A copy of this was to be sent to the Kaiser at Rominten.

Thus, from the hand of the Kaiser and the Chancellor the article reached the Undersecretary of State Stemrich, who passed it to Councilor Klehmet. The latter understood his task to be to examine the article and its contents by verification of the facts stated therein and in the light of the latest information available in the Foreign Office. With only slight alterations the article was then returned by Stemrich to Bülow in Norderney.

The Reich's Chancellor, in holiday humor, let it lie about for several days and then sent it on to the Kaiser with a note that the contents had been examined by his Foreign Office and that there were no reservations to discuss as regards its publication in England.

On October 28, 1908, the article appeared in the *Daily Telegraph* in the form of an interview. In it the Kaiser sought to show that he had always treated England in a friendly manner, as he would prove by four examples—namely, that in the first place he had declined to receive the envoys of the Boers, who had been feted in Holland and in France; secondly, that during the Boer War he had likewise refused to "humble England to the dust" by intervening in that war side by side with Russia and France; thirdly, that in the black week for British arms in South Africa he had worked out a plan of campaign which, after examination by his General Staff, he had forwarded to his grandmother, and that it corresponded very closely with the plan successfully operated by Lord Roberts; and fourthly, that a powerful German fleet was necessary in order to have a voice in the solution of the Pacific Ocean question in the days that were coming and perhaps were not far off.

The effect of this publication was very different from what Wilhelm II had expected. The newspapers united in a demonstration of hostility to the Kaiser that could not have been surpassed and overwhelmed him with abuse. Even the German press, reproducing the article in the *Norddeutsche Allgemeine Zeitung*, spoke of "unnecessary provocation and making the German people look ridiculous." That otherwise indulgent judge, Sir Edward Goschen, considered that "it now seemed doubtful whether His Majesty the German Kaiser was of sound mind."

In the German Foreign Office everyone completely lost his head. The Chancellor Prince Bülow, the Secretary of State von Schön and his Undersecretary Stemrich all sent in their resignations. The Kaiser was utterly disconcerted. He thought he had safeguarded himself against all eventualities by having the article examined and passed by his Foreign Office. Now he found himself disavowed and left in the lurch by those who had agreed to its publication.

All his bitterness, however, was concentrated against England, whom he accused of being malignantly disposed toward him, and of having picked out only what she could distort and misinterpret. In his rage he cried out in English, "They're mad—mad—mad as March hares!"

Three days after the publication in the *Daily Telegraph* Bülow found it necessary, in view of the continued excitement in England, to give an explanation in the *Reichsanzeiger* in the form of a detailed statement as to how the talks with Colonel Stuart Wortley had come about. In regard to the publication the intentions of the Kaiser were entirely pacific. He (Bülow) himself, he mentioned casually, had known nothing about the article, but it was obvious that if he had read it he would never have permitted its publication. However, as Reich's Chancellor, the responsibility was his and he was prepared to bear the consequences.

In fact, of course, the article had twice been in Bülow's hands before it was printed. Moreover, he knew of the talks with Colonel Stuart Wortley, knew their tenor and knew the subjects that were discussed at Highcliffe Castle. He now declared that he could not remember what they were.

In the German Foreign Office no one doubted that Bülow had played false. Those who knew him well considered that he had deliberately doublecrossed the Kaiser. In Doorn the Kaiser expressed a very unfavorable opinion of Bülow, and when distressed by looking back on it, spoke most bitterly about his perfidious conduct at this time.

The sitting of the Reichstag on November tenth—thirteen days after the article had appeared in London—became something like the sitting of a People's Court of Justice, the "November Storm." All parties and groups, with the exception of the Center party and the Poles, had mustered their full strength. The questions on the Order Paper related solely to "the *Daily Telegraph* Affair." The atmosphere of the House was gloomy and depressed. The first few questions were enough to show that no party was prepared to tolerate any repetition of such blundering "in the All-Highest place."

In order to give members a clear explanation of events, the Chancellor began with the antecedents of the matter and how the article had come about. He then went on to its contents. He called the Kaiser's Plan of Campaign for Lord Roberts "a mere aphorism on the conduct of war." The Kaiser's references to the Pacific Ocean implied no threat to Japan. On the whole, no great importance attached to the Kaiser's performance in the *Daily Telegraph*—it was only "harmless chattering."

Summing up, the Chancellor made the following declaration: "Realization of the fact that publication of the conversations he carried on in England—which failed to produce the effect that His Majesty desired—has caused, even in our own country, profound disturbance and painful regret, will . . . lead His Majesty to observe more closely, even in private intercourse, that reticence which is equally indispensable in the interests of consistent policy and of the authority of the Crown."

Replying to an interruption from the Left, he then stated, "Were it not so, neither I nor any successor of mine could accept responsibility." Concluding his speech, the Chancellor repeated what he had already given out in the *Reichsanzeiger*—that the article was a grave political blunder, for which he himself was not to blame, but for which he nevertheless wished to assume responsibility.

The bourgeois parties showed they were little satisfied by Bülow's speech; it did not reassure them. The Social Democrats made noisy demonstrations and repeatedly called on the Chancellor to resign. The most disconcerted of all were the Conservatives, who received the Chancellor's explanation in silence. It was a black day for them and for the monarchy. In their anxiety about the further maintenance of the dynasty they adopted the course of addressing an open letter to the Kaiser.

In this, the "pillars of the Throne" complained that because of certain blunders that had involved serious consequences, the popular desire for a curtailment of the royal powers and of personal rule was gaining ground and that to call anyone *kaisertreu* (loyal to the Kaiser) today no longer meant a recommendation.

Commenting on this pronouncement, the Conservative *Kreuz-Zeitung* wrote, "Undoubtedly the accumulated wealth of monarchical sentiment is very great, but the richest legacy can be dissipated if it be managed irresponsibly." In the Federal Council there was talk of putting the Kaiser under tutelage, and his abdication was also considered (as is confirmed by Baron von Schön in his *Memoirs*).

While this strife about the monarchy was going on in the Reichstag, Wilhelm II was once more away on his travels. He shot deer with the Archduke Franz Ferdinand in Eckardsau; after that he spent a few days with the Emperor Franz Joseph at Schönbrunn; then went on to hunt foxes at Donaueschingen. In spite of the dramatic events in Berlin and London, he completed his program unconcernedly. For that he was blamed afresh, though probably he had unintentionally done the right thing. His presence in the capital might well have served only to increase the general turmoil and to provoke hostile demonstrations.

In order to give the Kaiser some diversion, his host in Donaueschingen, Prince Max Egon zu Fürstenberg, tried everything in the way of shoots, trips in the Black Forest, concerts and even a cabaret in which the Chief of the Military Cabinet, Count Dietrich von Hülsen-Haeseler, though his figure was that of a Cuirassier, participated as a ballet dancer in a short tulle skirt. After this performance the General was on his way to his dressing room . . . but he never got there. He fell dead behind the curtain. The atmosphere in Donaueschingen was none the better for this fatality.

On November sixteenth the Kaiser arrived in Potsdam and the following day Bülow went there to make his report. His attitude was strictly formal and official. The Kaiser was at first embarrassed and could not hide how disappointed he was in a man he had regarded as a friend and as "the ideal Chancellor." Bülow had disowned and betrayed him in the Reichstag—that is, in public. His anger at this was further inflamed by the fact that Bülow, in the course of his report, had not uttered one word of regret or excuse, but on the contrary had presented his master with a list of that master's own frivolous activities.

When the report was concluded, Bülow placed before the Kaiser, for signature, a communiqué for the press which he had prepared beforehand and brought with him. Quite confused, the Kaiser scarcely glanced at it and signed. Its contents were as follows:

"In the course of the audience given this day to the Reich's Chancellor, His Majesty the Kaiser and King heard a report by Prince von Bülow, which lasted for more than an hour. The Reich's Chancellor depicted the state of public opinion in Germany with regard to the publication of certain matter in the *Daily Telegraph*. Moreover, he explained the attitude he had adopted in dealing with the interpellation in the Reichstag.

"His Majesty received the statements and explanations of the Reich's Chancellor with great seriousness and made known his intentions thereon. While not influenced by what he regards as unjustifiable and exaggerated public criticism, he perceives that his principal task as Kaiser is to safeguard the consistency of the policy of the Reich while observing constitutional responsibilities. His Majesty the Kaiser therefore approved the action taken by the Reich's Chancellor in the Reichstag and assured Prince von Bülow of his unabated confidence."

After admissions, concessions and humiliations, he had to give an explicit assurance of confidence in the man, who carried the major share in the blame in connection with this *Daily Telegraph* affair.

As the Kaiser admitted afterward in Doorn, he suffered severe mental agony in that month of November 1908. If he had been able, while in Donaueschingen, to treat "the people in England who had gone off their heads" and "those chatterboxes in Berlin" as being of no great importance, an atmosphere had now developed in Potsdam which had hitherto been unknown in the New Palace. People spoke only in whispers; His Majesty was not to be seen, and when the Kaiserin emerged from her rooms she was observed to have been crying. It was only in a choked voice that she could give the most necessary orders.

A week after the publication in the press of Bülow's communiqué the Kaiser was due to make a speech in the Berlin Town Hall. He had the speech written for him by the Chancellor, and what had never happened before, he read it from his notes. In it there occurred this sentence: "Uprising clouds must never cast their shadows so as to fall between me and my people!"

Almost four months passed without the Kaiser and his Chancellor meeting otherwise than officially. The social intercourse between the Schloss and the Chancellor's palace was suspended. The Chancellor made only formal and ceremonious appearances. After what had happened, the Kaiser did not see why he should take the first steps toward a reconciliation.

At last, on March 11, 1909, Bülow himself requested an interview. In recalling the occasion the Kaiser stated, "I went with Bülow into the picture gallery of the Schloss and we walked up and down under the portraits of my ancestors, the battle scenes of the Seven Years' War, and the Proclamation of the Kaiser in Versailles. To my astonishment he harked back to the events of the previous autumn, and sought to explain his attitude. I took the opportunity of discussing with him the events of recent months. His frank speaking and his satisfactory explanations eased the tension. The result was that he remained in office. He then asked me if I would accept an invitation to dine with him that same evening at his palace, in order to show the world at large that all was once again in order. I did so. A gay evening, the obviously delighted Princess at her most charming and the Prince overflowing with his usual vivacious and witty conversation, closed that memorable day."

Just as in the Eulenburg case the Kaiser had been accused of insufficient knowledge of men and of overreadiness to place his confidence in others, so again these defects are apparent in his association with the unscrupulous Bülow.

When long afterward the Kaiser asked the question, *"War alles falsch?"* (Was everything wrong?) the answer must be, looking back to the *Daily Telegraph* affair, that apart from the Kaiser's inability to understand the English mentality and his having acted on a misconception of it, the blame in this case attaches mainly to Reich's Chancellor Prince Bernhard von Bülow. If he had so wished it, that article would never have appeared in the *Daily Telegraph*. Bülow deliberately played false, because he was false himself.

68. THE KAISER AND AMERICA

IT WAS TOUCH AND GO that a second catastrophe did not follow after the *Daily Telegraph* affair. During the Kiel Regatta in 1908 the Kaiser entertained several guests from America on board the *Hohenzollern*, among them a journalist, William Bayard Hale, with whom he had been glad to have talks on current political questions.

In so doing the Kaiser was under the impression that Hale would keep these conversations to himself and not make use of them for publication. Hale, however, who, on his way back to the United States, had recorded these talks on paper, received such a tempting offer from *Century* magazine that he made up his mind to publish them. When they were already in type, there appeared in the *Daily Telegraph* the sensational interview with Wilhelm II, whereupon Hale stopped the printing at the last moment and so prevented their publication.

What the Kaiser admired in Hale and other Americans was their unceremonious and self-confident manners, their unfailing coolness and, above all, their genuine independence. Wealth had always made a strong impression on Kaiser Wilhelm II. So it came about that he tolerated familiarities from these self-made men that no German Prince ought to have permitted. Thus Mr. Armour of Chicago clapped him familiarly on the shoulder, and Vanderbilt called him in a large company "a good fellow." Pierpont Morgan and Theodore Roosevelt were equally familiar. About the latter the Kaiser once remarked appreciatively, "What I most admired in Roosevelt was the fact that of all the men I've known he showed the strongest moral courage!"

When the daughter of the President of the United States was chosen to christen the German royal yacht, its owner well knew that by this compliment he would win applause on the far side of the "Big Pond."

Rich Americans coming to Potsdam might well find that it was Wilhelm II in person who conducted them round the New Palace, showed them its treasures and made the kind of conversation usual between millionaires engaged in reciprocal evaluation of their possessions. "This malachite vase is worth a share in the Panama Canal," the Kaiser would declare eagerly. "It was a present from my cousin the Czar of Russia." . . . "This Wedgwood service comes from my grandmother, Queen Victoria of England. It is worth more than its weight in gold." . . . "This portrait of my friend the Emperor of Austria is by Winterhalter—he was once a woodcutter in the Black Forest and afterward became a millionaire."

Thus the Kaiser would stride with his guests through the Tamerlane and the Lace Rooms, through the Apollo Hall with its pictures by Rubens, Van Dyck, Reni and Pesne, all dutifully admired by the Yankees.

Then they would all go out into the park, where the Kaiser would hold forth about his ancestor Frederick the Great. One of these visitors was so impressed that he ordered a statue of old Fritz to be dispatched to New York, to be erected there, though the New Yorkers, as Republicans, could not quite see what they ought to do with a foreign king. After such a conducted tour the Kaiser's guests were very satisfied, and he himself was amused by their astonishment and the odd questions that they asked.

This display of affability toward Americans encouraged several millionaires to come to Berlin with their daughters so that these might be presented at Court to the Imperial couple, arrayed in the regulation gowns and long trains. Such ceremonies often led to a young Guards officer's falling in love with a "Dollar Princess" and asking for her hand in marriage. The Kaiser raised no objections if in such manner a nobleman's rusty coronet was made to gleam anew with dollar gold.

What the indulgent Kaiser could not endure, however, was the mania of the Americans to buy all kinds of things from him, for instance, his Star of the Black Eagle or the Kaiserin's ostrich-feather fan. One exceedingly wealthy damsel from Baltimore offered any price if only she could acquire a cuirass that had been worn by the Kaiser. A big farmer from Ohio wanted to buy the Achilleion, which he proposed to carry away piece by piece and re-erect somewhere in Florida. A captain of heavy industry made serious inquiries about the cost of the Brandenburger Tor. His name was O'Connor and he wanted to buy it for the World Exhibition in St. Louis.

Now and again, however, the Kaiser was able to turn his acquaint-ance with American millionaires to some advantage. When he heard that Pierpont Morgan possessed a letter of Luther's, he called the attention of his Ambassador in Washington to this: "There is a Mr. Morgan who possesses an original letter of Martin Luther's, for which he is said to have paid some 300,000 marks. . . . How did this Morgan come by it? . . . He is not sufficiently educated to appreciate its real value. . . . The proper place for that letter is in the Martin Luther Museum in Wittenberg. . . ." And there in due course the letter was placed, thanks to the Kaiser's perseverance.

As everywhere else, the Kaiser had enemies in America. Among them was Gordon Bennett, the newspaper proprietor, who waxed wrathful that his compatriots in Berlin, representatives of democratic America, should be attracted by such petty things as orders, titles and court dress.

Also in the Reich, and especially among the Conservatives, there was real concern about the Americanization of the Kaiser. The Conservatives feared that the All-Highest ruler might fall too much under the influence of money, the banks and industry, to the detriment of agriculture.

But these personal links with "the country of unlimited possi-bilities" were to remain merely superficial. In astonishment rather than in admiration, he thought of America as a far-off unknown Somewhere, where people sent undutiful sons to wash plates and dishes. Later on such threads as Wilhelm II had spun between him-self and the United States proved tenuous and short-lived. It was re-served for the second successor to Theodore Roosevelt to assist in the overthrow of "the damned German Emperor" and to consign the Hohenzollern dynasty to its grave.

69. BÜLOW DEPARTS

Und die Moral von der Geschicht
Zeigt sich bei jedem Zickzackwandern:
Der welcher schwankt, der merkt es nicht,
Das merken immer nur die andern! [1]

THIS APPEARED in *Kladderadatsch* at the close of the year 1908 in connection with a survey of Bülow's "tightrope dancing" policy. The attitude of the Reich's Chancellor had been one of vacillation all along the line, and especially in regard to the Austro-Hungarian desire for annexations of territory. This desire had been pressed with increasing vehemence by the Ballhausplatz [2] as being legitimate, so that for a long time the Wilhelmstrasse [3] had been preoccupied by the question of Bosnia and Herzegovina.

After making the necessary preparations in secrecy the Dual Monarchy [4] proceeded, on November 5, 1908, to occupy the territory claimed by it. This having been done, Wilhelm II, who had dreaded the danger of a Russian intervention, showed how glad he was that everything had gone smoothly and without any immediate signs of trouble.

When Franz Joseph thanked him for the friendly attitude of the Reich the Kaiser disclaimed any merit for following what was to him the obvious course. "We are only doing what Austria wishes and considers right." Speaking in the same key, the Chancellor declared that "We shall too, from now on, leave it entirely to Austria to regulate her conduct toward the Serbs exclusively according to her own interests and at her own discretion."

After the annexation, Serbia, embittered and exasperated, began to stir, though cautiously and secretly at first. Belgrade felt confident of the as yet unvoiced support of "her big Slav sister"—Russia.

---

[1] And the moral of the story
Appears at every zigzag lurch:
He who staggers does not note it,
But the others always spot it!
(Literal trans.)

[2] Site of Austro-Hungarian Foreign Office.
[3] Site of German Foreign Office.
[4] The Austro-Hungarian Monarchy.

With a view to counteracting the growing agitation of the Serbs, Bülow proposed, in February 1909, that all the Great Powers (with the exception of Austria-Hungary) should unite in a *démarche* in Belgrade. Wilhelm II approved of this suggestion, all the more as he already felt little sympathy for the Karageorgevich dynasty [5] on account of their "unkingly" conduct.

The Great Powers, when consulted, made evasive replies to this appeal from Berlin. Owing to her unfavorable political position, Russia did not risk displaying her pro-Slav and pro-Serb attitude openly. France held back because she was not yet ready with her rearmament. England and Italy appeared undecided. The one and only result was to make it plain that Russia had not yet recovered from her defeat in the war with Japan. For Austria-Hungary it meant that for the time being no undertakings regarding Greater Serbia could be reckoned with. Aehrenthal and Goluchowski could claim the outcome as a success for themselves, while their old opponent, Izvolski, had to pocket a rebuff.

The Kaiser took particular pleasure in giving credit to Goluchowski, who, in the Morocco crisis, had already shown himself a staunch ally. At that time he had sent Goluchowski a personal telegram saying: "You have proved yourself a brilliant second in this duel and you can be assured of the like service from me in any similar case."

Three years after that telegram, on February 9, 1909, came the signing of the Franco-German Agreement on Morocco. It contained the recognition of France's political predominance in Morocco, involving the abandonment by the Reich of the demand for "an open door," on which she had hitherto insisted, thereby ensuring that the door should virtually be closed against her. Germany had demanded this Morocco conference; now, after many dramatic moments and threatening dangers of war, it had come to an end with the German representative yielding and having to leave the conference table without gaining any essential point. Bülow's only success had been the so-called Casablanca Agreement—a mere plaster on the gaping wound that still remained.

France was triumphant. In their enthusiasm the French went so

[5] The pro-Russian ruling house of Serbia, which came to the throne in 1902 following the murder of King Alexander and Queen Draga by a group of young officers.

far—it looked rather like a gesture of disdain—as to confer the Grand Cross of the Legion of Honor on the German Ambassador in Paris, Prince Radolin, and on the Undersecretary of State von Schön.

The dilatoriness of the negotiations at Algeciras,[6] like the lack of positive results, had called forth pessimistic comments combined with violent attacks in the German press against the Reich's Chancellor and the foreign policy that he represented. People declared that his "patent solution" for the Moroccan affair was no solution at all—rather had his policy served to bring about the consolidation of the *Entente Cordiale*.

Houston Stewart Chamberlain, the self-confessed anti-British Englishman, states that "during the Morocco crisis he met the Kaiser, not often, but in particularly favorable circumstances not provided for by Court etiquette, for informal and secret exchange of views." As a result he spoke as follows about the Kaiser: "In this important personality two characteristics seem to me especially noteworthy as being the dominant factors in all his feelings, thoughts and behavior —a deep and never-failing sense of responsibility before God and, closely and strongly bound up with that, a strong, masterful, even violent, determination to keep Germany at peace; never to use Germany's strength (for which she has to thank his care) so as to bring about war, but rather to enforce peace on those unwilling to keep it.

"His actions prove it. Even during the last ten years, when the situation was almost too much for Germany's honor to bear—and England saw to that as far as she could—it was always Wilhelm II who ensured peace."

Peace had indeed been maintained by the Kaiser, despite the sometimes dangerous developments of the Morocco crisis. True, many expectations remained unfulfilled, many a striking pronouncement of the Kaiser's had evaporated into sound and smoke; so also had Bülow's challenge, "We seek to put no one in the shade, but we too demand our place in the sun!" At any rate, war was averted.

With the dexterity of a tightrope dancer, as *Kladderadatsch* had described him, Reich's Chancellor Bülow had balanced himself on a quivering wire all through the Balkan crisis, the Morocco crisis, the dissolution of the Reichstag and the *Daily Telegraph* affair. But none

[6] *See* Bülow in Appendix, page 437.

of those events was destined to bring about his fall from that unstable foothold. It was a matter of internal policy, and not even one of primary importance, a Legacy Duty Bill, that forced him to resign.

He would have mastered this crisis too, if only he had had to deal with the old Reichstag of Bismarck. Things were somewhat different now in the new building on the Königsplatz—there were forty-three Social Democrats sitting in opposition on the Left. The Center was apathetic; the Rights were wearied, disappointed and unsure of themselves—but just to show that they were still there, they would fight the Sozis over this bill. The gossip shop was turned into a rough house.

Bülow made his last speech in the Reichstag on June 16, 1909. It was a farewell summary of the happy years of his Chancellorship. The members could gather at once from his subdued tone that he was tired of office. A week later, in a plenary sitting, the Legacy Duty Bill was rejected on its second reading by 195 votes to 187. On July fourteenth he ceased to be Chancellor.

In later years Wilhelm II forgave his fourth Reich's Chancellor many things, but he never forgave his treachery in the *Daily Telegraph* affair. Once when Kaiser Wilhelm II, accompanied by his namesake King Wilhelm II of Württemberg, happened to pass by the place where Bülow had stood before him for the last time as Chancellor, the Kaiser remarked grimly, "It was here, on this spot, that I threw the rotter out!"

70. THEOBALD VON BETHMANN-HOLLWEG

PRINCE BÜLOW was now numbered among those who had been axed. A row of important victims lay alongside Bülow on the battlefield. Anyone who still stood up was all the more glad to be alive, one such being the Minister Viktor von Podbielski, who was in high favor with Wilhelm II. To most people this was hard to understand, since "Pod," as he was commonly called, was spoken of as engaged in speculative business and accused of being concerned in some shady affairs.

Besides the ever-unsuspecting Minister von Köller, the capable Baron von Schorlemer, Minister for Agriculture and Forests, was thought much of by the Kaiser, as was also von Maybach, the Minister for Railways. Maybach, however, had been reproached in the Right-wing parties for having neglected the East Prussian deployment zone, delayed the construction of the Vistula and Nogat bridges, and failed to satisfy the strategic requirements of the West by not improving the Rhine crossings. These deficiencies, which had been greatly exaggerated by the Conservatives, were put to rights by his successor, the brilliant organizer von Budde, and the able and politically farsighted Minister von Breitenbach.

But the man of genius among the ministers of Wilhelm II was generally reputed to be Johannes von Miquel, who had carried out the financial reforms in Prussia by legislation on income tax, property tax and business tax, and had thereby greatly encouraged the Kaiser in his huge canal projects. In him the Cabinet possessed its best and most acute brains, those of a man of wide knowledge, subtle yet courageous and prepared to speak frankly with the Kaiser. Unfortunately, as he himself confessed, he seldom had an opportunity of doing so—"If only the Kaiser would invite me to the *Hohenzollern!*"

The Minister of the House of Hohenzollern, Count August zu Eulenburg, was recognized as a thoroughly honorable man. Those who had to deal with him praised his devotion to duty and his sincerity. His colleague, Privy Councillor von Roux, praised Eulenburg's good influence over his subordinates. It was from the circle to which August Eulenburg belonged, from the ranks of the solid and reliable administrative civil servants, that came the new Reich's Chancellor, Theobald von Bethmann-Hollweg, recommended by Bülow to the Kaiser.

Wilhelm II had met Bethmann-Hollweg some thirty years before when taking part, as a young officer, in maneuvers. Afterward he described the occasion thus: "The host (the father of the new Chancellor) and his amiable wife received me with a hospitality that won my heart. I spent many happy hours with this sympathetic family. . . . As I had no civilian clothes with me at the time, Bethmann's long and lanky son lent me a shooting jacket of his, which hung on me like a greatcoat, to everyone's great amusement. The loyal and deeply religious atmosphere that prevailed in that household gave me endless pleasure and afterward drew me back frequently to Hohenfinow."

As Secretary of State of the Home Office, the new Chancellor had already proved his value, as he had also done when representing his Department in the Reichstag. On the other hand, he had had little opportunity of devoting himself to foreign policy, and he stressed this point when he was appointed. An upright and conscientious man moved into the Chancellor's palace; he was no friend of big social gatherings. He was circumspect, reserved, often given to meditation, averse to hasty decisions or, as the Kaiser put it, "he would go very thoroughly into everything before making up his mind how to act." There was something of the professor about him, nor was this belied by his personal appearance. He gave the impression of being a philosopher, but not a statesman. When the Kaiser, immediately after nominating him, invested him with the uniform of the Dragoon Guards, he soon became "the good Theobald" of all the comic papers, with his gaunt figure—he stood just at six feet three inches—his peg-top head, as the Berliners called his short-cut hair, all brushed back.

All these witticisms about Bethmann did much to obscure his real qualities and to give the public a wrong impression of him. Friedrich von Payer said afterward, "During the course of years I have been in close association with Bethmann-Hollweg and I have always found him to be high-minded and just. No one at home or abroad has ever contested his possession of outstanding statesmanlike talents, and now that he is freed from the strife of parties, nobody should deny it."

In office the new Chancellor made few friends. His solemn manner, his professorlike exactitude, irritated his counselors. Of course, they had to admit that his work was precise down to the dotting of the i's. The Kaiser called it "classical."

Whereas Bülow dashed off his improvisations without much preliminary spadework, Bethmann verified his syntheses by attested evidence and the testimony of unimpeachable authorities, as though he were working on a thesis for a doctorate. About this the Kaiser declared afterward, "The result was that as all the possibilities had been exhausted there remained only that solution which the Chancellor advocated as ideal and the only one conceivable. That in itself must imply an element of danger. So long as Bethmann himself was not convinced it was difficult to bring him to any decision. He showed a strong and increasing propensity to dominate, which in discussion often amounted to an obstinate and almost schoolmasterly dogmatism and laying down the law to anyone who differed from him. At school they had called him 'the Governess' ... and he was always teaching me lessons!"

The relations between the Kaiser and Bethmann were quite different from those between him and Bülow. While Bülow could deceive and persuade the Kaiser, Bethmann, supported by all his proofs, tried to convince him. As they strolled under the old trees in the Chancellor's garden, Bethmann strove to set out his proposals in such a way that the Kaiser would have to agree, while Wilhelm II did not want to be argued to death by his own Chancellor.

After such promenades the Kaiser would now and then stay to luncheon with the simple, goodhearted Frau von Bethmann; but, despite her domestic merits, she could not make him forget the clever, sparkling and vivacious Italian, Princess Maria Bülow.

In bad weather the reports were given in the Schloss. That was not nearly so amusing as in the open air. So it might happen that the Kaiser, bored by the length of Bethmann's performance, would play with his dachshunds, chase them between his Chancellor's long legs, or let them rush madly round the room. This no doubt irritated the statesman, but it did not put him out of his stride.

What Bethmann thought of his royal master was indicated respectfully by him in a pertinent criticism, differing from Bülow's, which he placed on record: "An exuberant imagination, quickly changing moods, and frequent intention of strongly influencing his listener in a certain direction. [This last being the same habit that the Kaiser had noted in Bethmann himself.] From different motives the Kaiser often threw a veil over his own thoughts and intentions, despite his urge to communicate them. In the case of outsiders who had no inkling of the Kaiser's complex character, many very strange conceptions of it arose directly from personal contact with him."

Despite all Bethmann-Hollweg's good qualities, the Kaiser soon came to the conclusion that his Chancellor did not fulfill what his work as Secretary of State had promised. The excellent civil servant Bethmann was out of place as Reich's Chancellor. Bismarck's warning had proved to be justified: "If there should come a Chancellor who has started right from the bottom of the ladder, it could only result in catastrophe!"

Ballin, the creator of the Hamburg-America Line, saw things even more clearly when, in spite of his personal regard and high esteem for the new Chancellor, he uttered these striking words, "Bethmann is Bülow's revenge!"

71. THE HALDANE MISSION

AT THE TIME the new Chancellor took office the external political situation was by no means favorable for the German Reich. In France chauvinism and the longing for revenge were increasing, largely because of the advantages secured at Algeciras. Russia, after the annexation of Bosnia and Herzegovina, had drawn even further apart from Austria-Hungary, and therefore also from Germany. Italy had always been, and still was, a doubtful factor, and could not be taken seriously into account as an ally. England, thanks to the energy and initiative of Edward VII, had been able to consolidate the *Entente Cordiale* without interference, and thereby had realized the Foreign Office policy of encircling the Reich.

In the summer of 1911 the eyes of Europe were once again turned toward Morocco. Unrest had occurred there and France had been obliged to send some troops to Fez. Undersecretary of State von Kiderlen-Wächter advised an immediate intervention by the dispatch of German warships to Moroccan waters. Bethmann hesitated, but eventually agreed, though reluctantly, to support Kiderlen's proposal with the Kaiser. But Wilhelm II would not hear of it. "It can only be to our advantage," he declared, "if the French get themselves seriously involved with money and troops in Morocco. In my opinion it is not in our interest to stop them. If they infringe the provisions of the Algeciras Agreement, we can leave it to the other Powers, Spain in particular, to protest. I suppose our wish to send warships will remain alive. But we could effect nothing, as Tangier is not threatened and the scene of action lies far inland. I beg you, therefore, to discourage any outcry there may be for sending ships."

Thus did Wilhelm II, the alleged warmonger, write to his Chancellor in 1911. Three years later it was broadcast to the world that "this man, throughout his reign, has missed no opportunity of kindling war and plunging Europe into confusion."

On June twelfth Kiderlen asked that "at least four warships" should be stationed off the coast of Morocco "as it was absolutely necessary to protect German interests." Although the Kaiser could not see that these interests were endangered to any great extent, he gave in at last to the pressure from his Foreign Office and sanctioned the diversion to Casablanca of a small vessel, the gunboat *Panther*,[1] which happened to be on passage home to Wilhelmshaven from Swakopmund. (Afterward people used to speak of "the leap of the Panther.")

France, startled by this threatening gesture, demanded fresh discussions by the Great Powers. These were begun, but after endless shilly-shallying, produced no results. Bethmann was partly responsible for this, as the directives he gave to the German negotiators were far from clear. The impression made on the Algeciras Powers by the deliberations was that the German Government itself did not really know what it wanted. This circumlocution was not at all to the liking of the Kaiser. "They talk and discuss and nothing comes of it! While we are losing valuable time the British and Russians are stiffening the back of the terrified Gauls and dictating to them what is the most they may be allowed graciously to concede to us! At the beginning of May the Chancellor explained to me in Karlsruhe the whole program of our handling of the negotiations. I expressed my agreement. And now, at the beginning of July, we are just where we were before! This kind of diplomacy is too refined and too lofty for my brain!"

Despite recognition of the fact that Bethmann had proved incapable of coping with this comparatively simple situation, he remained in office as Chancellor. There was nobody there to replace him.

In November 1910 the Czar Nicholas II had come to Potsdam on a visit. The Kaiser had taken the opportunity of assuring "Cousin Nicky" that he would see to it that there should be no further question of Austria-Hungary's territorial expansion at the expense of Serbia. Obviously relieved and pleased, the Czar then left Potsdam.

On the occasion of this visit Bethmann and Kiderlen had made

[1] *See* Agadir Incident in Appendix, page 433.

the acquaintance of Sazonov,[2] the Russian Minister for Foreign Affairs, who had only shortly before assumed office. While "agreement on all questions of foreign policy was reached" and the fact was announced in a communiqué, Sazonov, immediately after this visit to Potsdam, informed Hartwig, his Minister in Belgrade, of his own views, as follows: "I have the impression that Austria-Hungary, despite the German brotherhood in arms, is on her last legs. . . . Serbia's promised land lies within the orbit of present-day Austria-Hungary. . . . Under these circumstances it is a matter of vital importance for Serbia to put herself, by hard and patient work, in the position of readiness necessary to face the inevitable outbreak of future war."

Once again Kaiser and Czar met, in 1912, in Finnish waters off Port Baltic. The Czarina, whom the Kaiser did not like overmuch, was present and thought that "he had become very quiet." After the meeting had passed off amicably, Bethmann, who did not allow himself to be deceived as regards the real trend of feeling in Russia, drew up an exposé of the political situation which he handed to the Kaiser.

Bethmann's Views	*The Kaiser's Marginal Comments*
That war with Russia also means for us war with France is certain.	*I don't doubt it for a moment!*
On the other hand, there are many signs to show that it is at least doubtful whether England would intervene actively if Russia and France were to appear as plainly offering provocation, for then the English Government would have to reckon with its own public opinion.	*They will take good care that it won't appear so! With the help of the press bribed on both sides!*
Statements such as those of Haldane and the like point simply to this—that England would only intervene on behalf of a	*Haldane has expressly declared that the possibility of an overthrow would not be tolerated, so intervention by Eng-*

[2] Sergei Dmitrievich Sazonov, Russian Foreign Minister from 1910 until 1917, when he was preparing to go to London as Russian Ambassador but was prevented by the outbreak of revolution.

France already overthrown, that is, after the event, and at first only diplomatically.

land is absolutely certain to be immediate—and not "after the event."

Besides, as regards the word "provocation," even if we, for our part, were to avoid provocation, we should still be regarded as the provokers!

With experienced diplomats and a skillfully handled press, "provocation" can always be manufactured — for instance, the case of the candidature for the Spanish Crown in 1870— and this must always be kept ready to hand. Opinions about it will always differ on either side.

Owing to the difficult position of the Reich, Bethmann, who to the very end of his term as Chancellor clung to his mistaken ideas about England and English world policy, endeavored to induce the Kaiser to make a new approach to London, although it was clear from the first that any such attempt was doomed to be wrecked by the force of public opinion there. Bethmann's effort to escape from encirclement ended in a frigid rejection by Downing Street. Moreover, Asquith introduced a new Navy Bill in the House of Commons, alleging that he suspected, and was even convinced by incontestable evidence, that the Reich was building more warships, and building them faster than it admitted. In March 1912 Germany would have not thirteen but seventeen capital ships completed. Within the next six years they would have twenty-one (Balfour put the figure at twenty-five) modern first-class battleships. If the German Reich was sincere in desiring an understanding with England, said Asquith, Bethmann need only enter into an agreement about his shipbuilding program. Nothing would then stand in the way of friendly relations between the two countries.

Bethmann, like Wilhelm II, saw in the German fleet the one and only instrument capable of exerting continuous pressure on England. No reliance could be placed on Italy, with her obsolescent fleet. Still less could the fleet of the Dual Monarchy be counted upon, cooped up as it was in the Adriatic, without even a secure exit. His reply to the English proposal was as follows: "The program of construction for the fleet of the German Reich, which at any rate is permanently weaker than that of England, and, moreover, might come into conflict with the fleets of other countries, can only be regulated by agreement if the Reich be assured that during the currency of such agreement its arms shall not clash with those of England."

These preliminary heats, stoutly contested on both sides, induced King Edward VII to make a last attempt at clarifying the situation. He decided to pay his first official visit to Berlin, taking Queen Alexandra with him. He had hesitated as long as possible. The royal couple arrived in Berlin on February 9, 1909.

An incident that occurred on the Unter den Linden was popularly regarded as no good augury for the meeting. As the carriage in which Queen Alexandra and the Kaiserin were sitting approached the Lustgarten the battery of the 1st Guards Field Artillery Regiment began to fire a royal salute, and in the extremely cold air the sound was peculiarly loud. The horses of the Dragoon escort shied, and those drawing the four-horse carriage followed suit. A catastrophe seemed inevitable, but the Master of the Horse dashed in, checked the leaders and prevented the team from bolting.

On the occasion of this visit "Uncle Bertie" looked old and tired. It was destined to be his first and last visit to Berlin as king. Fifteen months later, on May 6, 1910, he died.

Even in his obituary notice the Kaiser could not forget his grudge against his "Uncle Bertie." "An outstanding political personality has suddenly disappeared from the European stage. . . . At such a moment one can forget many things. . . . I believe that on the whole it will make for more calm in European politics. . . . Apart from his own people, King Edward VII will mostly be mourned by Gauls and Jews."

Despite this strange expression of condolence, Wilhelm II went to London on May nineteenth to attend the funeral that was to take place the following day. The new King, George V, was clearly at pains to prepare a friendly reception for his cousin. An apartment in Windsor Castle was allotted him, one in which his parents had long ago stayed "and in which I often used to play as a youngster," as the Kaiser said afterward. "Many memories passed through my mind and reawakened the feeling of being at home that binds me to that place and has made these last years so hard to bear, in view of the political aspect." Then, in a revulsion of sentiment evoked by the memory of his grandmother, Queen Victoria, he added, "I am proud to call this place my second home and to be a member of this royal family!"

The ceremony of the lying-in-state in Westminster Hall made a deep impression on the Kaiser. On the gigantic catafalque lay the costly bronze coffin, guarded by officers of the Coldstream and Irish Guards, in their red tunics, bearskins on their bowed heads, and hands crossed on the hilt of their drawn swords resting point downward on the ground. High above the catafalque, in semidarkness, stretched the ancient Gothic roof of oak, while the only lighting came, broken into variegated colors, from the great rose window beneath which the somber files of mourning people passed slowly by.

A year later, in May 1911, Wilhelm was in London again, this time for the unveiling of the memorial to Queen Victoria. With him came the Kaiserin and Princess Viktoria Luise. Freed from the hated figure of "Uncle Bertie," the Kaiser showed himself more affable and almost friendly to his cousin George V.

After this amicable getting-in-touch came the so-called "Haldane mission," whose course the Kaiser afterward described thus: "On the morning of January 29, 1912, Herr Ballin was announced to me as requesting an audience. I took it that it was a matter of coming to offer belated birthday congratulations. So I was not a little astonished when Ballin, after a short expression of good wishes, informed me that he came as an emissary from Sir Ernest Cassel, the trusted friend and business adviser of the late King Edward. Sir Ernest, he said, had come to Berlin on a special mission and asked to be received by me. I inquired if it was a case of a political mission, and if so, why did not the British Ambassador ask for the audience. From Ballin's answer it appeared that, according to hints given him by Cassel, the matter was one of great importance; the reason for bypassing the Ambassador was that in London it was especially desired that this matter should not pass through the official diplomatic channels, either English or German. I declared that I was ready to receive Sir Ernest at once, but I added that should his mandate involve political affairs then I, as a constitutional ruler, must immediately summon the Chancellor. I was not in a position to deal, in his absence, with any representative of a foreign Power.

"Ballin then called in Cassel, who handed me a paper which had been drawn up 'with the knowledge and approval of the English Government.' I read the document through and was not a little amazed to find that I held in my hand a formal offer of neutrality in the event of Germany's being in future involved in any warlike complications, this offer being made conditionally on a definite reduction in the sphere of naval construction, which should be the subject of discussions and agreements."

In view of the importance of this memorandum, the Kaiser at once had the Chancellor called to the Schloss. He came immediately, but insisted on Admiral von Tirpitz' being also summoned. After some inconclusive discussion Bethmann proposed to draw up a note in reply, in the same style as that which Cassel had presented, to be written in English so as to obviate any chance of misunderstanding. The Kaiser declared that he was prepared to undertake the translation himself. He described the scene in Doorn. "I sat down at the desk in the A.D.C.'s room, the gentlemen standing round me. I read out a sentence from the note and drafted the reply, which was then read out. Thereupon Bethmann and Tirpitz started to criticize it— for one, my translation was too abrupt, for the other, it was too accommodating. It was remodeled, recast, improved and turned about. It was particularly the Chancellor, with his philosophical exactitude and his deep-searching thoroughness that took nothing for granted but carefully weighed and tested each word so that afterward there should not be any occasion for criticism. It meant for me many agonies over grammar and style. At last the answering note was signed and sealed."

Then the Kaiser went on: "Days of great tension passed before a reply came from London. Haldane, the Secretary of State for War, was to be entrusted with the negotiations and would arrive in Berlin as soon as possible. This caused us some astonishment, for it seemed obvious that Churchill, as First Lord of the Admiralty, should have handled this matter. Imagine that, *mutatis mutandis*, the Reich would have sent its Minister for War, von Heeringen, instead of Admiral von Tirpitz, to discuss naval affairs! Various explanations of the enigma were propounded, Bethmann being of the opinion that the choice of Haldane was a polite gesture by the English, for he was well known as a Goethe scholar and also for his knowledge of German philosophy, besides which he spoke German fluently. Tirpitz recalled that Haldane had studied for a time under General von Einem at the Ministry of War in the Leipzigerstrasse.

"Haldane arrived. As my guest he was received with especial honors. In the discussions that followed he showed himself well informed, skillful, and tough in debate, where his brilliant qualities as an advocate were very apparent. The conversations went on for several hours and led to a general clarification as well as to a preliminary understanding about the number of our new constructions and the times at which they would become ready for service. Tirpitz proved himself an able defender of our interests. After a few more talks, in which Ballin took part, Haldane departed. Ballin told me that Haldane had spoken to him as being well pleased with the outcome of his mission, and had said that in his opinion a rough draft of the agreement would be sent to us within a week or a fortnight.

"Eventually there came, not the draft of the agreement, but another document containing all sorts of questions and demands for information, to answer which called for much pondering and many consultations. Gradually the suspicion grew upon me that the English were not really in earnest, for the raising of one question only led to the raising of another. Details were asked for that had nothing to do with the agreement. England gradually withdrew more and more from her offers and promises, so that it all came to nothing.

"Next there started in Berlin, from both competent and incompetent quarters, a drive against the Supplementary Navy Bill, against Tirpitz and myself. That was quite senseless, for the Chancellor and I were both agreed that we should have to sacrifice part of the bill in order to better our relations with England and escape from the encirclement. What I could not agree to was that we should make concessions that came near to endangering our sovereign rights without any returns.

"Toward the end of March (1912) the battles about persisting with the Navy Bill, or letting it drop, became so acrimonious that the Chancellor came to Charlottenburg on March twenty-second, and asked to be allowed to tender his resignation. After talking it over, and on my assuring him that Dr. Burchard (Mayor of Hamburg) vigorously supported the Chancellor's views, Bethmann withdrew his request.

"A week later when I went to meet Herr von Bethmann in his garden, I found him quite crushed. By way of explanation he showed me a dispatch from London disavowing Cassel and his memorandum, brushing aside the idea of a treaty of neutrality, and ending with the scornful-sounding assurance that the Reich's Chancellor von Bethmann-Hollweg would continue to enjoy the complete confidence of the British Government. It was understandable that the Chancellor should not fall into raptures over a compliment of that kind, since it came from the worst of all his adversaries, one prepared to humiliate and make a fool of the Reich, at the expense of the Chancellor."

72. THE KAISER IN SWITZERLAND

AFTER HIS DISAPPOINTMENT over the "Haldane mission" the Kaiser was able (in September 1912) to realize his long-cherished project of paying a visit to the Swiss Confederation, his neighbor on the Boden See (Lake Constance) and the Rhine. An invitation came from Berne from the Federal President Ludwig Forrer, who had heard of the Kaiser's wish and was anxious to gratify it. He was not sure, however, whether it was a wise thing to do; to him, as to most of the democratic republican Swiss citizens, Wilhelm II represented a being from some other world.

Preparations for the reception of the German Kaiser were made deliberately and in patriarchal calm, with the aim of presenting a dignified appearance, but nothing more. Some questions did call for a certain amount of brain-racking, for instance, where were they to find a State coach for the entry into Zürich? After much searching they chose the open carriage of a lady of Zürich, who placed it at their disposal.

By September third they were ready to receive their exalted visitor. The leading men of the Government, arrayed in black frockcoats and tall hats, without decoration of any kind, were assembled in the main station of Zürich. The Federal President, who perhaps was feeling rather nervous about the unaccustomed ordeal that was to come, pulled at his short cigar and refused to part with it until the engine of the royal train came in sight.

Mindful of the fact that until 1857 the Rifle Battalion of the

Prussian Guards had been recruited from the Swiss of the Canton of Neuchâtel, which for some time had belonged to Prussia, and then had been under Prussian hegemony until this was voluntarily renounced, the Kaiser wore the uniform of that battalion on the occasion of this visit. Accompanied by Forrer, he drove to the Villa Rietberg on the Lake of Zürich, and from there attended each day the Swiss Army maneuvers held near Wil. The conduct of the maneuvers was in the hands of Colonel Theophil Sprecher von Bernegg, Chief of the Swiss General Staff. What the Kaiser and his generals saw there greatly surpassed their expectations. After the powwow when the operations ended, the Kaiser had a lively conversation with the Corps Commander, Ulrich Wille. In his spontaneous manner the Kaiser asked him, "What would you do, Colonel, if one of these days I were to march into Switzerland with one hundred thousand men?"

The Kaiser, who was expecting affright and embarrassment, was disappointed, for the Colonel calmly said what he would do. "And," asked the Kaiser eagerly, "suppose I came with two hundred thousand men?" After a second for reflection, Wille, with a roguish twinkle in his eyes, replied, "In that case, Your Majesty, we should just shoot twice!"

On the evening of September fourth the town of Zürich staged a farewell water festival on the lake, in honor of the Kaiser. From the shore thousands watched the rare spectacle. A splendid display of fireworks ended with a bouquet of three thousand rockets, the Kaiser viewing it from a lake steamboat.

After the visit to Zürich the Kaiser went on to Berne. Just as he was about to step out of the station into the station yard, there was an incident which nearly ruined all the careful arrangements for the reception. A farmer leading a cow by a rope took it into his head to try to pass between the police cordon and the band, but lost control of the maddened animal, which broke away, and rushed all over the yard until at last the happy thought struck it to vanish down a side street.

Yet another thing—quite harmless in itself—was to upset this reception in Berne. At the very moment when the State carriage moved off from the main station, a big flowerpot fell from a window sill onto the pavement. It sounded like the explosion of a bomb, and despite all the reassuring explanations of Colonel Held, the officer commanding the Swiss troops, the Kaiser declined to proceed with a trip into the Bernese Oberland that had been planned for him.

At the banquet offered to the illustrious visitor in the Federal capital, President Forrer, in proposing his toast, gave the assurance that Switzerland was determined always to maintain good-neighborly relations with the German Reich.

Replying to this toast the Kaiser spoke as follows: "Herr Bundespräsident, I was glad to accept your invitation to attend this year's maneuvers of the Federal Swiss Army. Since ancient times the inhabitants of the Swiss mountains have been known as fine and vigorous men. . . . It has done my heart good to see, as a soldier, that you Confederates of today, remembering your glorious history, are following as excellent soldiers in the footsteps of your forefathers. . . . Endowed with unique natural beauty, pressing assiduously forward in every domain, military, scientific, artistic, industrial, technological and economic, the Swiss State, lying here in the very center of Europe, has won for itself the esteem and respect of all. A large part of Switzerland clings, both in spirit and in character, to the German way of life and the exchange of ideas and material products is accordingly as extensive as it is natural. In Schiller, to name only one, you revere, as we do, a national poet who has spoken from his heart to your people as hardly any other has done. On the other hand, the works of your intellectual giants such as Gottfried Keller and Conrad Ferdinand Meyer, have come to be looked on by our people as common property. Hence it is understandable that Switzerland and the German Reich, with all their distinctive individualities as States, unaffected by the diversity of their historical developments, find themselves closely bound together, not only through the exchange of their commodities, but also by their spiritual life and their creative abilities, and it is understandable also that they should desire to stand by each other in cordial and confident friendship. For nearly twenty-five years I have been a good friend of Switzerland, and as far as I am concerned, I shall continue to be so!"

73. THE TORCHLIGHT DANCE

DOWN THE KÖNIGGRÄTZER-STRASSE, past gazing walls of spectators, trotted the escort of the 1st Guards Dragoons, sky-blue tunics with gold belts and nodding white plumes, preceding and following the carriage in which rode Queen Mary of England and the German Kaiserin. People knew but little of the English Queen beyond the fact that she came of a princely German House, yet was by no means a Germanophile. The May sun shone brightly despite some gray clouds as the cavalcade passed through the Brandenburger Tor on to the middle roadway of Unter den Linden.

At Entrance IV of the Schloss stood footmen in laced jackets. The one acting as lookout gave the signal, "Guard, turn out!" to the guardroom. Then the carriage swung through the gateway and round the curve across the courtyard to the entrance stairs at the foot of which the Kaiser and his cousin King George V, were awaiting their consorts.

The Queen was the last guest to be greeted on that tiring day, for the Czar Nicholas II, the Duke and Duchess of Cumberland, and all the other reigning princes invited to this marriage festival in Berlin, had arrived the day before.

On the morrow a marriage was to put an end to a long-standing feud—that between the old Guelphs and the young Zollern. Nearly fifty years had gone by since the Battle of Langensalza, where the blind King George V of Hanover had lost his kingdom to Prussia. On his deathbed he had made his son Ernst August swear that he would never renounce Hanover. After the death of his unfortunate father, however, Ernst August retired to Schloss Gmunden where, as Duke of Cumberland, he lived very quietly. His aversion for Prussia was fully shared by his wife, a Danish princess, who as a child had seen the loss of Schleswig and Holstein.

When the son of this marriage, also named Ernst August, wished to enter on a military career, it was a question of his joining the Austro-Hungarian Army, in which his father held the honorary rank of General. But the young Prince preferred to serve in a Bavarian cavalry regiment at Munich. There could, of course, be no question of Prussia.

But what matters the oath of a dead king when two young people are in love? The Hohenzollerns had always been practical people in their marriage arrangements, just as Wilhelm II had shown himself to be by marrying the daughter of the unjustly dispossessed Augustenburger. No objections of any kind were raised by Berlin when the only daughter of the Kaiser and Kaiserin announced her determination to marry the young Guelph prince. In Gmunden no one knew at first what to do. Then they came round and decided to drop all reservations and the obligations imposed by the last King of Hanover, in view of the fact that the young Ernst August would in any case become Duke of Brunswick, which of course implied renouncement of any claim to the Crown of Hanover and the Guelph treasures.

At this wedding in the Berlin Schloss the bridegroom's father, the old Duke Ernst August of Cumberland, was perhaps the most remarkable personality among the guests. He wore the uniform of an Austrian general, with its low red collar, so that his wrinkled neck, lean and long, stuck out far above it—"like a turkey cock," as the young pages whispered to one another. His ill-humored and discontented face showed how uncomfortable he felt at being there in that Schloss and at this wedding, which his father would never have permitted. The one thing that seemed to connect him with this Prussian environment was the new *moiré* ribbon of the Order of the Black Eagle, lying across his narrow chest and looking, in his case, like a long yellow sticking plaster.

Wilhelm II was all the more delighted to see not only a happy daughter before him but also that he had acquired a fine son-in-law. He paid special attention to the Duchess Thyra of Cumberland, who was not at all well disposed toward him, because she enjoyed great respect in the family circle. Among these were her sister, the widow of King Edward VII; her brother, King George of Greece, assassinated not long before in Salonika; another sister, the widow of the Czar Alexander III of Russia; and lastly her two nephews, King George V of England and the Czar Nicholas II, both of whom had been invited, and come, to the wedding.

The Czar had arrived without the Czarina. Everyone was particularly interested in the "Asiatic despot," but found his face pallid and rather puffy, his eyes veiled and strange—"Kalmuck eyes," some declared. Some saw in him a simple weakly child with a head like that of Janus, others called him a harmless and unhappy autocrat, but nobody in the Schloss could form any definite opinion about him, for his languid, delicate courtesy served him as a screen.

The face of the English King also looked flabby and puffy. Since both the Czar and George V wore pointed beards, were of about the same height, had heads of about the same shape and wore Prussian uniforms, they were frequently mistaken one for the other by the Court officials and servants, if they were not standing close together.

It happened that on this same day, May 24, 1913, Prince and Princess Heinrich of Prussia were celebrating their silver wedding anniversary. It was a sunny May morning, real "Hohenzollern weather." Flags were strung across the streets and waved from the houses, while the bells were ringing in all the churches of Berlin. The many princely guests began to assemble at an early hour, and they were followed by the generals, the ministers, royal households and their dignitaries. In all, over a thousand persons had been invited.

The bridal procession was marshaled in the gallery of the Schloss preparatory to traversing the venerable halls. A foreign and unbiased witness—Lord Frederick Hamilton—has written about these halls: "Their silk-hung walls, their pictures and the splendid pieces of old furniture they contain, redeem these rooms from the soulless, impersonal look that palaces wear. . . . When the Throne Room was lighted up at night the glowing colors of the Gobelin tapestry and the sheen of the great expanses of gold and silver produced an effect of immense splendor."

Passing the King's Company of the 1st Regiment of Foot Guards, the Castle Guard Company in their historic uniforms, and the special guards furnished by the Body Guard and the Kaiserin's Life Guards, over carpets on which were arranged magnificent vases and bowls full of pink carnations—the Princess's favorite flower—the bride and bridegroom reached the Chinese Salon, where the crown of a Prussian princess, brought from the Royal Treasury, was placed on the bride's head. Next followed, in the Elector's Room, the official registration of the marriage by the Minister of the House of Hohenzollern, Count August zu Eulenburg. Among the few witnesses was Prince Max of Baden. Five years later he was to be witness at a very different event.

In the chapel of the Schloss the nearest relatives, the representatives of sovereign houses and the highest officials of the Reich were awaiting the arrival of the procession. The bride wore a white silk dress with a train of silver brocade borne by four maids of honor. The young Duke of Brunswick wore the uniform of the Zieten Hussars. By the altar stood the Kaiser, the Kaiserin and next to her the Queen of England, who in honor of the occasion wore on her breast the incredibly large Cullinan diamond.[1] Then came the white-haired Grand Duchess of Baden.

In the background stood, like two pillars, the tall figures of the Reich's Chancellor von Bethmann-Hollweg and the Austro-Hungarian Military Attaché Baron Niemerth. Between them were ranged the Ambassadors von Szögyény-Marich, Cambon and Lichnowsky, the Princess zu Fürstenberg with her celebrated diadem of pearls, and the slender figure of the Crown Prince in the uniform of the Death's-Head Hussars, with his two small sons, Friedrich Wilhelm and Louis Ferdinand.

As the organ started to play and the choir chimed in, the sun came out and shed its rays on the motley of silk and velvet, on the clusters of lilac and the bunches of roses, on innumerable candlesticks and on the altar, before which the Principal Court Chaplain stood ready to read out the text, chosen by the Kaiser himself, on which he based his sermon.

As the rings were being exchanged the salute from the Guards battery in the Lustgarten crashed forth, making the stained-glass windows of the chapel tremble. The solemn wedding ceremony was over—the festive banquet could begin.

The Kaiser was obviously greatly moved as he rose to propose the first toast—that of his daughter and his son-in-law. "My dear daughter, on this day when you are about to leave our house, I thank you with all my heart for the joy and gladness that you have always given me and your mother, and for the years of radiant sunshine that you have represented in my home!" Then he turned to the young Duke and confidently entrusted his child to him as his life partner.

When the banquet was over a procession was formed for the entry into the White Hall. There, after fanfares by the massed trumpeters of the Guards Cuirassiers, began the traditional Torch-

---

[1] Cullinan diamond—found in Cullinan, South Africa, in 1907, and presented to Edward VII.

light Dance, a polonaise, in which the pages carried lighted torches.

While the ball in the White Hall was still going on, the Kaiser accompanied the newly married couple to the Lehrter Station. When the train drew out, peas and rice were thrown into the carriage in accordance with ancient custom. For a long time the Kaiser stood gazing after the departing train. It was no easy thing for him to bid farewell to his only daughter.

So the Hohenzollern-Guelph marriage was accomplished. Its fanfares and drum rolls could not drown the distant sound of drawn swords. Just when the German Government introduced a new Army Bill in the Reichstag, the Three-Year Term of Service was adopted in Paris. But this did not prevent M. Cambon from emptying a glass of champagne in the White Hall in honor of the peaceful relations between France and Germany. The King of England, too, spoke of peace and smiled graciously in his Prussian uniform, while at the same moment Sir Edward Grey, at a dinner party in his country house, was giving an assurance that "it shall never again happen that a Wellington should fight at the side of a Blücher!" While the Czar was making his bow to the German Kaiserin in the Torchlight Dance, people in St. Petersburg were making jokes about the "Family Party in Berlin," and gibing at the German press for so comically overrating the significance of the Czar's "private visit." While courteous "Cousin Nicky" deferred in everything to the Kaiser, Suchomlinov retained reservists under the colors and sent them to their garrisons on the German frontiers.

In the White Hall the torches were extinguished. Thousands of empty bottles and cartloads of dead flowers remained behind. The Bridal Dance in Berlin is over. The Death Dance in Europe can commence!

74. AN ALBANIAN INTERLUDE

THE CHOICE of Prince Wilhelm zu Wied to be Prince of Albania (in 1914) did not meet with the approval of Wilhelm II. He feared a fiasco which would turn ultimately to the detriment of the Reich.

The Kaiser would have preferred the choice of an Egyptian

prince, who would more easily adapt himself to the peculiar conditions in Albania, anyhow, better than a German prince from the Rhine. But this did not entitle him to forbid a prince of equal birth to make the journey to Durazzo.

When the young Ferdinand von Coburg-Kohary had asked Prince Bismarck whether he ought to accept the call to become Prince of Bulgaria, the old Chancellor had told him. "Do so by all means! In any case it will be something for you to remember later on!" The Kaiser dared not repeat this nonchalant advice even though the Bulgarian venture had turned out quite well.

When Prince Wilhelm zu Wied came to Berlin to pay his farewell call the Kaiser took the opportunity of warning this aspirant to the throne of Albania against the danger of taking wrong steps in certain eventualities. He advised him not to let himself be influenced by any foreign intriguers, and not to become involved in any armed disputes. He ought not to accept Durazzo as his place of residence, but should establish this in the interior, at Tirana or Scutari. Above all, he should listen to the natives, do what they wanted, and make himself liked by them. That of course meant a lot of money, silver money, to be thrown to his subjects as Haroun-al-Raschid used to do. That, no doubt, would be the best way at first to win popular sympathy in Albania.

Prince Wied disregarded all these hints and suggestions of the Kaiser's and also his warning about the dangerous Essad Pasha, a determined Albanian national, who could not fail to see in the German Prince a tyrant forced upon his country.

If Wilhelm II followed the course of events in this enthronement with anxiety and apprehension, nothing could prevent Queen Elisabeth of Rumania (who also came of the House of Wied) from composing and presenting to her nephew a hymn as a parting gift. "Carmen Sylva" (her pseudonym as a writer and poet) entitled her composition "Fairyland Will Have Its Prince." The title was wrong, for Albania was no fairyland . . . nor would it have the Prince.

What the Kaiser had predicted turned out to be true—money, much money, was the first essential for any success in Albania. Prince Wied, who did not possess any great fortune of his own, receiving only a meager sum from Albania, and that only in installments and irregularly, found himself unable to live up to the pompous standards that Orientals expect from their princes. Disappointments followed. The Prince realized, as he could not fail to do, that he was out of place here, that "his people" did not care for him and there was little hope of establishing a Wied dynasty in Albania. At the *Folies Bergères* in Paris they were already singing a ditty:

> *Les caisses sont vides,*
> *Le trône est Wied,*
> *Tout est vide,*
> *Le prince du vide!* [1]

75. SCHLOSS KONOPISCHT

DURING ARMY MANEUVERS in Bohemia the Archduke Franz Ferdinand of Austria-Este had been quartered in Schloss Konopischt. He took a great liking to the place and the wide expanse of rough grounds in which it stood, and in the end he bought the property, which had once belonged to Count Waldstein (or Wallenstein) and to the family of Lobkowicz. So as to be able to live there quietly with his family he bought more land adjoining it and thus threw a broad protective girdle around the Schloss.

A magnificent baroque fence surrounded the estate, with its old oaks, silver spruces and copper beeches, bright clumps of birch, its rose gardens, ponds with swans and lawns with peacocks and tame deer. In the center of all this stood the massive stone castle, fitted inside like a hunting museum with innumerable weapons and trophies of the chase.

Anyone who ventured to disturb the Archduke's peace at Konopischt by trespassing upon his land—as unsuspecting strollers from the neighboring town of Tabor sometimes did on Sundays—had to reckon with being shouted at by an irascible and almost apoplectic proprietor who would threaten to shoot anyone who dared to set foot on his ground a second time.

[1] A play on French and German words. The French word *vide*, meaning "empty," is pronounced like the German name Wied. A free translation would read:

> "The coffers are empty,
> Wied is on the throne,
> All is empty,
> The prince of emptiness."

His officials and staff had much to put up with owing to the Archduke's passionate temper. His outbursts were frequently so dreadful that people thought they were confronting a lunatic. After such fits of rage the Archduke was often depressed and felt ashamed of himself. But that did not prevent him from bursting out again at the next opportunity.

Franz Ferdinand knew only enemies and friends—black and white. Either he took to someone at once, in which case his friendship was lasting, or else he despised and hated him, in which case the feeling was profound. He was incapable of pretense in such matters. It was not in him to forgive and forget, if anyone had once opposed him. People called him "a born autocrat," or "a man of the seventeenth century." He was no weakling—he was afraid of nothing—"It's always a dangerous business to be afraid!" He stuck to that rule of life and remained a combative personality, a lonely fighter for his principles who found it hard to co-operate with anyone else.

Full of ambition, he strove with determination to reach his appointed goal, even if it appeared to be unattainable. His strength of will was based on his implicit belief in the doctrines of the Roman Catholic Church. The slogan "Away from Rome!" had for him the same meaning as "Away from Austria." He did not like to have Protestant officers in his entourage. In all this he was encouraged by his wife, who, the Viennese used to say, was more Catholic than the Pope.

Franz Ferdinand was inflexible. Whatever he had determined upon he carried out, whether it was the morganatic marriage or a dangerous journey against which he had been warned. His marriage with the Countess Sophie Chotek von Chotkowa und Wognin came after a supreme trial of strength, for it meant that he waged war on tradition and legitimacy, and therefore against the most powerful figure in the State—the Emperor.

If it had rested with the Empress Elisabeth there would have been no objection raised to this morganatic marriage. "Above all, no inbreeding! You should be glad that for once fresh blood comes into the family, instead of Spanish or Bavarian!"

For some time before this the Archduke Franz Ferdinand had so often been a visitor to the palace of the Archduke Friedrich that the latter believed his eldest daughter Maria Christine to be the chosen bride of the heir to the throne. All the more shocked and disappointed was the Archduchess-Mother Isabella when it turned out that his choice had fallen on Countess Sophie Chotek, Lady in Waiting to the Archduchess.

On the Emperor's orders Prior Marschall had endeavored to persuade the Countess into a voluntary renunciation, but was unsuccessful. Apart from being in love, she was just as ambitious as "Franzi." Marschall had to report the failure of his mission to the Emperor, who disdainfully remarked that "love makes people lose all sense of dignity!"

Regardless of the All-Highest's wishes the Archduke insisted on the marriage. It took place on June 28, 1900, in the Council Chamber of the Hofburg. A tall crucifix lit by wax candles was fixed to the wall, and before it stood the throne, on which the aged monarch sat like a graven image. To right and left of him stood the Privy Councilors, the Prince-Bishop of Vienna and the Prince-Primate of Hungary. The whole thing resembled a funeral rite. The loud rough voice of the Archduke rang through the room as, having removed his glove and laid his finger on the Gospels, he took the oath. . . . "This my marriage is a morganatic one, and shall now and evermore be regarded as such!"

Though the Countess was created Princess von Hohenberg, she soon found that at Court she was exposed to constant humiliations. The Chief Marshal of the Court, Prince Montenuovo, who was himself the issue of a morganatic marriage, laid down in a thick dossier the subordinate position that was to be hers. In all the Emperor's castles, on occasions of ceremonial entrance, only *half* the folding door was to be opened for her. She was denied the use of the Court carriages and horses, also of the royal boxes in the Opera and Burg Theater.

If the old gentleman in Schönbrunn could never recover from the shock of this blow dealt at the hallowed and now violated Law of Legitimacy within the House of Hapsburg, Wilhelm II, who was on friendly terms with the Archduke, could more easily accept it. On every occasion of his going to Konopischt, Miramare, Eckardsau or Vienna, he was especially punctilious in paying his respects to the Princess von Hohenberg, and at a ball in the Belvedere his attentions and his conversation with her were quite conspicuous. Possibly it was this attitude of the Kaiser's that induced the Emperor to raise her to the rank of Duchess and thereby to confer upon her a position of precedence over all unmarried archduchesses. When the Archduke Franz Ferdinand came to Berlin with his wife in 1909, she was expressly received as an Archduchess "of the blood," in which, however, the Kaiserin Auguste Viktoria made an exception and, regarding her as "not of equal birth," treated her coolly and condescendingly.

Wilhelm II had known the Archduke since the time of Crown Prince Rudolf's wedding in 1881. He had met him then in the palace of the Archduke Karl Ludwig, and afterward had got to know him better when shooting together. The Kaiser knew how to get cleverly round the difficult heir to the throne; it was not only that he treated the Duchess as an equal, but he understood how to fall in with Franz Ferdinand's peculiarities.

Despite his supple adaptability there were many things about Wilhelm II that were not to the liking of the Archduke. Much struck him as odd, or even repelled him. He thought him too nosiy and too provocative. For a time, too, he mistrusted him because he suspected —quite wrongly—that he encouraged the Pan-German circles in Austria against the Ruling House. He imagined that Wilhelm II had had a hand in it when a Deputy, in a session of the Vienna Reichsrat, called for cheers for the Hohenzollerns. Moreover, he had doubts as to the reliability of the German Kaiser as an ally. Twice already—in 1908 at Schönbrunn and again in 1912 at Springe—Wilhelm II had lent him support in his attitude to Serbia only subject to reservations. At another occasion, in Leipzig, there had been sharp differences of opinion in the Austrian delegation between the Archduke Franz Ferdinand and General Conrad, which had been composed by the Kaiser, whose guests they were. But the Archduke had departed in a huff, considering that he had been made to look ridiculous before his host.

With the object of making him forget the painful scene, the Kaiser decided to pay a visit to the Archduke at Konopischt. As to the form taken by the relations between Franz Ferdinand and the Kaiser after the Leipzig episode, Count Stürgkh, the Austrian Prime Minister, has written in his *Memoirs*, "That they were on friendly terms was undeniable, but my conviction was that no personal liking on either side was the reason for it. The Archduke Franz Ferdinand was far too much of an Austrian, and had grown up far too much under the influence of the traditions of his House, to confide his innermost feelings without reserve to a scion of the House of the Hohenzollern. He certainly could not forget the long score of enmity shown by that House toward the Hapsburg-Lorrainers for 160 years. Any friendship was based on this consideration—'We are in urgent need of one another, consequently we must be friends!' I firmly believe, too, that if Franz Ferdinand had come to the throne and been convinced that some other alliance would be more profitable for Austria-Hungary, it would not have cost him one heart pang to abandon Germany and her Kaiser."

Despite all the outward stressing of cordiality, the extent to which their association was forced is clearly apparent in their correspondence, in which it is striking how subserviently Franz Ferdinand, so well known for very different qualities, expressed himself in writing to Wilhelm II.

"I am, as always, following with the greatest admiration your policy, with which in all modesty and with the deepest devotion I should like to identify myself entirely." He ended with this: "Permit me, Your Majesty, to say how anxious I am to be allowed to discuss with you the latest political events, for which an opportunity may offer in Leipzig, where I shall have the honor of meeting you again, or at Konopischt. I could tell you much that in my humble opinion is interesting."

To this the Kaiser replied quite unaffectedly: "I thank you with all my heart for your kind and friendly note. You know how much I enjoy visiting you and how I look forward to being with you in that beautiful home that you have made for yourself! I hope that it will suit you if I come immediately after my wife's birthday, which seems a good time as regards the weather and climate. . . . I, too, am looking forward with the utmost interest and satisfaction to the early opportunity of talking many things over with you and I am very glad of the common understanding between us that you express in your letter."

Wilhelm II and the heir to the Austrian throne were in many ways alike. Both were self-willed, impulsive, obdurate and impatient of constitutional restrictions. Both looked on the nobility and the Army as the pillars of the monarchy. Anyone who attacked the monarchy, for instance the Social Democrats, was their enemy. Their monarchical sentiments were based upon their religious tendencies. For each the Church represented the co-ordinating power. In love of the Navy they shared a common interest. It was a proud day for Admiral Franz Ferdinand when he could accompany the *Hohenzollern* to Corfu, not with worm-eaten floating coffins dating back to the days of Tegethoff, but with real warships. Even in questions of art they thought alike, both were ever ready to join in a conversation as dilettanti, each called for changes according to his own taste, and for the rest looked on the artist as an instrument for glorifying his Emperor and the Ruling House.

In this friendship Wilhelm II played the predominant part. When he visited Konopischt in the middle of June 1914 his influence over Franz Ferdinand was so strong that he could venture to raise the difficult problem of Hungary. The heir to the throne did not at all agree with the policy of Count Stephan Tisza [2] toward the Rumanians. He feared that one day they might rise against the entire Empire and therefore should be held back. As he put it, the Emperor Franz Joseph "groveled so to speak on his stomach before Tisza," who unfortunately did everything to turn the Rumanians into enemies of the Dual Monarchy.

In Konopischt Franz Ferdinand reverted to the question whether Austria-Hungary could rely on the support of their German ally in the event of a grave situation's arising from the prolonged hostility of the Serbs and the dangerous activity of the *Narodna odbrana*. Again Wilhelm evaded giving a direct answer. He may have taken the same view as Bismarck, who said, "It is not Germany's business to promote Austria's ambitious designs in the Balkans!"

After such a tentative excursion into the field of politics came recreation—in the form of shooting. This also they each carried out in a similar way. In contrast to the old Emperor, who preferred shooting deer in the mountains, they stayed on the flat land because there it was easier and quicker to let fly with their guns. Although Wilhelm II held some records for popping off at game, the heir to the Austrian throne surpassed him in that. Count Adalbert Sternberg used to call those indiscriminate slaughterings "downright sadism."

No sooner had the Archduke started off for the scene of the day's

[2] Count Stephan Tisza (1861–1917), Premier of Hungary from 1913 to 1917. He vainly opposed the strong ultimatum that Foreign Minister Berchtold of Austria sent to Serbia, following the assassination of Archduke Franz Ferdinand on June 28, 1914, at Sarajevo.

operations than he would begin to fire through the compartment window, even at crows. It sometimes happened that in these wild discharges he hit people working in the fields, or a beater. At his stand, dressed in leather breeches and a Salzburger jacket, he exchanged gun after gun at such a rate that his loaders could hardly keep him supplied quickly enough. He liked to have "Soph, the good Soph" (his wife) standing behind him—firstly because he wanted her to see how he could shoot, and secondly because she "brought him luck." It was not at all uncommon to have eight hundred hares in the day's bag.

In Konopischt the Kaiser had every opportunity of noting the happy family life of the Archduke. Respect for the sanctity of marriage was another thing that bound them together. In the Schloss the thrifty mistress of the house saw to everything, haunted by the thought that her servants were robbing her. If either she or her husband had to journey anywhere there was an affecting scene of leave-taking, in which he would make the sign of the cross on her forehead. This family life in Konopischt was hidden from the eyes of outsiders. Scarcely any member of the Ruling House had anything to do with "the Este," either because they could not bear his intolerant ways, or because they feared to arouse the wrath of the stern head of the family in Schönbrunn.

For his part Franz Ferdinand had a very poor opinion of his relations: "They're stupid and thickheaded in so far as they're not crackpots!" He was not quite so severe as regards the little tubby, rosy-cheeked bookworm, Ludwig Salvator, and his cousin, Joseph in Alczuth, who was working on a grammar of the Tzigane language. "He'll never have anything stolen!" said the Archduke with a laugh. "The gypsies are guarding his Schloss!" The Archduke Ludwig was the only one with whom Franz Ferdinand was on good terms; but the day came when Ludwig, having had enough of Court life in Vienna, emigrated to Majorca, there to enjoy an idyllic existence, surrounded by his harem.

Hence, for the lonely Franz Ferdinand, a visit from the Kaiser was an important event. He made use of it to bemoan his fate every time they went for a walk or paced up and down the George Gallery. He had to stand by inactive and watch how his old uncle ruled, and according to him everything was being brought to ruin. When the Emperor fell seriously ill, in April 1914, the Archduke had his royal train kept standing day and night with steam up, so as to get quickly to Vienna should the old gentleman make room for him. But hope was again deferred; fate had duped him once more. "Thus I must wait, and be told less than the meanest bootboy in Schönbrunn. My position is like that of an expectant heir to an entailed inheritance who must look on quietly while the aged proprietor lets great properties be depreciated through dishonest management."

Once when Wilhelm was speaking of the Emperor, the heir to the throne burst out, "The old man only imagines that he governs! In reality he himself is governed by Metternich, from his grave, with moldy files and outmoded laws that only go halfway and are no longer valid."

Later at Doorn the Kaiser recalled the Archduke's "moody, dreamy eyes. He looked more like a man from Ferrara, from the homeland of the Estes, than an Austrian. What struck me once at a dinner in the German Embassy at Vienna was the tight fit of his uniform over his corpulent figure. When I expressed surprise at this, he confessed that for special occasions he had himself sewn into his uniforms. This craze, to satisfy his vanity, was to cost him his life very soon after my visit to Konopischt, for when struck down by those bullets in Sarajevo, they tried in vain to unbutton his uniform. When they found the strange reason for this and fetched a pair of scissors, it was too late."

As for the Serbs, Franz Ferdinand scarcely gave a thought to a move against Serbia—unless he was compelled to do so by Serbia herself. The best solution was, he considered, to use the Serbs as a counterpoise to the Hungary that he hated. He wished to put into practice the advice once given to Franz Joseph by Napoleon III— to make his Slav subjects the mainstay of the Austrian monarchy.

In this connection the historian Richard Bahr remarked that "Franz Ferdinand thought of making an end of the motley conglomeration of States that constituted the Dual Monarchy, superseding dualism by the so-called trialism, and setting up a Southern-Slav element of the Empire side by side with a predominant element comprising the Germans and Magyars. This idea was prompted largely by his hatred of Hungary. Such was his aversion to the Magyars that he never would receive their Prime Minister, Count Stephan Tisza."

This scheme of the Archduke's found favor and encouragement among the politicians. One of these was Karl Lueger, the Burgomaster of Vienna, who openly acknowledged himself to be a follower of "the Este." The old gentleman in Schönbrunn was not unaware of this. Shaking his head, he said to Beck, "There's nothing of *me* in the Este! No, he is not of *my* blood!" When a portfolio of papers, with enclosures giving the opinion of, or remarks by, Franz Ferdinand, was put before him in Schönbrunn, he sighed as he turned over the sheets. "It's unbelievable! He's now poking his nose into *this*!"

In his plans for reorganizing the Imperial Army, the Archduke stuck to the proven model—the German Army. As a guest at maneuvers in Prussia he had made its acquaintance. He was concerned, above all, to reform the General Staff. For that task he recommended, despite some earlier differences of opinion, General Conrad von Hötzendorff, "an outstanding soldier, but a poor judge of men." Conrad was, in his opinion, the only man capable of dealing with "those rascals."

With the object of putting his plans to a practical test, Franz Ferdinand decided to attend the maneuvers in Bosnia. This decision he mentioned shortly before the Kaiser's departure, and in connection with it the Archduke once more put the question, "What would you do, Your Majesty, if over Bosnia we got involved in Balkan disputes?"

Again the Kaiser evaded giving any direct answer, but he gave the Archduke to understand that in the event of such a conflict, which would beyond doubt bring Russia into the field at once, the German Reich never could or should engage in a war for life or death on two fronts.

That Wilhelm II did in fact make this explicit declaration at Konopischt in those days of June 1914 is today certain. Quite surprisingly it was calmly accepted by the Archduke. "You are right, Your Majesty! Even if we were victorious in the war against Serbia, all we should get would be a pack of thieves, ruffians, murderers and . . . a few plum trees!" [3]

"Murderers" was the word the Archduke used. While shaking hands with the Kaiser on his departure he was already a doomed man. Laughing, he invited the Kaiser to come again in the autumn, unconscious of the fact that this leave-taking on the station platform was a parting forever.

[3] Plums, as fruit and as providing alcohol, were an important source of both private income and government revenue in Serbia.

Not the slightest breeze was blowing. The folds of the black and gold (Austrian) and the black, white and red (German) flags hung limply from their poles, showing too much black between the lines of fan palms that had been set up, and giving the impression of a mourning display.

When the Kaiser's train had left, the Archduke and his wife got into their carriage to return to Konopischt. As they were passing a piece of fallow land the Duchess pointed to some ravens, birds that were seldom to be seen thereabouts in the month of June. "Ravens?" exclaimed the Archduke, annoyed and rising from his seat. "They are birds of ill omen for our House! That's strange! Just twenty-five years ago Rudolf was driving to Mayerling for the shooting, and some of those same birds alighted on the road! Rudolf was very upset by that incident! I remember that he is said to have repeated the words, 'Drive on, it's enough to send one crazy!' "

A few days later Franz Ferdinand left on the way to Sarajevo and his death. The Duchess was to follow him; she sensed the danger, but did not know that a stream of warnings was already pouring in from Bosnia to the authorities in Vienna. Some even came from the Serbian Government itself, who pleaded urgently that the visit of the heir to the throne should be postponed, as the present was not a favorable moment.

Franz Ferdinand, however, cared little about "unfavorable moments," about the Serbian National Festival Day (that of St. Vitus), about the anniversary of the battle of the Amselfeld, or even about the *Narodna odbrana*, that group of conspirators so dangerous to himself. His tremendous obstinacy, his determination to carry through to the end everything that he had planned, decided him to select precisely that day for his entry into Sarajevo.

There, on June 28, 1914, the fateful shots were fired, fourteen years to the day after the registration of the Archduke's morganatic marriage in Vienna and his act of renunciation. The victims of the outrage were Franz Ferdinand and the Duchess Sophie—the shots were in fact intended for Master General of the Ordnance Potiorek. The murderer was one Gavrile Princip—a name that may be read either as "the first" or as "a principle." He was the first to strike at the Dual Monarchy with a weapon, and thereby to make a principle of the destruction of everything Austrian.

Destiny was fufilled in Sarajevo as the result of willful defiance and exhibitions of petty vanity. Goethe had once written in his diary: "Nobody, save one who entirely renounces his own interests, is worthy to rule, or can rule." Franz Ferdinand could not comply with the first requirement and therefore was never to attain the position of ruler.

It must, however, be regarded as a tragedy that the very man who planned to rebuild the Dual Monarchy on a basis that favored the Serbs should be assassinated by a Serb. And it was just because parts of Serbia were to be incorporated into the Dual Monarchy, Princip confessed before his judges, that the Austrian had to die, in order that the greater Serbia might arise.

In Vienna the Chief Marshal of the Household was busy with his Book of Ceremonial, making ready for the burials. After a lengthy explanation that there could be no question of the Archduke and his morganatic wife being buried in the Capucine vault, he reached the conclusion that "the old-established laws of legitimacy should not be flouted. Conduct of that kind would be equivalent to irreverence." So the dead husband and wife were debarred from the mausoleum of the Hapsburgs. Even for the lying-in-state Montenuovo insisted that the coffin of the Duchess should stand one step lower than that of the Archduke. On the latter were laid the crown of a prince and the Archduke's plumed hat. On the coffin of the Duchess of Hohenberg lay only a fan and a pair of gloves.

Ostensibly on account of ill health the Emperor took no part in the ceremony. When the news of the assassination of the Archduke was first given him, he had remained unmoved. He merely remarked to his A.D.C., General Count Paar, that "the Almighty has restored the order that I, alas, was unable to maintain! God does not allow Himself to be defied!"

So the Archduke Franz Ferdinand, Inspector General of all the Armed Forces of the Empire, and his spouse were carried away in strict privacy to Amstetten. It was two o'clock in the morning when the cortège entered Pöchlarn just as a heavy thunderstorm broke. During the crossing of the Danube by ferry, flashes of lightning struck just behind the ferryboat. The heavy crashes of thunder that followed so frightened the horses of the hearse that they shied and reared up and one wheel was hanging over the water. It was only thanks to the strenuous efforts of the mourners that a catastrophe was averted. On reaching the far bank everything had to be

put to rights, and the wreath (which had fallen off), with its white
silk band marked with a golden W and the crown of the German
Kaiser, had to be restored to its place, before the journey to Amstetten could be resumed.

The political seismographs were beginning to tremble. The shots
of Sarajevo and the thunder and lightning of Pöchlarn had awakened
angry echoes. Only thirty more days were to pass before Europe
burst into flames.

76. THE GERMAN ARMY AND NAVY

WHEN THE SUPREME WAR LORD looked back on the development of his Army and Navy since his accession, he had every
reason to be content with the results achieved in those twenty-five
years—twenty-five army corps (including the new corps in Allenstein and Saarbrücken) had passed from the stage of paper estimates to that of realities. So Germany was prepared for war, even
for a war on two fronts. The General Staff was, of course, of the
opinion that three more corps were absolutely necessary, and these
were demanded by Lieutenant Colonel Ludendorff. He was unperturbed by the hostile clamor of the Social Democrats, who sought
to wreck this new bill with allegations of soldiers being ill-treated
and similar arguments.

As for the combat value of the Army, opinion was unanimous—
it was of the highest standard. An officer of the French General Staff
stated in June 1914 that "the German Army could bring France to
her knees in six months."

If Friedrich Wilhelm III could say, "I have jumped straight from
Brigade Commander to King," Wilhelm II could say the same of
himself, who before he was thirty, and having only ranked as a
General for a short time, had become King, and Supreme War Lord.
The words addressed by him to the Army shortly after mounting
the throne expressed his desire to remain thenceforth, as King and
Kaiser, a soldier in the first place. "So we are born for one another,
and so we intend to hold together indissolubly whether it be peace or
storm that comes by the will of God." Outwardly this was clearly

evident from the fact that the Kaiser wore uniform almost exclusively. He looked upon the Prussian Army as his own. He was not
at all pleased when this possession—even unintentionally—was disputed. When Major Wissmann, just back from Africa, began his
report by saying, "For the rapid success of the operations in the
colony, I have to thank the ability of my officers . . . ," the Kaiser
sharply corrected him: "They are *my* officers!"

Wilhelm II gratefully acknowledged the historical successes of
his Army. "What the Kings of Prussia accomplished in the past was
only made possible by their having a people who produced such in-
comparable officers and soldiers." He never missed an opportunity
of showing his regard for the old officers of the 1870's; thus he had
all the colors of the regiments that had served under von Moltke at
Paris paraded before the old Field Marshal, on his ninetieth birthday.

As there were very few young officers in the Army and their
average education standard was low—Field Marshal Count von
Wrangel had never been able to speak German properly—the Kaiser
endeavored to remedy both these defects. A colonel was not to
be over the age of fifty, and as far as possible young officers were
to be selected only from the *Abiturienten* (students who had passed
the final examinations of secondary schools). The Kaiser further laid
it down that the young officer was to be trained with a view to
strengthening his character and giving him an ideal and self-reliant
personality. Here he was thinking of Schlieffen, who had claimed
that character was more important than anything else in a military
leader.

In spite of His Majesty's clear-sightedness in these respects, some
people in military circles feared that besides the men already marked
out in the case of need, such as Ludendorff, Groener, Kluck and
Scholtz, "Court generals" and Federal princes might be entrusted
with important commands. This did in fact happen later on, but the
Crown Princes of Prussia and Bavaria, and also Duke Albrecht of
Württemberg, stood the test in the field beyond all expectations. The
employment of the "Court General" August von Mackensen [1]—even
as a general he used to kiss the Kaiser's hand—was regarded with

[1] Field Marshal August von Mackensen (1849–1941) commanded some of
Germany's most spectacular campaigns on the Eastern Front against Russia
in 1915, against Serbia that same year, and against Rumania in 1916.

misgivings. But this choice also turned out to be a happy one, for wherever Mackensen's Corps, or Army, fought later on, they were successful, whether it be that luck or Seeckt [2] turned the scales. Only results are decisive, and in the case of a general, only success.

Mackensen had become well known in the Army for his parade displays. The regimental and brigade exercises of his Death's-Head Hussars, and the charges in close order that he led himself, made a magnificent impression on a spectator but nevertheless were, as the Kaiser himself had to admit to the English Colonel Swayne, only of use for inculcating discipline. "In case of war, of course, such a charge as this would have been impossible, but all the same it was a grand spectacle—forty-eight squadrons galloping across that great plain. The thunder of the hoofs was enough to deafen one!"

The Supreme War Lord's admiration of such "playing at soldiers" was looked on with misgiving by responsible people in the Ministry of War and the General Staff. Heads were shaken at seeing the Kaiser losing himself more and more in external trappings, designing new uniforms and braidings or inventing cords and silver whistles for dispatch riders.

The normally tolerant younger Moltke remarked in this connection, "Different-colored cords are hung round the men's necks, as an insignia of good marksmanship, that will only interfere with the handling of their rifles. By countless external distinguishing marks ambition is incited, instead of developing the sense of duty. Uniforms are being made ever more bright, instead of being made inconspicuous for field use, and exercises are being turned into theatrical performances. . . ."

This incessant brightening-up of uniforms, with all the spit and polish involved, with new cuirasses, with finer fur trimmings, goldbordered saddle cloths and coral-studded bridles, cost a great deal of money. The young gentlemen of the nobility, as officers of distinguished regiments, found themselves faced with expenses for their equipment which they could no longer afford, unless they happened

[2] General Hans von Seeckt (1866–1936), Chief of Staff to Mackensen and originator of the break-through technique used by the Germans on the Eastern Front in the first World War and further developed in the *Blitzkrieg* campaigns of the second World War. Seeckt reorganized the Reichswehr after the defeat of 1918, worked closely with the Russians, laid the foundations for Hitler's armies, and served as an adviser to Chiang Kai-shek.

to be well-off, or did not mind plunging into debt as soon as their ensign days were over. On the other hand, fathers always wanted to have their sons serve in their own old historic regiments, and sought to prevent their being posted to inferior regiments.

A deep rift threatened to open between the officers, on the one side the Guards and the Cavalry, on the other the Infantry of the line, the Artillery, Pioneers and the despised Army Service Corps. Twenty-two years before this, Wilhelm II had sought to put a stop to the widening of the breach that even then existed, and to that end he issued (on March 29, 1890) the following decree: "I cannot approve of entrance into the Corps of Officers being made to depend on excessively large private means; this only prevents sons of less well-endowed families, who, however, in sentiment and conception of life, are closely connected with the Corps of Officers, from entering the Army. I consider it disadvantageous if the necessity for a private income in the Cavalry, and particularly in the Guards, has become so great that the landed proprietors will find it virtually impossible to let their sons serve in the arm that has become so dear to them. The Army cannot but be ill-served by such extravagant demands!"

But that well-intentioned appeal had long since been forgotten. Count Waldersee laid the blame on the Kaiser himself: "His Majesty knows only the Guards and the Navy!" Waldersee looked on "luxury and prodigality" in cavalry messes as threatening danger to the old Prussian spirit of the officer. As a warning he called attention to the motto that figured in the *Handbook of the General Staff Officer*—"*Mehr sein als scheinen!*" (Be more than you appear to be!)

In contrast to Potsdam and Berlin there could be no question of luxury or extravagance in the messes of the small garrison towns and villages. Here everyone had plenty to do, especially on the frontiers. Also, the scanty pocket money coming from home, and the Army pay of fifty marks a month did not admit of much expenditure. Conduct had to be exemplary in the eyes of the population, and one had to be always on duty.

Because of the privileged position accorded to the Army within the State it was no wonder that everyone wanted to be in it, even if it were only as an ambulance man, a stretcher-bearer or driver of a wagon in the train. The Kaiser took every opportunity of stressing this "especial esteem" enjoyed by his Army, "through whose School of Arms every physically sound German must be passed."

Bismarck had been a Cuirassier, Bülow a Hussar and Bethmann-Hollweg had been made a Dragoon, without any of the three having received a real military training. Naturally enough, every official wanted to be at least a "Summer Lieutenant" (reserve officer) and to wear a uniform as they did, so as not to be looked down upon as a civilian. But to become an officer in the Prussian Army it was necessary to fulfill certain conditions, for instance to furnish proof of good origin, and here the fact of having a father who was a shop-keeper was quite sufficient to ensure disqualification. An ambitious man in Germany could become a Commercial Councilor, or even a Privy Councilor, he could receive the Order of the Red Eagle or that of the Crown, he might even secure the ennobling "von," but to become a Reserve Lieutenant was not so easy. Indeed, His Excellency the Privy Councilor Dernburg, all-powerful in colonial matters, had first to pass the test on the barrack square before he could be finally promoted from Sergeant Major to Reserve Lieutenant.

By comparison with the Army, the Navy was less in evidence. The reason for this was that the naval stations were situated on the coast and the crews were frequently abroad. In the Navy there were no distinctions between officers, such as existed in the Army. Anyone who did his duty could get along, whether he was of noble or bourgeois birth, whether he had large or small private means. The Navy knew that it could hold its own with the Army, and also that the training of its officers and seamen was far superior. What alone impressed the German Navy was the British fleet, *the* Navy. Every German seagoing officer could speak English; he knew all the particulars of each British warship, its size, date of launching and the kind of use for which it was intended. If a unit of the Royal Navy happened to come into view of German telescopes, every movement was closely followed and afterward discussed in the messes. They still took the British fleet as their model.

In their Grand Admiral, Alfred von Tirpitz, the German Navy saw a representative from its own ranks. He, who had grown up with the German Navy, enjoyed the highest respect in naval circles, not only because of his talent for organization and his expert knowledge but also because of his dexterous handling of affairs in the

Reichstag. His speeches on naval construction were read with keen delight. From them they could appreciate the cunning with which he was able to keep the opponents of the bill in the dark. It was immaterial to Tirpitz by what means he got the bill passed, even if the excited member Liebknecht [3] did shout at him in the Reichstag, "You swindler!"

In the fleet Tirpitz saw not only a fighting force for the protection of coasts and colonies but also an instrument whereby new aims could be attained, and a crucible in which the several peoples of Germany could be fused together effectively. On this latter point he once expressed himself thus: "In point of fact none of the many measures taken by the German Reich since it was organized on a solid basis in 1871 has contributed so powerfully or in so many ways to fostering the idea of unity as the creation of the fleet. In the fleet, north and south, east and west, met, animated by the one determination: to give of their best and to create great things. Distinctions and differences of race, origin and dialect disappeared. Under the war flag of the Reich men learned to feel and to think as Germans. . . . One may state confidently, and what we know of the past in no way qualifies it, that the inception and the expansion of the Imperial Navy have not only increased the defensive strength of the German people but have also given an important upward impulse to its political development. The outlook of those who served under the war flag widened, the hinterland awoke, and through kinship with men in the Navy seafaring matters came to be discussed far from any coast line. Above all, the sense of community of interests, widened by the increasing comprehension of what is important in world politics, spread its roots more strongly and farther afield. Every seaman or stoker who went on leave from Wilhelmshaven or Kiel became in a greater or lesser degree a disseminator of these ideas. When he returned home from abroad, he found the most willing listeners for his yarns in places to which the breath of world understanding had not yet advanced. It is impossible to evaluate, in figures and statistics, the importance of this spontaneous work of enlightenment performed by the Navy. That it was of considerable

[3] Karl Liebknecht, Left-Wing German Socialist, son of Wilhelm Liebknecht, one of the founders of the German Social Democratic party. Karl Liebknecht was the first German Socialist to vote against war credits after war came in 1914 and he was murdered in 1919 with Rosa Luxembourg because of revolutionary activities.

importance and had a sound and healthy influence on the German people does not admit of the slighest doubt."

77. HELMUTH VON MOLTKE THE SECOND

WHEN COUNT ALFRED VON SCHLIEFFEN retired from his post as Chief of the great General Staff on New Year's Day of 1906, the Kaiser nominated General Helmuth von Moltke, a nephew of the great Army Commander, as his successor. He expected that this famous name alone would have a good effect on the service. He was, of course, aware that the second Moltke, despite his excellent military qualifications, did not come up to the level of "the Great Silent One." In connection with his nomination, people have ascribed to the Kaiser these words: "Now, my dear Moltke, don't worry! In war I shall myself be Chief of the General Staff, and you will very soon master the little bits of peacetime work!" The Kaiser never made this statement. It came from the Munich comic paper *Simplicissimus*, issue No. 41 of the year 1905.

Helmuth von Moltke was already a sick man when he was sent for. He himself pointed this out and asked to be excused. The Kaiser, however, would not hear of it, probably because there was no one else to whom he felt he could entrust that responsible post. The new Chief of the General Staff was one of the few at Court who dared to tell the Kaiser the truth. Moltke himself stated later that alone with the Kaiser, and in correct form, he could tell him quite unpleasant things. "He never bore me a grudge if I stood up to him frankly." Moltke's experience confirmed what Tirpitz and Ballin had already established.

Thus Moltke frankly opposed the Supreme War Lord's attitude to war games, which were reduced by him to the level of parlor games. "Your Majesty knows that the army led by you invariably encircles the opponent and thus, apparently, decides the outcome of the war at one stroke. That kind of war game, in which Your Majesty's opponent is, so to speak, delivered up with his hands tied, must give rise to entirely false conceptions that can only be pernicious when war comes. . . . I consider it as even more serious that because of the violence done to the war game, the large numbers of officers taking part find all the interest taken out of it. . . . But what I above all else deplore, and must tell Your Majesty, is that it deeply undermines the confidence of the officers in their Supreme War Lord. They say that the Kaiser is far too astute not to notice that everything is arranged so that he must be successful—he must therefore have wished it to be so!"

Anyone who saw Moltke in his gray cloak, erect as an athlete, broad shouldered and the very type of a Prussian General, would scarcely imagine that this heroic figure was a highly strung, sensitive man, moody, weak, and pessimistic into the bargain, with a bent for mysticism, in which he was not unlike Waldersee.

Moltke was greatly liked by those who served under him—they nicknamed him "Julius," and it suited him extremely well. He had learned his trade under the eagle eye of his great-uncle, and from him he took over the motto "First ponder, then dare!" Later on he was to ponder too much, and to venture on the decisive stroke too late.

In June 1914, when the fateful shots were fired in Sarajevo, he was taking the cure at Karlsbad. He felt ill, weary and run-down and complained of pains. Hardly able to muster enough energy for a walk to the pump room, he had to pack his bags and return to Berlin as quickly as possible.

78. THE CROWN COUNCIL IN POTSDAM

SUNDAY, JUNE 28, 1914, was Hamburg's Derby Day. In radiant summer weather the onlookers were crowding onto the course in expectation of the great sporting event. The red disk had already been hoisted, to show that the weighing-in was over. The horses cantered up to the starting point, when something quite unexpected happened: the number boards were lowered and the red disk removed, as also, a little later, was the name of the hot favorite Confusionarius, owned by the Austro-Hungarian financier Nikolaus von Szemere.

Immediately before the start of the Derby it became known in the stands why Confusionarius had been withdraw from the 100,-000-mark race—"The Archduke and heir to the throne, and his wife, have been assassinated in Sarajevo!" A troop of newspaper boys with special editions rushed among the crowds spreading the news. Many onlookers left the race course, convinced that this outrage must involve world-shaking consequences. In Hamburg people had always known how to react to the events of the day, how to weigh political news accurately, to make their arrangements, and to act in accordance therewith and not just because of the stock exchange!

From Hamburg to Kiel! On that Derby Sunday the Kiel Week had reached its peak. Surrounded by many yachts the slim white *Hohenzollern* lay at her moorings, dressed over all. Outside, off Laboe, lay a British squadron paying a visit to Kiel. The yachts that were still engaged in the race crept slowly up the fiord.

The Kaiser had sat down on deck under an awning in the *Hohenzollern* in order to study the program of the Regatta and to scan the sea with his telescope for the first yacht to come in. Suddenly a naval pinnace appeared alongside the *Hohenzollern*; an obviously excited officer stood up in her and called for the Officer of the Watch, at the same time holding up a telegram to show that it was urgent. The Kaiser, hearing the noise, got up and looked over the rails. When the officer saw him he made the pinnace turn sharply, snatched his cigarette case from his pocket, put the telegram inside and threw it onto the deck, where a sailor picked it up and handed it to the Kaiser.

When the Kaiser had read the telegram and learned that his friend the Archduke Franz Ferdinand and his Duchess had been murdered, he at once had the Imperial Standard lowered to half-mast. The Regatta was terminated and orders given for an immediate return to Potsdam.

Wilhelm II, of course, wanted to escort his friend on his last journey, but it was indicated to him from Vienna, as also to the Crown Prince of Rumania and his wife, that with regard to the state of health of the Emperor Franz Joseph, they would be grateful if the intention to go to Vienna would be abandoned. That would also serve as an excuse for preventing the unwanted King Peter of Serbia from appearing at the funeral.

On considering the new political situation that had arisen, Wilhelm II changed his attitude. He, who until then was opposed to "taking part in every Viennese folly against Serbia" now thought that it was time to make a firm stand against greater Serbian designs. Belgrade must be made to understand that the measure was now full. But he considered it questionable whether at the Ballhausplatz in Vienna they would take any decisive action, for the Foreign Minister, Count Leopold Berchtold, seemed totally devoid of energy. Wilhelm II considered a punitive action against Serbia as justified, but it must be localized, and above all must not bring Russia into the field.

In the period between June twenty-ninth and July sixth he stayed in Potsdam, waiting for any further developments; he then decided to start on his usual Scandinavian cruise. By so doing he wished to show that he trusted Russia and expected that St. Petersburg would show itself as disinterested in the events in Serbia as he was himself. The Reich's Chancellor, von Bethmann-Hollweg, approved of this voyage, because he too thought it would have a good and calming effect in Europe.

Before boarding the *Hohenzollern* the Kaiser received Admiral von Capelle and General von Bertrab to give them a short résumé of his appreciation of the political situation brought about by the crime of Sarajevo.

In reply to a request made by the (German) Foreign Office on October 8, 1919, Admiral von Capelle gave in evidence the following account of his conversation with the Kaiser. It is filed under the number A.S. 2139.

"On Monday the 28.6 1914 [a mistake on the part of Capelle], between 7 and 8 in the morning I received as Acting Secretary of State—Admiral von Tirpitz being on leave—a telephonic request to go at once to the Kaiser at the Neues Palais. I found the Kaiser in the garden, ready to start on his Scandinavian cruise. He walked up and down and he gave me a brief statement of the events of the previous day, Sunday. According to my recollection he added something like this: . . . he did not believe in any serious warlike developments. In his opinion the Czar would not side with the murderers in this case. Besides, neither Russia nor France was ready for war. He made no mention of England. On the advice of his Chancellor he would go on his northern cruise, so as not to cause any uneasiness.

Yet he wanted to inform me of the tense situation, so that I might think about it further. There was no consultation at Potsdam on July sixth of the military authorities, for immediately after his conversation with me the Kaiser left for Kiel."

The same record also contains the reply of General von Bertrab to a similar request. It is filed under number S.2194, October 20, 1919:

"I respectfully inform the Foreign Office that on July sixth His Majesty the Kaiser informed me personally and with no witness of his views on the situation that had arisen in consequence of measures taken in Austria, so that I, as the senior officer of the General Staff serving at the moment in Berlin, might inform the Chief of the General Staff, who was staying in Karlsbad. Present were, in the background, Her Majesty the Kaiserin, an A.D.C. and a footman. Immediately before, His Majesty had spoken, obviously to the same purpose, to a naval officer who left at once after the conversation. When the Kaiser dismissed me he got into his car to leave for his Scandinavian cruise. No instructions or orders were given me either during the conversation or following it. His Majesty even emphasized that he did not consider it necessary to issue any special orders, as he did not expect any serious developments as a result of the crime in Sarajevo."

The reception of these two officers, with the Kaiserin, one A.D.C. and a footman "in the background," must have been the cause for a serious statement by the Entente that a Crown Council had been held in Potsdam. The result of the council was to have been the decision to incite Austria-Hungary to take severe measures against Serbia, irrespective of the consequences which might provoke a war. It was said that after this Crown Council Wilhelm II had gone off on his travels merely to deceive the Entente and to lull it into a feeling of security. In fact, this frequently quoted "Potsdam Crown Council" was merely a malicious invention and has been recognized as such by objective and neutral critics. The simple truth is that the Kaiser, before starting on his journey, summoned the two senior staff officers who happened to be in Berlin, to make them acquainted with his own views on the existing political crisis.

On July sixth the Kaiser sailed. To his intimates he expressed himself as confident on the score of further developments between

Vienna and Belgrade. "I cannot imagine that the old gentleman in Schönbrunn will go to war, and most certainly not if it is a war over the Archduke Franz Ferdinand!"

79. SERBIA FACES A DECISION

THE CORRESPONDENCE that passed between President Poincaré and Izvolski in the years 1911–1914 shows that after the annexation of Bosnia and Herzegovina, Russia had but one aim—to exclude Austria-Hungary from the Balkans, if necessary by force of arms. In order to attain that object, Russian policy had to support Serbia, which had emerged from the Balkan wars with her territory considerably enlarged. Thus encouraged, Serbia could proceed toward the realization of an old dream—the creation of a great Southern Slav State. In this endeavor the Belgrade Government was encouraged by the Russian Ambassador Hartwig, who, like Izvolski, came from the school of Count Ignatiev.[1]

However, despite this strengthening, the Belgrade Government could not launch out as energetically as it would have liked. Their army had been decimated in two hard-fought wars and was no longer battleworthy. Almost everything needed for a war was lacking. Besides, spotted typhus and cholera were raging in the country. For these reasons alone the Serbian Government was not keen to embark upon a fresh war, especially against powerful Austria.

Today it is established that the Belgrade Government did not instigate the murders in Sarajevo. It must, however, be regarded as bearing a great part of the responsibility, in that it tolerated the *Narodna odbrana* and allowed it, without interference from Serbia, to make itself a nuisance to Austria-Hungary. Trained by these conspirators, Princip committed his crime.

[1] Count Nikolai Pavlovich Ignatiev (1832–1908) served as Russian Minister in Peking, where he gained territorial concessions from the Chinese, and as Ambassador in Constantinople, where his intrigues culminated in the Russo-Turkish war of 1877–1878. The disappointing results of this war, from the Russian point of view, caused him to fall into disfavor, but he continued to exert some influence on the next generation of Russian statesmen, who were largely responsible for their country's policies up to the outbreak of the first World War.

Von Wiessner, Councilor in the Security Section of the Vienna Foreign Office, who was entrusted with the investigations in Sarajevo, could only report to his chief Count Berchtold: "From what has been gathered regarding the period previous to the outrage, no evidence has been found for any propaganda being furthered by official Serbian authorities." He further telegraphed: "There is nothing to indicate, nor is there any reason to suppose, any complicity on the part of the Serbian Government either in procuring the crime, in preparing it or in providing the weapons. Rather is there evidence for regarding this as impossible."

This telegram was never made public by the Ballhausplatz. But it must have been known to the Emperor Franz Joseph, for on July 5, 1914, he wrote to the Kaiser that "it will probably be impossible to prove any complicity on the part of the Serbian Government in what happened at Sarajevo."

It was only while he was on his cruise that the Kaiser, after receiving further news from Vienna, began to have doubts about the optimism which he had felt. To be on the safe side, he ordered the German fleet, then lying off Jutland, to return to Wilhelmshaven and Kiel. This Bethmann-Hollweg called "overhasty." Whereupon the Kaiser replied, "The order to the fleet to prepare speedily for its return home was given by me . . . in view of the general situation and possible eventualities. I was all the more forced to do this, as I had not received any Foreign Office report on the situation, and I learned the contents of the Austrian ultimatum only through the newspaper reports from Norddeich, not through official channels." It was a mistake on the Kaiser's part, who ought not to have acted on news reports, but should have awaited information from his Foreign Office, even if the "official channels" meant delay.

As for the ultimatum sent to the Serbian Government from Vienna, the Kaiser approved of its wording. He also agreed with the action taken by Baron Giesl, the Austro-Hungarian Ambassador in Belgrade, but not with the subsequent attitude of Count Berchtold. Taking the opposite view to Berchtold's, he regarded the Serbian reply to the ultimatum as sufficient and satisfactory. "It's a great moral success for Vienna! But it means that there are no grounds for going to war, and Giesl might as well have stayed on in Belgrade! In the circumstances I should never have ordered mobilization! While we are prepared to fulfill our obligations as allies, we must decline to let ourselves be dragged by Vienna lightheartedly and without heeding our advice, into a world conflagration!"

In Vienna there was complete confidence in the German *Nibelungentreue*. If they behaved so boldly, it was only because they felt they could rattle the Kaiser's saber. Cartwright, the British Ambassador in Vienna, reported to London: "Here they rely on Germany, and base all their hopes on their powerful ally. It is certain that they believe there are only two alternatives, either to force Serbia to her knees, or sooner or later to be mutilated by her. . . . Everyone believes in the justice of their cause, so that to the people it seems unthinkable that any country could stand in their way."

When the Kaiser, still in Norwegian waters, received the report that the British home fleet, instead of dispersing as usual after the review at Spithead, was concentrating in the North Sea harbors, he decided to return to Kiel immediately. There were other alarming reports that startled him—news from Russia, according to which mobilization notices had been posted and railway lines torn up on the German frontier. Above all, it was the reports from Vienna and Belgrade that induced him to return to Berlin as quickly as possible in order to prevent "Vienna's continuing to act in this offhand manner."

"There seems to be sulphur in the air," remarked the Berlin banker Fürstenberg, pulling a wry face. "There is something in the wind," reported von Knorr, Naval Attaché in Tokyo, "rather like an expression of condolence about a sentence of death not yet pronounced! In Japan people in general are expecting an early war of the Entente against the German Reich, and frankly say so."

The most crafty monarch in Europe, Ferdinand I of Bulgaria, also had forebodings about this "tremendous July heat." He wrote in confidence to his friend Viktor Hahn, the editor of the *Berliner National-Zeitung,* "War can no longer be averted! I know it, and I know, too, who are guilty parties—Berchtold and Suchomlinov—the latter as cunning as he is unscrupulous, the other vain and foolish. Unfortunately, the German Ambassador in Vienna does not sufficiently restrain the Foreign Minister Berchtold. I certainly do not love my cousin, Kaiser Wilhelm, but I feel sorry for him all the same. Now he will be dragged into the whirlpool, be entangled, and he will have to fight, whether he wants to or not. That is all he gets out of his *Nibelungentreue!*"

80. MEDIATION BY ENGLAND

MUCH NOW DEPENDED on the *Nibelungentreue* that Czar Ferdinand had ridiculed. If Wilhelm could justifiably be reproached with anything during those critical days of July 1914, it would be first and foremost for his decision to keep faith with Austria-Hungary, in any and all circumstances, consistently and to the very limits of what was possible. On the other hand, he objected to "the utterly idiotic measures taken by the Ballhausplatz." His marginal notes to reports from Vienna show how these infuriated him. "*Nanu?*" ("What next?"); "*Blech!*" ("Rubbish!"); "They've already had plenty of time for it"; "*Kindisch!*" ("Childish!")—referring to some of Berchtold's orders.

While Berchtold was carrying on the business of the Ballhausplatz in a casual and "appallingly reckless" fashion, Franz Joseph was seriously following the swift development of political events. Conrad von Hötzendorff said of him, "He has taken the decision to go to war with Serbia, a decision made inevitable by Serbia's behavior, with the utmost seriousness and with the deep-rooted sense of duty proper to his nature, fully realizing the gravity of that decision." And the old gentleman said to Conrad, "If, then, the monarchy is doomed to fall, it should at least fall with decorum!"

There was reason for his outspoken pessimism. The aged ruler knew of the deficiencies in his lands, and also that the Dual Monarchy—as had been the case in 1866—no longer possessed an outstanding Army Commander. The maneuvers had proved that to him. The only General he had who came near to the standard needed was Conrad von Hötzendorff. But even regarding this officer he had doubts, for he considered Conrad as an ideologist and an innovator, or, on account of the reforms he had advocated, even a visionary to whom one could not entrust plenary authority. His doubts brought the gentleman to the point of considering whether the Austro-Hungarian forces should not be placed under the command of a German general. But the idea so horrified him that he soon abandoned it.

If the Emperor made up his mind to declare war on Serbia, it was only because Berchtold, and also Krobatin, the Minister for War, assured him that it would be confined to Serbia and would soon be over. The Foreign Minister, indeed, was so convinced of a quick end to the fighting that he made mistakes that afterward provided most effective material for propaganda against both Austria-Hungary and the German Reich. Wilhelm II later pointed out that one could not, on account of the mistakes made by Berchtold, lay the blame of the World War on the German Reich.

Events in Serbia were followed with strained attention in Paris. An opportunity seemed to present itself at last to escape from the prolonged anxiety of the German menace and, with the help of powerful allies, to banish the German peril. As the alarming news came in from Paris, Wilhelm II remembered Bismarck and his views about France. Later, in Doorn, he said: "The Prince was always aware of the great danger which threatened the existence of the German Reich, the youngest of the great Continental Powers, from its neighbors. He looked on French chauvinism as an irrevocable fact, which Germany had to, and could, put up with, so long as she succeeded in damming or diverting the pressure of Russian expansionism, which was directed westward by Pan-Slav aspirations and inner political ferment."

The price demanded by France for the satisfaction of chauvinism was indicated in a remark made by Prime Minister Barthou to the German Ambassador von Schön: "Give us back Alsace-Lorraine, Your Excellency, and we shall be the best friends in the world!"

While the political situation thus became more acute, the Kaiser received from Sir Edward Grey in London, on the morning of July thirtieth, a proposal for mediation. This he passed on immediately to Vienna, recommending it for "the urgent and serious consideration of the Cabinet in Vienna." He advised "to accept the mediation on the honorable conditions stated." For his part the Kaiser had done everything possible. He could not give orders to the Cabinet in Vienna.

By this intervention Sir Edward had hoped to succeed in what he had already announced in a Cabinet council as the aim of his efforts: "So long as there remains a prospect of a direct exchange of views between Austria-Hungary and Russia, I should like to hold back all other suggestions, as I entirely agree with the view that this is the most preferable method of all." The next day Sir Edward added to his declaration: "For Austria-Hungary and Russia to come to an understanding would be the best possible solution. I should press for no other proposal so long as there remains a possibility of this."

When Count Berchtold—greatly to the Kaiser's displeasure—rejected this suggestion of mediation by London, Sir Edward Grey [1] conveyed through the British Ambassador in Berlin the intimation that he now saw no other possibility except to leave Austria-Hungary and Russia alone to settle their accounts. That did not mean any immediate danger of war for England. But if France and the German Reich should become involved in the conflict, then the question would arise whether England must not comply with her obligations laid down in the *Entente Cordiale*.

When the Kaiser heard of this attitude taken in London he burst out: "So we're to break our faith, just because Herr Grey wants us to! Now you can see what that hypocritical nation of shopkeepers is driving at!" Summarizing all his bitterness in words he scribbled in the margin of a report from Prince Lichnowsky, his Ambassador in London: "Just as I expected! Grey, that utter hypocrite!" It was his old hatred for England that now flared up again. Forgotten were his love and reverence for his grandmother, Victoria. He closed his ears when he heard anyone speak of his mother's country—which, he declared, was determined to bring about his own downfall and that of the German Reich. He was so carried away by his indignation that he would scarcely allow his Chancellor to say a word. "This is too much! That infamous Mister Grey!" Then in his blind fury he threw out threats and warnings that sounded quite childish. "If we have to bleed to death, then, at any rate, England shall lose India in this war!"

It was the old tune—and always the old hatred! It was directed against a phantom, behind which stood the shadow of the dead Edward. In the Kaiser's view it was he who had worked for, and moreover had accomplished, the encirclement of Germany. "A magnificent achievement," his nephew acknowledged bitterly, "truly a magnificent achievement which awakens admiration even in the person who is meant to be ruined by it. Edward VII is dead, but though dead, he is stronger than I, who am alive!"

[1] *See* Appendix, page 441.

81. "I CAN DO NO MORE!"

JUST AS WILHELM II had forwarded and recommended Grey's proposal for mediation to Vienna, he now declared that he was prepared to play the part of "honest broker" between Austria-Hungary and Russia. When Count Pourtalès, German Ambassador in St. Petersburg, reported that an exchange of views was still possible, the Kaiser jumped at the chance and telegraphed to "Dear Purzel"—as he called him familiarly—that he "could scarcely expect Austria-Hungary to negotiate with Serbia, with whom she was already in a state of war, but that it would be a grievous mistake to refuse an exchange of views with St. Petersburg, as such conduct was plainly bound to provoke warlike intervention by Russia."

From the letters and telegrams of those weeks in July it appears that Wilhelm II was convinced that he could still save the peace. His endeavors were, however, conditioned by two suppositions, firstly that he must not break faith with his ally in Vienna, and secondly that "Serbia, with her murderers and bandits, must receive a condign punishment."

In spite of his readiness to mediate, the relations between Russia and Austria-Hungary deteriorated rapidly. In all secrecy the Czar's Empire was already making its first military preparations so as to gain an advantage from the start over the tardy working of the mobilization machinery in the Dual Monarchy. The validity of an old saying of a hundred years before was now being reaffirmed: "While the Austrian pleads, the Russian commands; while the former reproves, the latter lays on with the knout; while the Austrian haggles, the Russian freely dispenses purses well lined with gold."

As the deployment of the Austro-Hungarian troops on the Serbian frontier was making only slow progress, the tone of the Russian press was already exultant and helped to inflame the desire for war in St. Petersburg. It was in this threatening situation that Wilhelm II made yet another attempt at intervention, addressing his "friend and cousin" directly. This highly informative telegram, of July 28, 1914, was worded as follows: "It is with the greatest uneasiness that I hear of the effect produced in your country by Austria's advance against Serbia. The unscrupulous agitation which for years has been at work in Serbia has at last led to the abominable crime to which the Archduke Franz Ferdinand has fallen a victim. The same spirit that made the Serbs murder their own king and his consort still reigns in their land. You will surely agree with me that we two, and all sovereigns, have a common interest in insisting that all those morally responsible for this dastardly murder shall receive their well-deserved chastisement. In a case like this, politics have no part to play. On the other hand I can very well understand how difficult it is for you and your Government to oppose the currents of your public opinion. In consideration of the cordial friendship which for so long has bound us together, I am exerting all my influence to induce Austria to come to a satisfactory understanding with you, by immediate negotiations. I hope and trust that you will support me in my efforts to remove any difficulties that may yet arise."

Next day the Kaiser dispatched another telegram to the Czar, worded in terms no less urgent but somewhat less cordial, exhorting him "not to involve all Europe in a horrible war on account of Serbia."

"Your telegram received and I share your desire to preserve the peace. But, as I told you in my first telegram, I cannot regard Austria's advance on Serbia as an unworthy war. Austria knows from experience that Serbian promises on paper are entirely unreliable. In my view Austria's action is to be judged as seeking full security for any Serbian assurances' being translated into deeds. This view of mine is confirmed by the declaration of the Austrian Cabinet that Austria has no intention whatsoever of seizing any territory at Serbia's expense. Hence I suggest that it should be quite possible for Russia to retain the part of onlooker in this Austro-Serbian conflict. . . ."

While the Kaiser was thus striving to maintain the peace, there occurred an incident whose consequences were of grave importance. It came about through a stupid misunderstanding, which was seized upon by the enemy press as proof of the German urge to go to war. It concerned a telephone conversation that the German Crown Prince Wilhelm had with the chief editor of the *Berliner Lokalan-*

zeiger, just when the crisis was in its most acute stage. On the strength of some incorrect information the Crown Prince had informed the editor that Russia had already mobilized. The result was to rush out a special edition of the paper, which, after some thousands of copies had been sold, had to be hastily withdrawn. In its next edition the report of the Russian mobilization had to be denied, and a remarkable excuse was made—that the special edition had been published "owing to a mistake by a subordinate employee." But the damage had already been done, the news had been spread to every point of the compass and reached, only a few hours later, Vienna, Paris and London, where it caused tremendous confusion which nothing could then repair.

A few hours later the Czar did in fact order the mobilization of the Russian Army. This step was of special importance since by the terms of the Franco-Russian Agreement of August 1892, mobilization in one of the two countries had to be at once followed by similar action in the other. Nevertheless, Paris hesitated to issue the decisive order for mobilization. In order to induce France to act, Sazonov telegraphed to Grey with the request to assert a last pressure on France, for "if Russia is assured of the support of France, she will face all risks of war."

On July thirtieth the Czar's reply to the Kaiser's last entreaty was received in Berlin. In this telegram from St. Petersburg it was stated that "the military measures now in force were only taken with the object of defense in view of the Austrian preparations . . . and that these measures will in no way prejudice your office as mediator."

From the wording it was clear that the Czar, who would have preferred anything rather than war, was already under the influence of his cousin, Nikolai Nikolaievich, the party of the Grand Dukes and the Generals, who were openly pressing for war. They were only playing for time and trying to lull the German Kaiser to believe that there was still a chance of mediation.

The Kaiser now realized that he was no longer communicating with his "cousin Nicky," but with the Russian war party. There was no longer any purpose in mediating, for any intervention would prove farcical. The whole Russian Army was on the march against the Dual Monarchy, and probably against the German Reich as well.

"And all this when Austria-Hungary has only ordered a partial mobilization in the south against Serbia. Thereupon military measures have been taken by the Czar, as he states openly, which are already in force, and, moreover, have been for five days. Russia thus is almost a week ahead of us. . . . And these measures are supposed to have been taken solely as a safeguard against Austria, which is not attacking him at all! The Czar has mobilized secretly, behind my back! It is only a maneuver to keep us in suspense and to increase the advantage they have already gained. I can do no more!"

If Wilhelm II had to that moment clung to his belief in the possibility of a peaceful solution, he now had to admit that Russia was determined on war, and that war was no longer to be averted.

On account of military measures and movements of troops on the Galician frontier, the Government in Vienna decided to order general mobilization. This took place at 13.30 hours on the afternoon of July thirty-first.

To this countermove the Czar reacted once more and telegraphed to his cousin Berlin: "My hearty thanks for your mediation. It gives me to hope that all can yet be peacefully arranged. It is technically impossible to suspend our military preparations, which were made necessary by Austria's mobilization. Far be it from us to wish for war. So long as the Austrian negotiations regarding Serbia continue my troops will take no provocative action. I give you my solemn word for that! I place all my trust in God's grace, and I hope for the success of your mediation in Vienna for the welfare of our countries and for the peace of Europe. Your cordially devoted Nicky."

Mindful of the promise that as a young Prince he had made to his dying grandfather, never to let the linking thread with Russia be broken, Wilhelm II decided once more to warn the Czar. Over and over again he altered the wording of this decisive telegram, endeavoring to find the right tone which might influence his cousin toward peace and turn him from the insinuating counsels of his anti-German entourage. Early in the afternoon of July thirty-first the following telegram left the Neues Palais in Potsdam: "I am now receiving reliable reports of grave preparations for war on my eastern frontier. Responsibility for the security of my Reich compels me to adopt preventive defensive measures. I have gone to the utmost limit in my endeavors to preserve the peace of the world. Responsibility for the disaster that is now threatening the entire civilized world will not fall on me. Even at this moment it is still in your power to avert it. No one is threatening either the honor or the might of Russia, who is surely in a position to await the result of my mediation. My friendship for you and for your Empire, bequeathed to me as a legacy by my grandfather on his deathbed, has always been for me a sacred charge. I have often stood honestly by Russia when she was hard pressed, notably during her last war. The peace of Europe can yet be preserved by you, if Russia consents to suspend the military measures that threaten Germany and Austria-Hungary."

This telegram speaks clearly and convincingly of the Kaiser's honest and sincere will to avoid the war that was threatening. No flourishes crept into it, and it is devoid of any sentimentality.

The Czar's reply to this telegram of July thirty-first was non-committal and evasive. It strengthened the impression that the Grand Dukes and the Generals were out for war, and that the Czar was now only a puppet in their hands. That reliance could no longer be placed on his word was proven by reports of Russian troop concentrations between Kovno and Mlawa. Passengers arriving at Eydtkuhnen confirmed this.

In order to prevent Russia from gaining any further advantage and to make it clear that Germany would no longer allow herself to be duped, the Kaiser instructed Count Pourtalès (at 15.30 hours on July thirty-first) to announce to Sazanov that he had proclaimed "a state of threatening danger of war" throughout the Reich, and that mobilization would follow should Russia not cease all warlike measures against Austria-Hungary and the German Reich within twelve hours. By proclaiming "a state of threatening danger of war"—an invention of the Kaiser's not to be found in any of the textbooks of a German General Staff Officer, he sought to create at the eleventh hour an intermediate stage, before ordering mobilization. However, thanks to this conceding of time for reflection the Russian Ministry of War gained another twelve hours for their already mobilized Army, while in Berlin only the first steps toward it were being taken. Further, the Kaiser waited for a full seven hours after the expiration of the time limit before signing the order for mobilization.

In order to put this on record the Kaiser sent one last telegram (dated August 1, 1914) to Nicholas II: "Thank you for your telegram. Yesterday I indicated to your Government the only way in which war can now be averted. Although I requested a reply by noon today, no telegram has up to now reached me from my Ambassador, giving the reply of your Government. I was therefore compelled to mobilize my Army. An immediate, acquiescent, clear and unmistakable answer from your Government is the only remaining possibility of avoiding endless misery. Until I receive that answer I regret that I am not in a position to entertain the matter you refer to in your telegram. I must earnestly request that you immediately order your troops not in any circumstances to commit the slightest violation of our frontier. Willy."

This was language different from that which Wilhelm II had hitherto used in addressing the Czar. Speaking afterward in Doorn, he said: "At that time I could do no more—any other course would have meant degradation. I tried in every possible way to induce my cousin, the Czar, to turn back, and to prevent the outbreak of war. I had waited, prayed, even begged, and with entreating words pointed out the immense misery which such a war would involve. When I realized that I was not having any success with the Czar, I warned and threatened. At that time I was already convinced that this war would be synonymous with the destruction of the monarchy in Russia, indeed on that day of August 1, 1914, I foresaw that the other monarchies also would be subjected to the severest stresses."

82. GREY'S DOUBLE GAME

THERE COULD NOW BE no question of drawing back, not even from the final step—a declaration of war. "Had Germany given way in August 1914," said the Kaiser twenty years afterward, "Pan-Slavism, unrestrained, could have launched out on the destruction of Austria-Hungary. They could have succeeded in this, because the structure of the Dual Monarchy was decaying, owing largely to the subversive attitude of Czechs and Serbs. After the loss of that ally we should have found ourselves in a very weak position vis-à-vis Russia. We should have had to choose then between a desperate struggle on our own territory, or capitulation, which would have meant an inglorious end to Germany."

After the mobilization of the Russian Army all doubts as to the attitude of France were removed. The *démarche* of the German Ambassador, Baron von Schön, made to the Quai d'Orsay on the afternoon of July thirty-first, requesting a reply within eighteen hours to his inquiry as to whether the French Government would remain neutral in a Russo-German war, elicited promptly the explicit answer that "France would act as her interests required."

Almost simultaneously an inquiry from London reached Berlin as to whether the German Reich would refrain from an attack on France in the event of France declaring for neutrality. The Kaiser was at once prepared to give a suitable assurance, namely, that he would slow down the westward movements of his armies. Moltke, together with those of the General Staff responsible for these movements, protested against this intention of the Supreme War Lord, declaring that the inquiry from London was only a trick to ensure that the French moves could be carried out with less interference. Apart from that, it was out of the question to delay and overthrow the deployment of the five armies (according to the Schlieffen Plan), as this must result in terrible confusion.

Accepting Moltke's representations, the Kaiser telegraphed back to London to King George the same day (July thirty-first) as follows: "For technical reasons the mobilization on two fronts, East and West, which I ordered this afternoon, must proceed in accordance with the preparations made. Counterorders cannot be given, since unfortunately your telegram arrived so late. But should France offer me her neutrality—which must be guaranteed by the British fleet and Army—I should naturally abstain from attacking France and should employ my troops otherwise. I hope that France will not become nervous. The troops already on my frontier are now being detained by telegram and telephone from crossing the French frontier. William."

Grey made further soundings, asking Paris if France would respect the neutrality of Belgium. This was answered in the affirmative. The same question was addressed to the Wilhelmstrasse, but the Undersecretary of State von Jagow avoided giving an answer. This meant, for Grey, that Britain—to whom the thought that the German Reich might settle in Belgium and on the Channel coast was wholly unacceptable—would certainly be dragged into the whirlpool of events.

Thus began "Grey's double game." The German Ambassador in London, Prince Lichnowsky, never saw through it. His optimism, which accepted credulously whatever was told him at the Foreign Office, was to blame for the Wilhelmstrasse's expecting that England would remain outside the conflict. Every little sign that he looked on as favorable was joyfully reported to Berlin during those critical days, until the moment came when, confronted with realities, he was thunderstruck.

Shortly before being handed his passports, the German Ambassador had a last brief interview with Sir Edward Grey. The Prince made use of this opportunity to complain bitterly of the false protestations of friendship made by the Government in London. He felt that he had been deceived by Sir Edward. The Englishman replied coldly "that political conclusions should not be drawn from social favors."

With the outbreak of war, English propaganda set in immediately accusing Wilhelm II and the Germans as being alone to blame for the kindling of this world-wide conflagration. Much later the English historian, G. P. Gooch, after many years of careful research, came to the conclusion that "no proof of any kind can be found that the German Government or the German people wished for, or planned, a world war."

Armed force spread like a gray-black thundercloud over "unworthy Europe." The monarchs had failed; it was a victory for the cabinets urging on a war whose mathematically worked-out game Wilhelm II had never really seen through. Hinzpeter had already said of his pupil: "Mathematics is not his strong point!" But the peoples, also, had failed; for, as Cowper remarked, "War is a game at which kings could not play, if their subjects were wise."

83. THE FIRST BATTLES

Now BEGAN what Bismarck once called "the gory game of might and chance." The Kaiser had no doubt whatever that the war would be a long one. Afterward, when recalling those first months of the struggle, he said, "It had almost become an article of faith that a modern war, affecting the entire life of an entire people down to its deepest roots, could not continue for long. It was a dogma which the economists, more than anyone, subscribed to." Later, in a conversation with Niemann, he enlarged upon this, saying, "A modern war of peoples cannot be measured on the scale that applied to wars of the previous century. The campaign of 1870–1871 was, by and large, fought out by those young men of the two countries who were capable of bearing arms. In the World War it was not a matter of one army against another, but of mankind versus mankind, and with all their national and native bonds. The soul of one people fought against the soul of another, culture against culture, one philosophy of life against another, one economic system versus another, technique against technique, and material against material. Ideas of space and time expanded in proportion to the number and quantity of the forces employed."

If "the soul of one people was struggling against the soul of another," it was, above all, the German versus English, for England was generally held by the Reich to be responsible for the war. France's attitude was to some extent intelligible to Germans, for she sought revenge for 1870–1871 and if possible to recover her lost provinces of Alsace and Lorraine. But that England, a Germanic people, whose royal House was of Hanoverian origin, and was moreover closely related to the Hohenzollerns, should stand by the side of sworn enemies and Slavs, seemed incomprehensible to the German citizen, as incomprehensible as it was to the Kaiser himself, who in his bitter disappointment disowned the country of his mother and resigned his honorary ranks of Field Marshal and Admiral in the British Army and Navy, respectively. The men in the street understood this gesture. Anxious to show that they shared the Kaiser's feelings, they gathered in front of the British Embassy in the Wilhelmstrasse, where all the windowpanes fell victims to a hail of stones.

Nevertheless, it was characteristic of Wilhelm II that, despite all his scorn for her, he went to war with "perfidious Albion" in two minds. Thus, one day he suddenly and surprisingly gave orders to his Zeppelin commanders that they were not to bomb the royal palaces. So restricted were they by these orders that worth-while bombing over London became scarcely possible. When the Kaiser happened to read the words of the song *Hassgesang* (*Song of Hatred*) he was much amused, but afterward banned it from General Headquarters.

Germany declared war on Russia at 17.00 hours on August first. It has been imputed to Bethmann as a grave error that he allowed himself to be hustled into the declaring of war by the aggressors. The one who issues the challenge will always be stamped with responsibility for the war. The Chancellor was also reproached for permitting the violation of Belgian neutrality. If he had to accede to the demands of the Army Staff, then he ought to have backed up his action in the Reichstag, and not admitted openly that *de facto* a breach of international law had been committed by the German Reich.

So, on August second, a German ultimatum was sent to the Belgian Government with an inquiry whether it would permit German troops to traverse its territory, if undertakings were given by Germany that such troops would not engage in hostile action in that country, that everything requisitioned would be paid for in cash, and that all damage done would be made good. Further, an assurance was given in the ultimatum that on the conclusion of peace Belgium would be evacuated and the independence and sovereignty of the Kingdom of Belgium would be guaranteed.

The reply from Brussels was—"No!"

The sequel to this German inquiry in Brussels was that Sir Edward Goschen, the British Ambassador in Berlin, was instructed by Grey to demand his passports in the event of the Secretary of State von Jagow not giving, before twelve midnight, a satisfactory assurance that the advance of the German troops toward the Belgian frontier had been stopped.

On this day of August fourth half the population of the Reich's capital (in so far as the men had not already been called to the colors) was afoot; the Linden became a surging sea of excited, enthusiastic people pressing on toward the Schloss to see the Kaiser. They had to wait for some time in the Lustgarten until the doors of the balcony over the great entrance were opened and the Kaiser, already in field-gray uniform, stepped out. His words, which so often had something of a trumpet call in them, at this hour sounded excited, filled with emotion: "I commend you now to God. Go into the churches, kneel down, and pray for help for our soldiers!"

Although people in general regarded the war as having been forced upon them and accepted with devotion and enthusiasm all sacrifices demanded of them, the Left Wing of the Social Democrats would not pass the war credits in the Reichstag. They would, of course, agree to the bill "for national reasons," but since the Social Democrats were only "fellows without a fatherland" and were "a gang unworthy to be called Germans," they felt in no way authorized to vote the credits.

When the Chancellor heard of this he suggested to the Kaiser that he should make some reconciliatory announcement. Rather reluctantly he produced this: "In peacetime I have indeed been attacked by one party or another, and this I forgive with all my heart." A few days later, however, on the occasion of reading the Speech from the Throne in the White Hall, he expressed himself more clearly: "I know no more parties, I know only Germans!"

After that Wilhelm II left Berlin for the Supreme Headquarters, established at Koblenz, but soon transferred (at the end of August 1914) to Luxemburg.

The successful capture of Liége, largely due to the brave action of Ludendorff, followed by other successful operations in Belgium and Lorraine raised great hopes of an early defeat of France. However, much as this news contributed to stimulating their spirits at Supreme Headquarters and to strengthening the confidence of the Kaiser, it was soon discounted by news of fighting with *francs-tireurs,* whose suppression was giving rise to all sorts of stories of atrocities. In war things do not proceed on a basis of delicacy or tenderness, as Tilly[1] knew when he said that "you cannot carry an army across a country in a sack." Excesses by individuals may certainly have occurred, but the mass of the German soldiers behaved correctly, as was freely admitted after the war on the part of their enemies, in so far as these were not intractably malevolent.

If the celebrated pastels by La Tour can today be admired, intact and unharmed in the Paris Louvre, it is due solely to the brave conduct of German soldiers who, at the risk of their lives, saved them out of the burning Museum of St. Quentin—this only as an example.

If developments on the Western Front seemed favorable at first, the situation in East Prussia was menacing. The Russians had already invaded the province and driven back the armies of General von Prittwitz und Gaffron. When Prittwitz telegraphed to the Kaiser that he was retiring to the Danzig-Thorn line, he promptly received the reply: "*You* will retire!" To replace this army commander, General von Hindenburg was hastily summoned from Hanover, where he had been living on retired pay, and with him went Ludendorff. They managed to inflict a decisive defeat on Samsonov's army at Tannen-

[1] Count Johan Tserclaes von Tilly, 1559–1632, German general in the Thirty Years' War.

berg and compelled Rennenkampf to withdraw. This success was equalized by the Russian invasion into Galicia. A breakthrough on the line Gorlice-Tarnow and the ensuing capture of Lemberg (Lvov), Przemysl, and afterward of Warsaw, Ivangorod (Deblin) and Brest Litovsk for some time removed the danger from the Russians to which the far-stretched Eastern Front was exposed.

The year 1915 was afterward designated by the Kaiser as the most successful of the whole war. In the months that followed the spring offensive in Galicia he was confident, and even convinced, of an early and victorious ending of the vast struggle.

The dramatic culminating point of the whole war was, however, the Battle of the Marne, seen by the Kaiser from Supreme Head-quarters in Luxemburg. In his view it was essential that the battle for Paris should be fought out and a decision reached there, and the sooner that happened the less chance the French Command would have of bringing their reserves into action, and especially of utilizing their African colonial troops. The fact that the French Government had already left Paris and fled to Bordeaux, while Hussar patrols of Marwitz's Cavalry Division were within sight of the Eiffel Tower, must have greatly strengthened optimism in Luxemburg. But in this case Paris was not France. What lay to the west and south of Paris constituted the essential territorial backbone of the Republic. That was the experience which the other Moltke had had forty-four years previously. This time, as then, the French Army was not yet beaten. This impression prevailed also in the mind of Lieutenant Colonel Hentsch, who had been sent to the front by Moltke to view and re-port on the situation. On the ground that a considerable gap was forming between the 1st and 2nd German Armies, and having full authority given him by the Chief of the General Staff, he ordered both the armies to retire beyond the banks of the Marne, in order that touch might be regained with the corps on the flank of the ad-vance, and that the rearward communications, which had fallen into confusion, might be restored. The ailing Moltke allowed himself to be convinced by this pessimistic view of Lieutenant Colonel Hentsch. To the astonishment of the German corps that had been pressing forward successfully, they found themselves obliged to break off the battle on the Marne that had been going so well for them, and retire on Rheims.

By breaking off the battle on the Marne, and by the evasion of a decision, "for tactical reasons"—about which Napoleon had never worried at critical moments—the German Reich lost the game on the most important battlefield, and with it the chance of winning the war. At best, it would only be a case of a *partie remise*. Moltke, who had to be replaced by General von Falkenhayn as Chief of the General Staff, confessed when, in a state of deep depression, he was leaving the Supreme Headquarters: "How different it was a few weeks ago when we opened the campaign so brilliantly. Now comes bitter disappointment! We are bound to be suffocated in the fight between the East and the West!"

The epilogue to the tragic fate of Colonel General Helmuth von Moltke had been written, unwittingly, by his great namesake. In his works he wrote about his successor: "The reputation of a commander in the field is decided above all else by his success. How much of it is due to his own real merits is very difficult to determine. By irresistible force of circumstances even the best man may be wrecked, and by it again an ordinary man may be sustained. But in the long run luck goes only with ability."

84. THE SUPREME WAR LORD IN THE FIELD

THE DOUBTS that had been expressed regarding his capacity for the appointment of Chief of the General Staff in succession to the highly gifted Schlieffen, when Moltke was nominated, were now shown to be in fact well founded. But there was no foundation for the fear that the Supreme War Lord might elect to play the part of Chief of General Staff himself. Even Waldersee had referred to it as a possibility: "Should the Kaiser wish to take over the command himself in time of war, in fact and not merely formally as his father and grandfather had done, it would be a calamity!" However, the words "in war I am myself my Chief of Staff!" remained, what in reality they were, a joke.

To everyone's surprise the Supreme War Lord refrained from all interference in military measures. He confined himself to approving whatever was put before him by Moltke, then by Falkenhayn and later by Hindenburg.

Ludendorff wrote in his *Reminiscences of the War:* "The Kaiser was the Supreme War Lord. In him was vested supreme authority over Army and Navy. The highest commanding officers in the Army and the fleet were subordinate to him. The Chief of the General Staff conducted the operations of the armies in the field independently, in accordance with the will of His Majesty. Vital decisions required the Kaiser's consent. The Chief of the General Staff did not possess over-riding authority."

Hindenburg has expressed himself in a similar sense in his *Reminiscences:* "In the case of the more important decisions, I myself undertook the duty of presenting them and requesting, in so far as it was necessary, the Kaiser's approval of our plans."

Thus, despite his "supreme authority," the Kaiser at Supreme Headquarters maintained an attitude of reserve and restraint that so often had been found lacking in him before. It was realization of the fact that he understood very little about the conduct of military operations that made him afraid of committing mistakes which were bound to affect himself most seriously. But even so he would not by any means admit what *The Times* said of him—that his military abilities "might be taken as equivalent to those of a Staff Trumpeter."

In the General Staff they were well pleased with this judicious attitude of the Supreme War Lord; but it was different with Tirpitz, who complained that the holder of supreme authority "would neither take any decisions nor be willing to bear any responsibility."

As the war went on the Kaiser figured less and less at Head-quarters as Supreme War Lord. Some reports from the front he saw for the first time after the General Staff had taken action on them, and often not until the evening meal.

After the favorable events of 1915 came the time when no more victories were won, and then the Kaiser's confidence gave way to pessimism. Carefully he marked on his maps every minor success on the vast front that stretched from Ypres to Mesopotamia. But where was the final decisive victory? Again and again he would reach for his horn-rimmed spectacles, study the telegrams and reports from the armies, map in hand, read the press commentaries and those of the Austrian Colonel Eisner-Bubnar. A new battle was about to begin. Would this intention again be betrayed by deserters and spies?

Victor Hugo once wrote: *"Attendre, c'est la vie! Rêver, c'est le bonheur!"* To dream, and dream, was the only thing that made it possible to endure this torment of waiting.

Thanks to his dreaming, the Kaiser's apprehensions reverted to the extravagant optimism that had already brought Moltke to despair: "This hurrah mood of the Kaiser's turns vague hopes into accomplished facts!" It sufficed to mention the Austrian 35-cm. mortar or a Zeppelin and he had at once a vision of bombarded Amiens in flames, or Woolwich Arsenal reduced to ruins. Any report by an officer of a patrol boat, any statement made by a prisoner, any favorable piece of news from a neutral source, would cause him to judge the situation as surpassingly satisfactory. Rosy-tinted optimism of this kind served only to silence his own insidious doubts. "Yesterday evening," noted Tirpitz in his diary, "it was again very dull. Conversation dragged on and on. The Kaiser sees great victories everywhere, but only in an attempt to cover up his uneasiness, I think."

Maurice Paléologue, the last French Ambassador at the Court of Nicholas II, once said: "There is a well-known psychiatric phenomenon, self-kindling autosuggestion, an innate tendency to indulge in deceptive illusions, in which vanity has free play, the features of the scene assume different forms, and the contours of things are obscured in fog. All that is then required is the application of a stimulus coming from outside such as that of some favorable event, and the brain begins to work in the direction here indicated."

"The stimulus coming from outside" took the form of whatever the Chiefs of the Cabinet insinuated into the ears of the Kaiser. Tirpitz called them "the watchmen on the wall with which the Kaiser has surrounded himself." The endeavor of the Chiefs of Cabinet was to "keep His Majesty in a good humor" and to keep away from him as much unpleasantness as possible. The "watchmen" accordingly proceeded on the understandable assumption that the only role allotted to the Supreme War Lord was to infect the guests at Headquarters with his own self-confidence and assurance, and especially officers arriving from the front and returning to their units with the impressions they had gathered. Those who stage-managed this play acting included, besides Valentini and Marschall, Admiral von Müller, who, though melancholy as an owl, tried his best to see that His Majesty did what he himself could not do—smile!

There were often hours at Headquarters when the Supreme War

Lord, in spite of his numerous suite, was alone. The Chief of the General Staff would excuse himself, through an A.D.C., on the grounds that important news had just come in; even the report to His Majesty must therefore be postponed. Everything seemed to be of more importance than the Supreme War Lord himself. He had to sit as though in a box in a theater, and wait before the lowered curtain, until it was raised and the arranged scenery was revealed to him. Then, when Falkenhayn did appear to make his report, the Chief of the General Staff had to reckon on being interrupted by his impatient War Lord, who could not tolerate that his own illusory view of the situation should be destroyed. The Chief would defend himself against this failure to appreciate reality, saying that though the situation was not unfavorable, it was not as His Majesty appeared to see it.

Even though such frank corrections were attempted in front of the Kaiser, he mistrusted those who reported to him at Headquarters, being uncertain as to whether they were telling him the whole truth. In the evening, if anyone spoke in a whisper at table or round the fireplace, he would suspiciously try to catch a word here and there, immediately convinced that they were trying to hide something from him. Had the breakthrough failed again? Must the Front be withdrawn back to the old positions, or even farther?

Wait—and dream! In such dreams the hope always revived that these men, who were working indefatigably for their Kaiser and their Reich, would bring about and win the final victory. In his restless nights, lying awake and hearing every hour strike, there appeared before his eyes a vision of the Brandenburger Tor in Berlin. Forty-three years before, he had been there to see the entry of his triumphant grandfather. The victors had been received with flags, flowers and rejoicing. So it will be again one day when he, Wilhelm II, with his warriors, enters Berlin, victorious. Beside him would be the Duke of Tannenburg (Hindenburg) with his gleaming Blücher Cross, and Count von Gilgenburg (Ludendorff).

To dream is bliss! and it was the only possible way to endure this waiting.

85. WILHELM II, ITALY AND THE BALKAN STATES

THE KAISER'S HOPE that the successes at the beginning of the war would bring him new allies turned out to be delusive. Italy regarded herself as not obliged by the terms of the Triple Alliance concluded in 1882 to come in on the side of the German Reich and Austria-Hungary, since those States had not been attacked but were themselves aggressors by the fact of their own declarations of war. Here again Bethmann's mistake proved disastrous.

This defection on the part of allied Italy was received with surprise and anger by the German people, though their Foreign Office had never expected any other attitude. How firmly commanders of detached German forces believed in Italian co-operation is shown by what happened at Messina in the early days of August 1914. The German cruisers *Goeben* and *Breslau* had put in there, and their Admiral Souchon had at once got in touch with the Italian naval authorities, trusting that he was dealing with allies. He almost disclosed the secret German signal code, but at the last moment, in reply to an inquiry, a wireless message was received from Norddeich which explained the situation and prevented this being done.

In Rome, Baron von Flotow represented the German Reich, and Baron Macchio the Dual Monarchy. Both found themselves accused at the Palazzo Chigi of having given the Royal Italian Government insufficient and tardy information of the course of events and the intentions of their own governments during the month of July. This offense alone against the Treaty of Triple Alliance was sufficient to permit Italy to remain neutral. Secretary of State von Jagow knew well how glad they were in Rome to have such a plausible excuse. He was enraged by this "unreliability of the Romans, on which the Bible had already had something to say."

The real beneficiaries of Italy's attitude were, in Rome, Sir Rennell Rodd, British Ambassador, in his embassy near the Porta Pia, and Camille Barrère in the Palazzo Farnese, where the French Embassy soon became the center of all the efforts to draw Italy to the side of the Entente. King Victor Emmanuel III could see little objection to this, for Wilhelm II had all his life been a stranger to him, despite outwardly friendly relations and a few meetings in Venice or Berlin.

Rumania, too, was disappointing, owing to her hesitant attitude. King Carol I, of the Catholic line of Hohenzollern-Sigmaringen, in whose veins, however, ran more French than German blood, a one-time officer in the Berlin Guards Dragoons, and a Field Marshal in both the Prussian and the Russian armies, found himself, with his conflicting titles and his recollections of Königgrätz and Plevna, in a most embarrassing dilemma. He felt that Germany had lost the Battle of the Marne, but realized at the same time that the Russian invasion across the Carpathians constituted a most serious menace to his own country. Relations between Sinaia and Berlin had always been correct, but no more than that. They had been restricted to the customary courtesies, varied by the exuberant letters and poems with which Queen Elisabeth ("Carmen Sylva") used to afflict the Kaiser. Her nephew, the heir to the throne, felt himself even less drawn to Wilhelm II. He had got to know the Kaiser when serving with the 2nd Regiment of Guards Field Artillery in Potsdam, but this had only strengthened his dislike.

When Conrad von Hötzendorff [1] extolled the merits of the old King Carol and pointed out that within the space of forty years he had created a well-ordered country out of a neglected vassal state of Turkey, this praise did not extend to the heir to the throne. What Conrad found fault with in Ferdinand of Rumania was his irresolution and his timidity. As King, too, he showed himself lacking in self-confidence, hesitant and mistrustful. He looked insignificant and sickly. His face was thin, his skin yellowish like that of one suffering from a chronic liver complaint. His hair was brushed back, his eyes were wandering and helpless. In uniform he cut a poor figure—especially when he wore his cuirassier helmet with the horsetail plume pulled far down over his face.

All the more decorative looked his wife, the beautiful Princess Marie, later to be Queen, in her white uniform of the Roschiori Regiment. As a niece of Edward VII, and a daughter of the Grand-

[1] Conrad von Hötzendorff: *Aus meiner Dienstzeit* 1906–1918. Leipzig, 1927.

Duchess Maria of Russia, she was no friend of Wilhelm II, and made no secret of it. Her memoirs supply proof of that. Ambitious and determined to influence Rumanian policy, as granddaughter both of Queen Victoria and the Czarina Maria of Russia, she represented the Entente in Bucharest.

For King Carol, who had always looked on himself as German, the alliance with Austria-Hungary and the German Reich, fixed by treaty, was to remain inoperative. In Parliament it was represented to him that the Central Powers must be regarded as aggressors, that therefore the treaty was devoid of application, especially as it had not as yet been ratified by Rumania.

In the Crown Council, summoned immediately after the outbreak of war, the King—supported only by Carp—implored those present to assume at least a benevolent attitude toward the Central Powers, saying: "Situated as we are between two power groups, who are disputing for preponderance in the Balkans, we can never gain the friendship of Russia—because it is an historical impossibility—and risk to lose forever the friendship of both Austria and Germany. I declare myself decidedly opposed to a policy of adventure, because, if we assist in the dismemberment of Austria-Hungary, we shall hasten our own end. The dismemberment of Austria-Hungary would mean the extinction of Rumania!"

But nobody in Parliament except Peter Carp would support the King's policy. Even Marghiloman, a good friend of Carp's, would have nothing to do with "benevolent" neutrality. At best, he would vote for "strict" neutrality.

The fact that King Carol could not carry his point came as a great disappointment to Wilhelm II. In his cousin he saw, not "Carol of Rumania" but "Karl of Hohenzollern," the Prussian Field Marshal. If he did the King an injustice, it was because he had been wrongly informed about events in Rumania by the perplexed German Ambassador, von Waldthausen. Waldthausen had been relieved on the outbreak of war. As, however, his successor, Baron von dem Bussche-Haddenhausen, had not yet arrived from Buenos Aires, the active and impulsive Ambassador of the Dual Monarchy, Count Ottokar Czernin, temporarily took over the charge of German interests during those fateful days of August 1914.

Czernin's activity, his suggestions and threats, alarmed old King

Carol, of whom Czernin demanded no less than the dismissal of the Crown Council and the signing of a new Treaty of Alliance with the Central Powers.

The long process of attempts to influence King Carol was largely responsible for his falling gravely ill at the end of September 1914; worn down and embittered, he languished away. The last audience that he granted was to a German, the author of this book.

On the death of King Carol his nephew ascended the throne as Ferdinand I, and Rumania's attitude veered toward an open breach with the Central Powers and an alliance with the Entente. Soon after this, however, the troops of Mackensen and Falkenhayn succeeded in smashing the Rumanian Army and effecting the dissolution. King Ferdinand, who had completely lost his head, turned to Vienna and begged that he might be granted asylum in Austria as a private individual until the end of the war. Without informing his German allies of this request the Emperor Karl, who had succeeded Franz Joseph, sent Lieutenant Colonel von Randa to King Ferdinand with a cordial invitation to come to Austria. "Deeply moved, and with tears in his eyes," Ferdinand was about to accept, when suddenly the energetic Queen Marie intervened and insisted that the King must remain in his country and go with her to Jassy, from where she would organize Rumania's resistance to the enemy. By this determined action Queen Marie managed to rescue the Rumanian crown for the Hohenzollern-Sigmaringen dynasty.

If Wilhelm II was disappointed by the behavior of his Sigmaringen cousins in Rumania, the attitude of the Coburg Czar Ferdinand of Bulgaria must have been an agreeable surprise to him, all the more so as it was no secret that this Czar, in whose veins ran more foreign blood than German, was personally not at all well disposed toward the Kaiser. They had never got on together, and had taken no great trouble to establish friendly relations with each other.

It was because Czar Ferdinand in October 1915 looked on it as being of advantage to himself that he came in on the side of the Central Powers. He was guided only by prosaic considerations, and even then he was so cautious as to reserve for himself, on entering into this political marriage, the possibility of a separation. The alliance was only to be for a war of short duration, and at most until the autumn of 1916.

With Bulgaria's entry into the war, the long-desired bridge was established with Turkey, who had declared for the Central Powers as long ago as October 1914. That decision had not been a voluntary one on the part of either the Sultan Mohammed V or of his Grand Vizier, Prince Said Halim, but was due rather to a daring stroke by Captain Humann, the German Naval Attaché, who was assured of the support of his friend Enver Pasha in what he did. On the day of the Feast of Kurban-Bairam the German Ambassador, Baron Wangenheim, was able to send to the Kaiser from Terapia the news he had been awaiting impatiently, that the Ottoman Empire had decided in favor of the Central Powers.

During the war Wilhelm II confined himself to maintaining conventional relations with the Sultan; he paid him one visit. Otherwise they could only exchange good wishes and swords of honor, and bestow iron crosses and gold medals on each other.

The proclamation by the Sultan of a "holy war," on which the Kaiser had set great hopes, soon proved to be disappointing. For anyone who knew the Orient, that was to be foreseen. However well disciplined and brave German soldiers proved themselves to be, in the "holy war" they were, in Turkish eyes, only "unbelievers."

86. THE KAISER IN CHARLEVILLE

SINCE SEPTEMBER 1914 Supreme Headquarters had been established in Charleville-Mezières. While the military offices, command posts and staffs were lodged in Mezières, the Kaiser's quarters, his suite, the three cabinets and the civil authorities, as well as the representatives of neutral Powers, were accommodated in Charleville.

The Kaiser lived in Charleville in the villa of a French industrialist. Those who had met him previously and now saw him here had to admit that he seemed more subdued, more serious, and that he had aged. Housekeeping in Charleville was plain and simple. Only when there were guests, and especially guests who were not to be allowed to notice any restrictions, were there printed menus with many courses and choice wines. Next day there could be seen again, as usual, the little slate on which was written in chalk "Pea soup with sausages—fruit." There were carafes of red and white wine, also water, on the table. It was no different from an infantry mess in Prenzlau or Osnabrück. No one would suspect from the clean uniforms of the officers sitting at table that they had only just returned in their cars from the Front, dusty and bespattered.

When the meal was over, the tablecloths were removed and lighted candles, boxes of cigars and ash trays placed on the table by the orderlies. Those who smoked cigarettes had to draw on their own cigarette cases. Then restraint was relaxed, they drew nearer to one another, jokes were made, and experiences of the day and impressions gathered at the Front were related. So long as the Kaiser was present these reports were toned down to suit him. From time to time many would secretly cast an eye at the clock, rise, make their bow to the Kaiser, and leave so as to be punctual at their work. Others would be called out and not come back. They were all busy, were needed and useful. In the end the Kaiser with a few of his personal staff, who tried to keep him company, would be the only ones left. The Kaiser would be gazing straight before him into the crackling fire, in meditation. There were periods of silence, interrupted only by the low whimper of Senta lying at her master's feet and dreaming of hunting, of which she had so long been deprived.

Sometimes the Crown Prince would come over from his headquarters to visit his father. He, also, with his slim figure in the laced field-gray Hussar jacket, did not make any remarks or references which might depress his father in any way. But the never-ending protraction of the war, without any positive results, made him thoughtful also. Every day that passed favored the other side and made one's own situation worse. He tried to talk about commonplace things—the old oak at Oels had been struck by lightning, or Captain Walter Kirchoff (who was a concert singer) had sung the *Gralserzählung* for him the previous evening. There were plenty of officers at Supreme Headquarters who disliked the Crown Prince and called him a *Windhund*[1] whose mind was set only on superficial things. Others looked on him as underrated and misunderstood, and defended him, and not only on account of his excellent conduct as an Army Commander. But both friend and foe were at one in agreeing that the Crown Prince—as had already happened in the Eulenburg

---

[1] *Windhund* means greyhound and also a thoughtless or empty-headed person. The English equivalent would be "windbag."

affair—was the only person who, whenever it became necessary, could tell the Kaiser the truth.

At night the Kaiser often took a sleeping pill. In spite of it, he would remain standing by a window, gazing for a long time into the darkness of the night. On the horizon tracer bullets would rise and, for an instant, light up the darkness. Like the distant roaring of a sea, like the mighty rolling of thunder, the infernal music of the Front drifted over to him.

What would the new day bring forth?

87. THE KAISER, HINDENBURG AND LUDENDORFF

As THE WAR WENT ON it became increasingly clear that the supreme military leadership and the political chiefs were not working harmoniously together. Rather were they at loggerheads, and even worked against one another. All attempts to make the war leaders and the politicians work in harmony had been in vain. The Kaiser was doing his utmost to smooth over and eliminate the ever-increasing tensions, and particularly that between his Chief of Staff and his Chancellor. Often, however, he found himself confronted with views so conflicting that he was at a loss himself what to suggest to bridge the gaping gulf.

He had for some time realized that his Chancellor Bethmann was no longer capable of coping with the demands of the situation. Despite this awareness, the Kaiser—for reasons of foreign policy—did not venture to get rid of him. Possibly he may have thought of "Uncle Bertie's" advice: "Never change the jockey during the race!"

The once-erect Guards Dragoon Reich's Chancellor had become, owing to his being overloaded with work and worry, a weary and bent old man. When he was alone he would pull on his cloak and smoke cigarette after cigarette, glad that he had not to put in an appearance at any of those many conferences where he was either ignored or laughed at. He put up with this treatment, like a school-teacher who is content if his pupils are not preparing any worse humiliations for him.

What exasperated the soldiers, and especially Falkenhayn as Chief of Staff, was the fact that in spite of all the malice of the Entente, all the stories of atrocities, and the denigration of the German generals, the Chancellor still enjoyed a relatively good repute in the enemy press. That was enough to cause fingers to be pointed at him. Just imagine: the people in Paris and London are satisfied with that lanky fellow! You can figure out for yourselves what kind of a German he must be!

Bethmann knew about gibes of that sort. He made careful notes. He put down what he thought of Falkenhayn: "He is as slippery as an eel, a place hunter, and a brainless devourer of men." He accused Falkenhayn of being responsible for the debacle before Verdun: "Since when does one attack the enemy at his strongest point?" Later on, strategists of the other side put the same question to the German Chief of Staff.

Ballin once asked Bethmann why he did not make it a condition of his continuing to remain with the Kaiser that his adversary Falkenhayn should go? To which the Chancellor replied, nervously passing his hand over his clipped hair, "But, my dear Herr Ballin, I could never do that!"

The elegant Chief of Staff wore his hair clipped short, just like the Chancellor. He, too, had gone gray, for the worries with which he had to contend every day were no less onerous than those of the Chancellor. But in contrast to the weary Bethmann, Falkenhayn, through his brisk, vigorous and assured way, appeared more convincing and to better advantage. The Kaiser would not consent to part with his "able Chief of Staff," whom he was ready to defend against all criticism.

Clausewitz, who, despite the fact that the technique of war changes and develops from year to year, always appears to remain quotable, once said: "The conduct of war, in its great features, is policy itself, which takes up the sword in place of the pen, but does not on that account cease to think according to its own laws."

The political chief (Bethmann) was, however, during those years of war 1915–1916, in no position to enforce his own laws in opposition to the preponderance of the soldiers. When, in August 1916, Hindenburg and Ludendorff took over the military leadership, this appeared in a still stronger form.

When Hindenburg came to Supreme Headquarters, many things

changed for the better. Tirpitz, who had already complained to the Kaiserin that the Supreme War Lord was surrounded and shut in by a weak crowd composed of Bethmann, Müller and Treutler (to which the Kaiserin replied: "Yes, alas, that is so"), declared that he was highly pleased, for now at last "the only right man" was taking over military control. "The simplicity, loyalty and the character of Hindenburg were really refreshing to one's heart, after coming away from that accursed den." This remark was made, with satisfaction, by the Grand Admiral.

The "accursed den" had been transferred to the gigantic Schloss of Prince Hans Pless. The lady of the house, the ever-beautiful Princess Daisy Pless, was an Englishwoman and as such an object of deep suspicion to Tirpitz. For that reason he scented danger in the choice of Pless as the site of Supreme Headquarters. If he did not look on the Princess as an agent of the British Intelligence Service, he feared her influencing the Kaiser and causing possible indiscretions in the direction of London. What further displeased the Admiral about the new Headquarters was the luxury he found there, luxury such as—it had been a pleasant surprise to visitors from the Front and the homeland—had not existed at Charleville. On the other hand, Schloss Pless, with its hundreds of rooms, was particularly suitable for the housing of Headquarters; it provided separate self-contained suites of apartments, with separate staircases up to the attics, so that the servants and batmen were in direct communication with their officers' rooms.

For anyone coming to Pless it was at first astonishing to see hardly any soldiers except the few on guard at the main entrance and possibly one or two riders in uniform cantering along the avenues of the park.

After entering the great lobby with its many trophies, one came to the reception hall, hung all round with red damask. From this hall great French windows led to the park, with its artistically laid out flower borders, ponds and beautifully green, mown lawns such as one seldom sees except in England. It was delightfully peaceful at Pless.

These were the surroundings in which Hindenburg and Ludendorff set to work on their new plans for the operations in the East. Even though Hindenburg was now the real Supreme Army Commander he never failed in his respect for his Imperial master. By comparison with the broad-shouldered, tall and erect Field Marshal the Kaiser seemed almost slight. When Hindenburg with his harsh, almost blustering, voice began a report, speaking in short precise sentences, the Kaiser must have thought of his grandfather's paladins. Roon had spoken harshly like that, and old Moltke had used just such short precise sentences. But Hindenburg had something affable about him, almost suggesting the man of the world—though in fact he had seen little of the world. When, in soldierlike fashion, he "most humbly took leave of his Imperial master," he remained the man of noble blood whose forefathers had owned their bit of land up there on the Vistula. Before leaving the Kaiser's presence he would look at him steadily, as though wishing to encourage and reassure him—I'm here, you can trust me! with God's help we shall surely bring it off! After such a visit by Hindenburg, the Kaiser felt safe and at ease. For the first time in his reign he had a man at his side who reminded him of that great man from the Sachsenwald, Bismarck.

Like Hindenburg, Ludendorff—Quartermaster General—was a product of the Cadet Corps. A soldier from the age of ten, a man of the middle class and without private means, without any favoring from above, he had only his own ability, his own self-education and his own hard work to thank for advancement in his career. Driven on by his never-flagging energy and burning ambition, he had got into the great General Staff, already then singled out for great tasks. When Ludendorff looked at his companions in Pless, the Courtier Generals, and the "children of protection" from the elegant Guards or Cavalry regiments—even Hindenburg came from a Berlin Guards regiment, while he himself had served in line regiments on the frontiers—then he could smile and treat their arrogance with contempt.

Ludendorff was not liked at Supreme Headquarters. In Pless he was a solitary figure. No one ever heard him speak of a friend. It was very seldom indeed that he addressd an old colleague in the familiar second person (*"Du"*). Had he received the Order of the Black Eagle and with it the ennobling "von," he would still have remained the "middle-class officer." He was "sick and tired" of the counts and princes, with their Orders of St. John and Maltese Crosses, hanging about at Pless, and even more of the courtly gentlemen of the three cabinets, whom he hated from the bottom of his heart.

The Supreme War Lord was often annoyed with his Quarter-master General without ever being able to catch him out in an error. To Ludendorff work for the Front was of far greater importance than the performance of ceremonial duties, such as greeting the Kaiser on his return to Pless from shooting in Fürstenstein. Then Ludendorff would send an aide-de-camp to apologize for his absence on the score of pressure of work, and remain invisible. He did the same when one of the Federal princes came to Headquarters and asked that the Quartermaster General be presented to him. "I'm no showpiece," said Ludendorff, and entrenched himself all the more obstinately in his map room.

Ludendorff worked with the demoniacal energy of the scholar who has nearly reached the goal, achieved success, and who makes a last great effort to attain it. He was like a magician obsessed with the idea that fate had singled out him alone to win victory.

When the Quartermaster General had to appear before the Kaiser to make a report, he tried to bring it to an end as quickly as possible. He spoke fast, crisply and emphatically, always coolly and to the point, with few gestures. His explanations were spoken as if he were in a hurry; he looked on them as unnecessary and a waste of time. His reports seemed to exclude all possibility of misapprehension; he carried conviction, even if his audacious ideas sometimes made the Kaiser think that perhaps, after all, his enemies were right, and he was really only an ingenious gambler.

If the Kaiser asked a question, Ludendorff would clap his monocle in his eye, bend over his map, mark off distances with the compasses, which the Kaiser would follow with his beringed finger. In the meantime Ludendorff detailed the names and numbers of divisions, times of attack, and the objective aimed at. He would point to the arrows marked on the map which he had drawn to show the directions of the advance planned, then hurriedly roll up the maps and await the hint to withdraw.

Then he would stand by the door with the *Pour le Mérite* on his collar, his lips pouting, as always, and await the sign of dismissal from his War Lord, who would keep him standing there for a few seconds just to enjoy, if only for a moment, the triumph of still being able to give orders. At last would come the signal, then there was a click of spurs, an effortless about-turn—no walking backward for him!—and the Quartermaster General returned to his work. Undoubtedly a very gifted man was this Erich Ludendorff, but not an easy one to deal with.

Strained relations and all manner of discord continued to be a frequent occurrence at Pless. Tirpitz tells of fresh disagreements between Hindenburg and Bethmann, and between Bethmann and Helfferich. For a time there was even unpleasantness between the War Lord and Hindenburg, but this was removed by the mediation of the Kaiserin, then at Oels. Similar troubles had occurred in the past—Roon had not always got on well with Bismarck and Moltke, nor had Blücher with Gneisenau, nor had either of them with the Prince State's Chancellor von Hardenberg.

War is not only a struggle between States. Enmities born of it can only too easily infect those who have to conduct the war. But for the one whose task it is to maintain and ensure unity in State leadership, for Wilhelm II, the dictum of Friedrich von Gentz remained valid: "To grasp the whole with a mighty hand, and at the same time to deal gently and carefully with each separate component: those are the actions that we, in modest longing, expect of our Prince."

88. THE EMPEROR KARL THE FAITHLESS

TOWARD THE END of the autumn of 1916 the life of the eighty-six-year-old Emperor Franz Joseph began to flicker and fade. His last thoughts were not hopeful, although news coming from the various fronts was only read to him in the form of selected extracts from the more favorable items. When in his daily round, on his way to his little dining room, he passed by the portrait of the Archduke Karl, the victor of Aspern, then he would think of his own successor, that other Archduke Karl, and the others who would rule Austria-Hungary after him.

When General August von Mackensen asked to see him on passing through to Serbia, he was so taken with the Prussian Commander that, quite against all the drastic rules of the etiquette observed in Schönbrunn, he invited him to dinner so as to be able to have longer talks with him. When Mackensen was leaving, the old gentleman gazed after him, nodding his head, and said, "Ah! With men like that you'd never have any nasty experiences!"

On November fifteenth the German Ambassador, Baron von Tschirschky und Bögendorff, died. Six days later, the Emperor Franz Joseph passed away. The Kaiser, who had been kept informed of the progress of his fatherly friend, was not surprised to hear the news of his death.

The general public knew little about the Archduke Karl, who now came to reign. They knew a good deal more about his father, who had given the old Emperor not a few shocks by his loose way of life in Vienna. The Viennese had many a song about the gay Archduke Otto and his remote little Schloss Schönau. He was very popular with them, although on account of his pranks he had been sent away by the old Emperor to command the Elfer Dragoons in Galicia, and after that could only seldom visit Vienna.

His son Karl had little of his father's disposition to take everything lightheartedly. He was rather reserved and serious. As nobody had taken much notice of him during the lifetime of Franz Ferdinand, although he then stood second in succession to the throne, his spiritual education had been neglected. Before the outbreak of war the sturdy and vivacious figure of the Este (Franz Ferdinand) had been so prominent in the foreground as heir to the throne that it was possible to lose sight of the Archduke Karl. This was to have unfortunate consequences. Apart from his life as a Dragoon in a frontier garrison, the Archduke Karl had only studied law in Prague for a few terms. Even after his marriage with the ambitious Princess Zita of Bourbon-Parma, he had been sent to a frontier corner of the Empire, to Kolomea, where he had to spend his honeymoon. Not until November 1912 had he been promoted to Major in the 39th Regiment of Hungarian Infantry, in garrison in Vienna, where on the Emperor's instructions he set up house in the little Schloss Hetzendorf near Schönbrunn.

Here it was soon apparent that the Archduchess Zita had the deciding voice in everything at her little court. More energetic and more healthy than her brothers and sisters, aunts and uncles, many of whom, owing to generations of inbreeding, were sickly and even mentally unsound, she had managed, with the help of the influential dignitaries of the Catholic Church, to establish and make good her position at the Hapsburg Court. Then—when the tragic destiny of Franz Ferdinand was fulfilled in Sarajevo—came the hour longed for, but already despaired of, often prayed for and well prepared for, when she attained the status of wife of the heir to the throne of the Dual Monarchy.

For the unhappy position of that monarchy at the death of Franz Joseph, her young husband and she were in no way responsible. The alliance with the German Empire and the friendship of Wilhelm II had not been sought for or decided by them, indeed the Empress Zita hated the Kaiser wholeheartedly. Like the Empress of Russia she, too, wished that "Germany and the Kaiser should be punished," the more and the sooner the better, so that she could cut loose and be free. In this the Empress Zita was thinking of a separate and favorable peace for Austria-Hungary. The propensity of the House of Parma for playing a part in European intrigues showed itself again here. Firstly, soundings were taken in Paris, to ascertain on what terms such a separate peace could be arranged. In doing this they failed to see what harm they were preparing for themselves and their German allies. That, however, did not concern the Empress Zita very greatly. For the mission to Paris she had chosen the "prodigy of her family," her brother Prince Sixtus. The fact that Prince Sixtus was a captain in the Belgian Army worried neither her nor the Emperor Karl overmuch. Contact with him was quickly made. Delegates representing the Emperor and Empress met him in Switzerland and then, feeling more confident, invited the Belgian captain to come to Austria.

To begin with, the Emperor had to find the right man to conduct these secret and important negotiations. Finally, he decided on Count Ottokar Czernin. The tactics chosen by Czernin cut out the German ally completely—at the suitable moment the ally would be told of the steps taken. Then the gentlemen in Pless could do nothing but accept the *fait accompli*. When they heard in Pless of the Emperor Karl's arbitrary actions—without, however, having any tangible proof—they were angered to find that "since Karl had become Emperor, the Austrians were doing what they liked, and were 'dancing on their own.'"

In this two-handed game, in which both parties played with concealed cards, Karl had, for a time at any rate, some pangs of conscience that he did not hide from Prince Sixtus. The latter, however, dispelled any such qualms with the invented statement that according to reliable news from Paris Wilhelm II himself had already put out feelers for peace there, naturally at the expense of the Dual Monarchy. Russia was to have the Bukovina, Rumania was to get Transylvania, Poland would get Galicia, Serbia would acquire Croatia, while Trent and Trieste went to Italy.

The Kaiser had no knowledge at all of these things imputed to him, and was equally ignorant of Prince Sixtus's activities. His main concern was to be on the best possible footing with the successor to his paternal old friend. In 1915 the Archduke Karl, then heir to the throne, had been in Charleville to explain the old Emperor's negative attitude regarding the German demand for the cession of Trentino to Italy. The impression that the young Archduke had then made on Wilhelm II was not unfavorable, though evidence had been put before him to show that the Austrian heir to the throne displayed little liking for the Reich or for the alliance with it. In this connection, mention was made of the enmity that existed between the Archduke Karl and the Archduke Friedrich, a proven friend of Prussia.

On the Kaiser's fifty-eighth birthday (January 27, 1917) the Emperor Karl came to Pless. The Kaiser paid him a return visit in Vienna on February twelfth. On this occasion there was no frank discussion, for Karl evaded all his ally's questions and tried to veil his real intentions.

No one could blame the young Emperor for wanting an early peace in the interest of his own dominions, even if it meant renouncing the German brotherhood-in-arms. But in that case he ought to have frankly informed his ally of his plans, above all he ought to have disclosed the missions that his Parma brothers-in-law were already engaged upon. That he did not do, but instead he deceived Wilhelm II all the time, in accordance with the principle that he had himself laid down as a guide: "When I have to deal with the Germans I agree with them about everything; but when I am back at home I do as I think fit!"

While, in Pless, the Emperor Karl was proposing the toast of fidelity to the German Reich, his brothers-in-law Sixtus and Xaver were on their way to Paris to treat with President Poincaré on the subject of a separate peace for Austria-Hungary. The French President received them, listened to their proposal and, without referring to it at all, made the general statement: "France wants nothing from Austria-Hungary. On the contrary, she is concerned for the preservation of the Dual Monarchy, and even for its aggrandizement by the inclusion of Bavaria and Silesia, at the expense of the German Reich. With the German Reich we shall not conclude any peace until it has surrendered unconditionally."

This declaration of Poincaré's caused Prince Sixtus to warn his imperial brother-in-law, on March 16, 1917, against being drawn into this matter of unconditional surrender. "It is my duty to call your attention to this essential point—nobody will treat with the Reich until it is beaten. If the Reich persists in trying to force a peace on the Entente, it will try to conclude this peace at the expense of Austria and Turkey. Therefore it will be necessary to act quickly and resolutely. Soon the whole world will be against the German Reich. Then it would become impossible for us to conclude an acceptable peace if our own fate remained linked with that of Germany."

Under pressure from the three Parmesans (Zita, Sixtus and Xaver) who ruled over him, the Emperor Karl announced on March 24, 1917, that "he would support the legitimate French demand for the return of Alsace-Lorraine in every way. . . ." In this instance he was prepared to inform his ally personally of his attitude. He decided to call on Wilhelm II at Homburg, taking the Empress Zita, Count Czernin and General Arz von Straussenburg with him to the Taunus. They knew well how difficult it would be to reach a voluntary renunciation of Alsace and Lorraine.

Richard von Kühlmann made the following remarks about this Hapsburg demand: "An ocean of hatred separates us from France. To make any concessions worth mentioning in this matter of Alsace-Lorraine would be out of the question for a Germany that had not been utterly defeated. Thus we have nothing to offer France. Therein lies the weakness of the whole plan of the Austrians and of Czernin: that they hope or believe to be able to detach France from England, while on calmer consideration they must realize that they themselves have nothing to offer to France and that they could not, in any circumstance, force Germany to give up enough that would in some degree compensate for their lack of bargaining power."

What ought to be done was summed up by Kühlmann in these words: "We shall never get to the end of it if we cannot by some means or another manage to drive a wedge into the coalition of our opponents, just as the Entente is trying to drive a wedge between us and Austria."

The Crown Prince Wilhelm expressed himself even more emphatically against the Emperor Karl's suggestion, saying, "The German people would stone a Reich's Chancellor who proposed to sacrifice any territory of importance in Alsace-Lorraine." Even Bethmann-Hollweg, who usually passed his judgments with philosophic calm, was enraged at this presumption: "I cannot see why the Reich, which drew the sword on behalf of Austria-Hungary, should into the bargain have to surrender voluntarily an entire *Reichsland*!" And he added, "Count Czernin declares that he couldn't cede a square meter of Austrian soil to Italy. But we're supposed to give the French Alsace and Lorraine!"

At this meeting in Homburg the Kaiser endeavored to encourage his ally and make it clear to him that all that mattered now was to preserve their unity, and put full confidence in the further development of their common action in war, and no longer to listen to Czernin's pessimism. Surprisingly enough, the Emperor Karl agreed with this, saying, "That is quite right! Czernin always exaggerates, even when he is pessimistic!"

As Czernin had failed over the matter of Alsace-Lorraine, he was anxious to return to Vienna with at least some other point gained. So, shortly before they left, Czernin brought up the Austro-Polish problem in order to put forward the name of the Archduke Karl Stephan, whom he had in view for nomination as Regent. But neither the Kaiser nor Bethmann was prepared to give any decision on a matter thus broached, so to speak, "on the front doorsteps." They needed time to think over a proposal of such importance.

When Ludendorff heard of Czernin's request, he remarked disdainfully, "The Austrians are like a sieve—what you put in at the top runs out again at the bottom!" After this visit to Homburg, the German Quartermaster General felt so doubtful about the reliability of the "black-and-gold brother" that he took up a proposal put forward by the Bulgarian delegate, Gantschev, that the four Central Powers should be bound by a special treaty among themselves not to conclude any separate peace.

With the increasing deterioration of the prospects of the Central Powers, Wilhelm II was setting all his hopes for peace on the intervention of Pope Benedict XV, of the King of Spain and the Queen of Holland. Bethmann's estimate of the Pope's attempt at mediation on June thirteenth (1917) was too optimistic, because he assumed that the Pope had already put out feelers directly to the Entente, which was not the case. This, like all the other interventions for peace, was nipped in the bud.

After the strenuous German efforts in search of peace, Briand voiced what the whole world was thinking: "The call for peace is only the voice of weakness!" And Czernin received from Ribot the unmistakable answer that "the Austrians will ask for peace not, as they do today, hypocritically and by suspect and devious ways, but openly and directly. Then we shall make peace on terms that suit France. If they do not request this peace, we shall compel them to do so!"

Lloyd George expressed himself in much the same way in a speech made in Glasgow in June 1917. He declared the main aim to be the annihilation of Prussia as a military power, and that England could only make peace with a free Germany that respected the freedom and independence of other peoples.

More pessimistic, but all the more resolute for that, the old "Tiger" Clemenceau declared (on June 4, 1918), "I'll fight in front of Paris, I'll fight in Paris, and I'll fight behind Paris!"

The former Austro-Hungarian Ambassador in Rome, Baron von Mercy, had already uttered warnings against "begging for peace." "Every offer of peace, which is really a request for peace, strengthens even a war-weary opponent and only serves to prolong the war." A similar suggestion was made by the Secretary of State Zimmermann: "We must not let them notice that we are tired, otherwise we attain precisely the opposite of what was intended."

However this "peace-mouthing," as the enraged Ludendorff called it, did not die down for a long time. In spite of his unsuccessful attempts the Emperor Karl wished to show the Entente again that he was ready to give in, if only the war could be brought to an end on tolerable terms. On January 2, 1917, he wrote to Kaiser Wilhelm:

"The answer of the Entente, so far as we know it, is certainly not pleasing in its conclusions, but it does not exclude a continuation of the thoughts for peace. My endeavors—which I am certain you approve—are directed to nursing the strong desire for peace that exists throughout the whole world, and in that way, in course of time, to reach the stage of serious peace negotiations. I greatly fear, however, that the Army and fleet orders proposed by your supreme war leaders must have the result of making our enemies definitely break off the thread of peace. Please forgive if your faithful friend and ally— so much your junior—turns to you with the request that you might make another diplomatic attempt before we speak to our soldiers— and by so doing finally break off all connections which might lead to an understanding."

In Homburg Wilhelm II had already declared bluntly to Count Czernin, "Nobody longs for peace more keenly than I do. But we hear every day that the others want no peace until Germany is shattered." And the Kaiser was not willing to discuss the idea of an unconditional surrender. He looked on the situation as being not so unfavorable that the game must necessarily be lost. That estimate of the situation at the time was afterward shown to be correct, for Ribot, to cite only one witness, himself declared frankly that "Wilhelm II and his advisers did not realize what trumps they still held in their hand."

Soon after the meeting in Homburg the Kaiser and Kaiserin paid a return visit to Schloss Laxenburg. If the two Emperors could discuss things together, the two Empresses found they had nothing in common. What separated them was their respective attitudes toward politics. While the Kaiserin scarcely concerned herself with politics, the Empress Zita occupied herself incessantly with them. They were alike only in their deep piety, though they were of different confessions, and in their display of arrogance, which can perhaps be explained by the fact that they both came from minor princely houses.

After the visit of the Kaiser and Kaiserin to Laxenburg, Prince Sixtus resumed his activities. He went even further and promised the French not only the *Reichslande,* but also the left bank of the Rhine. In order to make his brother-in-law take an interest in the mission, he promised him possession of "Prussian Silesia."

As Prince Sixtus was bound to see that fulfillment of his promises must be long delayed, he demanded of his brother-in-law Karl that he should once and for all challenge Wilhelm II "to state definitely how long he and his generals thought of going on fighting." Besides this, the Prince intrigued with the Kings of Bavaria and Saxony against Wilhelm II, promising them the preservation of their kingdoms if they would cut adrift from the German Kaiser.

It was then, for the first time, that the Kaiser was given precise details of the infamous game that was being played, with himself and the Reich, behind his back. In the strongest terms he addressed Vienna and demanded a cessation of "this suicidal and criminal behavior." Czernin then found himself obliged to modify and to abandon his demands for the time being. On December sixth he declared before the Foreign Affairs Committee of the Hungarian Delegation, "We are fighting for Alsace-Lorraine, exactly as Germany has been fighting for Lemberg and Trieste." Ribot, on hearing of this declaration of Czernin, refused to meet Prince Sixtus again, for, as he put it, "in Vienna they seem to have entirely lost their heads. The question remains whether one can call this sort of shilly-shallying politics at all!"

The sum total of the co-operation of the Kaiser with the successor to the old Emperor Franz Joseph amounted to a few pleasant exchanges and no good results of any kind. The Reich had drawn the sword on behalf of the Dual Monarchy and had kept its *Nibelungentreue* inviolate. Now came the "thanks from the House of Austria," about which the Duchess Elisabeth Charlotte of Orléans had already complained that "It is characteristic of the House of Austria that they are never grateful!"

89. THE U-BOAT WAR

COMING AMONG so many setbacks the courageous conduct of the German fleet at Jutland gave Wilhelm II great satisfaction. It is true that this battle against British warships was, from the point of view of experts, an indecisive one, but it was an undeniable fact that the British Navy had been hard hit and had suffered severe losses. For the German Navy, only twenty years old, this trial of strength against the best fleet in the world constituted a success.

Although the British Navy was weakened in its fighting power by this loss of ships, it still remained so greatly superior to the German fighting fleet that a further open battle at sea could not be contemplated by Germany. Tirpitz, too, realized that the German battle fleet could not again be exposed to losses on such a scale. He and the

German Admiralty Staff looked on unrestricted U-boat warfare as the best means of dealing a decisive blow to England. They calculated that by this daring method of warfare they could bring England to her knees within six months. Supreme Army Command concurred in this interpretation and announced in the Charlottenburg Council of March 5, 1916, that "unrestricted U-boat warfare was inevitable, if they did not want to perish."

Even Falkenhayn declared that such a measure "was the only remaining measure capable of saving the situation."

The Kaiser agreed, although he considered a strict carrying out of the plan hazardous on account of the United States of America. They might one day intervene to England's advantage on the ground that their trade was being endangered. In this opinion he was supported by Albert Ballin, who already had a vision of "the unchaining of the hatred and fury of the whole world"—a natural consequence of which would be the end of his Hapag [1] fleet. In an attempt to avert this new menace, Ballin pointed to false statements of the German Admiralty, who, as he said, delighted in exaggeration and optimism and submitted incorrect statments to the Kaiser. He referred to reliable returns to show the small number of U-boats in fact available. With so few boats, he declared, one could not start upon such a hazardous adventure, which "might perhaps scratch England's skin, but could not force her to sue for peace."

However, if the total number of U-boats was in fact small, in Kiel and Wilhelmshaven they looked forward confidently to further developments. If only "the civilians" would not interfere! New and bigger U-boats were already lying at the wharves; building went on feverishly by day and by night. In the officers' messes the efficacy of unrestricted U-boat warfare was greatly overestimated. The humorous periodicals adopted this feeling of optimism and were already representing John Bull as starving and on crutches. Such a confident attitude might, however, be necessary, in order to speed up and spur on the spirit of the new weapon. Determined men like Weddigen were ready to take it on, although the technique of these boats was imperfect, and their radius of action small.

Through the adoption of unrestricted U-boat warfare the Reich's Chancellor von Bethmann-Hollweg found himself in a difficult posi-

[1] Hapag: *Hamburg-Amerikanische-Paketfahrt-Aktiengesellschaft.* Full name of the Hamburg-America Line.

tion. He stood between a cross fire from the admirals and generals on the one side, exhorting him to acknowledge himself firmly in favor of the U-boat war, and, on the other side, from the members of the Reichstag and the diplomats who entreated him not to sanction "this new piece of insanity," which would result in the complete ruin of the Reich. Secretary of State Zimmermann was assailed in much the same way by people who insisted that he should put a stop to this "pirate war" and not permit that the Law of Nations should be degraded to a mere "scrap of paper." Zimmermann said one day to von Flotow, head of one of his sections, "If I could only see a way for us to come to a reasonable peace, I should be the first to condemn this kind of warfare."

When the Emperor Karl rather surprisingly gave his approval to unrestricted U-boat war, there was a palace revolution in Laxenburg, with the Empress Zita and above all her brother Prince Sixtus of Parma insisting that the Emperor should withdraw his consent. Shrugging his shoulders, Karl replied: "There is nothing else I can do. The Germans will do as they like in any case!"

Tirpitz began the U-boat war with, at first, not quite two dozen boats, as he himself admitted afterward. He quoted an old artillery general who once said: "If I went to war and only had one gun, I'd fire it, and not wait until I had a hundred!" The sudden use of the U-boats did not fail to have its effect on England; it was, in fact, stronger and more serious than had been expected. An unbiased witness for the German success is the United State Admiral Sims, who at the time came to the conclusion, from a study of the shipping lists, that the British Empire would have to surrender unconditionally within four or five months, if it could not find a means of protecting itself against the U-boat plague. Sims added that the compilation shown him by Admiral Jellicoe indicated an appallingly great success for the German U-boats, three or four times greater than the figures given to the public.

If people in America had hitherto placed little reliance on the German reports of the success of their U-boat weapon, the account given by their own Admiral actually caused dismay. The statistics he had supplied were confirmed by cable by their Ambassador, Mr. Page.

In the one week of April 16-22, 1917, no fewer than eighty-eight vessels, totaling a quarter of a million tons, had fallen victims to the German U-boats. It was Ambassador Page, too, who in cables had entreated Wilson and Lansing to intervene as quickly as possible, as Germany would otherwise win the war at sea.

In Washington they were still hesitating as to whether they should allow themselves to be drawn into this European war, when on January 19, 1917, a telegram from the German Foreign Office to its Chargé d'Affaires (von Eckhardt) in Mexico was intercepted. Its wording caused an immense agitation in the United States. The telegram read thus:

We intend to begin unrestricted U-boat war on February first. In spite of this we are intent on remaining neutral with the United States. Should this intention, however, prove impossible, then we recommend an alliance with Mexico on the following terms: to make war together, and to make peace jointly. In general we shall guarantee monetary support, and we intend that Mexico shall reconquer her lost territories in New Mexico, Texas and Arizona. Details are left to your discretion. Your instructions are: to inform the President of Mexico of the above under pledge of the most complete secrecy, as soon as there is no longer any doubt of war with the United States, and to suggest that the President should on his own initiative get in touch with Japan, with the object of inducing Tokyo to support this plan, at the same time offering to mediate between Japan and Germany. Kindly call the attention of the President of Mexico to the fact that the adoption of ruthless U-boat warfare promises to compel England to make peace within a few months. (Signed) ZIMMERMANN

On April 6, 1917, the United States came into the war on the side of the Entente. Apart from the Mexico telegram there were other weighty reasons to induce President Wilson to take this decisive step. His resolution was decided primarily by Germany's unrestricted U-boat warfare, which already seriously damaged the commerce of the United States, and was even beginning to paralyze it.

Although the Kaiser would not believe that the United States could send any large contingents of troops to Europe—relying on various expert opinions—he freely acknowledged the moral and material strengthening of the enemy by the American action. More than ever he had to look on his U-boat weapon as the *ultima ratio regis*.

Tirpitz had tendered his resignation in March 1916. What he now could glean, in his peaceful abode in the Black Forest, might often have made him turn red wth rage, but also with shame, for instance, when the Reichstag member, Matthias Erzberger, spoke publicly about "the continual failure of the U-boats." Tirpitz might have had the same opinion as the writer Fester when the latter remarked, "What would the American Admiral Sims have thought, if he had been a witness of how a German member of the Reichstag, using faked tables, disputed the calculations in the hands of the Admiralty Staff—which proved to be very near the truth—and went so far as to deny the success of the U-boat war?"

That Admiral Sims's judgment was sound is witnessed by two Englishmen—Lloyd George and Winston Churchill. In a speech made by Lloyd George in 1920, he frankly announced that the Germans did not know for some time the effect of their own U-boats. England found the means of dealing with them, but it was a near thing. However, he had simply believed in the justice of the cause and in victory for it. But never again should England rely on that.

Even more clearly did the former First Lord of the Admiralty, Winston Churchill, express himself: "We only just got through. The more one knows about the struggle, the more one realizes on what small, narrow, perilous margins our success turned. At the first onslaught France was within an ace of being destroyed. A very little more and the submarine warfare, instead of bringing America to our aid, might have starved us all into absolute surrender. . . . It was neck and neck to the very end. Let us be thankful!"

90. TWO NEW CHANCELLORS

REICH'S CHANCELLOR VON BETHMANN-HOLLWEG had expected that there would be useful opportunities for opening up new peace discussions after the retirement of Admiral von Tirpitz. They never materialized. And now his own retirement was demanded as an absolute necessity if the war was to be continued.

It was not, however, the Fatherland party—which Tirpitz had

helped to found—that succeeded in giving Bethmann the *coup de grâce*. It was Hindenburg and Ludendorff, who insisted in the strongest terms that the Kaiser must get rid of this Reich's Chancellor, with whom the two Generals declared categorically they declined to co-operate any longer. Otherwise they themselves would be obliged to hand in their own resignations. So Wilhelm II found himself compelled to dismiss his fifth Chancellor and seek someone to replace him.

A violent struggle, in which Prince Bernhard von Bülow was involved, broke out for the successor to Bethmann. The gentlemen in the Ballhausplatz in Vienna were up in arms against the candidature of von Bülow who, they alleged, when German Ambassador in Rome, had unscrupulously trafficked in Austrian possessions— Trent and Trieste. But it was precisely in this objection by the Black-and-Golds that the Prussian Generals saw the advantage to themselves that Bülow's candidature would offer. If they would have nothing to do with Bethmann it was first and foremost because in their opinion he was entirely in tow with the Parma-Czernin clique, and acted like one who was Chancellor "by the grace of the Hapsburgs." To try to stave off the threatening danger of Bülow's appointment, Czernin appealed to the Kaiser through the Emperor Karl "to refrain from appointing Prince Bülow to the chancellorship out of regard for the feelings of the Austrian people."

This request of Czernin's came quite opportunely for the Kaiser. The thought of working together, in such difficult times, with the man who had once so disloyally exposed him before the Reichstag and the people (after the *Daily Telegraph* affair) seemed to him unbearable.

As the generals and chiefs of the cabinets could not agree on any one candidate, a full week passed in which the Reich was without a Chancellor in the middle of a world war. In the end the choice for the highest office in the State fell upon a man whose name was to most people as good as unknown, but served just to provide a solution in the embarrassing circumstances. A short list had been presented to the Kaiser by von Valentini, Chief of the Civil Cabinet, showing the short-listed candidates; the name of Georg Michaelis had been pointed out, as an experienced civil servant whose abilities had brought him to the position of President and Prussian State Commissioner for Food. The Kaiser agreed to this nomination, though Michaelis' career hitherto seemed to him not quite a sufficient preparation for the many-sided and difficult office of Chancellor, especially in wartime.

There now came to Supreme Headquarters, in place of the tall and spindly Bethmann, a friendly and benevolent-looking man. He had something of the clergyman about him and, as the satirical papers put it, reminded one of a hostel warden, or "the administrator of an orphanage, in which thanks to God were assiduously offered morning, noon and night." *Kladderadatsch* depicted him as a lay preacher in a black coat carrying a white lily in his hand, while a journalist could not rid himself of the impression of a "schoolteacher shuffling about in carpet slippers." In fact Michaelis was a devout man, a pietist.

The new Chief brought with him, as his subordinates had to recognize, a good deal of self-confidence and also of presumption, openly displayed. This found expression in the fact that Michaelis immediately moved into the Reich's Chancellor's palace with bag and baggage, and there proceeded to turn everything upside down, even making the historic study, in which Hohenlohe, Bülow and Bethmann had labored, into a salon for his wife. Perhaps it was intended to show that a new era was beginning which the new Chancellor emphasized by refusing to sit at the same desk as his predecessors.

However, all too soon it was apparent that the tubby Chancellor Michaelis in no sense attained the stature of the lanky Bethmann. His inadequacy became so quickly apparent in the ninety-nine days (July-November 1917) that he held office that complaints against him poured in from all sides. He took these rebuffs with the humility proper to a pietist, and in accordance with the words of the Bible that enjoin anyone receiving a box on the cheek to turn the other cheek also. No one in the ever-growing band of his opponents failed to appreciate the good qualities of the new Chancellor's character . . . but with them alone one could not cope with a world of enemies.

When Michaelis made his maiden speech in the Reichstag it met with little approval, and with none at all on the part of the generals at Supreme Headquarters. They were told by the man they had chosen that he considered the U-boat weapon to be "the last resource of the Reich," which indeed was correct, but should not have been so openly admitted, because of its usefulness to enemy propaganda. So, too, his remark that Austria-Hungary had dragged the Reich into war showed little sense of fitness or political tact. It also was true, but should not have figured in a speech by the Chancellor of a power allied to Austria-Hungary.

In Vienna they were all the more annoyed and disappointed by this statement because of the high hopes they had set upon this rival candidate to Bülow. With the object of effacing the bad effects of this speech in the Reichstag, Count Botho Wedel, German Ambassador in Vienna, proposed that Chancellor Michaelis should come to Vienna and have talks with the responsible authorities there and also with the Emperor Karl. Count Wedel thought that a meeting between the Chancellor and the Emperor was expedient for, as Wedel put it, "formerly one suffered from worn-out old age, but now from inexperienced youth; old age was the lesser of the two evils!"

Another thing that was fatal for Chancellor Michaelis was his ambiguous attitude toward the peace resolution, to which he had only shortly before given his approval, assuring the party leaders that it should be carried through. His failure to fulfill that promise raised against him a storm to which he succumbed. In November 1917 he handed in his resignation, which the Kaiser accepted without opposing it.

When, after Michaelis' departure, attempts were made to determine who had been responsible for this blunder, many hands were raised in disgust and protest, for nobody wanted to admit having had anything to do with the appointment of this Chancellor. The Kaiser was greatly embarrassed that he had to find yet another Chancellor. That successor must offer a guarantee that so brief and barren a chancellorship should not be repeated. The Kaiser had indeed plenty of well-qualified officers and conscientious civil servants, but the outstanding statesman whom he needed at that time of peril was lacking.

Even before the choice of Michaelis the Kaiser had approached the Bavarian Prime Minister, Count von Hertling, and asked him to take over the office of Chancellor. At that time, Hertling could not be persuaded to do so and had flatly refused the offer. Today it is known that the old gentleman did not feel himself strong enough to stand up to the generals, and to Ludendorff in particular. When, for the second time, the Kaiser called upon him, urging him "not to deny your services to the Fatherland," he at last gave way. If Michaelis, on first taking office, had been tolerated by the parties because they wanted to see how the new man would turn out, Count Hertling was from the first opposed by almost everyone who could claim a say in the matter, even by one of his own camp—Matthias Erzberger.

In Hertling the Kaiser found a man at his side who, as regards origin, training and age, reminded him of Prince Chlodwig zu Hohenlohe-Schillingsfürst, except that Hertling, so far as clarity of comprehension and finesse of execution were concerned, did not nearly approximate to the standards of the Prince. Each had been Prime Minister in Bavaria before being called to the chancellorship. Hertling was a *grand seigneur* of the old school. Despite war, Social Democracy and ration cards, he attached particular importance to social formalities. He never forgot to insert on his cards of invitation to evening receptions at Supreme Headquarters the words—*Uniform, or evening dress*.

Anyone who watched the elegant little Count, a Papal Chamberlain, with the stars adorning his breast, had to admit that he seemed just as much at home at Supreme Headquarters as on the parquet floors of his Munich residence. Even at critical moments he was never ruffled. It was known at Headquarters that no one could easily confuse the Count.

This then was the seventh Chancellor of the Reich, a man with his active career behind him, determined to end his life with honor, but who was already too worn out to be able to save a dangerous situation by bringing drastic measures to bear.

To this, unfortunately, was added the fact that Hertling, a South German, knew nothing about the Eastern problems, which were just coming into the foreground. "Although officially the link with Russia had been severed," as the Kaiser said afterward in conversation, "there remained possibilities for concluding peace while the Czar still reigned. Our sounding did, however, not lead to any tangible results. It appeared that Rasputin was at that time the one who was supporting the idea of peace in the Court of the Czar. Ranged against him stood the party of the Grand Dukes, the parliamentarian, nationalistic *bourgeoisie*, and the English determination on war, represented in St. Petersburg by their Ambassador Buchanan and Colonel Knox, who was invested with full powers on the military side.

When these people realized the increasing influence of Rasputin, they took action—Rasputin was murdered."

In any case the position of the Entente was worsened to the advantage of the Central Powers by the defection of Russia. That fact must be used, peace with Russia must be so concluded that it could serve as a reasonable basis for other arrangements. This commendable definition of his aims by the Kaiser met with the full approval of the new Secretary of State for Foreign Affairs, Richard von Kühlmann, who drew up the following peace terms for Russia:

(1) Surrender of a strip of land east of Thorn as a security for that fortress;
(2) surrender of the Bendzin coal fields;
(3) autonomy for Congress Poland.[1]

Kühlmann's proposals, however, were not to Hertling's liking. Being already dependent on the military party at Headquarters, he rejected the reasonable plans of his Secretary of State.

It was soon clear that Count Hertling no longer decided the foreign policy of Germany—and internal policy had long since been taken out of his hands. Bethmann already had been more afraid of the enemy within the gates than of the enemies on the war fronts. The end of 1916 saw the beginning of serious difficulties in providing food supplies, and of the so-called "turnip winter." Serious doubts arose among the people whether there was any sense in holding out. The first signs of unrest, distrust and rebellion were becoming apparent. In every war it has been proven that the stomach problem is the most important and the most decisive of all. Those who have the best nerves win the war. But for the strengthening of those nerves good nourishment is needed. True, in the towns food that had become scarce could still be had at great cost, but few could afford such expenditure. It led to outbursts of indignation against "wanglers and war profiteers." Karl Liebknecht took advantage of this mood and made a speech of May first on the Potsdamer Platz, in which, before an audience of many thousands, he openly indulged in sharp attacks against the Government, and more especially against the Kaiser. Liebknecht was arrested. In the next sitting of the Reichstag the Left Wing unchained a storm against Liebknecht's

[1] Congress Poland refers to Poland as established by the Congress of Vienna in 1815.

arrest, which once again developed into a series of most bitter attacks on the Kaiser, which the Pan-Germans and Conservatives were hardly able to avert. It was reserved for a Socialist—Philipp Scheidemann [2]—to put up a defense of Wilhelm II against the majority of the House.

In the spring of 1915 a memorandum on the reform of the Prussian Electoral Law had been submitted by von Loebell to the Kaiser, who, willy-nilly, had agreed to it. But before Wilhelm II could make up his mind about a message to the people, in which a promise of universal suffrage, after the conclusion of peace, was to be made, he summoned the Crown Prince to Headquarters in order to discuss these questions with him as being heir to the throne. The Crown Prince agreed with his father's decision.

This project as well as differences of opinion about the parliamentary system were the cause of the fall of the seventh Reich's Chancellor. When Hertling learned from one of his party comrades that the majority of the Reichstag had decided to deny him a vote of confidence he forestalled that intention by handing in his resignation.

Once again the already shrunken list of candidates had to be consulted. This time it was no longer Valentini who made the proposals —the war leaders and the Fatherland party had already brushed him aside—it was Fritz von Berg, the "gloomy castellan," who put forward names that were still to be considered, although he knew well that they were little suited for the office of Chancellor. Those shortlisted were the supple Richard von Kühlmann, behind whose back people at Headquarters raised their eyebrows and whispered Anglophile; then there was the cosmopolitan Count Bernstorff and the quiet Count Brockdorff-Rantzau; and lastly Prince Paul Hatzfeld, Prince Max of Baden, Wilhelm Solf, Adolf Wermuth and Admiral Paul von Hintze. These were excellent men . . . but not necessarily as Reich's Chancellors.

The problem was discussed and gone into, argued and considered, without coming to any definite conclusion or any choice of a Chancellor. The Kaiser was condemned to wait and look on patiently, seeing the parties at loggerheads with one another, frittering away their energies in jealous disputation.

[2] Philipp Scheidemann, moderate leader of the German Social Democrats in the Reichstag who subsequently proclaimed the German Republic and headed its first government.

91. A TRIP TO THE FRONT

ALREADY, in the days of the Marne, it had been regarded by the older officers as a matter of course that the Supreme War Lord and his Headquarters ought to be established closer to the Front. Now, after three years of war, it had become a necessity. "The Kaiser must be with his Army on enemy territory! His soldiers must see him!"

Supreme Headquarters was for the time being located in Bad Kreuznach. The Kaiser's entourage would not hear of its being moved farther west. The Kaiserin was living in the old ivy-clad Schloss Homburg, to be near her husband. She was anxious about him, because she heard and got to know many things that were hidden from him. Apart from a few warnings which she had communicated to the Kaiser—especially in the days before Admiral von Tirpitz's retirement—she sought to keep away from political matters.

Whenever the Kaiser decided to make a trip to the Front, this involved all kinds of preparations. The lines over which the royal train was to pass had to be guarded, and the place had to be cleared of their inhabitants for the duration of the journey. The coaches of the old royal train had been turned into regular living rooms. In order to get into them, steps had to be fixed by which one reached a longer corridor, very dimly lighted on account of danger from aircraft.

If the train stopped on one of these journeys, it was for the purpose of picking up dispatches from the Front brought by orderly officers, who were to inform His Majesty of the latest events in that section of the Front which he was going to visit.

The Kaiser worked in his cedar-paneled study, on one side of which hung a large map of northern France. The desk stood facing a wide window which made it possible for him to take in the landscape as it rushed past—burnt-out villages with the scorched ruins of walls between trees, no longer green but pointing skyward like blackened arms emerging from the churned-up soil.

At the final halt cars stood waiting, the first one displaying the yellow Imperial Standard, its chauffeur with the double-eagle badge, just as if they were going for a drive on the Linden. The object of the journey was usually a post on the battlefront that had to be carefully chosen, firstly as being screened from direct view of the enemy, and secondly as allowing something of the actual front line to be seen. Surrounded by his suite, with his standard-bearer and staff trumpeter, two guardsmen of the Royal Rifles carrying his map case and field glasses, the Kaiser followed what was happening through a periscope, throwing back the cape of his cloak and pushing his camouflaged helmet off his forehead. From under the rim protruded a tuft of gray hair. Wilhelm II had aged visibly. On his temples and around his mouth were wrinkles. He had lost much of his vivacity and was more serious and more thoughtful. Knowing that everyone would be eying him, watching every expression of his face, searching for some clue to the general situation, whether things were going well or badly on the various Fronts, he strove to infuse confidence. He clung to the latest news from the Western Front, where in the summer of 1917 the enemy had had to put in colored troops to suppress mutinies. Painlevé had been obliged to sign 150 sentences of death, and whole regiments, together with their officers, had been withdrawn from the theater of war and sent away to the colonies. Unfortunately, similar occurrences were reported from the Austrian Front, where Czech regiments were said to have gone over to the Russians. Other units of the Austro-Hungarian Army were said to have refused to go on fighting. How different was the behavior of the German troops, standing waist-deep in water opposite Ypres or living in holes in the ground on the Somme, badly fed, often short of ammunition, but still offering stout resistance to a superior enemy.

These trips to the Front generally comprised a visit to units that had been withdrawn for resting. Then the Kaiser in person would distribute Iron Crosses. An eyewitness of one of these visits describes it thus: "The Kaiser, on foot, covered the whole extent of the great hollow square in which the troops were formed up by Hassavant Farm in thirty-four minutes, a pace that severely tried the older officers, who had to keep up with him. After that came the presentation of orders and decorations to the troops, with some two or three hundred handshakes, each given with full use of the muscles and full intensity of the accompanying look into the eyes of the recipient. In conclusion the Kaiser gave an address, which took fifty-five minutes to deliver, on the campaign in Poland that culminated in the capture of Warsaw. Owing to the intense heat of the day one of the generals fainted."

Then, usually late in the evening, came the return to Kreuznach, past the ruined villages and the field hospitals, overtaking a trainload of prisoners or meeting an oncoming convoy, whose piebald-paint camouflage gave it an almost ghostly appearance in the twilight. On the horizon rose the first star shells and tracer bullets; increasing thunders in the far distance showed that on the Front the battle still went on. How would that battle end? How would this war, that had now dragged on for years, end? The wheels rolled onward through this land that belonged to France. Would they finally subdue the French as his grandfather had succeeded in doing in his time? The Kaiser's thoughts wandered away over France and the Channel to his cousin George V and his English relatives. Their very names were now for him taboo—yet he thought of them often in his sleepless nights. But he never spoke of them to anyone. His was the silence of unutterable bitterness of heart!

92. BEFORE THE COLLAPSE

THE KAISER'S THOUGHTS now centered on one single aim—Peace! Peace on tolerable terms! Even he dared not believe any more in a victory for German arms. In his opinion the intervention of America had already given a decisive turn to events and had thrown the Reich back on both the strategic and the tactical defensive.

In the summer of 1917 the Papal Nuncio, Eugenio Pacelli,[1] had paid a visit to Kreuznach. After his conversations with the Kaiser it had been an open question whether or not the Vatican would once again appear as a mediator for peace. In any case Wilhelm II had shown that he was prepared to make further concessions. In 1917 he had already told Kühlmann, "Now you have a free hand. Show what you can do and get peace for us by Christmas!"

[1] Eugenio Pacelli, later Papal Secretary and finally Pope Pius XII.

In July 1918 the Kaiser declared that "he no longer wished to stand in the way of a restoration of Belgium" and that he would even be ready to accept corrections of the frontiers of 1871.

To bring these additional concessions to the notice of the Entente various means were employed. These, however, led to no serious paving of the way toward peace. Nor did the efforts of Queen Wilhelmina of Holland, frequently appealed to as a mediator, or those of the Spanish diplomatist Villalobar meet with any success either in London or Paris.

From the place of exile Tirpitz declared that this continual begging for peace would have fatal results and would soon bring with it a bitter revenge. "Anyone who goes searching too urgently or too openly for an agreement only reduces his chances of attaining it, and anyone who does not uphold the national dignity above all else inevitably exposes himself to the severe self-discipline of all his neighbors, and thus brings about a progressive decline of the national welfare and prospects."

Severe self-discipline was already evident in France, personified in the inexorable figure of Georges Clemenceau who, when asked to state his war aims, replied categorically: "My war aim is to be the victor!" Hard as iron, he kept to that aim with the persistence that Napoleon had already declared to be the foundation of all success: "In war persistence is everything. I have to thank it alone for my victories."

While in France and England confidence in final victory was steadily gaining strength, in the German Supreme Headquarters opinion was continually wavering. When the German onslaughts of May 27, 1918, penetrated deeply into the French Front, and German shells fell in Paris, there was optimism. This sank away suddenly when the French, three months later (on August 8, 1918), succeeded in seriously threatening the German flanks. When the Kaiser at that time went to the Front at Avesnes, to see the situation for himself, Ludendorff explained to him in a few short, concise sentences that serious reverses had been suffered and that the situation was causing anxiety, because the troops could no longer be regarded as reliable and were becoming susceptible to revolutionary agitation. It was to be regretted, he concluded, that by every means, such as strike slogans, the soldier was deprived of his belief in victory.

Scarcely had Ludendorff made his report on the situation when Hindenburg announced the receipt of a telegram from Count Kageneck at the Austro-Hungarian Headquarters stating that the Dual Monarchy was on the point of collapsing. The news, too, from Turkey and from the Bulgarian Front left it to be inferred that there also a catastrophe was to be feared. All that the Kaiser could do was to resign himself to admitting, "I can see that we shall have to close the account. We are nearing the end of our tether—the war must be brought to an end!"

In those critical summer months of 1918 Hindenburg and Ludendorff were made painfully aware that they were being hampered and obstructed in all their military measures. "We do not give orders, we are ourselves being ordered about!" declared one of Ludendorff's aides-de-camp, referring to the alleged interference by the Social Democrats in all matters of moment.

Nevertheless, and despite all setbacks and disappointments, the Kaiser never abandoned hope of obtaining an acceptable peace. Casting his mind back to those days he said afterward in Doorn: "In August 1918 I had decided to hasten the opening of peace negotiations on the basis of the *status quo ante*. In agreement with the Chancellor I had given the Secretary of State for Foreign Affairs directions to get in touch with the Entente through a neutral power that was prepared to act as mediator. That naturally needed time. It was clear to me from the first that the Entente might be more disposed to listen to our proposals after the strength of their attacks, which had been directed against our entire front in a continuous series since August eighth, had lost momentum. The crisis of September twenty-eighth scattered all such calculations to the winds. It engendered the idea in the minds of our enemies that our powers of resistance were waning. The Army leaders of the enemy could not be blamed for preferring decisive victory in the field to a military *partie remise*."

To the bad news that, during August and September 1918, was coming in from all Fronts of the Central Powers were added violent attacks directed against Wilhelm II personally, showing clearly that they aimed at his elimination. The French Prime Minister, Alexandre Ribot, had already succeeded in forcing King Constantine and his heir to the throne to leave Athens. The King was the Kaiser's brother-in-law, and his abdication operated like far-off lightning that portended a coming catastrophe. A further worry was added for the Kaiser personally when he learned that the Kaiserin had fallen seriously ill as a result of the great excitement she had suffered. At this difficult moment he looked to God for support. It was known to his aides-de-camp that he sought relief in lengthy prayers. Lieutenant Colonel Niemann, of the Supreme Headquarters, made the following note about him: "I have experienced his truly great, human qualities; his noble mind and his idealism. I have myself seen how many things beset him, what mountains of mental labor he had to overcome in order to keep in touch with the life and activities of the entire State and be capable of making decisions, and again I saw how inexpressibly heavily there weighed upon his mind the welfare and the woes of his seventy million people."

During these anxious days of the late summer the Kaiser was compelled to appoint yet another Chancellor. He found one in Prince Max, heir to the throne of Baden.

Slowly but irresistibly old Bismarck's prophecy was being fulfilled. His curse accompanied the crumbling of the Empire he had helped to found. The eighth and last Chancellor of Wilhelm II was destined to witness the decline of that Empire in all its stages. A quarter of a century before, he had been at the Lehrter Railway Station when the fallen Reich's Chancellor Prince Bismarck had to leave Berlin. Now he was to be a witness when Wilhelm II, made powerless, lost his throne.

93. PRINCE MAX OF BADEN

BISMARCK ONCE SAID, "A Government must be consistent. Firmness and even severity, in an authority that governs, is a guarantee of peace both without and within. . . . No Government is so harmful for a country's interests as a weak one. . . . A Government that suffers from a propensity to avoid conflicts, to shirk strong measures when necessary and to give way continually to foreign demands, slides irretrievably to its own destruction. It very soon finds itself able to survive only by dint of concessions, each leading to yet another, until nothing more remains of the authority or influence of the State."

The Kaiser was concerned with restoring and strengthening this authority of the State which, under the chancellorship of Count Hertling, had fallen seriously into decline. Above all, he would no longer tolerate interference by the various groups in the Reichstag. The parties of the Left were proving especially recalcitrant, determined not to submit to any restraint and concerned only with making their party doctrine the supreme law. What the Kaiser had declared before the members of the Reichstag in August 1914 might, after four years of war, be varied to read, "I see now only parties, but not Germans!"

After the dismissal of Count Hertling, General Ludendorff went to report to the Kaiser. Speaking harshly and with some impatience, he inquired as to the successor to Hertling: "I ask Your Majesty, most dutifully, if there is still no appointment of a new Chancellor and a new Government." The Kaiser replied with equal curtness: "Your Excellency, I cannot produce them by magic!"

Hertling, who for so long had been obliged to renounce "his rightful allowance of sleep" was succeeded by Prince Max of Baden, who was immediately styled "Chancellor of the Revolution" by the Peace party. The new Government formed by him on October 3, 1918, differed but little in futility from its predecessor. It took no decisive action to remedy the prevailing muddle and confusion. There was much speechifying, but nothing was done. In his role of Chancellor, Prince Max felt no more comfortable than Hertling. He subsequently said that when he took over the office he felt "like a man who had been sentenced to death and had forgotten it in his sleep."

Collaboration with the Kaiser, as Prince Max soon found, could be satisfactory only if he was assured of the implicit confidence of his imperial cousin. His aim was to exert a greater influence and make him more tractable than either of the last two Chancellors had been able to do.

After a visit to Supreme Headquarters in July 1918 Prince Max had formed quite a favorable opinion of the Kaiser and had made some notes about this meeting. "The Kaiser has a strong and even overbearing will, which makes him diabolically impatient, yet he is susceptible to good advice. His self-control is astonishing." Now, in

October, his opinion was even more favorable. "The Kaiser is no longer so temperamental—he is well-meaning and friendly . . . and he shows a heroic readiness to recognize facts."

Prince Max, coming from a House of equal standing to his own, was from the first more acceptable to the Kaiser than either Herr Michaelis or the Bavarian Hertling. Moreover, Prince Max was heir to the throne of Baden, and, like the Kaiser, had something to lose.

As early as September twenty-ninth, because of the unfavorable reports from the various Fronts, the Supreme Army Command had requested the opening of negotiations for an immediate armistice.

The reply which came from America was discouraging, especially for the Kaiser, who now had to recognize the fact that the matter also concerned him personally. "After the arrival of Wilson's second note," he said later, "I realized that it was the aim of the Entente to smash the powerful position of Prussia and the unity of the German Reich as personified by me, and to achieve the great military victory which it had not been possible to achieve in battle, by the removal of my person."

Since it was sought to conceal from him the real course of events and the details of their further development, he had himself to grope for the bitter truth. Speaking in Doorn of those days of October 1918, he said: "Many hours of reflection in deep solitude have allowed my life's work to be spread out before me. To find an answer to the many questions put to me by fate was my chief concern. Many riddles were solved, but many new ones appeared: such is the fate of man. Those final enigmas we shall never solve here below. The Almighty Ruler of our destiny knows the answers. That must suffice."

94. THE FIFTEENTH POINT

THE SELECTION of Prince Max of Baden as Reich's Chancellor marked the first occasion of the appointment of a representative of the Parliamentary Democrats to that office.

Social Democrats figured as secretaries of State in his Government and that had never happened before. On October twenty-first the

Kaiser summoned the members of the new Government to the Schloss Bellevue in Berlin. He declared himself to be "in the service of the people," and demanded "unity and the will for resistance." On the advice of Undersecretary of State Scheidemann this speech of the Kaiser was not made public. The Kaiser took an immediate dislike to Philipp Scheidemann; perhaps he already divined that despite a show of good will, Scheidemann would prove his most bitter adversary and would one day be the instrument of his undoing.

The Social Democrats were determined to accept any peace offer the enemy might make. The *Vorwärts* quite openly voiced its intentions in the issue of October 20, 1918: "Germany must—this is our firm determination—strike its war flag forever without having brought it home victorious this last time."

From this article it also became clear that they were trying to place the blame on some other shoulders than their own. A scapegoat had to be found. It was Wilhelm II. And here, as in the case of Tirpitz's downfall, the hope for more favorable peace conditions was a decisive factor in the party's speculations. The Social Democrat Noske quite openly admitted that "if the Kaiser goes, we shall get a better peace."

The *Fränkische Tagespost*, in particular, was prominent in this agitation against Wilhelm II. Speaking for both Social Democrats and Independents, it wrote: "In Wilhelm II we see the last German military monarch. It was he who brought about the greatest war the world has known, a war that comes to an end in the breakdown of the military system. Wilhelm II is still German Emperor and King of Prussia; but he himself must realize that he can no longer be what he intended—an 'instrument' appointed by God. It must be a strange experience for Wilhelm II to have to select and appoint ministers from among the names submitted to him by the Social Democratic party of the Reichstag and by the General Council of the German trade-unions. The Kaiser wishes to remain at all costs. The entire constitution is changed, but Wilhelm II remains Emperor, or at least that is his intention." The phrase "willingness for sacrifice" was mentioned, and in connection therewith it was stated that the Kaiser "had always demanded the greatest patriotic sacrifices from his subjects; the time had come for him to make some sacrifice himself."

This article created a sensation. But it called forth no reply;

nobody defended the Kaiser. Not even the censor took cognizance of it. The fact encouraged other Socialist papers to drop their long-practiced restraint. The *Leipziger Tageblatt,* for instance, two days later appeared with the headline: "Our aim—the Socialist German Republic."

While Left-Wing and even Democratic papers agitated against the Kaiser and by their demands for "peace at all cost" weakened the Government, newly assembled divisions went in to attack the Western Front. In spite of exhaustion, privations and diminished confidence, the impact of these attacks was strong. Field Marshall Haig admits in his memoirs that around the middle of October 1918 German resistance was still very strong. And André Tardieu, a friend of Clemenceau's, supplemented this estimate by admitting that "in the war council of October 25, 1918, Foch, Pétain, Haig and Pershing advocated the concession of acceptable conditions for the Germans, as they themselves had come to the end of their strength." Even the United States was impressed by this flare-up of German resistance. They, too, were tired of the war. Colonel House afterward remarked that it seemed almost like a miracle that the authorities in Germany had been unaware of this, and that it could only be assumed that the enemies of the monarchy believed that victory for Germany would have jeopardized the chances of a revolution—and that they preferred revolution and defeat to victory.

In the propaganda of the German revolutionaries the name Woodrow Wilson became more and more important. On him and his sense of justice even the German citizen fixed his hopes. He was convinced that Wilson would put everything right again; he dared to hope that even the subscribed German war loans would be repaid in good American dollars. This was a propaganda story set in motion by the revolutionaries. The Germans relied on Wilson's assurances because they believed in his good will. They read his book, *The State,* which a Berlin publisher brought out in a vast edition. In this book Wilson voiced his views on Prussia: "Prussia has endeavored to be more perfect than any other European State in her administrative organization. Prussia's administrative system serves as a type of the highest development of local government. The Prussian judges stand in a position of substantial independence." In the same work, a few pages before the above quotation, he referred to France: "The most conspicuous trait in all branches of administration is the 'tutelege.' . . . French administration has suffered . . . profound corruption. . . . Ministerial responsibility has rapidly degenerated in France, during the past few years, into government by the Chamber."

A person who could think as objectively as Wilson must indeed be a suitable mediator for the unraveling of the confusion in Europe. Wilson's Fourteen Points were accepted and considered as a suitable foundation for peace talks. The man in the street did not doubt the President's sincerity.

From the first, however, the Kaiser lacked confidence. With great anxiety and apprehension he watched the exchange of notes between Wilson and Prince Max. The Reich's Chancellor's willingness, in particular, to put a stop to all further sailings of U-boats appeared to him premature and uncalled for. In later years Wilhelm II commented on this: "The reply to Wilson's notes by my War Council showed the direction in which we were traveling. I used all my personal influence with Prince Max of Baden in order to prevent the cessation of the U-boat war. On October twentieth I left Potsdam for Berlin and by appointment called on the Chancellor. I found that Prince Max had asked the Bavarian Minister to be present at the conference. Both men declared categorically that all members of the Reich's Government were agreed that U-boat warfare had to be discontinued in order to obtain a sympathetic reception of our truce offer. I pointed to the degrading words of Wilson's note and entreated the Prince not to give away the most effective means of warfare at our disposal at that time, without binding guarantees on the part of the Entente."

But the Kaiser was already excluded from official business. The Reich's Government even avoided the mention of his name to Wilson in their endeavor to assure the President that the Government was authorized by the German people: "The present German Government, which is responsible for the peace offer, has been formed after consultation and in agreement with the great majority of the Reichstag. In every one of these actions the Reich's Chancellor, supported by a majority decision, speaks on behalf of the German Government and the German people."

In further notes from President Wilson it became apparent that some of his Fourteen Points had already been abandoned. When the Germans realized this, their mood changed. Feeling deceived, they indignantly turned against the "mad professor" who was no longer an "honest mediator of peace" but an "artful hypocrite." Ludendorff turned down Wilson's new proposals abruptly. Later, in a proclamation to the Army, he described these proposals as "unacceptable to us soldiers."

Confronted with this attitude Prince Max of Baden threatened to resign should the General again frustrate the policy adopted by the Chancellor. As Ludendorff insisted on the right to speak his mind, the Chancellor declared that he could no longer co-operate with the Quartermaster General. The Kaiser tried to keep the peace at Supreme Headquarters, but it was impossible to mollify the opponents. To one of his adjutants he admitted despondently: "For weeks I have worked with all my strength to weld the parts together. Now the whole edifice threatens to collapse. It is an impossible state of affairs when proclamations such as this can be published without my, or the Chancellor's, knowledge. I see no other way than to comply with the Chancellor's request."

Upon this Ludendorff declared that in any case he was going to tender his resignation. A government that no longer backed its Supreme Command created an impossible and intolerable state of affairs. So Hindenburg had to part with his Chief of General Staff who had worked with him for four years and had so greatly distinguished himself. His place was taken by General Wilhelm Groener.

Ludendorff's defeat was received triumphantly abroad and by the Left-Wing press in Germany. In German military circles it produced a bad impression, even consternation. They felt that in difficult times such as these a leader of the unflagging energy and determined grip shown by Ludendorff was more essential than ever. But the Social Democrats were not satified with the downfall of Ludendorff; the Kaiser's removal was the next goal of the revolutionaries and the Entente; it was indeed Wilson's Fifteenth Point, though not actually included in the list. Wilson advised the acceptance of this demand to promote the benevolent mood of the Allies. With biting sarcasm the Kaiser commented on this suggestion, "I think that, on the whole, it is always wiser not to follow advice offered by your enemy."

On the Kaiserin's birthday, October 22, 1918, the popular press for the first time used the phrase "the Kaiser's abdication." Dulled by four years of war, this demand was received with comparative indifference. The average citizen remembered how honored and esteemed had been this man who had stood at the head of the Reich. It was remembered that for a quarter of a century, in spite of the Boer War, the Moroccan crisis, the Russo-Japanese War, in spite of the danger of war after the annexation of Bosnia and Herzegovina, the Kaiser had preserved peace for the German people. They had no proof that he was personally responsible for this war, as the Entente would have them believe. During many years the Kaiser had been glorified; foreign countries, such as France, had envied the Reich its ruler; he had been popular and had been acclaimed. Now all this was to be thrown aside, obliterated, and taken as a crime, just because such was the wish of the enemy? With these and similar practical observations the German citizen tried to counter the propaganda onslaught.

But retrospection was not viewed favorably by the Left-Wing press. They increased their agitation against Wilhelm II. "Where is Hindenburg?" they asked. "Hindenburg knows His Majesty through and through and cannot be in doubt about the real war situation? Where is Hindenburg, and why does he not go to the Kaiser and inform him of his last duty as Supreme War Lord?"

Perfectly calm in all this commotion, Hindenburg remained unperturbed. In his gruff voice he said to Niemann, "We must never forget that the Kaiser is a truly noble man."

In England the question of Wilhelm's abdication was debated with especially lively interest, for the Kaiser's close relationship to the English Royal House added considerable importance to the matter. There were two opposing parties: one, with the *Daily Chronicle* as its mouthpiece, considered the deposition of the Hohenzollerns as undesirable. They maintained that by this act all gates and doors of Europe would be opened to Communism. The other party favored deposition. This view was supported by the *Manchester Guardian* in particular, which, in accordance with Wilson's theories, proclaimed: "No peace with the Hohenzollerns. So long as the world is not rid of the Hohenzollerns, we cannot make peace with Germany." The *Daily Express* said they thought Prince Max was endeavoring "to save the dynasty of the Hohenzollerns and the Junkers." The *Daily Mail*, however, deliberately enumerated all the difficulties opposing a removal of the Kaiser, for "Wilhelm II still holds the power in Germany."

In Germany the Conservative party, led by Heydebrand and Westarp, opposed pressure from abroad and from the German Social Democrats for a removal of Wilhelm II. In the *Kreuz-Zeitung* Westarp entreated his readers to remember "the blissful years of 1888 to 1914, the good days . . . which the German people have experienced in rich measure. The time has come when we can show that what we said and sang in those glorious days was not just a collection of empty phrases." A proclamation from Count York von Wartenburg, in the name of the *Herrenhaus* (the Prussian House of Lords) demanded that the Kaiser "should find his people faithful even in the darkest hour." On October thirtieth the Christian trade-unions in Düsseldorf voted for a "people's emperor" (*Volkskaisertum*); even some republicans from the entourage of Prince Max endorsed this with the same argument that Secretary of State Haussmann had given the Reich's Chancellor: "I am a democrat, but a nation must not, at the order of the enemy, reject its Kaiser."

In the course of further developments and under pressure from foreign States and the German revolutionaries, Prince Max of Baden found it inevitable that someone must suggest to the Kaiser that he should abdicate. But all those whom he approached to carry out this difficult mission emphatically declined. General von Chelius explained his refusal by stating that the Kaiser's abdication would mean "the dissolution of the Army and the Reich." The Chief Chaplain also declined "the execution of any mission which he could not back with conviction."

On the evening of October twenty-eighth the Kaiser declared to his Reich's Chancellor: "I shall remain in my place and co-operate loyally with the Government."

95. JOURNEY TO SPA

THE DAY PREVIOUS to making this declaration, Wilhelm II received news in Berlin of serious signs of disintegration in the Austro-Hungarian Army. It was rumored that the Vienna government had asked for a truce. This news, as also the necessity of discussing other important questions which could only be settled at General

Headquarters, decided him to leave the capital for Spa, then Supreme Command Headquarters. Later, he thus explained this decision: "Soon after that, at the urgent request of Field Marshal von Hindenburg, I traveled to Spa. Important military decisions had to be made, decisions which—owing to our allies all forsaking us—necessitated exhaustive discussion. Moreover, I considered it my supreme duty in such critical times to be with my troops, who were engaged in the fiercest of battles."

In Government circles the Kaiser's sudden departure was received with surprise. It was considered ominous, for in view of the many rumors that were circulating and the general state of affairs, a variety of conclusions could be drawn from his action. The Left-Wing press was quite outspoken; they talked of a "guilty conscience" and "flight." The *Berliner Tageblatt* said, "The departure of the Kaiser had taken all official and political bodies completely by surprise. . . ." However, this journey prevented any immediate discussion of the abdication question for the time being.

Even before Wilhelm left Berlin the Reich's Chancellor had tried, over the telephone, to make him change his plans. The Kaiser, however, remained adamant. "You have dismissed Ludendorff," he said, "now I have to introduce Groener." The Chancellor's objection that "in times like these the War Lord was indispensable at home" was countered by the observation that Germany was at war and his place was with his soldiers. Prince Max replied very tartly that he was well aware that they were at war; but as the Kaiser was set on leaving Berlin, it was imperative that the Chancellor should be given an opportunity for discussing matters before his departure. This request was curtly refused on the grounds that the Kaiser's physician would not permit him to visit the Chancellor for fear of infection, for Prince Max was at that time in bed with influenza.

In his sickroom the Chancellor pondered on the best course of action. Should he resign, or should he, by offering his resignation, try to exercise some pressure over the Kaiser and Supreme Command? He made one more attempt, however, to cause the Kaiser to return to Berlin, by telegraphing to Spa a request for an immediate and urgent consultation. Offended by the Chancellor's peremptory tone, the Kaiser instructed Delbrück to reply for him.

It was in a letter to Prince Max from the Undersecretary of State, Scheidemann, that the question of abdication was brought up again.

In his letter Scheidemann set down the demand "which could not be made in the press," but which would have to be considered, and considered by the Chancellor himself. At a Cabinet meeting the following day (October thirty-first) the Chancellor frankly announced that for days the question of the abdication of His Majesty the Kaiser had continuously been foremost in his mind; however, he wished to declare most emphatically that His Majesty's abdication could and must be voluntary.

It was after this Cabinet meeting that Prince Max's condition began to deteriorate, and in order to restore him to health as soon as possible, his doctor prescribed a drastic cure. To this the Chancellor submitted, and after thirty-six hours' sleep his temperature was down and he was well again. During these vital thirty-six hours further attempts were made to propose to the Kaiser the advisability of abdication; but they were fruitless. Both the Grand Duke Ernst Ludwig of Hesse—who was far from being one of the Kaiser's friends—as also Prince Friedrich Karl of Hesse emphatically refused to undertake the mission. Two of the Kaiser's sons, Prince Adalbert and Prince August Wilhelm, who came to the Chancellor for information about "the wild rumors circulating in Berlin," indignantly rejected the request for their help in the abdication question. Prince August Wilhelm remarked that "Max should fix that himself."

At the same time (October sixteenth) Viktor Naumann suggested to the Crown Prince that he ought to induce his father to take the necessary step. "It is only after having conscientiously searched in my mind for a different solution," Naumann's letter ran, "that I am putting this suggestion to you. We must now expect from His Majesty the high-minded decision to renounce his office. I cannot believe that His Majesty would be able to accommodate himself to the new times—even if he wished to, it would be difficult for him. His attitude in the past would hardly permit one to expect a complete transformation of his character."

Prince Max did not wish to make any decision in the matter of the abdication without having consulted the Federal princes. He therefore invited those members of the Federal Council who were entitled to vote to the Bavarian Embassy in Berlin on the morning of November first. Before the meeting he had requested those present to inquire, by telegram, from the various Federal princes whether they agreed to Wilhelm's abdication. Moreover, the Chancellor said, that as the Crown Prince's renunciation of his claim to the throne could not be avoided, it was suggested that his eldest son should become Kaiser under the regency of a Prussian prince.

One of the first replies to arrive was from the Grand Duke of Baden, the Chancellor's cousin, who declared himself in favor of Wilhelm II: "At this hour the place of the German princes is behind the German Kaiser." The other princes sent ambiguous replies; some implied, however, that they were confident that their affairs were being well taken care of by Prince Max.

Nobody seemed greatly in favor of the throne's passing to the young Prince Friedrich Wilhelm. Even to the Prussian representatives the thought of preserving the monarchy by means of an eleven-year-old child was an unhappy one. Some suggested the House of Wittelsbach, but later, and for different reasons, changed their choice once more in favor of the eleven-year-old boy. He was, however, no longer to be under the regency of a Prussian prince, but with Prince Max of Baden as Reich's Administrator. This solution was, however, rejected by the Chancellor himself, who justified his attitude by saying that he was a relative of the Kaiser's. "For me," he explained, "the situation is more difficult than for anyone else."

Bad news came pouring in. On November first the Ottoman Empire sued for peace. On the following day, Austria-Hungary submitted unconditionally to Wilson's terms. Then reports of open rebellion arrived from different sectors on the German front. At the same time news was received from Kiel that mutiny there had spread to the battle fleet, making it impossible for vessels to put to sea. Several officers, such as Captain Weniger, were murdered when opposing the mutineers, while others died a yet more dreadful death. On November fourth the first Workers' and Soldiers' Councils were formed in Kiel, based on the Russian prototypes. From that time onward the revolutionaries in Kiel obeyed only Liebknecht's instructions. At the urgent request of the Independents, and under pressure from the Spartakus League, Liebknecht had been set free on October twenty-first.

When the Kaiser heard that red flags were flying from leave trains and that they were also carried by ships of the German fleet, he came near to a nervous breakdown. "What has wounded me most deeply is the fact that the rebellion should have broken out first in my proud fleet, *my* creation!"

Impressed by the occurrences in the different front sectors and in Kiel, the Supreme Command viewed the future with dark misgivings. They could no longer subscribe to the Chancellor's policy of appeasement to the dissident parties, for this seemed only to increase their craving for power, especially among the Left-Wing parties in the Reichstag.

At last a man was found willing to suggest abdication to the Kaiser: it was the Home Secretary, Drews, who appeared at General Headquarters and was received by the Kaiser. When Drews, without faltering, had acquitted himself of his task, the Kaiser regarded him silently. Suddenly he advanced. "And you dare to suggest this to me! You, a Prussian official, sugggest this to the King to whom you have sworn the oath of allegiance? You can tell Prince Max, who has sent you, that I shall return home with my Army and shall dutifully remain at my post."

After this interview with Drews the Kaiser discovered an ally in his new Quartermaster General Groener, who, like Hindenburg, was opposed to the abdication. Prince Bernhard Bülow, too, protested against this solution. He had suddenly reappeared in order to proclaim has attitude (in the *Norddeutsche Allgemeine Zeitung* of November 4, 1918): "The notion of a democratic Emperor guarantees the undisturbed development of this process of evolution. I have spent a great part—the greatest part, perhaps—of my life abroad; you may take it from me as one who knows Europe inside out that the changes in our Constitution will for the time being suffice for Germany. . . . We entered into this war in full discipline; demobilization must take place in the same spirit of unconditional discipline, otherwise we shall experience unforeseeably grave consequences that will affect every German citizen alike, whether he may have declared himself for or against the Kaiser."

In those critical November days the Crown Prince proved himself a man of prudence and consideration. On November third he traveled to Crown Prince Rupprecht of Bavaria's headquarters to induce the Bavarian prince to sign a document, addressed to the Reich's Chancellor, in which he demanded that the Kaiser should remain on the throne. But the Wittelsbach prince refused his signature on the grounds that he, as Commander in Chief of an army, could not meddle in political affairs. His war diaries, which were later published, showed that he already held the opinion that "the German princes should jointly approach the Kaiser . . . and suggest his abdication."

So the ring was closing around Wihelm II; the only path open to him was the voluntary renunciation of his throne. Vice-Chancellor von Payer and Secretary of State Solf now considered this "unavoidable." Even the representative of General Headquarters at the Foreign Office, Colonel Hans von Haeften, declared: "If His Majesty should not decide to abdicate immediately, all that will remain to be done will be to break with Wilson. Then it will be: Remove helmets for prayers!"

For the last time the Reich's Chancellor begged His Majesty to return to Berlin, as his presence in the capital was essential on account of an expected new note from Wilson. But Wilhelm II suspected that this was a trap to separate him from his generals, most of whom, he noted with satisfaction, would not hear of his resignation. And now the Minister of War Scheuch declared that "abdication means force and will always mean force. The Army is closely connected with the Supreme War Lord and would suffer great damage through the Kaiser's abdication!" Quoting the opinion of his Minister of War, the Kaiser repeated the declaration he had given to Drews, namely, that he would "only yield to force."

On the evening of November sixth the fourth Wilson note arrived, according to which Marshal Foch was empowered to receive representatives of the German Government with truce proposals. Secretary of State Scheidemann, the first to examine the note, could not find in it "any mention of negotiations" or any allusion to the imaginary Fifteenth Point: the abdication of the Kaiser. By this time Scheidemann had already seized power into his own hands; for while Prince Max still placed full confidence in his Secretary of State, this man had in fact deceived him and laid plans for his downfall.

Later in Doorn, when talking about Prince Max's last days in office, the Kaiser said: "When one views, as a whole, the attitude of the Reich's Chancellor Prince Max of Baden, the following facts appear: first a solemn declaration to protect the imperial throne with the new Government; then suppression of the speech at the

Bellevue which might have favorably influenced the public; then exclusion of the Kaiser from all important work; surrender of the person of the Kaiser through the abolition of censorship; nonintervention on behalf of the monarchy in the abdication question, and finally the attempts to persuade the Kaiser to abdicate voluntarily. The whole development clearly showed the dangerous game played by Scheidemann, who had the Chancellor completely under his influence. He did not inform his fellow ministers of his real intentions, drove the Prince from one step to the next, justifying himself by saying that the leaders no longer controlled the masses. In this way he forced the Prince to surrender his Kaiser, the princes and the Reich, and thus made him the destroyer of the Reich."

The Reich's Chancellor was, in fact, already in the power of the Social Democrats. This was obvious from the manner in which Scheidemann and Ebert treated him. On the afternoon of November seventh they telephoned the Prince from the Reichstag to announce their ultimatum; this demanded in Clause 5 "the abdication of the Kaiser and the Crown Prince before noon on Friday, November 8, 1918." The same evening Ebert repeated this demand: "The Kaiser must abdicate immediately," he said, explaining this request by party-political reasons: "otherwise the whole crowd will go over to the Independents!"

The Independents had made their headquarters in the Russian Embassy in Unter den Linden. In spite of strict supervision by the Headquarters staff, cases with Bolshevik inflammatory literature came in daily from Moscow, marked as "diplomatic baggage." These were received through back doors and distributed over the whole of Germany, to the very front lines. This underhand conduct of Russia, contrary to all diplomatic customs, was eventually stopped by a trick. At the Schlesische Railway Station in Berlin, when unloading a container, one of the cases addressed to the Russian Embassy "accidentally" slipped and dropped down a lift shaft into a storage room, where the case broke open and revealed the leaflets. The following day the Russian Ambassador Joffe found himself obliged to leave Berlin in a hurry.

But the International in Moscow and the Independents had achieved practically all they had set out to do. Revolution flared up through Germany. The main towns were Wilhelmshaven, Cologne,

Hanover and Brunswick. In Munich Eisner [1] proclaimed the Bavarian Free State: King Ludwig III, as the first of the German Federal princes, had to leave his capital under cover of darkness. The
next was Duke Ernst August of Brunswick, who, after short reflection, signed his abdication in front of the Workers' and Soldiers'
Council. This happened only five years after the splendid Guelph
wedding in the Schloss in Berlin; the young Duke had ruled his
country only five years.

On November eighth the revolution spread to districts behind the
fighting lines; on the previous day the insurgents had occupied the
Rhine crossings. Alarming news came in from Berlin: mutinous
sailors were said to have entered the Berlin Schloss and to have
plundered it. The whole town appeared intoxicated; the population
was wild with joy, for "splendid times" were about to dawn. Field-
gray soldiers without shoulder straps but with stolen officers' badges
and decorations roamed the streets, often accompanied by women
with red ribbons in their hair and Spartacus [2] cockades on their
bosoms.

But in spite of the terrible news that arrived in Spa, Hindenburg's
attitude was unchanged. He had sent word to Scheidemann through
Groener [3] declaring, with regard to the question of abdication, that
"he would consider himself a rogue if he forsook the Kaiser." But
though the Field Marshal remained firm and unshaken, a change
was taking place in Groener. During a short visit to Berlin he had
had occasion to sample the mood of the capital; what he learned was
that people were absolutely opposed to the Kaiser, and declared him
guilty of causing the war. Groener had therefore come to the conclusion that Kaiser and Crown Prince must be sacrificed for the sake
of a reasonable settlement. Thus, the Quartermaster General now
declared himself in favor of a regency for little Prince Friedrich Wilhelm; but he considered Prince Max most unsuitable as regent, and

[1] Kurt Eisner, former Socialist editor who headed a short-lived revolutionary government at Munich until murdered by Freikorps troops in 1919.

[2] A group of Socialist extremists, under the leadership of Karl Liebknecht
and Rosa Luxembourg, called themselves Spartacists, after the Roman slave
Spartacus who led a revolt of the slaves.

[3] General Wilhelm Groener commanded the German armies after the abdication of the Kaiser and the signing of the Armistice. He did not belong to the
Prussian aristocracy and had risen to the top in the Army on the basis of sheer
ability. After the defeat, this gave him more prestige in the eyes of the soldiers and the people.

at the suggestion of Scheidemann, nominated either Prince Eitel-Friedrich or Prince Oskar.

From the evening of November eighth onward event followed event in breath-taking succession. News from the Reich reported further revolutionary movements in Königsberg, Karlsruhe, Essen and Breslau. The telephone did not rest at Villa Fraineuse in Spa where the Kaiser was staying. At nine o'clock in the evening a call came through from Berlin: the Reich's Chancellor wished to speak to the Kaiser personally. As soon as Wilhelm had picked up the receiver, Prince Max urged the Kaiser seriously to draw his own conclusions from recent events, and to abdicate; there was still time to do so honorably and the nation would appreciate his sacrifice.

When the Kaiser again rejected this demand the Chancellor asked for his immediate release. The Kaiser replied: "That is impossible. You made the truce offer; you must now receive the conditions!"

After a telephone discussion lasting nearly an hour the Prince realized that he could achieve nothing with the Kaiser; during the course of the night he therefore wired a situation report to the Kaiser. From this report it appeared that the Chancellor felt that he had been left in the lurch by the behavior of the Social Democrats: "I considered an abdication of Your Majesty and a renunciation of the succession by His Imperial and Royal Highness the Crown Prince, under pressure from the Social Democrats—and both are demanded before noon on Friday in a party broadsheet distributed today—as so great a danger to the dynasty and the conception of the Reich, that all my endeavors went toward preventing them by my approach to Your Majesty and the War Cabinet. But I consider a government without, or in opposition to, the Social Democrats an even greater danger. This would now only be possible in the shape of a military dictatorship which inevitably would result in a bloody civil war and in the destruction of the German people by Bolshevism."

In conclusion the Prince asked once more for his release from office.

That night, while the two cousins were holding their last conversation, the Workers' and Soldiers' Councils assumed power. The Independents had reason to be satisfied with their old opponent Philipp Scheideman; he had saved them the trouble of an unpleasant job. Triumphantly Hugo Haase announced to his comrades:

"Crowns are rolling in the dust: the crown of King Ferdinand of Bulgaria, the crown of Czar Nicholas and the crown of the Emperor of Austria-Hungary. Even those crowns which had already been considered safe have vanished like phantoms: the crowns of Finland, of Courland and Lithuania!"

There was only one missing . . . !

96. NOVEMBER 9, 1918

IT WAS A ROUGH, raw day. Autumn was no more and winter was already setting in with a chill whistling wind that shook the trees in the grounds of the Villa Fraineuse, stripping them of their last brown leaves until they stood pointing to the sky like so many exclamation marks.

The Kaiser had been up and dressed since an early hour. He was pacing uneasily up and down his room, every now and then going to the window to look out over the avenue, swept clean by the wind. From the ground floor came the incessant clanging of telephone bells —that had gone on all the night—the hurrying tramp of officers and orderlies, the clank of sabers and the clink of spurs.

He knew that on that day he would hear the decision that would determine his fate. He thought again of how, in that restless night now ended, he had made an irrevocable vow—not to abdicate but to remain at the head of his Army and to restore order in the Reich.

The previous afternoon Hindenburg and Groener had broken it to him that the reliability of the front-line troops could no longer be guaranteed. There was no lack of proof that this was so. The evidence had been collected and collated by Colonel Heye before that interview. But it was mainly composed of reports from front-line officers, not from the generals in command, whom the Kaiser had expressly required to be consulted. Nevertheless, these reports had, by the early morning of November ninth, been confirmed by other front-line officers specially summoned to the Kaiser's Headquarters. After these had made their reports at the Hôtel Britannique, the following telegram in cipher was despatched to Berlin at 9:15 A.M., with the instruction that it was to be kept secret.

"The Supreme Army Headquarters Staff has decided to inform His Majesty at once that the Armed Forces will not support him in the event of civil war and that because of supply difficulties the Army is not in a position to carry on a civil war."

After that, the A.D.C. on duty reported to the Kaiser that Field Marshal Hindenburg and General Groener were ready for a conference. Reports were being received both from the Front and from Berlin that Hindenburg had made up his mind to recommend the Kaiser to abdicate, and that Groener had urged him to take that course.

When the Kaiser entered the conference room the Field Marshal found that he was not able to carry out his intention to make clear to the Kaiser the necessity of his renunciation. In a low voice, which, though low, sounded in other respects rough and abrupt, he asked to be allowed to resign his commission on the ground that "as a Prussian officer he could not say what he now had to say."

Shivering with cold and looking worn out by a sleepless night, the Kaiser stood before the fireplace and searched the face of his loyal old comrade, who must now repeat to him what "the others" —the civilians—had already advised.

The embarrassed silence was broken by the arrival of von Hintze, Secretary of State, and General Count von der Schulenburg, the Chief of Crown Prince Wilhelm's General Staff, who came with General von Plessen.

As someone had to say something, General Groener stepped forward. In concise sentences he described the gravity of the situation —the line of the Rhine and all its depots were in the hands of the Workers' and Soldiers' Councils—no trains were allowed to pass through to the Front—the armies were cut off from their lines of supply.

At this, the Kaiser declared: "In that case I shall place myself at the head of the units that remain loyal and I shall restore order."

Groener: "That would mean civil war, Your Majesty—and war within the Army itself in addition."

The Kaiser: "I don't believe that!"

Groener (*undisturbed*): "The Army will march back obediently and in good order under its own generals, but will not do so under the command of Your Majesty."

The Kaiser (*moving toward Groener*): "Your Excellency, I must have this from you in writing! I must also have reports in black and white from all the generals commanding telling me that the Army will no longer stand behind me as their Supreme War Lord. Has not the Army sworn the *Fahneneid*?" [1]

Groener (*coldly*): "The *Fahneneid*? That is only a story now, Your Majesty!"

The Kaiser blanched. He was on the point of making some cutting rejoinder, but controlled himself. Hindenburg remained silent. His silence at that moment was the equivalent of assent, endorsing all that Groener had said.

The next to speak was Count von der Schulenburg, who showed himself in that hour to be not only the straightforward mouthpiece of the officers determined to remain loyal, but also to be the calm and prosaic General Staff man seeking ways and means to save the Kaiser.

He, too, stated that in part at least the troops were seriously demoralized, but maintained that if they knew that the Kaiser and the Field Marshal were putting themselves at their head to restore order they would develop a fresh *élan*. He summarized his proposals thus: "No yielding to revolutionaries in the homeland! No abdication, but strike with a firm hand! Restore order in one city after the other! The Army would respond to that call, would rally to the Kaiser, and preserve its discipline!"

The Kaiser, listening at last to a proposal that did not involve his abdication and that had been presented with such earnestness and confidence, agreed with Count von der Schulenburg.

Plessen, too, declared that he looked on Schulenburg's plans as providing the only possible basis for further action.

Then Hindenburg cast aside his reserve. He said that Schulenburg's proposals would also be his, but for the fact that the general situation called imperiously for other measures necessary to prevent useless bloodshed. In his position he could not assume responsibility for a civil war in which his troops would inevitably be drawn into fighting one another. That was why he and his Quartermaster General must unite in solid opposition to Schulenburg's solution.

Although these words of Hindenburg's sufficed to seal his fate, the Kaiser did not lose his nerve. Before closing the discussion he

[1] The oath of loyalty and true allegiance sworn on the regimental and other colors. It is a combination of the words *Fahn* (flag) and *Eid* (oath).

declared: "I want all the principal commanders to be questioned as to the feeling among their troops. If they report to me that the Army will no longer stand by me, then I am prepared to go . . . but not before."

He then left the room and went out alone for a walk in the grounds. He would await the reports from the principal commanders and would gain time to make it possible for him to talk with his eldest son, the heir to the throne, and finally make up his mind what to do.

Luncheon, toward one o'clock, was a painful affair. Scarcely one of them could swallow a morsel. All were oppressed by uncertainty as to what would happen within the next few hours. Immediately after the meal Colonel Heye came in with the latest reports from the Front. Most of the commanders of sections were unwilling to vouch for the reliability of their troops.

It would appear that the Kaiser assumed these to be the reports that he had called for from the Principal G.O.C.s, a mistake that afterward had an important effect on his own decisions.

Then came alarming news from Berlin. In the capital there was riotous clamoring for his abdication. The Secretary of State Hintze had been charged with handing to the Kaiser a notification of this. It was plain that it was intended as an ultimatum from the Government.

For what happened at that interview, which took place in the presence of Hindenburg, we are dependent on the notes made by the Crown Prince Wilhelm:

"When Hintze finished speaking, the Kaiser gave a curt nod of his head and his eyes sought those of Hindenburg as though, in his agony of mind, he hoped to find in them strength and aid. But there was none there—motionless, deeply agitated, in helpless silence, the great old man stood by and allowed the destiny of his King and master, whom he had served so long as a brave and loyal soldier, to fulfill itself."

Deserted now by everyone, the Kaiser decided to yield to the pressure brought to bear on him and to allow the Berlin Government to be informed that "His Majesty is prepared to abdicate as German Kaiser if by that means further bloodshed can be avoided. But he wishes to remain King of Prussia. He will lead the Army back to the homeland in perfect order."

Scarcely had this message been handed in for transmission to Berlin when, crossing it, came the announcement that the Reich's Chancellor, in order to allay the disturbances in the capital and throughout the country, had already, at approximately one o'clock, given out through the Wolff Telegraph Agency the news that the Kaiser and King had decided to vacate the throne. The Chancellor would remain in office until questions arising out of the abdication, the renouncement of his succession by the Crown Prince, and the setting up of a regency, had been resolved.

When General von Gontard came in with this message the Kaiser became wildly excited. He spoke of Prince Max's treachery and wanted to insist on his immediate withdrawal of that arbitrary declaration. But it was now too late. About two P.M. the Secretary of State, Philipp Scheidemann, proclaimed from a window of the Reichstag to the expectant masses of people below: "The Kaiser has abdicated! The people have won a complete victory! The monarchy has collapsed! Long live the German Republic!"

While at Supreme Headquarters the generals were debating what should be done about the now-deposed Kaiser, the latter had ordered his own servants to prepare the Villa Fraineuse as he had no intention of making his escape, as had already been suggested to him.

"If only a few of my gentlemen remain loyal to me, I shall fight to the end, even if we are all killed. I have no fear of death! I am remaining here!" He told General Gontard: "I want to stay on with my Army to the last and take my chance of living. They are trying to induce me to abandon the Army. That is an unheard-of piece of presumption! I am staying here!"

Toward evening, Secretary of State von Hintze arranged for a representative of the Foreign Office to advise the Kaiser that he should make his way over the near-by frontier to a foreign country, as that solution would obviate all the difficulties that his presence in person must involve. The other officers also urged him to accept this advice of the Government, since "no one can know how things may develop. It might be too late to come to any decisions at all later on."

Secretary of State von Hintze was afterward accused of misusing Hindenburg's name in his attempts to persuade the Kaiser and to ensure that he was got away into Holland. That accusation did

Admiral von Hintze an injustice. Four years later Hindenburg, when writing to the exiled Kaiser (his letter was dated July 28, 1922), made the matter perfectly clear: "On the afternoon of November ninth I myself, speaking in the name of all of us, advised [the Kaiser] that to cross into Holland was the last possible way out.

Moreover, it is established that on the same afternoon of November ninth Hindenburg, as Chief of the Supreme Headquarters Staff and the senior officer there, handed the Kaiser a note signed by himself which said: "I cannot take the responsibility for Your Majesty's being carried away to Berlin by mutinous troops, there to be handed over as a prisoner to the revolutionary Government. On that account I must advise Your Majesty to go to Holland."

This was advice which the Kaiser, by reason of the personality of the giver, the force of the argument and the danger involved for the Reich, could no longer reject. But it still needed some painful hours before he could make up his mind to accept it.

After fifty months of war against a superior force consisting of four-fifths of mankind, the German people had broken down, divided among themselves and impoverished. The Army was disbanded—the Navy broken up by mutiny. The Kaiser himself was a refugee without aim or future, an outlaw whose handing-over, wherever he might be, was demanded by the Entente.

With Wilhelm II, after 507 years and in its nineteenth generation, the reigning house of Hohenzollern had come to an end.

97. AND IT WAS WRONG!

IT WAS ON the afternoon of November ninth that Field Marshal von Hindenburg advised the Kaiser to cross the Dutch frontier, adding the proviso that it must be considered as "the last possible way out." Many people had regarded Hindenburg merely as an old soldier, a second Blücher, a man without qualities in any other sphere. If, on account of his education and military schooling, he could not be a politician, he was, however, able to view many things more soberly and clearly than the diplomats. People who knew and disliked the Field Marshal saw in him an ambitious, realistic man, often acting without consideration and even with cunning, determined to go his own way to his own advantage. The Kaiser may have heard this unfavorable judgment of his Field Marshal. On this November ninth he must have been astounded to find that the redoubtable warrior Hindenburg had succumbed to Groener's influence and finally—contrary to his original views—declared himself in favor of the abdication.

At the Kaiser's request, Hindenburg subsequently confirmed in writing that, as chief military adviser, he was fully responsible (and would always consider himself so) for the Supreme War Lord's decision to go to Holland. "I am asking Your Majesty . . . to be allowed to confirm once more that throughout my life I have stood, and shall always stand, behind my Kaiser, King and master; I am willing to declare, always and everywhere, that I share the responsibility for the decision taken on November ninth. . . ."

For his part the Kaiser admitted, "I have fought a fierce inner battle, for I did not wish to expose myself to the reproach of cowardice in forsaking any part of my Army that may have remained faithful. I would have preferred to die fighting with them."

After four years of war and continuous excitement the Kaiser was now on the verge of a nervous breakdown. There was none left to advise him; none wished to stand in opposition to the Field Marshal. Had Kessel still been alive, he would not have forsaken him in this difficult situation; then "perhaps the ninth of November would have taken a different course!"

On that evening, while the Kaiser was being assured by those around him that a tolerable peace could only be attained by his sacrifice, and that the German people would be grateful for it, troops returning from the Front marched into the German towns. Banners hung across the streets with the slogan:

> *Seid willkommen, tapfere Streiter,*
> *Gott und Wilson helfen weiter!*
> (Valiant fighters, welcome home!
> God and Wilson will carry on!)

In Paris Marshal Foch declared that he was proud of his victory over "the most splendid army in the world." When the Kaiser learned of Foch's remark, he renewed his refusal to leave: "They want me to leave that splendid army and repay their heroic deeds by taking myself to a foreign country. My wife is holding out and I am made to go to Holland! I shall not do it; it would be the same as a captain abandoning his sinking ship."

His A.D.C.s seized on his mention of the Kaiserin to remind him that only from Holland would he be in a position to look after her. This consideration may have had a decisive influence in inducing him to give way at last to the urgent requests of those around him.

Bismarck, who, after his dismissal, was not in the habt of talking favorably of Wilhelm II, once remarked at Friedrichsruh: "Given the fact that there was someone able to drive the Kaiser into a desperate situation, I am convinced that he would rather die than give in!"

Wilhelm II had seriously considered the possibility of death rather than yielding to Hindenburg and Groener. As a result of his reflections he had to admit that he could not see "the advantage of performing such a heroic act. The days are past when the king as commander-in-chief, sword in hand, led his warriors into the last decisive battle." He might have added: What a triumph it would have been for the French to have captured the German Kaiser fighting at the Front!

Critics—among them Groener—said that the Kaiser ought to have "made an end," by which they meant he should have committed suicide.

"Apart from the fact that I am the First Bishop of the Evangelical Church," the Kaiser remarked later, "I condemn all temptation of God, including even suicide for moral reasons. Had I committed this desperate act, it would have been tantamount to an irrevocable admission of guilt."

As for the Entente, it would have enabled them to say: You see, the Kaiser himself has drawn the proper conclusions and has evaded his earthly judges. Later, in Doorn, the Kaiser once said: "Had I employed the weapon against myself, they would have said: 'The coward! Now he is evading all responsibility!' The commission appointed in Paris to examine the question of war guilt would certainly have taken up this argument and interpreted it in their own way."

Others, who would not listen to suggestions of a heroic suicide, wanted the Kaiser to return at the head of his faithful regiments. The argument against this was that the German Government, owing to the conditions imposed by the Entente, would have been obliged to hand over the Kaiser to the Allies.

In spite of all this, and the unfavorable opinion his Field Marshal held of his doing so, Wilhelm II would have been right if, in his capacity of Supreme War Lord, he had placed himself at the head of his faithful troops. He should have shut his ears to the voices of those generals whose course was already determined by Parliament. He should have listened alone to the inner voice of the soldier who, in that hour, might have asked him to remember the 1st Guards Regiment, the Army, Potsdam, his ancestors and Frederick the Great; to remember that once he was a commander of a regiment himself, and that the time had again come to place himself at the head of any regiment, battalion or company and march with them, as every private had done for him for four years; that he must not listen to those advocating the easy way out and in this way clearing a path for themselves; that the old Potsdam motto must still hold good: *Semper talis*!

What, then, would have been the right course? The Kaiser ought to have followed the Crown Prince and Count von der Schulenburg, his Chief of General Staff, and ought, for the time being, to have remained with the army division *Deutscher Kronprinz*.

The end of the Hohenollern dynasty was at hand. The German people accepted it with almost uncanny indifference, an occurrence unknown in German history (with the exception of the decline of the Hohenstaufens). "November 9, 1918, was the day of judgment," Schüssler said. "The sentence was of unprecedented severity. Once again Bismarck's dictum was confirmed, that all political mistakes are punished sooner or later, and that history is more particular in its reckoning than even the Prussian Audit Office."

In his letter of January 6, 1888, Bismarck had written to the then Prince Wilhelm: "I look for firm support of the monarchy . . . in a kingship whose bearer is determined to co-operate industriously, not only in peaceful times, but who in critical times would rather die fighting, sword in hand, on the steps of his throne, than give in. No German soldier will forsake such a master!"

It was this Bismarckian determination that the Kaiser could no longer muster. He, who, as a rule, carried out his ideas without faltering, now hesitated and gave in; his nerves were worn out after the long, heavy strain. He clung to the suggestions put to him and in the end believed that there was no other path open to him than crossing into Holland.

In that night of the ninth to the tenth of November, he was no longer free to dispose, even of himself. In the early morning, surrounded by his retinue, one narrow path only was open to him, the path to the throbbing motor outside the house. "Should I have resisted?" the Kaiser later asked in Doorn. "I could not very well start fighting my A.D.C.s!"

A door closed, the wheels began to turn and, saluting, the responsible Headquarters' officers remained behind. Hindenburg was absent; he had remained in his room. In spite of his concession he did not wish to witness the departure of his Imperial master. It was a parting filled with the tragedy of destiny and guilt.

The question of war guilt and the decision of November ninth to cross into Holland repeatedly occupied the Kaiser's thoughts. Though he had no occasion to regret his decision, he may have doubted the wisdom of this step as Supreme War Lord.

When, in November 1935, we came to talk about this question, he tried to justify his action by an eloquent defense. But it was obvious that he himself was unconvinced by his reasoning. Suddenly he stopped in the midst of the conversation. "I know what you are thinking! Do say it!"

"What happened then, Your Majesty, was wrong!"

We did not continue our conversation that day.

98. EYSDEN

IN THE EARLY HOURS of November tenth nine motorcars left the General Headquarters at Spa with fourteen persons, not counting the drivers. Although there had been plenty of time to pack, it had been done in such a hurry—owing to the general excitement and agitation—that necessary and useless things had been thrown together without consideration.

It was getting on for seven o'clock in the morning when the column of motorcars reached the Dutch frontier, not far from the village of Eysden. It was Sunday, and no frontier guard was in evidence at that early hour. After repeated hooting, a sleepy sergeant emerged from the Custom House; at the sight of German officers in full uniform he decided at once not to lower the chains which barred the road. In accordance with instructions he asked for passports. Although the resplendent officers could produce service identity cards with illustrious names and titles, they none of them possessed passports. The sergeant declared that without a passport no one was allowed to enter Holland.

General von Gontard undertook to negotiate with the guard; he explained that they were bound for an exceptionally important conference at The Hague which must not, under any circumstances, be delayed. The sergeant, however, remained firm: without a passport no one was allowed to pass.

By now frontier guards and customs' officials had appeared and, following the sergeant's orders, they took up position alongside the barrier, staring at the many glittering decorations on the collars and chests of all the officers but one. He was addressed by all others with great respect.

After renewed discussions a German general approached the sergeant and declared that the fourteen German officers wished to be interned. Luckily the word "internment" figured in the Dutch manual of instructions, together with the instruction that in every case superior authority should be informed. So the sergeant telephoned to Maastricht, where the call was received by Major van Dyl, who immediately realized that he was faced with something quite out of the ordinary. Accompanied by a junior officer he hurriedly set off for Eysden.

One glance at the gold-braided shoulder straps and red ribbons showed him that he was in the presence of the highest officers in the German Army; but when he recognized the Kaiser, he decided—as something had to be done—to take on himself the responsibility of granting the request, and suggested accompanying the Kaiser and his suite to the neighboring railway station. Furthermore, he ordered the frontier at Eysden to be closed to all further traffic.

They walked the short way to the station, the cars following slowly. Shortly afterward the royal train from Spa rolled in; for the time being it was to serve as the Kaiser's residence. But efforts were made that very Sunday to find a dwelling place for Wilhelm II in Holland; after some consideration he decided on Amerongen, the residence of Count Godard Bentinck, whom he asked for shelter.

That Sunday, Count Bentinck had returned from hunting somewhat earlier than usual on account of the rain. He and his daughter were having tea by the fire when the telephone rang. An official of the Ministry of Foreign Affairs inquired from The Hague whether the Count would be willing to receive at Amerongen the German Kaiser, who had crossed the Dutch frontier the same morning. In return, Bentinck inquired how many guests he was expected to put up; the reply was fourteen at first, but later the number would be increased, though it would not exceed thirty. On hearing this Count Bentinck was obliged to tender his regrets, for his house could not possibly accommodate so many visitors.

Then a letter arrived at Amerongen in which the Kaiser asked his fellow Knight of the Order of St. John to give him sanctuary in accordance with their knightly vow. At this Bentinck said he was prepared to receive Wilhelm II and his suite in his house.

On the afternoon of November eleventh Wilhelm II and Count Bentinck met for the first time. The place of their meeting was the little railway station at Maarn, near the small town of Rhenen, the church tower of which has become famous through a Rembrandt etching. The station was closed to the public. Only the Governor of the Province of Utrecht, Count Lynden, was present at the Kaiser's arrival. A few railway officials and curious villagers leaned on the wooden gates outside the station. Thick fog lay over the country; rain was falling continuously, adding to the general feeling of depression.

In a car with drawn blinds the Kaiser started on the short journey to Amerongen. In the entrance hall members of the Bentinck family received and greeted him. His host then conducted him to his rooms. When they were left alone the Kaiser asked Count Bentinck a few questions, among others whether he was a Freemason. When the Count replied in the negative the Kaiser said, "I am glad to hear it. —What do you think of it all?"

Silent, the Count stood before the Kaiser.

In an effort to overcome the embarrassing situation the latter remarked with a smile: "And now, my dear Count, I should like a cup of tea, hot English tea!"

99. CHRISTMAS AT AMERONGEN

THE STAY at Amerongen was to have lasted only a few weeks; but in fact it extended over eighteen months.

Count Bentinck had had four lofty rooms on the first floor of the castle prepared for the Kaiser and the Kaiserin when she came. He furnished them with exquisite pieces of antique furniture, including a richly carved bed in which Louis XIV had once slept (in May 1672). In this bed the Kaiser passed his first night in the Count's house.

Eager to obtain sensational news, to observe what was going on in the Schloss and, if possible, to take photographs, crowds of journalists tried to climb the park walls or crawl through the hedges of the kitchen garden. In order to stay the onslaught Count Bentinck asked The Hague for a bodyguard, which was granted. The guards had strict instructions to admit no one without a pass and to keep the gates closed throughout the night.

The Kaiser's suite still consisted of fourteen officers: General von Plessen, General von Gontard, Lord Chamberlain von Platen, Major Generals von Frankenberg, von Litorff, von Grimmen, Colonel Count Moltke and Major von Hirschfeld. In addition there were Surgeon General von Niester and Captains von Ilsemann, Seiss, Knauff, Schaderberg and Grutsche. Not all of them could be accommodated in the Schloss.

They soon settled down to a strict timetable: at seven in the morning the Kaiser rose and went for a walk in the garden, wearing a blue civilian suit such as he used to dress in aboard the *Hohenzollern* or in the sailing clubs at Kiel or Cowes. During his walk he would stop and talk to the gardeners about rose cultivation and the growing of orchids. At eight-forty-five there was a religious service in the picture gallery, the Kaiser himself reading the lesson. After breakfast he occupied himself in his study with the mail, which at that time contained many insulting and threatening letters from all over the world. This done, he devoted himself to the study of the

Dutch language, which he mastered quite well after a few months. Weather permitting, he took exercise in sawing and chopping wood in the grounds of the Schloss. At four-thirty tea was served; dinner was at eight o'clock.

The first evening meal at Amerongen was dull, everyone at table was in low spirits. In vain the Kaiser tried to entertain his companions, who pensively stared at the plates in front of them and replied absent-mindedly.

Slowly they became used to their life in exile, which Count Bentinck tried to make as agreeable as possible. After dinner they began to assemble in the library, where matters of topical interest were freely discussed. The Kaiser avoided touching on the most recent events, or mentioning names such as those of Prince Max or Groener.

The daily routine, fixed by the Kaiser, was broken on November twenty-eighth, when several men dressed in black asked to see Wilhelm II. They came at the request of the Council of the Peoples' Delegates. The leader of the delegation was Count Ernst zu Rantzau, twin brother of Count Ulrich von Brockdorff-Rantzau. From his briefcase he produced a large white document, headed with the Imperial eagle. Then followed the typewritten text of the abdication. This he submitted to Wilhelm II. The document read as follows:

> "I herewith renounce for all time my right to the Crown of Prussia, and to the German Imperial Crown connected therewith. In doing so I release all officials of the German Reich and Prussia, all officers, noncommissioned officers and men of the Navy, the Prussian Army and the troops of Federal contingents from their oath of allegiance which they have sworn to me as their Emperor, King and Supreme Commander. Until the institution of a new order in the German Reich I expect them to assist the holders of the actual power in Germany to protect the German people from the dangers threatening through anarchy, famine and foreign rule."

After some reflection the Kaiser placed his signature and seal beneath the words: "Signed and sealed by our own hand and the affixed Imperial seal. Given at Amerongen, November 28, 1918. Wilhelm."

The name "Wilhelm" is signed large and in a vigorous hand, as if to show that the demand of the Republic had not broken his strength or taken all hope from him.

After the departure of this somber delegation, the Kaiser repaired to his host; he wished the Count to be the first to hear of the act that had been performed under his roof.

That same day the Kaiserin Auguste Viktoria arrived at Amerongen. She came from Berlin, accompanied by her Lady-in-Waiting, Countess Keller. The latter had been her constant companion throughout her married life, and she was unwilling to leave her mistress now, at a time when the Kaiserin was in special need of loving care, for in addition to heart disease, she was suffering from the memory of the dreadful scenes she had experienced in Berlin. Drunken sailors had forced an entry into her rooms in the Villa Liegnitz and had been prevented from harming her only by her determined attitude. That the Kaiserin appeared to have aged considerably and often felt exhausted was partly due to what she had gone through. Very rarely did she leave her rooms to appear at the dinner table. The events of the last weeks seemed to her some bad dream, which, on waking, she had yet to accept as cruel reality. She talked of the "incomprehensible," the "inexplicable," for which she could find no explanations. She seemed to suffer more under the changed conditions than the Kaiser, whose vitality and optimism helped him to bear his many humiliations. When, however, the Kaiserin appeared at the dinner table, dressed in simple black, upright and dignified, she never failed to impress those present.

Christmas was approaching, the first Christmas in exile. Most of the gentlemen of the Kaiser's suite had left Holland, which they found too expensive to live in. Among those who remained was the sixty-year-old General von Gontard, who in Potsdam had been nicknamed "Parrot." He was an honorable man, but showed an exaggerated deference toward his Imperial master. Cheerful young Captain Ilsemann, from Darmstadt, was a very different personality; he soon became the favorite of the whole household, including the host, who later gave his consent to the marriage of his daughter and Ilsemann.

The year 1918 was drawing to its close. What a year it had been! How few of the companions of happier times had remained! The Kaiser's relatives were scattered over the earth; many had died; "Nicky" and "Alix" had been murdered. Moltke was dead; Falkenhayn, Bethmann, Jagow and Tirpitz were still alive but hiding somewhere in the country or in the mountains. Ludendorff was in Sweden,

and in the midst of tumultuous revolution the Field Marshal was
trying to demobilize what remained of the Army.

The Kaiser's rooms at Amerongen were splendid with tapestries
from Flanders and furniture by Cressent, but in spite of such valu-
ables, these surroundings remained alien. There was nothing to remind him of the old days. The mutinying sailors had stolen much
from the Berlin Schloss; other things had been lost during the riots,
such as valuable correspondence or trifling souvenirs which possessed no value whatever for strangers. Among the treasured me-
mentos lost was the golden sovereign that his grandmother, Queen
Victoria, had once given him as a reward. In spite of all its comfort
and hospitality, Schloss Amerongen remained strange to Wilhelm II,
a little fort, a place of refuge, an exile, at the gates of which guards
patroled day and night, keeping watch over him as if he were a prisoner. From the lower windows the Kaiser looked on the guards in
their foreign uniforms. He could see the holes cut in the ice of the
moat, which were to prevent strangers from getting into the Schloss
at night by crossing the ice-covered water. This Christmas Eve his
gaze traveled beyond the moat and bridge, beyond the trees of the
park to the bright silvery line on the horizon. It was the Rhine and
beyond it lay Germany—the Republic!

100. THE STRUGGLE FOR THE KAISER

IF, DURING THE FIRST MONTHS at Amerongen, Wilhelm II
had been asked what was foremost in his mind, he would doubtless
have answered: "The question of war guilt." With great assiduity
he studied the numerous White, Yellow and Blue Books, also the
numerous memoirs of former statesmen in responsible positions.
These he studied in order to complete the "Comparative History
Tables" he was compiling, as well as to prove that neither he nor
his government could have caused the outbreak of the war, and that
they were therefore free of any guilt in that direction.

In the course of his researches he came across material exonerat-
ing him personally from blame. Phrases by Izvolski: *"C'est moi, qui
est le père de cette guerre!"* or Sazanov: "The German Kaiser's love

of peace is an assurance that we may fix the time for the war ourselves," were of great use to him. Some German statesmen expressed similar views in their reminiscences. Tirpitz came to the following conclusion: "I can produce a further, valid proof for the fact that our Reich's leadership did not want the war, namely, that from the beginning they were convinced that we could not be victorious. You may credit them with great ineptitude, but never with the criminal act of wishing for a war, the hopelessness of which was, in their eyes, a foregone conclusion."

In January 1920 the Supreme Council in Paris took cognizance of Articles 227–230 of the Versailles Treaty which demanded the surrender of nine hundred Germans. These were to include the Crown Princes of Prussia and Bavaria, Hindenburg, Ludendorff, Bethmann-Hollweg, Tirpitz, Scheer, Mackensen and—most important of all—Wilhelm II. The Supreme Council declared that for legal reasons they could not depart from their demand, as no less than fifty thousand indictments against the Kaiser had been lodged with the English Public Prosecutor alone.

The indictment formulated by the Versailles Treaty read as follows: "The Allied and Associated Powers publicly arraign Wilhelm II of Hohenzollern, formerly German Emperor, for a supreme offense against international morality and the sanctity of treaties." A court of law was to be instituted in which Great Britain, France, Italy, the United States and Japan were to be represented by one judge each and this court was to be "guided by the highest motives of international policy . . . and fix the punishment it considers should be imposed." At the same time a request for the Kaiser's surrender was sent to the Netherlands Government.

The Kaiser is a German, and this fact was recognized even by the Weimar Republic. For once they put aside their feelings and came forward in defense of the ex-Kaiser. Even his bitterest enemies declared that it would be "an inexpiable outrage," if the erstwhile representative of the country were to be handed over to the enemies like some criminal. Four years earlier Prince ("Erni") zu Hohenlohe-Langenburg had written: "In the Entente countries an agitation against the Kaiser has been carried out so cunningly and systematically that in the public opinion of these countries—America included—he is considered the embodiment of all real and invented horrors of this war."

The editor of the *Süddeutsche Monatshefte* turned against these suppositions and the request for surrender: "Nowadays not even savage tribes are being treated in such a manner." Count Rüdiger von der Goltz, who was not willing to hand over his "Baltic Warriors" appealed indignantly against the demand of the Entente: "I commenced my career as a man of character; I do not intend to end it as an opportunist. The question of surrender cannot even be considered by the Germans."

It was left to a Czech, Karl Kautsky, a friend of Scheidemann's, to appear as the chief witness for the prosecution against Wilhelm II. The Weimar Republic entrusted him, a foreigner, with the task of sorting out and editing the papers of the German Foreign Office concerning the antecedents of the World War. Before this supposedly official version was published a private edition of the material appeared, in excerpts and with marginal comments by Kautsky, wherein he asserted that it was Wilhelm II who should be made responsible for everything concerning the outbreak of war, for it had been proved that he bore the major part of the guilt. The appearance of Kautsky's publication came at an opportune moment for the tribunal that had been instituted, for it could now bring a charge against Wilhelm II based on a German report.

The Dutch Government was at first undecided as to what attitude should be taken about the Entente's demand that the Kaiser should be handed over. They sought to base their standpoint on a declaration by Lord Cecil of November 16, 1918, to the effect that in law the surrender of Wilhelm II could not be demanded but merely requested. Furthermore, The Hague was of the opinion that, as the Netherlands were not signatories to the Versailles Treaty, they could not be required to abide by it.

The Allies, however, were unwilling to accept this refusal from so small a country as Holland, all the more as it was in the interest "of the whole world to call to account the responsible originator of the war." In a special note the attention of the Royal Netherlands Government was drawn to the risks which they were running if they allowed Wilhelm II and the Crown Prince (who had, meanwhile, also arrived) to remain within their frontiers, as they were the representatives of the German "Military party." The note benevolently pointed out that the Allies were prepared "to relieve the Netherlands of the irksome care for the internment of both persons."

In the exchange of notes that followed some dramatic climaxes were reached. At first, as we have seen, Paris tried to obtain the surrender of the Kaiser by friendly means: "It is not a question of prestige, nor an infringement of the Netherlands sovereignty if the surrender of Wilhelm II be insisted upon. In this hour the Netherlands must not fail us; on the contrary, they must, in unity with all other civilized nations of the world, fulfill their duty, which is to deliver up the accused to the court of law entrusted with the prosecution of international criminals."

In a further note the Supreme Council reminded the Netherlands Government that they ought to consider "that to this man's politics can be attributed the deaths of nearly ten million human beings, brutally murdered in the flower of their youth; three times that number of men have been most dreadfully maimed; thousands of square miles of rich industrial, peaceful and happy land are lying destroyed and waste. A war debt of one thousand milliards remains unpaid . . . all this due to the terrible consequences of the war unleashed by Wilhelm II."

Without taking up these accusations, the Netherlands Government replied on January 23, 1920, that they had to persist in their refusal; the German Kaiser was enjoying the hospitality of their country and a surrender could only be considered from a wider and international aspect.

This reply was received with great surprise in Paris. It was decided to renew and insist on the demand. The next note, of February 14, 1920, concerned the Netherlands in particular. It recalled that a great number of Dutch citizens had died on the high seas as a result of German U-boat activity. It referred to the glorious history of the Netherlands, in itself a proof that justice had always been held in high esteem in that country. Finally the great Dutch humanist Hugo Grotius was called as a witness who, two hundred fifty years earlier, had demanded the expiation of crimes: "Lawbreakers have to be punished or destroyed or to be kept in safe custody."

But this last note did not receive a different reception from its predecessors; so the Supreme Council had to become more outspoken. They threatened the Netherlands Government with measures which would have serious consequences, should they continue to protect a man who had put force before justice and on whose being rendered harmless they (the Allies) had to insist. If the Netherlands

Government should persist in their refusal they would become participants in the Kaiser's guilt, "thus creating a baneful precedent that is likely to render ineffective all proceedings of an International Court of Justice against guilty persons of high standing. . . . The Netherlands Government will be aware of the seriousness of the situation, if only for the reason that the present domicile of the Kaiser is in the immediate neighborhood of the German frontier and that 'surprises' may be expected at all times." This note of February 17, 1920, ended by saying "that the Allies would—in the eyes of the whole world—make the Netherlands Government alone responsible for the mortal danger resulting from their refusal of surrendering Wilhelm von Hohenzollern to his judges."

While this controversy was raging the Kaiser was himself considering the possibility of voluntarily placing himself at the disposal of the Entente. But he soon dropped this idea; he had no intention, he said, "to play the part of Vercingetorix, who trusted in the magnanimity of his enemies, and surrendered himself in order to attain better conditions for his people. The behavior of the Entente during the Peace Conference was hardly such as to assure me that they would act with more magnanimity than Caesar, who had Vercingetorix chained and lated executed, but treated his people none the better for this sacrifice."

There were other reasons for this change of heart in the Kaiser: he saw that accuser and judge were united against him. The Tribunal meant to base its case exclusively on Entente documents and those of Kautsky, without considering the material evidence produced by the defendant. The prospect of years of imprisonment in a French penitentiary—and therefore appearing all the more guilty in the eyes of the world—may have finally dissuaded the Kaiser from giving himself up to the Allies.

The Dutch newspapers, which the Kaiser read every morning, reported at great length, and with extensive comments, on the exchange of notes between The Hague and Paris. Some papers advocated the surrender, others were opposed to it. Although he had no real apprehensions, this haggling over his person, this insecurity and uncertainty as to what was to become of him, ended by making him very nervous. The Kaiserin also suffered. Again and again she asked her companions whether they thought that the Netherlands Government would hold out and remain firm; would they protect her husband to the last? She slept very badly and it may well be true, as one of the inhabitants of the Schloss reported, that she often woke from her uneasly sleep at night and called for help.

101. A NEW YEAR'S EVE JOKE

BEFORE THE NEGOTIATIONS for the surrender of Wilhelm II were concluded, an incident occurred which, in spite of its comical side, might have had serious consequences. While at Amerongen everyone was endeavoring to make as few difficulties as possible for the Netherlands Government, and do nothing that might upset the Ministers at The Hague, a plot was hatched in Luxemburg, aiming at the forcible abduction of Wilhelm II.

The idea was conceived by an American, Colonel Lukas Lia, who, with his unit, was stationed in the small Luxemburg town of Tuntange, awaiting transport back to the United States. Little was happening in Tuntange and the enterprising Colonel was just bored. So he determined to do something to surprise Tuntange, Luxemburg and the world in general.

It was on New Year's Eve—under the influence of too many glasses of rum punch—that he conceived his plan to abduct the German Kaiser. He confided the scheme to his seven officers (some of whom were very young men), who were only too willing to assist in a *coup de main* to fetch Wilhelm II from near-by Holland and "give him as a present" to President Wilson, who was at that time in Paris. The cheerful session lasted well into the early morning; in their imagination these officers already saw the pleased and surprised expression on the faces of Wilson, Pershing, Clemenceau and Foch when they appeared with Wilhelm II. As a reward for their troubles they expected nothing less than the *Légion d'honneur* and Victoria Cross. Before breaking up the party, which was not until the New Year had dawned, they pledged to keep the plan strictly secret. No one was to know of their mission, with the exception of one person in Brussels who was to procure eight passports and the necessary papers for two cars. It has never been ascertained who this person in the Belgian capital was; it is certain, however, that it was not the U.S. Ambassador who endorsed the officers' passports for Holland.

In the afternoon of January fifth two cars crossed the Dutch frontier near Elten. They met with no difficulties, for the passports were in order, and the frontier guards put the officers on their way to Arnhem and Amerongen. Late that night the Americans stopped in front of the locked gate to the Schloss. As all the bedroom windows looked on the inner court, the outer front of the building lay in darkness.

The Colonel was the first to leave the car. He rang the doorbell. An old caretaker appeared and asked what the late visitors desired. They wished to speak to the Kaiser on very important business, was the answer. Upon his request to know who the gentlemen were, Lia replied curtly and explicitly that they were here at the request of higher personages.

Slowly windows lit up in the Schloss. An A.D.C. came to the gate to interview the strangers, who made a somewhat strange impression on him. They did not look in the least like emissaries with a high mission, most of them appeared far too young for any such employment.

The Americans were, however, ushered into the library, where they were kept waiting for some time. Eventually Count Carl Bentinck entered to tell them that both his father and His Majesty the Kaiser had already retired and could not receive anyone as late as this. Upon the officers' insistence that it was absolutely essential for them to speak to the Kaiser, Bentinck asked the Colonel some searching questions, to which he received only confused and contradictory replies. By now Count Godard Bentinck had put on his clothes and he came to the aid of his son. But the replies he received to his precisely worded questions were no more satisfactory, so he asked to see their credentials. Lia produced the passports and pointed out that they were explicitly made out for Holland and Amerongen; that in fact they constituted credentials. Count Bentinck was not to be misled by these bold assertions; he demanded to see properly valid credentials such as are customary in the diplomatic service. These Colonel Lia could not produce.

By this time the Count was convinced that it was a hoax, if not worse, so he asked to be excused for a few minutes as he wished to consult with His Majesty. In the meantime the Kaiser also had got dressed, ready to receive Count Bentick and receive his report on what was happening. When the Count had told him everything the Kaiser sent word that he was prepared to see the American officers if they would give a declaration, on their word of honor, in the presence of witnesses, that they had come to Amerongen at the request of the Paris Peace Conference, with the knowledge of President Wilson or General Pershing.

Colonel Lia did not dare to give such a binding assurance as this. He began to stammer, made excuses and looked for assistance from his junior officers, who were even less capable of dealing with the situation that had arisen. A footman entered with wine and sandwiches, and Count Bentinck took the opportunity to slip out of the room. He went to the telephone and asked the Mayor to send some stalwart villagers to the Schloss.

The Mayor of Amerongen was a smart man and not easily deceived. Immediately on arrival at the Schloss—as the representative of law and order in Amerongen—he began to cross-examine the Americans as to their intentions and what they meant by coming and waking an Emperor in the middle of the night! In his embarrassment Colonel Lia started pacing nervously up and down the room. As he passed the window he saw a great commotion in the torch-lighted courtyard: police and military detachments had arrived. The game was up!

To secure for himself and his companions an honorable retreat, Colonel Lia announced that he would reveal the purpose of their visit if he and his fellow officers were guaranteed a safe withdrawal. This was granted, and Count Bentick and the Mayor were told how the Americans had wanted to take the Kaiser with them to Paris, as a surprise present for the Supreme Council.

That confession made, the Americans had to leave their comfortable armchairs and the Schloss. Passing down a lane of police and hefty villagers they reached their cars and quickly drove away, escorted by troops as far as the frontier—the Dutch wanted to make quite certain that the uninvited guests left by the shortest possible route.

When General Pershing heard of this occurrence, in his first burst of indignation he determined to call a court-martial in Paris. He was shown a list of the offenses with which the accused were to be charged, which included desertion, violation of international law, attempted deprivation of liberty, constraint, breaking of the peace, acting under false pretenses and theft (one of the officers had taken one of the Kaiser's cigarette holders as a souvenir). On seeing this formidable indictment General Pershing decided on disciplinary procedure, the sentence of which did not have to be publicized. It was impressed on the judges and the accused that they must never, in any circumstances, breathe a word to anyone about the incident and the trial. In view of the foolishness of this prank the sentence was a lenient one: the eight delinquents were sentenced to be sent home; in America they were sent to prison for a few weeks to give them time to ponder over their enterprise and to come to the conclusion that—as the Mayor of Amerongen had said—you cannot just go and wake an Emperor in the middle of the night in order to steal him.

After this cowboy prank the Netherlands authorities felt compelled to increase the police force of Amerongen; for the more urgent the Supreme Council in Paris became in their demand for the surrender of the Kaiser, the greater was the risk of similar attempts being repeated.

The Government at The Hague remained firm. The replies sent by the Netherlands Foreign Office to Paris were masterpieces of diplomatic phrasing: polite, but courageous; giving way in words only, but unshaken in their standpoint that they intended to continue their hospitality to the German Kaiser.

The exchange of notes went on until March 24, 1920. The last note was signed by Lloyd George, and laid upon the Royal Netherlands Government the exclusive responsibility for any possible future complications. After that the question of surrender was slowly forgotten and the Kaiser once again began to breathe freely.

He could now think of settling permanently in Holland and of leaving Amerongen. When looking for a suitable home the first choice had been Belmonte, a house belonging to Baroness Justine Constant and her sister-in-law Countess Pückler. But he soon changed his mind and decided on the mansion at Doorn, only half an hour from Amerongen, which had formerly belonged to the Labouchère family. In May 1920 he moved to Doorn.

A small hospital, equipped with all modern installations and apparatus, was erected in Amerongen as a parting gift from the Kaiser to the place whose inhabitants had come to like him. The villagers were so deeply impressed by the white hospital with its many large windows that it was some time before they dared venture into it. It was an offering of thanks to those who had given the Kaiser a temporary home in his darkest hours.

102. DOORN

WHEN A CITIZEN of the small town of Doorn (it had eight thousand inhabitants) was asked the way to "Schloss Doorn," he corrected the inquirer and pointed the way to "Doorn House." It was, in fact, no more than a roomy country house, large enough for the Kaiser, his wife, their servants and, at most, six guests. A large park surrounded the main building. Rooms had to be arranged in the gatehouse and above the stables for the Marshal and the A.D.C.s. After the builders had been called in by the Kaiser these rooms became quite comfortable.

The Kaiser had always had a particular liking for Holland, partly owing to his connection with the House of Orange. His grandmother, Queen Victoria, had been a descendant of William the Silent, the first *Stadtholder* of the Netherlands, and Wilhelm II was proud of this forefather. He was also a descendant of the pious Princess Henrietta of Orange, who, as a young woman, had come to Brandenburg to become the wife of the Great Elector, Friedrich Wilhelm. "The Great Elector is the one forefather to whom I am most deeply devoted; ever since my youth I have looked up to him as to a shining ideal." Before the World War, as an expression of his admiration for these members of the House of Orange, the Kaiser had their statues erected on the terrace of the Schloss in Berlin. Thus Holland was no strange country to him. He knew and loved it, perhaps also because it reminded him of Brandenburg, his home.

In order to make the house more comfortable he ordered furniture, pictures, china and bronzes to be brought from Germany. Among these things were many that reminded him of happier days. He himself supervised the furnishing of Doorn; he wished to be surrounded only by things to which he felt some personal relationship. He made every decision, no matter whether it concerned the arrangement of his library or the hanging of a picture. This occupation diverted him and made him feel more at ease; here at last he would be able to live undisturbed.

Slowly life at Doorn settled down to a fixed routine. The day started with a morning service; as in Amerongen the Kaiser read the lesson. Breakfast followed and after that, weather permitting, a walk in the park or wood sawing; old Schulz or Vieke would stand by, holding the master's coat, watching this new occupation with astonishment. They had been in the Kaiser's service for more than thirty years, having waited to the last on his sick father at the Villa Zirio.

The Kaiser had the park at Doorn rearranged and replanted. There was no need to sow grass for lawns in the English style, for the lawns were already there. A little copse of rare conifers—gifts from admirers from all over the world—and a rose garden enriched the beauty of the park.

Wilhelm rarely left his estate. When he did go out of the park, however, and walk to the village, it was quite unceremoniously, accompanied only by an A.D.C. and an official. The passers-by, on bicycle or on foot, gave him a friendly greeting; to the citizens of Doorn the close neighborhood of this illustrious man had become quite profitable. The only restriction imposed on the Kaiser in Holland was that he had to inform the police whenever he wished to leave his estate, in order that measures might be taken for his safety.

At Amerongen it had rarely been possible, out of consideration for Count Bentinck, to invite relatives, children and grandchildren, or friends; now, in spite of the limited space, this had once again become possible. Those guests who could not find room at Doorn House were put up at the gatehouse, or—if that was full—at an hotel in neighboring Utrecht. Meals in large company had once more become stimulating and interesting. Most of the visitors came from Germany, but foreign guests also arrived. They were surprised at the ease with which the Kaiser mastered their languages, changing from one to another without for one moment losing the thread of the conversation.

After dinner the Kaiser withdrew to his study situated in a tower. There he took some of his chosen friends to talk, which was still his favorite recreation. One unwritten rule, however, had to be strictly observed: for reasons of tact political events that had taken place after November 1918 were not to be mentioned. The Kaiser himself once confirmed this rule by saying: "I myself refrain from all critical comment on conditions in Germany after the revolution!"

Anything that had happened before the revolution could be frankly and freely discussed with him; nor did he mind hearing criticism of his former decisions and measures. At such moments he might gaze at the speaker with a mocking, superior smile and say, with a shade of irony in his voice: "Do you really think so!" or, slightly contemptuously: "No, really!" But he would soon again be in a better mood, and once he started talking it was difficult to interrupt him, a fact he admitted himself.

Through this exchange of views Wilhelm sought to make life at Doorn as interesting as possible. He became more indulgent as he grew older, more understanding and more kindly. While reading the memoirs of Admiral Tirpitz, he put aside the book that attacked him so viciously and unjustly and said: "Even that cannot affect the high opinion I hold of the man."

Subjects for conversation passed rapidly in review: history and art, military matters and philosophy, music and literature, travel and archaeology—all this might be discussed in the course of one evening. If archaeology were the subject, the Kaiser was in his element; everyone else just sat and listened.

When relatives were up with him in the Tower the Kaiser, as head of the Hohenzollern family, was asked for decisions and advice in family matters; he never gave decisions until he had informed himself thoroughly of every detail of the case in question. He was greatly interested in everything concerning his grandchildren and well informed about all relatives, near and far; he knew what his daughter and her children were doing in Gmunden or how his nephew, son of his brother Heinrich, was getting on in Guatemala. When someone mentioned Heinrich, the Kaiser would relate how Prince Heinrich liked to bind his own account books, an art that he had learned at school in Cassel.

In all matters concerning the Royal House, Count August zu Eulenburg, Minister of the House of Hohenzollern, had formerly acted as the Kaiser's attorney. For decades all questions of the family, law and finance had rested in his hands. Now this old man of eighty-two left the master whom he had served faithfully for so many years; others who were once unable to protest too emphatically their loyalty for their Kaiser kept aloof, sending no letters or congratulations on his birthday or at Christmas. Had not the Kaiser promoted them, singled them out, believed in them and believed also that they would stand by him in hard times? The recollection of his former relations with statesmen or relatives made the Kaiser bitter and suspicious.

But on every January twenty-seventh, without fail, a letter arrived from Field Marshal von Hindenburg. The envelope disclosed the writer's identity by the large, firm handwriting. He never forgot to add to his congratulations the assurance that he would never, in whatever position he might find himself, sever the ties which bound him to his Imperial master.

With the help of correspondence and the newspapers Wilhelm watched developments in Europe, particularly in England. He expressed his hopes that the country of his mother might treat him more fairly and might now recognize the injustice they had done him. He often read aloud important passages from English newspapers; sometimes he lowered the paper in the middle of a paragraph, took off his horn-rimmed glasses, wiped them and observed how much he admired the great suggestive influence of the press on his mother's country, dominions and colonies. When Winston Churchill, in his speech of June 28, 1920, in the Commons, uttered a warning against the weakening of Germany, as she constituted a dam in Europe against Bolshevism, the Kaiser nodded approval: "Bravo!" he said. "That is sensibly spoken. I wish all Englishmen thought the same."

Time and again the Kaiser was aroused by the often-repeated accusation in the English press that Germany alone bore the guilt for the World War. He would revert to his "Comparative History Tables" and try to prove in long discourses that the accusation had no factual basis and that it was a fabrication which could not be repudiated strongly enough. Once, when the Kaiser was asked who, in his opinion, bore the major part of the guilt in starting the war, he retorted that such an attribution of war guilt would be most difficult. If, however, someone had to be named, it could only be a member of the Russian War party, perhaps Suchomlinov, the War Minister.

In 1920 the Empress Eugénie died. She had witnessed Wilhelm I's destruction of her husband's empire; and now it was France that had destroyed the German Reich of Wilhelm II. Such is the uncertain and inconstant fate of States and their rulers.

When the Empress Eugénie and her journeys to Biarritz and Baden-Baden were mentioned one evening at Doorn, one of the guests took up the name of Baden and asked the Kaiser whether he did not agree that it had been a clear case of high treason that Prince Max of Baden had committed in the November days of 1918. There was a pause, and then the Kaiser slowly rose from his armchair and, fixing the inquirer with piercing, almost disdainful eyes, replied: "You do Prince Max a great wrong by such a supposition. I am convinced that he did not act against me intentionally; one of the reasons for my conviction is that for a member of so ancient a German princely house such an act would have been quite impossible."

103. DEATH OF THE KAISERIN AUGUSTE VIKTORIA

IN THE ROSE GARDEN at Doorn were many bushes of a whitish-green rose, which thirty years earlier had captured the world under the name "Kaiserin Auguste Viktoria." When these roses were in bloom in the garden at Doorn, a bunch was placed on the desk in the Kaiserin's little drawing room every morning.

Here she would write letters home about her sorrows, and often pious words which were her spiritual consolation in this strange country—for to her Doorn had remained alien. "We, the Kaiser and I, have resolved to share all our griefs," she wrote in a letter to Silesia. But she was weighed down by grief far more than the Kaiser, for she lacked his adaptability. Her old pride rose and revolted against accepting without any opposition all that had happened. Quite apart from the last sad political events, there had been occurrences in the family which she, a deeply religious woman, could not accept. Foremost was the suicide of her youngest son, Joachim, whom she had greatly loved and whose loss affected her deeply.

The steady weakening of her heart forced the Kaiserin to keep to her bed for days on end. She was faithfully attended by Countess Keller. Shortly before her death she mentioned to the Countess that she wished that the Kaiser should not remain lonely but should remarry. On April eleventh she passed away peacefully in her sleep.

Her last wish had been to be buried at home, in Postdam. Sadly the Kaiser assented; he knew that he would never see his wife's grave. The Weimar Government suggested placing the sarcophagus in the little "antique temple" erected by Frederick the Great, close to the Neues Palais. In this little temple, Auguste Viktoria, third German Kaiserin, was put to rest not far from the place where she had spent the happiest years of her life as a young wife and mother.

What the Kaiser felt in his bereavement he gratefully expressed in these words: "All that the deceased Kaiserin has been to me as my life companion, and to my people as their sovereign, during four decades of good and bad days, has been indelibly engraved in my heart. Words cannot express the gratitude and reverence I owe to the late Kaiserin."

104. INTERMEZZO: VILLA MALTA

WHILE THE KAISER was occupied at Doorn with the completion of his "Comparative History Tables" and preparing further publications for his own justification, his former Reich's Chancellor, Prince Bülow, was also busy writing his reminiscences.

In former years Prince Bülow used to spend the summer months in Flottbek or at the Villa Edda in Norderney, belonging to Count Botho Wedel. Now he stayed in Rome, at the Villa Malta, where he found more warmth and sun than on the damp and foggy banks of the Elbe or the wind-swept North Sea island. He rarely traveled to Berlin, and when he did so it was only to arrange business matters or to collect material needed for his work.

Villa Malta was situated on Monte Pincio, between the Trinità dei Monti and Villa Medici; from his house the Prince had a magnificent view of the Eternal City. Goethe had once stayed here and had planted a palm tree to commemorate his visit, and Alexander von Humboldt had been a guest in the house. In the 1870's the Russian aristocracy had held splendid fetes in the villa; eventually the property had been sold to Bernhard von Bülow.

It was from Villa Malta that the ex-Chancellor, having once more been appointed German Ambassador in Rome, in the winter and spring months of 1915, endeavored to prevent Italy's entering the war on the side of the Entente. "The doctor was called in too late" had been his comment, when, unable to effect his object, he had left Rome by the last train running to the Swiss frontier.

Under the Peace Treaty he had personally been informed that Villa Malta had been declared "a national cultural monument of Italy," and that the villa must not be sold to any other than an Italian citizen. The Prince and Princess were to be allowed to live there for the rest of their lives. For the Prince the "national cultural monument," with its illustrious past, became an oppressive place of confinement. Behind every column or palm he seemed to see death lying in wait.

Although Bülow was now more than seventy years old, he was mentally very alert; it never caused him a moment's embarrassment when asked for names and dates. The Princess, however, once a temperamental woman, was confined to her armchair; she was very nearly deaf and no longer able to follow the trend of the conversation. The grand piano in the salon had been closed for a long time and covered with a rug; on it were placed numerous photographs in costly frames surmounted by little coronets.

While his eyes rested on the dome of St. Peter's, on the city— every stone of which spoke of history—which had harbored Tasso, Julius II and Michelangelo, the Prince liked to talk of the past. Whether walking in the grounds of Villa Malta, or sitting in the salon under the Lenbach painting, he seemed a different being to those who had known him only as Reich's Chancellor. He no longer wore the high stiff collars or white waistcoats, but made use of the privilege accorded to old age of dressing less formally. He now wore a white scarf round his neck, a comfortable coat and a soft, wide-brimmed hat which made him look like Bismarck at Friedrichsruh. (When the Kaiser was told of this, he laughed and made some sarcastic remarks.)

Bülow often compared himself with his instructor, Bismarck; his opinion of the person of Wilhelm II coincided with that of his old teacher. But though in outward appearance the former Reich's Chancellor might have altered, his character had remained the same. He still talked as if he were addressing the Reichstag, frequently pausing for effect and seeking to hide his unshapely hands in the folds of his coat. As he spoke he slowly developed his theme, skillfully increased his voice to a crescendo, and then again lowering it to a whisper. He proved himself still a master of rhetoric.

Every remark Prince Bülow made showed that he was embittered beyond measure. Part of his bitterness was due to having to live in his beloved house on sufferance, "watch in hand," as he said. More important still, he "had been prematurely unharnessed." The daily increasing number of his contemporaries' memoirs added to his annoyance. The authors did not spare the Prince's feelings and he found himself described as a "tightrope dancer" or a "juggler." The greatest insult was from Count Anton Monts, who described him quite openly as *"une vieille cocotte."*

The assertion that he had apparently been unsuccessful as Ambassador in Rome he declared to be "an insolent lie." What caused even more annoyance was the fact that he had not been re-elected Reich's Chancellor after Bethmann's resignation. It was a favorite pastime of the lonely old man to imagine what might have happened had they recalled him into office. "I might have managed the Kaiser better after the fall of Bethmann than I did before. After realizing all the shortcomings of that worthy administrator, he might have given me a freer hand."

Looking back to the days when he had actually been Reich's Chancellor, he said: "It was a difficult task to follow a uniform policy for the whole of the Reich, as a successor of Hohenlohe. I was expected to back the plan for the building of the fleet; on the other hand, I had to remain conciliatory toward England and keep her in good temper. Bethmann, who succeeded me, had a much easier task, for when he became Chancellor our fleet and the Reich were strong enough to ignore the fact that occasionally we displeased England." But he strongly criticized his successor, and called all his measures an unbroken series of mistakes. All his accusations started with: "How could Bethmann . . . ! How could he have committed such a folly as to ignore the unique opportunity—I am referring to the calling of a conference of the big powers at the end of July 1914. In the first instance, he should have rapped the gentlemen of the Ballhausplatz in Vienna over the knuckles and reminded them that the Serbs had accepted the proposed terms—what more did they want? With regard to the violation by the Reich of Belgian neutrality, I admit that this was a disastrous mistake. We should have waited for France or England to commit this breach—then all the trumps would have been in our hands. Furthermore, I would scarcely have consented to the unrestricted U-boat warfare; instead of that I should have worked more actively toward a peace with Russia. The silliest mistake of all was the restoration of Poland; by this act Bethmann completely undermined his already shaky position. What can I say about the Government's begging for peace, or of the Kaiser's tearful letter to his Chancellor?"

That started him talking of Wilhelm II. "By nature the Kaiser was endowed with the best of tendencies and talents; if only all rulers were thus gifted! Unfortunately, he did not make use of these talents, nor did he widen his interests by careful study. The advisers he chose encouraged this tendency to superficiality. With few exceptions they were all servile creatures. I will not mention Eulenburg, because he has been a friend of mine; nor will I talk of Holstein—a *chose négligeable*—whom the Kaiser found already in office."

The Prince would then turn to people who had been his collaborators and friends for many years. "Dear old Lichnowsky unfortunately proved a 'blank,' particularly in the 'London lottery.' And what can I say of Flotow or even little Jagow, who never managed to view the world freely from above his high stiff collar? He might have become an able government administrator in a small provincial town, but he was quite out of place in the responsible post of Secretary of State at the Foreign Office."

The Prince's criticism of Gottlieb von Jagow might find its explanation in the fact that in 1915 it had been Jagow who did not wish the Prince to be sent as Ambassador to Rome and who had fought against this appointment tooth and nail.

"I will admit that the Swabian Kiderlen was a tolerable diplomat, also Marschall, though to him this attribute applies only with reservations. But as for Monts! . . . that man Monts! . . ." Here the Prince was overcome by coughing. Then he continued: "Now who really was that man Monts? He was made by me, he was my protégé, they said in Berlin. That may have been so, but what thanks did I get for my protection? At every opportunity he disparaged me, annoyed me, not least by his articles in the *Berliner Tageblatt*, which he directed against me and the policy that I followed."

Unceasingly the Prince went on. The memoirs of Anton Monts had put him into a violent temper that also reflected on his own views about Wilhelm II. "The Kaiser had a startling habit of singling out indifferent people and keeping them around him. There was, for instance, that servile court pastor, Adolf Harnack, whom he even raised to the nobility. It was with people such as Harnack that the Kaiser surrounded himself throughout his life, with the result that he became conceited and boastful. These people told him from morning to night what a mighty ruler he was, and he accepted this quite seriously. He had not even the strength of mind of that great Pope who built St. Peter's and knew what to make of such hymns of praise: 'I know they flatter me,' he said, 'but I like to listen just the same.' Often the Kaiser seemed to me like a child; he should have been accepted and treated as a child. I found out that with the Kaiser it was very important to seize a favorable opportunity; if the moment did not appear opportune, it was better to wait and defer important decisions."

In reply to the question whether it would not have been possible to exert influence over the Kaiser at such an opportune moment, perhaps in order to warn him, or to draw him away from this entourage of flatterers, speaking to him openly and working toward a deepening of his character, the ex-Chancellor would throw up his hands in resignation: *"O sancta simplicitas!* Win influence over the Kaiser! That was very difficult! As far as I was concerned, I was always glad to put forward and carry out my own wishes, which, owing to my position as Chancellor, were varied and difficult. At any rate, I had not been appointed as guardian for other people; everyone had to find out for himself how best to cope with H.M."

The thought of these "other people" seemed to make the Prince uncomfortable. With his stick he crossly poked the old dachshund Waldi, who was sleeping at his feet; he did not want the dog to sleep all day as he would only frighten the poor Princess by wandering through the rooms at night. The "Reich's dog" was no longer a powerful Great Dane but a gouty dachshund who would slowly get up and trot away.

"I understand," the Prince continued, "that the Kaiser still considers the Treaty of Björkö as his doing and a masterpiece of diplomatic art. That treaty was a contradiction in itself and worth no more than a farthing!"

Listening to Bülow's criticism one could not help wondering whether he judged the Treaty of Björkö so harshly because it had not been he who drew it up or countersigned it. That privilege had been reserved for Tschirschky, whom the Kaiser had taken to Finland instead of Bülow.

During the course of conversation the ex-Chancellor touched on his dismissal; while talking about it he fixed his eyes on the paneled ceiling as if the story of the past was recorded up there.

"When I thought I could no longer shoulder the responsibility, I tendered my resignation and asked the Kaiser to relieve me of my post as Reich's Chancellor. I must tell you that King Edward VII entreated me to remain at my post; so did the Czar, who shortly before, as a proof of his trust in me, had presented me with the High Order of St. Andrew with diamonds. Cambon, the French Ambassador in Berlin, almost begged me to stay. And I have heard people say that even King Carol of Rumania was quite shocked when he heard of my intention to retire. They all realized that there was no one worthy to become my successor."

At this moment Privy Councilor Franz von Stockhammern entered the room and placed some pages of typescript on the Prince's desk; on the top there was a sheet of notes in the Prince's fine, thin German handwriting. "That is the chapter about the 'block politics,'" the Privy Councilor whispered and turned to withdraw. "I must not keep the Privy Councilor today," the Prince said. "He is going to hear the Cantata tonight at Santa Maria delle Anime; I think Stockhammern will one day become a friar." Then, glancing at the typescript, he took up the theme of "block politics."

"As I am writing down my memoirs of those days—when I was greatly in favor of block politics—I must again confirm how right my decisions were; undoubtedly they helped to pave the way for the parliamentarian idea in Germany, for it was I who, for the first time, managed to bring about a majority party in the Reichstag by merging two parties, the Conservatives and the Center party."

It became obvious that all that Reich's Chancellor Bülow had done appeared right in his eyes; and all that Wilhelm II had presumed to do had been wrong. That was the aging Prince's principle upon which he wrote his *Memoirs*. What the Reich's Chancellor Bülow had once said about his Kaiser, with tears of emotion in his eyes, no longer held good. "We cannot be thankful enough to have such a ruler who always recalls to me the heroic Salic and Hohenstaufen Emperors of medieval times." Another time he had said: "Our Kaiser is such an important man. Together with the Great

Elector and the Great King he is by far the most important member
of the House of Hohenzollern that has ever lived. In a way, never
before known, he combines the gifts of genius—a genius of the pur-
est and most original kind—with a clear *bon sens*. His great phantasy, which enables him to rise, on eagle's wings, above all trifling
matters, is combined with a sober appreciation of what is possible
and attainable. And what energy! What a memory! What quick and
sure apprehension!"

Obviously the Prince's own way of thinking was no longer borne
on those "eagle's wings"; his thoughts had become earth-bound,
caught in a mass of trifling details; he now appeared "talkative and
quarrelsome," so that it seemed as if the Kaiser's famous "Mephi-
stopheles" had turned into a scheming, gossiping old woman.

When the Prince felt well enough he dictated to his young secretary; and much of what he had to say became even more pointed in
the course of dictation. Sometimes it happened that in his bitter
mood he would ask one day to be given back what he had dictated
the previous day, because in a sleepless night he had thought of a
new way to hit yet harder, to characterize more appropriately the
person over whom he was sitting in judgment.

It is easy to say after the event, if I had done this or that in such a
way, all would have been well. But apart even from such subsequent
reconstructions the material Bülow used in the four volumes of
reminiscences was open to criticism, because it presented a one-
sided view and was partly unverifiable. Besides, Bülow's unrestrained language and his disrespect of even the highest lady in the
empire added to the annoyance of many of his readers when the
books were eventually published.

The obvious question to ask is whether the aged Prince did not
yield to his feeling of disappointment and hatred and write these
memoirs against his better knowledge, in the secret hope that, even
after his death, their publication might once again direct the eyes of
Europe toward him. It seems tragic that a man, famed throughout
the whole world as the prototype of the *grand seigneur*, should give
the lie to his reputation in his old age.

The four volumes of these "unmemorable memoirs" were published immediately after Bülow's death by Baron von Stockhammern. They caused great excitement in Germany, not only because
it was feared that they would create a bad impression abroad, where

Prince Bülow's publication might be used to make him the crown witness against his own country, but also because of the bad effect produced in Germany, where, at last, voices were raised in an effort to prevent people from using the recent past as a battlefield for their personal feuds and disparagements.

Even those few initiated persons who had known that Bülow had been engaged in writing his memoirs were shocked when they read these spiteful outbursts; they had expected Bülow—a true disciple of the Old Man of the Sachsenwald—to distribute blows; but in this case the blows appeared to be more in the nature of stabs in the back.

105. THE TOWER

VILLA MALTA and Doorn House had become political antipodes. In the South it was the ex-Chancellor who, to revenge himself on his Kaiser, made himself spokesman of Germany's enemies; in the North the Kaiser, unperturbed, extended and completed his "Comparative History Tables." When Wilhelm II heard of Prince Bülow's death in Rome he asked von Grancy, his former Naval Attaché, to represent him at the funeral at the Villa Malta. Later he received the four blue volumes of Bülow's *Memoirs* which were added to the library in the Tower. "I have read them," the Kaiser observed calmly. "I was surprised to see what can happen to a gifted man and a good diplomat when he loses control of himself and becomes embittered. Bülow will not succeed in vindicating himself from disloyalty by the publication of these four volumes— far from it. He should have backed me in the Reichstag; the fact is, unfortunately, that we Germans fight one another instead of standing together in the moment of danger. He was not the only one of my counselors who let me down at the crucial moment. The blame for everything was put on me, particularly when these valiant counselors were uncertain what to do and were at loggerheads among themselves. In England this state of affairs would be unthinkable, almost impossible! In face of political danger the English know no personal fear; they are concerned only with the protection of their common interests. To understand my character and nature you must not forget that I am half English. I have never been able to think like a Continental, and that is why I have so often been misunderstood or misjudged. Undoubtedly, my mother had great influence on my nature; it was due to her education that I could so easily get on with the English. I came to understand their character and I am convinced that if they had published the speech I made during my last stay in England it would have made a good impression and might have influenced favorably England's attitude to us in August 1914. Unfortunately, however, the text of my speech was not made available to the English public; there was nothing I could do about it; I could not demand publication, for I was a guest in England. Throughout my reign it has been my unremitting endeavor to maintain good and lasting relations with influential Englishmen. I need only mention Lord Russell, British Ambassador in Berlin, an excellent man, who—to my great regret—was recalled all too soon because he was too Germanophile. But let us leave such bitter retrospects—and Bülow—to be buried in the past."

One of the greatest surprises the visitor encountered on entering the Tower was the saddle stool which the Kaiser used instead of a chair when he sat at his desk. The Kaiser's pride throughout his life had been his Army and his own part in its training and perfection. In the saddle at the head of his troops he realized one of the ambitions of his life. Now that this could no longer be, a vicarious sensation was possible, sitting in the saddle at his desk—a memory of former greatness. There were many photographs on his desk, mostly family pictures. Glancing at a photograph of a woman in ball dress, the Kaiser began to talk about women:

"The most beautiful woman I ever met in my life was the Empress Elisabeth of Austria. Although she was past her prime when I saw her for the first time, she was still a beautiful and charming woman. Her smile was positively captivating. I cannot name a single *beauté* who, so far as looks and appearance are concerned, approached her in any way, and—believe me—I have seen a great many beautiful women in my time. Queen Marie of Rumania and the Princess of Pless would certainly be called beautiful, but they lacked the natural conquering dignity that was part of the Empress Elisabeth's character. Queen Marie and the Princess of Pless have now published their reminiscences; I am afraid the value of these two books compares unfavorably with the value of the famous pearl necklaces these two ladies owned. The pearls of memory which they have strung together in their reminiscences appear of little beauty; they lack the luster and hue of genuineness. One of the books by the Princess of Pless is called *What I Left Unsaid*. I cannot understand why she did not do so!"

About some other publications the Kaiser talked less reservedly. "My former Court Marshal, Count Robert von Zedlitz-Trützschler, has also published his memoirs. They abound in indiscretions, tactless remarks and breaches of confidence. I do not mind being attacked; it is anybody's right to do so, provided he furnishes proof for his accusations. But in this case we are concerned with a member of the ancient Silesian nobility, who—on account of his descent and upbringing—was chosen by me for a confidential post. You cannot toady to the master you have yourself chosen to serve, accept all the benefits he may load upon you and then desert him in the hour of his misfortune, attacking him, too, in such a disgraceful way!"

In order to forget these disappointments, Wilhelm II began to write his own memoirs in which—as was only to be expected—he discussed these attacks against him. A year after the completion of the "Comparative History Tables" (*Vergleichende Geschichtstabellen*) his *Ereignisse und Gestalten* appeared. In 1926 his autobiography, *Aus meinem Leben 1859–1888*, followed, covering his youth to the time of his accession. In addition to these publications a book was issued by his Leipzig publisher, which was meant to serve as a reply to lampoon against the House of Hohenzollern.

These books were not memoirs in the usual sense, as they were all very slim volumes. They were jotted down in a hurry and the contents were rather episodical. Much that he found disagreeable the Kaiser passed over lightly, in order to place in the foreground quite immaterial things. Moreover, the reader was wearied and bored by countless repetitions, as by the monotonous style in which they were written. While Bülow interspersed his narrative with well-timed and well-told jokes and anecdotes, the Kaiser introduced anecdotes and allegedly humorous stories without consideration and often in the wrong place, and the reader would constantly have to ask himself: what might be the connection between this little story and the events just described? Astonishing, too, were the strange conclusions which were often reached quite arbitrarily, likewise the stress laid on unimportant events or formalities of ceremony. How far the author was removed from the new developments in Germany was shown by the fact that he dedicated his childhood memories "To the German Youth." In the struggle of everyday life the German youths of that day were unlikely to show much interest in personal experiences of seventy years ago. To young people the Kaiser appeared as some fabulous creature, about whom they knew less than about Frederick the Great. The Kaiser had no objection to seeing himself described as a "fabulous creature"; he did, however, object to "fabulous animal," as one author entitled his book on Wilhelm II!

The details given in Wilhelm's writings often seemed improbable, particularly when he tried to reconstruct conversations he had held a lifetime ago and of which he had made no notes at the time. He was lavish in the use of exaggerated and exuberant expressions, especially when touching on his relations with his parents; his style was often full of false pathos and sentimentality and was all too free in the use of superlatives. Tears came readily to his eyes; and the reader would be informed that the author was overcome by emotion.

When, however, he wrote in his capacity of Supreme War Lord, the tone was changed: "I always felt completely at ease with my soldiers—the sad experiences of autumn 1918 have not weakened my confidence." To read a sentence such as this, one is set wondering at the Kaiser's line of thought, which set out from completely wrong premises. But apart from this peculiar personal attitude, he always endeavored to think factually, as far as that was possible for him; above all, he tried to avoid attacking anyone. He even went so far as to try to speak objectively of the Versailles Treaty: "One must not be hypocritical. After a world struggle for life and death the severity of the conditions imposed by the victorious side are, to a certain extent, the natural result of the feeling of relief at having escaped a deadly peril."

This gesture of forgiving and forgetting was perhaps the most sympathetic characteristic of the aging Wilhelm II. When the deaths of Alfred von Tirpitz and Prince Max of Baden occurred, he had wreaths placed on their coffins in his name. He himself admitted that age had made him more tolerant: "During these long years of exile one becomes more critical of oneself. I am grateful to all those who have stood by me as firmly in my misfortune as they did when fortune was on my side. I can esteem those whose honest convictions lead them to oppose me." He still had many enemies, as his mail proved to him every morning; threatening and abusive letters never ceased to arrive. Other unpleasant news was, for instance, the confiscation or expropriation of one or the other of his estates. Among these losses ranked the confiscation by the Greek State of the Achilleion at Corfu.

Wilhelm's memories of Corfu (of Corcyra, as the island was originally called) went back a long time. The excavations undertaken by Professor Wilhelm Dörpfeld had awakened his interests. He had originally taken up archaeology rather superficially, but he now resolved to devote himself to serious studies. With characteristic intensity he began with the history and nature of the science. The study of the works of Dörpfeld, Schliemann and Humann fascinated him to such an extent that it was not long before large numbers of books on the subject towered by the side of his armchair. At the same time he began to correspond with outstanding archaeologists who were prepared to assist him in his new studies. Thus it was that in 1933 the *Doorner Arbeitsgemeinschaft* (Doorn Study Group) was founded with Wilhelm II as its President. The aim of the group was to investigate and describe subjects which had not been hitherto treated, especially in the province of research into Babylon in Biblical times. It was laid down in the rules that once every year the members should assemble at Doorn in order to report on their researches and the results achieved, to exchange views, and hear lectures on special subjects. The first subject treated by the Kaiser as archaeologist was *The Gorgon*. He dealt with the Gorgon's head that had been found in 1911 near the Achilleion in Corfu, beneath the remains of an old Doric temple dating back to approximately 780 B.C. At the time of the discovery Dörpfeld, backed by the opinion of other experts, had realized that the temple must have been a shrine dedicated to the Gorgon. This opinion was shared by Professor Leo Frobenius, who became a frequent visitor at Doorn and helped the Kaiser in writing his monograph on the Gorgon.

The essay started with a description of the Gorgon: the circular face, with protruding tongue and snakelike curls. He then described the two sons of the Gorgon, both winged, like the Gorgon herself. He concluded by saying that in his opinion the arm and leg, bent to a right angle, constituted nothing less than the archetype of the swastika. Eminent historians fought against such arbitrary and fanciful interpretations. Leopold von Ranke expressed his opinion that, especially in the interpretation of prehistoric finds, one had to guard against the danger of jumping to wrong deductions. "Prehistory is either natural history or religion; there are only two ways open to us: either we confine ourselves to the description of the remarkable works of art which prehistoric man created or we silently pay homage to their mysterious manifestations."

Another subject for a treatise was suggested to the Kaiser by the chance examination of a prospectus of the Northern Pacific Railway. Prince Friedrich, one of his grandsons, brought this prospectus to Doorn from New York. The device of this railway was an emblem, similar to the well-known sign on the arms of Korea—a circular symbol, consisting of a large ring into which two smaller rings were placed. The Kaiser said in his essay on "The Chinese Monad" that again in this circular symbol he believed he had found the archetype of the swastika. The essay concluded with the words: "In the movement we find symbolized by the monad and the swastika, as also in solemn ceremonies we must recognize 'Energy divine, that liveth in all and worketh without end.' " [1] From this the Kaiser further drew the astounding conclusion, expressed in obscure and complicated phraseology, that monad and swastika "were sun symbols as well as symbols for the sun revolving around himself and across the sky, that is, movement symbols of the sun." He added that he considered the monad to be a "swastika reduced to a comma," and ended his essay on "The Chinese Monad" by expressing the newly gained knowledge that "symbolism was the veiled language of prehistoric man; it does not reveal its world of thought in intelligible picture signs or written letters, but its sincerely religious phantasy manifested itself in an artistic expression of form to the searching scholar dedicating himself to the understanding thereof."

These studies, written in a baroque style and intended to read like scholarly treatises, were followed a year later by his "Comparative Tables of Time" (*Vergleichende Zeittafeln*), not to be confused with the "Comparative History Tables" (*Vergleichende Geschichtstabellen*). This new work was concerned with the first epoch of human culture in the high steppes of Western Asia (ap-

[1] The quotation is from Goethe's *Faust I*, translated by Graham and Tristan Rarson. London: The Bodley Head.

proximately 8000 B.C.) and extended to the golden age of Baby-
lonia and the Roman Empire. His great love of Babylonian history
induced Wilhelm to write yet another work: *Kingship in Ancient
Mesopotamia* (*Königtum im alten Mesopotamien*). In this he was
mainly concerned with the legislation of Hammurabi. It is probable
that Leo Frobenius assisted actively in the writing of this book,
which proved to be the last work of this great scholar, for he died a
few months later.

In his "Chinese Monad" the Kaiser had declared that the exemplary scholar should "search devotedly" and thus he wanted to
dedicate his years of old age to a science which would enable him
to live in the distant past, to forget the present, and to look into the
future with an easier mind: a future ruled, as he said, by the symbols
of "Divine energy" and formed in accordance with eternal laws,
like the path of the sun moving across the sky.

106. HERMINE

WHILE AT the Cassel Gymnasium, the fifteen-year-old
Prince Wilhelm, an enthusiastic admirer of antiquity, had written
a Greek tragedy. The main figure in this drama had been a woman
whom the schoolboy had endowed with all the noble and beautiful
qualities his youthful mind could imagine. This lady of his heart,
this figure of light in an otherwise somber tragedy, he had called
Hermione.

Nearly fifty years later the name was to resume importance in his
life. It was chance that brought together the Kaiser and the widowed
Princess Hermine von Schönaich-Carolath. On the occasion of the
Kaiser's birthday the Princess's eldest son had sent his congratulations, which the Kaiser reciprocated with an invitation to Doorn. In
this way the Kaiser again met the Prince's mother, after an interval
of many years.

With every letter that reached him from Saabor or Greiz, he became increasingly convinced that Princess Hermine, a highly cul-
tured woman, was the right companion for his old age. She was
of equal birth to his own, for she was a member of the ancient,

wealthy, princely family, the House of Reuss, the older branch of which was to die out with her and her sisters. Her marriage to Prince Johann Georg von Schönaich-Carolath-Beuthen had been a happy one. Widowed at the early age of thirty-three, she had to bring up five young children as well as manage her large estate, Saabor, in Lusatia.

It was natural that a woman of her energy and temperament, gifted with her sympathy and sensibility and who had gone through the hard school of life, should appeal to the Kaiser as the embodiment of all he could desire. He asked for her hand. For her part the Princess may have hoped for a new life in the interesting atmosphere of Doorn; moreover, the knowledge that she could brighten the old age of that lonely man must have appealed strongly to her. For there is no gainsaying the fact, the Kaiser was a lonely man. The insulting and threatening letters that constantly came by post always upset and depressed him; they weighed him down to such an extent that sometimes he was unable to formulate a continuous sentence during his morning walk; sometimes he even forgot to acknowledge the greetings of the gardeners. He never discussed these letters with strangers, rarely with his confidants, Lieutenant General von Dommes or Count Schwerin; so the suppressed anger grew within him like some cancerous disease. To hide his feelings he would force a smile, but even his gestures appeared forced and insincere at such moments.

All this was to change. If he were to be alone no longer, even the interminable winter evenings at Doorn would be easier to bear. There were many things he would be able to discuss with a sympathetic wife, things about which he had spoken to no one. Although after the death of the Kaiserin the Duchess Viktoria Luise of Brunswick and the Crown Princess Cecilie had tried to lighten the heavy loss by their presence, they had been able to stay for limited periods only, for their presence was needed by their large families at home.

A number of Court formalities had to be attended to before the marriage could be performed. The wish had been expressed—by an interested party—that the Kaiser's marriage should in no way affect financially his children or grandchildren. Any fear of this was dispelled by a declaration by Princess Hermine that her children had their own fortunes and would, as a matter of course, renounce all claims to the Hohenzollern fortune.

The news of the impending second marriage of Wilhelm II—only a year after the death of the Kaiserin Auguste Viktoria—caused some excitement in Germany. Conservative circles in particular, without taking into consideration the reasons advanced by the Kaiser, took offense at this second "hasty" marriage. Many entreating and protesting letters arrived at Doorn, only to remain unanswered.

Finally, a delegation of the nobility residing east of the river Elbe went to Doorn. Headed by an old warrior, the delegation begged the Kaiser seriously and sincerely to give up the idea of a second marriage. They reminded the Kaiser of what he had said at the death of his wife. But he would listen to no objections. He reminded the delegation of his great-grandfather, King Friedrich Wilhelm III, who had married again after the death of the greatly loved and revered Queen Luise. At this, one of the gentlemen of the delegation observed that Friedrich Wilhelm had not married again until fifteen years after the death of Queen Luise. Without entering into this, the Kaiser replied angrily that this marriage was his own affair, and that he would not stand any interference by any third party.

At this the spokesman of the delegation gave one last warning: through this rushed second marriage the Kaiser would lose the last sympathies that people might have preserved for him in Germany, while the respect in which the monarchy had hitherto been held would be severely damaged. But this was equally unavailing to alter the Kaiser's decision.

Countess Harrach, second wife of Friedrich Wilhelm, had, on her marriage, been given the title of Princess Liegnitz, with the rank of "Royal Prussian Highness." The same style of address was accorded by Wilhelm II to his second wife, when the wedding took place at Doorn on November 5, 1922.

It seemed as if the heavy veil that for so long had rested on Doorn House had been lifted by the entry of Princess Hermine. A happy, even gay tone prevailed. A number of new guests were received, some of them the Princess's own friends, who filled the house with new life and interest.

Happenings in the world outside were now the concern equally of the Kaiser and his second wife, as were also all events taking place within the Imperial family, the members of which, after initial doubts, had soon felt drawn toward the new member of the circle. The first great family celebration after the Kaiser's second marriage had been the wedding of Princess Friederike of Brunswick with Crown Prince Paul of Greece. Again, as when the Kaiser's sister Sophie went to Athens to become Queen, a member of the House of Hohenzollern went to Greece as the wife of the heir to the throne. In May 1938 followed the wedding of Prince Louis Ferdinand of Prussia to the Grand Duchess Kira of Russia.

But there were also occasions for grief and sorrow. After the passing of Hindenburg, came the death, on December 20, 1937, of Ludendorff; the Kaiser was represented at his funeral by General Field Marshal von Mackensen. Almost the entire family of the Grand Duke of Hesse lost their lives in October 1937 in an air accident in Belgium. The Grand Duke of Hesse and his family had been related to him by their descent from Queen Victoria.

The Kaiser had always entertained a profound admiration for his grandmother, who had been succeeded on the throne by "Uncle Bertie." Then his cousin, George V, had ascended the throne, followed by his eldest son as Edward VIII and finally, after Edward's abdication, by the next son as George VI. Wilhelm had thus seen four generations on the throne of England. His own nearest relatives had long been dead. Relations and friends, diplomats and comrades of the old army—many of them much younger than he—had long been buried and were almost forgotten. Only he still lived on, old and becoming ever more and more a legendary figure.

107. A VISIT TO WILHELM II

THE MOTORCAR that took me from Utrecht to Doorn each morning stopped in front of the gatehouse. The civilian official on duty knew me quite well. On the first visit to Doorn House you were ushered into the main hall where visitors wrote their names in one of the two red leather-bound volumes with the gold letters W. and H. on them which lay on a desk. The books contained a great many confessions of loyalty, often expressed in touching words, but also a lot of empty phrases and laudatory verses.

There was a moat in the park in front of the house, spanned by a bridge. This was populated with ducks, which the Kaiser liked to feed himself. In winter, when the moat was frozen over, it became a skating place for the grandchildren. When I had crossed the bridge, the glass doors in the main entrance were opened and footmen in simple black livery showed me in.

On the ground floor were the drawing rooms and the dining room. They were tastefully furnished, though perhaps a trifle overloaded, and they contained many souvenirs from Germany. In the salon, in the place of honor, was the life-size portrait of the young Queen Luise.[1] From the center of the ceiling hung a magnificent poreclain chandelier from the Berlin factory. Snuff boxes that had once belonged to Frederick the Great lay in glass cases; on the piano stood the rust-colored terra-cotta bust of Wilhelm II with pointed beard and the Garde-du-Corps helmet on his head—a combination which had never actually existed.

On a console table was the photograph of the Emperor Franz Joseph and behind this, filling the corner completely, a marble bust of the late Kaiserin Auguste Viktoria. On another table stood the photograph of King Friedrich August of Saxony: the only one of the Federal German princes to be represented.

Every room was decorated with flowers in vases and bowls of china and copper. Two large portraits hung in the hall depicting a prince and his wife of the House of Orange. Maps lay spread out on a huge table.

To reach the first floor one had to climb a narrow spiral staircase. Immediately facing the head of the stairs was the sitting room of the Kaiserin Hermine. There she might be found sitting on the sofa knitting garments destined to be sold in one of the charity bazaars which she used to arrange in an outbuilding. Each winter she distributed woolen clothes to any who needed them. The first time I met her she was wearing a red dress, which contrasted well with her already white hair.

It soon became apparent in conversation how well-read the Kaiserin was and how familiar with all questions concerning literature.

[1] Luise, Queen of Prussia (1776–1810), was daughter of the Duke of Mecklenburg-Strelitz. She was a woman of great character, as was shown by her vigorous attempts to obtain concessions from Napoleon when the Treaty of Tilsit was being signed, 1807.

Suddenly, in the middle of our conversation, she rose and walked over to one of the flower-filled vases where she selected a few flowers and handed them to me. Crossing a short dark passage we entered the room where the Kaiserin Auguste Viktoria had died. The windows were heavily curtained and in the semidarkness one could just make out a simple bed with a white counterpane on which lay little bunches of withered flowers. I added my offering. Over the bed—where one might have expected to find a religious picture—hung an engraving of the Saracen fortress at Rapallo. The writing desk by the window was just as the Kaiserin left it. Rows and rows of photographs of her nearest relatives, of children and grandchildren, stood on it. "Is it not sad to think," the Kaiserin Hermine said in a subdued voice, "that this German woman had to die in a foreign land? She suffered unspeakably here in Doorn; but very few people know about that. It will soon be twenty years since the Kaiser came to Doorn." After this ceremony—the homage paid by the second Kaiserin to the first—we returned to the salon, and in a few moments the Kaiser entered, lively and animated.

Tea was served and a conversation began in which the Kaiser did most of the talking. It was only when he put in his mouth a piece of toast or a spoonful of black cherries, of which he was particularly fond, that anyone else had a chance to say something.

Bismarck was the first subject of the conversation. "I read your biography of Johanna von Bismarck. She was not nearly as important a woman as you have made her appear; neither was she as lovable as you would make us believe. She was quite ugly and very short. When the Bismarck couple entered a room together, he a giant in the uniform of the Cuirassiers, with that tiny person at his side, people wondered how such a pair were ever attracted to each other. For one thing, however, I must give her credit: the Princess never meddled in political affairs. For me personally she knew nothing but hatred. It was she who set the tone of their domestic life in Friedrichsruh. Sometimes one seemed to be in the house of Pomeranian peasants. I shall never forget the servants holding the wine bottles between their knees to draw the corks, or the Prince putting his plate on the floor to feed his dog. I, for one, could not get rid of the idea that it might be I who would eat from the same plate the next day."

Then the Kaiser touched on the delicate subject of Herbert Bismarck's relations with Princess Schönaich-Carolath. "You may know," he said, "that the Princess is a relative, by marriage, of my wife. From what I heard, Herbert Bismarck did not behave at all well." Here the Kaiserin intervened: "There is no doubt that the Princess Carolath loved young Herbert Bismarck. Originally she was not at all a lady of the world; it was old Bismarck who made her into that. He spread this invention about her because he wanted at all costs to prevent this marriage of his eldest son. As Herbert Bismarck had promised to marry her and she obtained a divorce on his account, he ought to have accepted the consequences. The reason he did not do so was that he dared not oppose his father."

From Herbert Bismarck the conversation moved on to Heligoland. "Herbert Bismarck had been charged by his father," the Kaiser related, "to negotiate in London on our behalf for the acquisition of the island. But he did not attain his object. If you want to negotiate with the English, you must never let out the secret of what you are interested in, particularly not if that something belongs to them. On the contrary, you must try and explain that you know quite well that they wish to part with that particular object because it is of no value to them. The important point is to wait for an opportune moment and then make your offer. Before I started negotiations for Heligoland, I had obtained very useful information from consuls and experienced businessmen in East Africa regarding the value of our protectorate of Zanzibar. From that information it became clear to me that, owing to the increasing importance of the ports on the Tanganyika coast, Zanzibar was of value only as a port of reshipment." The Kaiser mentioned a few of the harbor towns on the African mainland, including Pangani. "By means of my proved tactics in dealing with the English, I achieved the exchange of the two islands.

"Prince Bismarck was livid, for I had succeeded, without serious difficulties, where his son had failed. The Prince published numerous articles in the *Hamburger Nachrichten*, emphasizing the great importance of Zanzibar and exposing to criticism and ridicule the acquisition of Heligoland as senseless and useless. Today nobody has any doubts about the value of Heligoland, or the successful negotiations which regained for us this important island close to the mouth of the River Elbe.

"Looking back, many things concerning Prince Bismarck now

appear to me in a different light. You must believe me when I say that, having grown up in his era, it was impossible not to revere and admire Bismarck. As Prince of Prussia and as heir to the throne, I felt a glowing admiration for him; but no sooner had I succeeded to the throne than he seemed to have but one desire, which was to make clear to me that he had been first and intended to remain first. It was with a heavy heart that I had to part with him, for I could not permit two governments side by side. His son Herbert could have made many things easier for me had he not been so completely under his father's influence; I never cared much for Herbert Bismarck. His brother Wilhelm was quite different: he was much more accessible, and I never had any difficulty in talking to him."

Apart from these teatime conversations, there was always a possibility that I might be invited to the Tower at night; but that was a rare exception, for as a rule the evenings were reserved for members of the family. But sometimes I was asked to accompany the Kaiser during his morning walks in the garden. Such engagements, however, were liable to be canceled at short notice; for one thing, the Kaiser liked to alter his timetable on the spur of the moment; and often unexpected events interfered with the scheduled program. The morning walk might have to be canceled because a Minister from The Hague had announced his arrival; or the teatime conversation might be upset because the Kaiser had driven out to tea.

It was a special favor to be asked to lunch. A little before one o'clock everyone assembled in the hall of Doorn House, and punctually at one the Kaiser descended the narrow staircase. The guests bowed and curtsied; the host politely acknowledged the greetings. Then lunch was served. The simple menu usually consisted of three courses; red and white wine stood on the table; a silver goblet was placed by the Kaiser's place, with a mixture of red wine and mineral water. After lunch coffee was taken standing, as the Kaiser liked to walk around informally and talk to his guests.

The Kaiser's memory was remarkable. Very rarely was he at a loss for a name, and then the Kaiserin usually remembered it. "You see, Her Majesty knows everything," he would say with a smile. If a visitor did not take this hint, he would repeat "Her Majesty" so often that at last the thoughtless guest realized that "Royal Prussian Highness" was not used for the Kaiserin Hermine at Doorn.

When the Kaiser went for a walk in the garden, he did not seem an octogenarian. Usually he was dressed in an elegant gray suit; he wore a gold pin in his tie and in his buttonhole the miniature medal *Pour le Mérite*. He walked briskly, with light, elastic steps, and was always willing to discuss any subject. He spoke with a frankness that was astonishing, and the question remains open what would have happened if an evil-minded person had got hold of some of these frank remarks and indiscreetly had passed them on.

Much of what he said was filled with bitter irony. "There are people who write thick volumes about me," he said, "without ever having seen me, let alone spoken to me. I can well understand the wish to write about me and there is nothing I can do to prevent it; but I should at least be given an opportunity to present my point of view. I have been told that a Herr Lamprecht has written a voluminous work about me. Never in my life have I set eyes on this Herr Professor, nor probably has he ever seen me. The same goes for Professor Haller, in Tübingen, whom I have never met personally. Unfortunately, many inaccuracies have crept into Haller's biography of Prince Eulenburg. Looking back on Eulenburg, I am bound to admit that he was one of the most charming persons I have ever met. There is no doubt that he was a very talented musician; he was also an expert art historian and was never in doubt about the style in which a work of art had been executed, or why any ornament had this particular form and no other. He was an excellent talker. If you traveled with him, he would pick on some little insignificant happening of the journey and make it into an arresting story; you had to listen spellbound and the train journey passed in no time. But his biographer, Professor Haller, committed the error of wanting to make too much of Eulenburg. You should never exaggerate your hero or disregard his shortcomings. Whatever blame may attach to Prince Eulenburg, I will always remember him kindly, for he invariably proved himself my friend."

During one of the morning walks, Wilhelm II spoke of Adolf von Menzel. "In your biography you gave a very pleasant description of that great painter's—or should I call him a draftsman?—seventieth birthday. But what really happened on that day was even nicer." And the Kaiser, in an excellent mood, recounted the story. "I had requested the 'Little Excellency' to reserve for me the afternoon of his seventieth birthday. After lunch I sent one of the carriages to the painter's house and had him driven to Potsdam. The carriage stopped below the stairs leading up to Sans-Souci. On each step stood guards, dressed in the uniform of the soldiers of the time of Frederick the Great; they looked exactly like the little figurines Menzel had drawn. The little man slowly ascended the stairs, inspecting the stripes, tassels, headgear and boot laces of each of the soldiers; then he nodded contentedly and eventually reached the terrace at the top of the stairs. On the terrace I had posted an officer with a company of men specially chosen for their height; they also wore uniforms of the time of the Great King. Menzel was quite obviously satisfied with this reception; I had an opportunity of observing him unnoticed from one of the windows. As if he had done nothing else all his life he gravely reviewed the line of grenadiers, the little man's head on the level with the men's chests. It was a fine summer evening and all the French windows of the Schloss were open; the rooms were lit by candles only. The 'Little Excellency' entered by one of the antechambers, where some of my gentlemen were sitting playing cards, also dressed up for the occasion. Menzel accepted this as if it were the most natural thing in the world. In the next room I met Menzel and greeted him; I was dressed in the uniform of a general of Frederick the Great and had my mustache dressed differently. He eyed me suspiciously and scrutinized my uniform to see if everything was right. It was only then that I spoke to him and welcomed him to Sans-Souci. His eyes fixed me searchingly above the lenses of his spectacles; but he knew immediately who I was representing. I must confess that I did admire Menzel at that moment when he said to me very seriously: 'Am I right? Have I the honor of addressing General Lentulus, Adjutant to the Great King?'

"Then I recited a prologue written for me for the occasion by Max Grube. Wait a moment, this is how it started." And the Kaiser began to recite the prologue—hesitatingly at first—which he had spoken on the occasion of Menzel's birthday a quarter of a century ago.

"When I had finished the prologue I led him into the music room at Sans-Souci, which presented an enchanting *tableau vivant*: 'The Flute Concert' just as Menzel had painted it. The room shone with candlelight which was pleasantly toned down by the cedar paneling of the walls. In place of the Queen sat my late wife, and a young

Benda was at the spinet where many years before one of his fore-fathers had played.

"At sight of this picture Menzel stood still; he quickly composed himself, however, looked round leisurely, less at the persons than at the candles and the walls. He then turned to me and said in his gruff manner: 'At the time when I painted the picture the Lord Chamberlain's office refused me the use of candles, for reasons of economy, they said. I therefore had to imagine the lights and shadows and paint them as I thought they would look, including the reflections from the chandeliers. This is the first time that I have seen the room in actual candlelight. But I made no mistake when I painted the picture; it can remain as it is.' "

A gardener passed and greeted us, and after giving some instructions about some newly arrived roses, the Kaiser continued:

"I think the reason people like reading biographies is that nobody nowadays has the time and leisure to plow through all the volumes of a world history. History ought to be so written that it appears plastic and dramatic. That is how my biography should be written; there will be no lack of interesting detail. What has been published about me so far has been mostly of inferior quality, perhaps because the authors were foreigners. I need not enumerate them. What the American Viereck has tried to do was quite amusing: in his book, *The Kaiser on Trial,* I was handed over to the Entente and put in the dock. What does 'the Kaiser' say?—Well, in Mr. Viereck's case, of course, there is nothing but reconstructions and hypotheses; the reader must inevitably get tired of that kind of thing, for all the time he is conscious that it is all fiction. No, my biography has yet to be written, and above all it will have to be fair! What was right once will always be right; by which I do not mean to say that everything I did was right, but everything I did during the thirty years of my reign cannot have been wrong. The title of that biography will have to be very carefully chosen; it would have to express my wish and desire for objectivity and justice. If necessary, I myself would think up such a title; everything else, however, I would leave to the writer whom I will entrust with my biography."

108. THE KAISER AND
NATIONAL SOCIALISM

AFTER HITLER'S seizure of power the Kaiser felt that he ought to be more careful, not only on account of the members of his family in Germany but also because of the revenues which he received from the Third Reich. The often-careless, overfrank "Wilhelm the Talker" turned into a "Wilhelm the Silent." In spite of all caution it sometimes happened that in the heat of an argument he would make a remark which, contorted and exaggerated, reached the public. Then there would be inquiries, reproaches and hidden threats on the part of the Ministry of Propaganda, which were sometimes pacified only with the greatest difficulty by personal intervention of the Kaiser's son, Prince August Wilhelm, a member of the National Socialist party.

A particularly serious situation arose when in 1937 the *New Yorker* published an interview with Wilhelm II, which the Kaiser maintained he had never given, and which must therefore be a fabrication. In this supposed interview the Kaiser was said to have passed disapproving judgment on some of the leading men in the Third Reich. One of the sentences in this interview was: "What have these fellows of the Third Reich made of our nation of poets and thinkers?" In reply to a very sharp request from Berlin demanding an explanation, the Kaiser saw himself obliged to publish a denial. In this he gave his assurance that he had never made the published remarks to foreign journalists. But in spite of this denial, discord and suspicion remained.

In 1934 an agreement had been signed between the Prussian Minister President (Göring) and the representative of the Imperial House (Berg) according to which Wilhelm II and his family had been granted an annual revenue, a compensation so to speak, for the great losses of personal property they had suffered. Although the Kaiser never disclosed to strangers any particulars of this agreement, it was apparent from allusions he made that the payment of the revenue was conditional on the Hohenzollerns' making no comment whatsoever on the National Socialists and their policy. Taking into consideration the impoverishment of various of the branches of the House of Hohenzollern, it was natural that they should try to avoid any action that might endanger the payment of the revenue.

After 1934 visitors to Doorn House were asked to refrain from any mention of present-day Germany in their conversation. An old countess, who must have misunderstood the instructions and was endeavoring to do the right thing, started talking disapprovingly about the National Socialists at the dinner table. Deadly silence ensued; to break this the Kaiser took the youngest princess on his knees and handed her the menu: "Let's see whether you can read out to me what we shall have to eat. Duck? I do hope it isn't one from the moat outside the house!" Thus the conversation was changed and led back into less dangerous paths.

It was obvious that the Kaiser could not be a friend of the National Socialists: his high birth and education, his unconditional belief in God, culminating in the idea of the divine right of kings, all this stood in marked contrast to Hitler's teachings. The Gestapo, concentration camps and the persecution of the Jews were in the Kaiser's eyes a disgrace to Germany. Among trusted friends he would sometimes speak very disapprovingly of the generals who, in order to attain personal advantages, had attached themselves to Hitler in a spineless and undignfied manner.

After saying all this it might seem surprising that in spite of his sincere dislike of Hitler the Kaiser did, later on, send Hitler a telegram congratulating him on the occasion of his victories in France in 1940. The only explanation is that it must have been done for the purpose of settling disagreements which were again threatening. In any case it would seem that this telegram was drafted by the Kaiserin Hermine, of whom it was known that she kept up relations with National Socialists. When she went to Berlin she invited suitable officials to visit her in one of the side wings of the old Wilhelm Palais. She made the most of such occasions in order to safeguard her own interests with regard to her estates in Lusatia, as also the Kaiser's interests. When one of the negotiations proved unsuccessful from her point of view, she nevertheless felt it had been worth while as she had been able to gather important information which she intended to use to the best advantage after her return to Doorn. She even received Hitler and Göring in this side wing of the palais. Göring made some requests, mainly concerned with the satisfaction of his vanity; some of these requests were granted, but not—one may safely assume—without an assurance of some suitable return.

Advised by the Kaiserin Hermine, Wilhelm II maintained an attitude of forced restraint. He never liked to practice pretense, and in order to have to do so as seldom as possible he admitted into his presence only those friends whom he could trust not to contort the meaning of any of the remarks that he might drop accidentally. But all his good intentions came to nothing when, on the occasion of the launching of the battleship *Bismarck*, he heard over the wireless a speech made by Hitler: "Intriguing females [the mother and grandmother of Wilhelm II] forced Bismarck into a struggle against the Court Camarilla. . . . The Second Reich ended as he himself had foreseen it in the most tormenting presentiments. He was miserably rewarded, he, to whom the German nation owed everything, who, after long years of shame and disgrace, had once again raised the name of our people to the highest esteem, he who gave the empire might and strength and world-wide connections through colonial possessions. His removal from office and the subsequent attitude of certain politically hostile circles remain a disgraceful chapter of national ingratitude. . . . But Providence has proved more just than men had been, for princes and dynasts are no more!"

Such defamation by the "Bohemian lance corporal" roused the Kaiser's unrestrained anger, an anger that was only increased by the fact that he had to look on impotently while the other reigned in his place. Added to this jealousy was injured pride.

109. EIGHTIETH BIRTHDAY

WHEN THE OLD KAISER looked through the Army list he found that few among his generals were still alive or on active service. The time had come to cross out the name of his former Commander in Chief, the seventy-three-year-old Duke Albrecht of Württemberg, who had been spending the last years of his life in peaceful retirement at Schloss Althausen; Admiral von Müller also, his former Chief of Admiralty, had been buried. Professor Dörpfeld was one of those whom the Kaiser particularly missed, for to the very end he had been a member of the Doorn Study Group and had acted as an adviser. Only two of the Kaiser's contemporaries were still alive: August von Mackensen and Crown Prince Rupprecht of Bavaria.

Although the Kaiser had remained surprisingly vigorous, which was, no doubt, due to his good constitution and his healthy way of life, shortly before his eightieth birthday a visible decline of strength set in. It seemed as if the active resistance he had so long maintained had given way to irresistible weariness—weariness of living. No longer upright and elastic, he now walked with the aid of a stick, bent and slow. His gray hair turned white, and many wrinkles appeared on the youthful face.

The walks in the garden still continued: once the Kaiser was nearly killed by a falling tree. But soon these walks, too, had to stop. The saddle stool by his desk was replaced by a comfortable chair which, however, was seldom occupied as the Kaiser was wearied and preferred to go to bed.

On January 27, 1939, Wilhelm II celebrated his eightieth birthday. His relatives did what they could to make the day a festive one, in the face of difficulties raised by the German authorities when guests wished to leave Germany to visit him. Some members of the family were even forced to give up the journey to Holland. To make up for any who could not come, nearly ninety-year-old Field Marshal von Mackensen appeared. Also the Kaiser's other contemporary, Crown Prince Rupprecht of Bavaria.

From early morning the Imperial Standard fluttered from the roof of Doorn House, by the side of the black and white flag. The day was opened with a morning service in the flower-decked hall. The Court Chaplain, Doehring, preached the sermon. Afterward the Kaiser received congratulations.

In the afternoon a gala dinner was given. The ground-floor rooms presented a colorful picture which in a small way reminded those present of the good old days in Potsdam: the ladies were in *grande toilette*, the gentlemen in dress uniforms, the Kaiser himself wearing the gala uniform of the Hussar Body Guards. At the table were sons, daughters-in-law, his only daughter with the Duke of Brunswick;

grandchildren, among whom were the Crown Princess Friederike of Greece and her husband, Crown Prince Rupprecht, the Grand Duke of Mecklenburg, Grand Duke Vladimir of Russia and Prince Friedrich Christian of Saxe. Queen Wilhelmina was represented at the dinner by Baron von Hardenbrock and the Province of Utrecht by Yonkheer Bosch Ridder van Rosenthal. During the banquet cables and telegrams were read out, including those from the King and Queen of England and Queen Mary; the silence that had lasted for many years was thus broken.

After dinner a film—*The Life of Frederick the Great*—was shown, and this was followed by a ball preceded by a presentation of birthday wishes. As had been done many years earlier in the White Hall, guests in uniforms of bygone times bowed in front of His Majesty; it was like some weird ballet to illustrate the theme: "When the gods have left, the ghosts arrive."

The German press confined itself to short reports without further comment. The foreign press, however, seized the opportunity of the eigthtieth birthday to give a review of the life of Wilhelm II, in the course of which the difficulty was emphasized of doing justice to the former German Kaiser. Not that this was owing to any lack of material; on the contrary, there were many sources, but the information that issued from them was rarely impartial. Only the French press showed open hostility, stigmatizing the old man as the "real originator of the World War." On January 26, 1939, the *Eclaireur de Nice* printed a photograph of Wilhelm II with the caption: "This is the eighty-year-old Herr Wilhelm Hohenzollern, guilty of the premature deaths of many millions of young people."

110. 1940, A SECOND 1914!

WITH THE OUTBREAK of war against Poland in 1939 Holland was plunged into a state of feverish nerves. Rumor followed upon rumor with lightning speed; frontier incidents were reported and exaggerated to enormous importance. Foreign consuls advised their compatriots to leave Holland as speedily as possible. In order to preserve order in the country the Foreign Minister van Kleffens addressed an appeal to the population in which he assured them in the name of the Government that the country would not be surrendered and that "the independence of the Netherlands would be defended to the last drop of blood."

In these uneasy days many people wondered what the German Kaiser would do. But only once did he break his silence when, on the occasion of the sinking of the Dutch steamer *Simon Bolivar*, he telegraphed to Queen Wilhelmina his sincerest sympathies. In Berlin this alleged tactlessness raised indignant comments. To subdue the rising wave of anger the Kaiser wired through the good offices of the German Embassy at The Hague to Hitler, congratulating him on his having survived the attempt on his life. Hitler thanked him in friendly words.

The Kaiser followed the fighting at the various Fronts with the utmost interest; he did not spare his criticism. Much of what happened appeared to him too daring from the military point of view, and without perspective when viewed from a political angle. In January 1940 he wrote to his old friend Poultney Bigelow that in his opinion "all European States should unite to fight Soviet Russia, which would soon endanger Europe and the world."

During the fateful days of April 1940 the Dutch Minister Kan visited Doorn House and informed the Kaiser that he need not consider himself an internee and that he might leave the country at any time and for any destination.

On the morning of May fourteenth advance troops of the Infantry Regiment 322 under Colonel Neidhold reached Doorn after having succeeded during the previous night in breaking through the Grebbe position at Rhenen. Again the question arose of what would happen to the Kaiser. Queen Wilhelmina offered him a refuge on one of the Dutch islands, but the Kaiser declined this friendly offer, thanking Queen Wilhelmina from the bottom of his heart. He said that on account of his great age he preferred to remain at Doorn "and face his fate."

Then a semiofficial voice declared in Berlin: "The question has arisen, in connection with the possible occupation of Doorn by advancing German troops of what will be the fate of the German ex-Kaiser Wilhelm. It is thought in political circles that the Government will accede, as far as possible, to the wishes of the former Kaiser. Should he desire to return to Germany, it is believed that this would be permitted; but no objections would be raised should the ex-Kaiser desire to settle in a neutral country."

At the order of Colonel Neidhold a guard of honor, consisting of one officer and fifteen men, was posted at the gatehouse. When the Kaiser stepped out of his house German soldiers saluted him for the first time in twenty-two years.

As soon as Hitler heard that vast numbers of members of the armed forces were visiting Doorn House he had this declared out of bounds to officers and men until further orders. The guard of honor was withdrawn and ordinary guards substituted. As such orders could not remain secret in Holland, new rumors started according to which the Kaiser was going to leave Doorn and settle on one of the Dutch islands. Some papers reported that "Wilhelm II had given in to National Socialist pressure" and intended to move to Cadinen. It was not until the sensational news was published that a Prussian prince had been executed and the Crown Prince had been taken into custody, that the latter found himself compelled to make a statement which was published by the German News Agency as a letter from the former German Crown Prince Wilhelm: "A number of assertions have recently appeared in the anti-German foreign press which are so absurd and insulting that it is with reluctance that I take notice of them. Neither myself nor my brothers or sons, nor any member of the House of Hohenzollern, or any other German princely house, have been arrested or executed, nor been restricted in our personal liberty. The extent of the ignorance of the slanderers is shown by the fact that they have resurrected Prince Max of Baden, who has been dead these ten years. I need only point out that all members of German princely houses who are of military age are serving at the Front."

Fifteen princes of the House of Hohenzollern were at the Front; the first to die in action was young Prince Oskar. Shortly afterward he was followed by the eldest son of the Crown Prince. As Hitler feared that the bravery of the princes might make them appear as martyrs in the eyes of the Germans, and that this might strengthen the monarchistic idea in Germany, he then had all princes removed from the armed forces.

It was not surprising that the Kaiser should compare the war of 1940 with 1914. What would be the outcome of this second World War? Would the other succeed in achieving victory where he had failed? In leaps and bounds the little markers on the maps in the hall were moved in all directions. But had it not been the same in 1914? One evening, after hearing the favorable news from the various battle fronts the Kaiser said: "Herr Hitler has not learned anything; the others have the supremacy at sea, but he will not believe it. It is this fact, however, that will decide the outcome of the war, which he must lose. My heart grows heavy when I think of what is to happen, for once again the whole world is against us!"

111. THE LAST PARADE

DURING the spring of 1941 the Kaiser felt ill and exhausted, frequently complaining of pains and fatigue. He caught a cold which developed into pneumonia. The press was quick to report that he had been given up by his physicians, but it was not until May thirty-first that his condition really caused anxiety. There was an embolism of the lung and this caused the old man rapidly to lose strength. On June third he became unconscious. Kaiserin Hermine, the Duchess of Brunswick, Prince Louis Ferdinand and Princess Henriette were at his side when, at eleven-thirty in the morning of June 4, 1941, Wilhelm II drew his last breath.

In his will the Kaiser had expressed the wish to be buried in the park of Doorn and that the funeral should be a simple one, confined to the family circle. One of the first telegrams of condolence came from Hitler, addressed to the Kaiserin Hermine.

The funeral was fixed for Monday, June ninth. To facilitate the journey to Doorn Hitler put a special train at the disposal of the relatives.

The standard was flown at half-mast from Doorn House. Sons and grandsons took turn in keeping watch at the coffin, as it lay in the hall. The park outside was in rich bloom: rhododendron, lilac and laburnum bushes gave the impression that great masses of flowers had been heaped for the occasion beneath the dark green beeches.

On this Monday the roads in Doorn were lined by villagers who watched the arrival of the guests for the funeral. German police were in charge of the traffic regulations. Punctually at ten o'clock the guard of honor, commanded by Colonel von Gersdorf, took up position in front of the house. Immediately afterward Hitler's representative, the "Reichskommissar for the Netherlands," Seyss-Inquart, arrived and presented Hilter's condolences to the Kaiserin and the Crown Pince. After him old General Field Marshal von Mackensen approached the coffin, which was covered by the Imperial Standard; he fell on his knees, and embraced the coffin which contained the remains of his Imperial master as if it were itself some beloved person. Lieutenant Colonel Niemann and Major Giese hastened to assist the old Field Marshal to rise to his feet; but with an angry gesture he pushed them aside. Leaning heavily on his sword, he managed to get up unaided. It was an incident no one who witnessed it would easily forget: the old Army bidding farewell to its Kaiser.

The service was conducted by Court Chaplain Doehring, who took for his text some words from the Bible that the Kaiser himself had chosen. The coffin was then carried to the car by footmen while the military band played a hymn. When the coffin appeared in the doorway the guard of honor presented arms, to the accompaniment of the muffled roll of the drums.

Many splendid wreaths were carried in front of the coffin. General Count von der Goltz carried on a red cushion the Kaiser's Field Marshal's baton and Count Moltke bore the orders and decorations. They were followed by the Court Chaplain, the Kaiserin on the arm of the Crown Prince and the other members of the family; after them came Seyss-Inquart, Field Marshal von Mackensen, Colonel General Hase, General Christiansen and the Admirals Densch and Canaris, representing the armed forces.

Under the old trees of the park the guard of honor formed a line for the last parade at the graveside. Another hymn was played, to the accompaniment of drum and bugle, and, while salvo after salvo was fired, the coffin was lowered into the temporary grave. The throb of a military march concluded the funeral parade of him who had been Wilhelm II, Kaiser and King.

EPILOGUE

IN THIS BIOGRAPHY of Wilhelm II an attempt has been made to answer the question "Was everything wrong?"; to answer it as impartially as is humanly possible; and to view it in the light of contemporary events. "Love and seriousness" was what Goethe, in a conversation with Heine, laid down as the fundamental conditions and justification for writing about the character and events in the life of a human being.

The task was to consider the for and against in the right proportions, to draw conclusions and pass judgment in such a way as not to tip the scales in the hands of justice. This was the author's guiding principle in writing this biography. If the goal has been reached, or even partly reached, something will have been achieved.

Much that happened during the reign of Wilhelm II was doubtlessly wrong. But it must not be forgotten that under the German constitution the Kaiser alone could not be held responsible for every decision taken. The Reich's Chancellor and his ministers, who were at liberty to approve or otherwise, must share any blame and together with him bear the responsibility.

Within a period of fifty years the young German nation, hitherto unused to political thinking, became one of the great powers of Europe. The nation was thrilled by the same ideas and ideals as their young Kaiser who, in his speeches, only expressed what was in the minds of his subjects: to achieve a "place in the sun," protected by strong "shining armor." Had Wilhelm II died before the outbreak of the World War, the whole German nation would doubtless have mourned his passing as that of one of the most illustrious rulers of the House of Hohenzollern.

Many of Wilhelm's adversaries endeavor to picture his reign as one of lasting chaos. They ignore the fact that the nation enjoyed a quarter of a century of profound peace, followed by a brilliantly organized, indomitable fight against half the world—a struggle that lasted four years. Count Hans von Pfeil, the valiant defender of his Kaiser, pertinently asks whether the Kaiser's rule over the German

Reich for so many years was solely to the country's harm and misfortune: "If that was so, why did not the ministers, one after another, the public servants and active generals, hand in their resignations? Why did not the German princes, under the leadership of the King of Bavaria, as the second largest Federal State, make representations to the Kaiser or the Reich's Chancellor in order to save the Reich from decline? Why, on the occasion of the twenty-fifth anniversary of his accession, did all the most eminent scholars and experts in all the big towns of the land rise to make speeches at gala dinners and gatherings, glorifying, celebrating and praising the Kaiser's excellence in almost every branch of monarchical activity?"

It cannot be doubted that Wilhelm II seriously endeavored to prevent the outbreak of the World War. If events, hastened by the dangerous game played at the Ballhausplatz in Vienna took him by surprise and forced him to adopt hurried countermeasures, they were taken only in fulfillment of his royal obligations. During those dramatic days of July and August, 1914, Kaiser, Czar, King and President succumbed to a power that they had not reckoned with: the power of Fate. Had it not been for that, the war would never have started; for, quite apart from any other reason, the Czar, as well as the two Emperors, must have known that an unsuccessful war would most certainly deprive them of their crowns. There was another reason that affected Germany particularly, for, as Tirpitz had once emphasized, any martial entanglements, involving fighting upon two fronts, were from the outset doomed to failure.

"The side possessing the better nerves will win," the Kaiser once said during the war. Unfortunately, the truth of this was exemplified at the cost of his own people who, owing to pressure from outside and being cut off from the rest of the world, had to suffer more than any other nation involved in the war. It was indeed possible to perceive the increasing nervous deterioration of the peoples of all the powers engaged in combat. The first of the Central Powers to break down was Bulgaria; Turkey followed, then Austria-Hungary and finally the German Reich. We know today that the sequence might have been different. It was but a question of hours.

As in the Lay of the Nibelungen, where the struggle was broken off "with great sorrow" and the verses end in sadness and lament, so also the epic of the World War. It was the end of an epoch, complete in itself. Those who had grown up in it survived to find themselves in a new world in which they must remain outsiders. Postwar developments found them divided and perplexed. Added to grief for their sorely afflicted Fatherland were their own misfortunes, which Wilhelm II shared with them. He complained once that Providence had treated them harshly; that relentless and hard had been the fate of those who, so short a while before, had enjoyed their young lives gaily and untroubled. He may have been thinking of his cousins, the Czar and Czarina, the members of the House of Hapsburg, or of Coburg and of all those who, like himself, had had to withdraw from the stage of world events.

The unhappy conclusion was provided by the peace of Versailles. The words in which Leopold von Ranke, the German historian, concluded one of his works would equally well apply to this peace: "The great business of peace that was to bring calm to Europe began like an intrigue in a comedy."

The German Empire was shattered. After a rapid rise there had followed an almost equally rapid decline. Bismarck once prophesied that after the German decline that he foretold, there would rise a new Germany: "A generation that has taken a thrashing is always followed by one that deals out the thrashing; the first is doomed to decline, the latter to rise." When someone asked Wilhelm II what, in his opinion, would be the effect of these wars on the future German generations, he replied with some hesitation: "My great-grandfather, King Friedrich Wilhelm III, led his Prussian nation to a great catastrophe. Those who lived through it rightly called it a terrible national disaster. Today we know that precious, new German life blossomed forth from that catastrophe; regarding it from a historical distance we must ask: Was it really a national disaster?"

It was with reflections such as these that the Kaiser sought to cling to what had been good in the years of war and to banish the somber ghosts that surrounded him during his hours of loneliness. It would be misleading to assume it was his real nature to treat as trifles and dismiss airily anything that was disagreeable. On the contrary: all this was merely an attempt to cover up the self-accusations that crowded on him. His complacency was not by any means what his adversaries tried to make out. The truth was that he who had always had such unbounded self-assurance now suffered immensely under the events that had taken place, though he invariably hid his feelings with a smile.

Every revolution and breakdown of a nation will be followed by an evolution toward improvement, though this can never be accomplished by the person who has been made responsible for the catastrophe. This applied to Wilhelm II.

"Great events create a feeling of reverence," the Kaiser confessed once; and it was this knowledge that made him forgive even his slanderers, who would have liked to "morally annihilate him while he was still alive."

Even to this day there are many inside and outside Germany who have nothing good to say of Kaiser Wilhelm II, though this is largely because it became a habit to do so after the first World War. German Social Democracy above all has sought to lay the blame for everything on the former bearer of the crown. But in simple justice it must be admitted that even in those circles there were men who—although insisting on the dethroning of Wilhelm II as an essential measure—nevertheless treated him with fairness. It was the Social Democrat and Minister of Justice Landsberg who, at the National Assembly in Weimar on February 20, 1919, said: "Far be it from me to attack a man who has been greatly stricken by misfortune and whose intentions have always been good and pure."

Wilhelm II's intentions had indeed been "good and pure," even if his problematic character did not always admit the carrying through of these intentions. A problematic character is but a first step on the way to genius. That the Kaiser did not reach this state of genius and remained, in many respects, the ingenious dilettante with all the faults and consequences that ensued from this, was the tragedy of his life.

Politically, Wilhelm II's fate drew to its inevitable conclusion. Men have sought to accuse, to defend and to explain. But the last true judgment will have to be passed by history itself.

HOHENZOLLERN FAMILY

SHOWING THE DIRECT DESCENT OF WILHELM II

The Burgrave Friedrich von Nürnberg was enfeoffed in the Mark Brandenburg by the Emperor Sigismund. He reigned (1415–1440) as Elector Friedrich I. There followed: Friedrich II, Albrecht Achilles, Johann Cicero, Joachim I, Joachim II, Johann Georg, Johann Sigismund, Georg Wilhelm, followed by his son, Friedrich Wilhelm. Then:

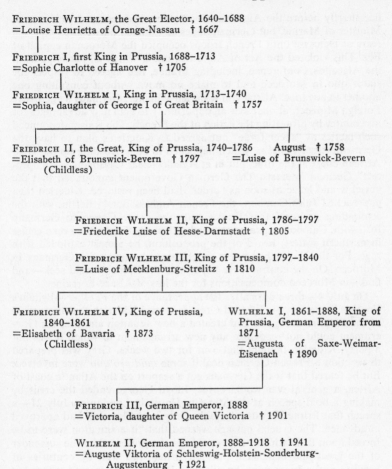

FRIEDRICH WILHELM, the Great Elector, 1640–1688
=Louise Henrietta of Orange-Nassau   † 1667

FRIEDRICH I, first King in Prussia, 1688–1713
=Sophie Charlotte of Hanover   † 1705

FRIEDRICH WILHELM I, King in Prussia, 1713–1740
=Sophia, daughter of George I of Great Britain   † 1757

FRIEDRICH II, the Great, King of Prussia, 1740–1786   August   † 1758
=Elisabeth of Brunswick-Bevern   † 1797   =Luise of Brunswick-Bevern
   (Childless)

FRIEDRICH WILHELM II, King of Prussia, 1786–1797
=Friederike Luise of Hesse-Darmstadt   † 1805

FRIEDRICH WILHELM III, King of Prussia, 1797–1840
=Luise of Mecklenburg-Strelitz   † 1810

FRIEDRICH WILHELM IV, King of Prussia,   WILHELM I, 1861–1888, King of
   1840–1861   Prussia, German Emperor from
=Elisabeth of Bavaria   † 1873   1871
   (Childless)   =Augusta of Saxe-Weimar-
                                                  Eisenach   † 1890

FRIEDRICH III, German Emperor, 1888
=Victoria, daughter of Queen Victoria   † 1901

WILHELM II, German Emperor, 1888–1918   † 1941
=Auguste Viktoria of Schleswig-Holstein-Sonderburg-
   Augustenburg   † 1921

APPENDIX

AGADIR INCIDENT is the name generally given to the crisis provoked by
the dispatch of the German cruiser *Panther* to the little Moroccan port
of Agadir, in the summer of 1911. In February of that year, Joseph Caillaux, who favored an understanding with Germany, became Finance
Minister in the French Government and presently supplanted Monis
as Premier. Théophile Delcassé, who had quit the French Foreign Of-

fice shortly before the Algeciras Conference, had returned to power as Minister of Marine, but German hopes of Caillaux outweighed German fears of Delcassé until French troops occupied the Moroccan capital of Fez. This violated the Act of Algeciras, under which all participants in the Algeciras Conference, including France, had agreed to respect the status quo in Morocco and to make no move without consulting one another in advance. Alfred von Kiderlen-Wächter, Germany's aggressive Foreign Minister, at once saw an opportunity to gain new advantages for his country by protesting the action of the French. The Kaiser denounced such tactics as "sheer farce" but agreed to Kiderlen's plan to have the German cruiser *Panther*, which happened to be proceeding up the West African coast at the time, put in at Agadir—near Casablanca—to "protect" German interests. The German Government announced that the vessel would leave as soon as "order" had been restored. Kiderlen then approached Jules Cambon, the French Ambassador in Berlin, with the astounding proposal that France cede the entire Congo to Germany forthwith. Cambon appeared stunned. When the Kaiser, then on a cruise in northern waters, heard of the proposition, he almost exploded with rage. For the Kaiser had never sought any advantages for Germany in Morocco. On the contrary. He hoped that the French would seek—and find—in Morocco compensations for the loss of Alsace-Lorraine.

On July 4—three days after the appearance of the *Panther*—Britain's Foreign Secretary, Sir Edward Grey, informed Kiderlen that the arrival of the *Panther* at Agadir had created a new situation and that his Government could not recognize any new arrangement to which it was not a party. Kiderlen thought that over for two weeks. Grey was prepared to sanction a Franco-German deal if some *quid pro quo* were involved. But he feared that if the Germans got a seaport on the Atlantic coast of Africa, a general war would ensue. Lloyd George ended the crisis by making a bold speech at the Mansion House in London on July 21—a speech that Prime Minister Asquith, Grey, and Churchill had approved in advance. The crucial passage warned that "if a situation were to be forced upon us in which peace could only be preserved by the surrender of the great and beneficent position Britain has won by centuries of heroism and achievement, by allowing Britain to be treated where her interests were vitally affected as if she were of no account in the cabinet of nations, then I say emphatically that peace at that price would be a humiliation intolerable for a great country like ours to endure." The Germans at once informed the British they had no thought of establishing a port in Morocco. Soon afterward they scaled down the demands they had made upon the French.

The Agadir crisis had made two things clear: first, that Britain would support France in a war against Germany; second, that a clear, firm British warning to that effect could preserve the peace. Kiderlen drew the correct conclusions, but died within a year. The Kaiser drew other conclusions and was therefore unable to prevent war in 1914 or even to understand what had happened when it came.

THEOBALD VON BETHMANN-HOLLWEG (1856–1921) came from two West German families who had distinguished themselves in banking and the law. Prince Bülow, his immediate predecessor as Imperial Chancellor, had made his mark in the world of diplomacy. Caprivi, who succeeded Bismarck in 1890, was a general. Although the Kaiser referred to Bethmann-Hollweg contemptuously as his "civilian" Chancellor, it was Bethmann-Hollweg's nonmilitary, non-Prussian background that brought him to the top. And it was his vacillating personality that kept him there from 1909 to 1917. For the Kaiser, thanks to his hereditary position and his natural energy, could not abide a strong Chancellor, and the generals and admirals had to wait until war came to throw their weight about. Prior to August 1914, Bethmann-Hollweg's vacillations did more to involve Germany in war than any deliberate firebrand could have accomplished. But after war came, he soon fell into the discard, and Hindenburg and Ludendorff became the real masters of Germany. Bethmann-Hollweg, in his simple-minded honesty, frankly admitted that Germany regarded its pledge to respect the neutrality of Belgium as a "scrap of paper," thereby earning for himself and his country the contumely of the outside world. Admiral von Tirpitz, whose big-navy program Bethmann-Hollweg opposed before 1914, blamed Bethmann for the declaration of war on Russia. "Bethmann-Hollweg was throughout those days so excited and irritable that it was impossible to talk with him," wrote Tirpitz. "I can still hear him as with uplifted arms he repeatedly emphasized the absolute necessity of the declaration of war and put an end to all further discussion." With the outbreak of war, Bethmann-Hollweg boasted of German invincibility and rejected any suggestion of a compromise peace. Before the war he had antagonized the militarists; during the war he antagonized the moderates. On the question of unrestricted submarine warfare he told the Kaiser in January 1917: "I can give Your Majesty neither my assent to the unrestricted U-boat warfare nor my refusal. I must submit to Your Majesty's decision." Six months later, divested of all support in any direction, he submitted his own resignation when Hindenburg and Ludendorff demanded a showdown with the leaders of the various political parties over the question of the terms on which Germany would agree to make peace.

OTTO EDUARD LEOPOLD VON BISMARCK (1815–1898), the chief creator of the German Empire over which Kaiser Wilhelm II later ruled, came of an old Prussian family. He was educated for a diplomatic career, traveled and read widely, and as a young man held liberal political views. But when he entered public life in 1847, he defended the rights of the Hohenzollern dynasty which had ruled the Kingdom of Prussia for more than four hundred years. From 1858 to 1862 Bismarck served as Prussian Ambassador to Russia. After a few months as Ambasador to France, he was summoned back to Berlin by King Wilhelm I of Prussia and appointed head of the government and Foreign Minister. Although opposed by a majority in the lower house of the Prussian Parliament, Bismarck remained in power, solely because he had the backing of the King. His control and his conduct of foreign affairs made him indispensable. He made common cause with the Russians to crush a rebellion in Poland. He made common cause with the Austrians to strip Denmark of the provinces of Schleswig-Holstein. In 1866 he turned against Austria and, as the result of a lightning seven-weeks' war, drove Austrian influence from northern Germany and established Prussia as the head of a new confederation of North German states. He took the title of *Bundes-Kanzler* and in 1870 turned against France. As a result of an even more spectacular series of victories, culminating in the defeat of the armies of Napoleon III at Sedan, Bismarck forced France to surrender the provinces of Alsace and Lorraine, and in 1871 King Wilhelm I of Prussia proclaimed himself Kaiser Wilhelm I of a new German Empire, with Bismarck in the post of *Reichs-Kanzler.*

Having, by force and guile, created a new German Empire around a hard Prussian core, Bismarck concentrated on trying to stabilize this new Empire in a new Europe. At home he entered a long-drawn-out struggle, known as the *Kulturkampf*, with the Catholic Center party. The roots of this struggle went back to the Protestant Reformation, the Thirty Years' War, and the rivalry between the Protestant Prussian House of Hohenzollern with the Roman Catholic Austrian House of Hapsburg. In Bismarck's time this struggle had to do mainly with control of education and of the clergy. By the time Kaiser Wilhelm II came to the throne, the *Kulturkampf* had ended with a substantial victory for the Church. Bismarck met with sharper opposition from the growing Social Democratic party. At first he tried repression. Then he tried to beat the Socialists at their own game by sponsoring a few "welfare state" measures. Neither Bismarck nor the Social Democrats can be said to have scored a victory, and Bismarck's successors continued the battle, using many of his methods.

But it was still in the field of foreign policy that Bismarck made his most characteristic contributions. In his view, Germany's paramount interests lay in eastern and central Europe, but he had no territorial ambitions in those directions and declared that all the Balkans were not worth "the bones of a Pomeranian grenadier." In 1878 he presided over the Berlin Congress, acting the part of "honest broker," as he called it, between the rival claims of Russia and Austria. By taking a stand against Russia's acquisition of Constantinople, Bismarck gratified the British as well as the Austrians. Disraeli returned to London from Berlin boasting that he had brought back "peace with honor." But Bismarck had antagonized Russia and had committed Germany so much to Austria that he soon had to sign a mutual assistance treaty with the Austrians promising to aid them against a Russian attack in exchange for their promise to aid Germany if the Russians struck in that direction. In 1882, Italy joined, and from then on the arrangement, which remained in force until the outbreak of the first World War, was known as the Triple Alliance. But Bismarck distrusted the Austrians; he respected Russian power. Shortly after Italy joined the Triple Alliance he quietly signed a secret Reinsurance Treaty with Russia under which each state promised to observe benevolent neutrality if either one were attacked by another. Technically, this did not violate the Triple Alliance, which called on German aid to Austria only if Austria were the victim of attack. Practically, however, it put some restraints on Austria and made it unlikely that Russia would enter into an anti-German alliance with France.

Bismarck became a belated and reluctant convert to the program of colonial expansion on which his country embarked shortly after the Franco-Prussian War. He hoped that the French might find compensation in Africa for the loss of Alsace-Lorraine and his hearty and consistent respect for Great Britain made him slow to recommend any moves that might lead to an Anglo-German conflict. But Bismarck had builded better, or more dangerously, than he knew. In the early years of his chancellorship, Prussia's military aristocracy and the newer industrial aristocracy of the Ruhr and Rhineland valleys supported his foreign policy, which was essentially continental and European. But by the time Kaiser Wilhelm II came to the throne, the ambitions of Germany's soldiers and the appetites of Germany's industrialists had increased. And a new generation of traders, shippers, and bankers had appeared who looked to the new Kaiser rather than to the old Chancellor. Bismarck in his first speech as Prussian Prime Minister, back in 1862, had declared: "The great questions of the day will not be settled by resolutions and majority votes—that was the mistake of the men of 1848 and 1849—but by blood and iron." With blood and iron he had made Prussia the foremost German state and Germany the first nation in Europe. And though he wanted to stop and stabilize what he had gained, a new generation used the same means to seek new ends. Not for the first time in history— or the last—had the means become ends in themselves.

BERNHARD HEINRICH KARL MARTIN VON BÜLOW (1849–1929) served as Imperial Chancellor for the Kaiser from 1900 to 1909, the longest period that any man except Bismarck ever held the position. Bülow came of a distinguished North German family, fought in the Franco-Prussian War, entered the diplomatic service, served in Paris, St. Petersburg, Bucharest, and Rome. In 1886 he married the Italian Princess Camporeale, whose first marriage to Count Karl von Dönhoff had been annulled two years before. Thanks to the intervention of Eulenburg, the Kaiser sanctioned the union. "I do not possess your erudition," Bülow wrote Eulenburg at the time, "but belong more to the intuitive diplomatists. Therefore I might in certain circumstances be dangerous, and only my self-knowledge protects me. You walk along the broad highway of erudition and experience; I on a tightrope, and have to take care not to lose my instinctive balance." In 1895 Eulenburg was telling the Kaiser that Bülow was "the predestined Imperial Chancellor of the future." But before the Kaiser appointed him to that high post in 1900, he made him Secretary of State in charge of foreign affairs.

Bülow, at the start of his chancellorship, wanted to protect the power of the Kaiser for the same reason Holstein, in the Foreign Office, wanted to whittle it away. Bülow believed that, through flattery, he could make the Kaiser his tool. Holstein wanted foreign-policy-making shifted from the Kaiser's hands to his own. But Bülow, in his laziness, followed Holstein's lead. Both Kürenberg and Professor Johannes Haller, in his life of Eulenburg, also suggest that Holstein was able to blackmail Bülow into doing his bidding. Kürenberg points out that Bülow, in 1905, left the reluctant Kaiser no choice but to pay a provocative visit to the Sultan of Morocco at Tangier. But it was Holstein who put Bülow up to it. As an immediate consequence of this sudden German intervention in a French zone of influence, Théophile Delcassé, the anti-German Foreign Minister of France, had to resign, which gave the Kaiser such pleasure that he made Bülow a Prince. But Holstein, who had planned it all, could not stop there. Having eliminated Delcassé, he proposed to torpedo the Anglo-French alliance by sponsoring a conference on Morocco that would isolate France and establish Germany's position as the dominant power in Europe.

But the conference that assembled on January 16, 1906, in the Spanish city of Algeciras ended by isolating Germany and cementing the *Entente Cordiale*. The chief German delegate, acting under Holstein's instructions, made himself so offensive to the British that he had to be withdrawn. Bülow took over the direction of the conference from Holstein and then accepted Holstein's resignation from the Foreign Office post that he had held for thirty years. Nevertheless, Holstein had the last laugh, two years later, when he furnished the material that led to the trial of Eulenburg on homosexual charges. Bülow, fearing that he too might come within Holstein's line of fire, did nothing to save his old friend, and Eulenburg's disgrace and banishment from the Imperial Court meant that the Kaiser had lost his one outspoken, impartial, and rational adviser. And Holstein's revenge on his lords and masters became complete when the Kaiser, at the same time, had to yield some of his powers to Bülow as a result of the tactless interview he gave to the *Daily Telegraph* of London that would never have had appeared but for Bülow's own laziness and negligence.

Before Bülow fell from power in 1909 on a vote about the budget, he committed one final blunder that contributed to the outbreak of war five years later. In 1908, Austria defied the decisions reached at the Congress of Berlin in 1878 by seizing the South Slav Balkan provinces of Bosnia and Herzegovina. The Young Turk revolution had suddenly weakened Turkish power in the Balkans, while the Russians, having recently suffered defeat at the hands of Japan and barely suppressed the 1905 revolution, could do nothing. Bülow not only failed to restrain or rebuke his Austrian allies, he rubbed salt into Russia's wounds by demanding approval of Austria's violation of the Berlin accords. The Russians had no choice but to accept, and if they behaved highhandedly in July 1914, it was partly because they had not forgotten the way Germany and Austria behaved during the Bosnia-Herzegovina crisis of 1908.

Bülow did not again play any political role until he went to Rome as German Ambassador shortly after the outbreak of the first World War. Here his wife's Italian connections served him well. Thanks in part to Bülow's influence, Italy did not declare war on Germany until a year after declaring war on Austria-Hungary. Bülow lived on until 1929, writing his massive memoirs in four volumes, for which he was paid—and paid handsomely—by the word. They gave a vivid and detailed picture of a man who played a great part in his time and succeeded in learning nothing from his experience.

PRINCE PHILIPP ZU EULENBURG (1847–1921) was for ten years perhaps the closest personal friend of the Kaiser's and certainly his most outspoken adviser. He was the son of a hard-bitten Prussian soldier and of an artistic and accomplished mother whose ancestors came from Silesia. To the surprise of his father, Eulenburg won the Iron Cross in the Franco-Prussian War and might have made a successful career as an architect, musician, or dramatic impresario, but went into diplomacy, representing the Imperial Government at several German courts until appointed Ambassador to Vienna in 1895, remaining there for eight years. He always found time to see the Kaiser often, and he wrote to him constantly. The humorous weekly *Kladderadatsch* called Eulenburg "Count Troubador." He staged and performed pageants, sometimes dressing himself up in women's clothes. In 1894 he was mentioned as a possible Chancellor, but he wrote a memorandum stating he had "very urgently begged the Emperor, when my candidature was being much discussed, *never* to give me that appointment, for which in many ways I am entirely unsuited."

Eulenburg and Bülow had first become friends when they were both serving in the German Embassy in Paris in 1881. Later Eulenburg's reports attracted Holstein's favorable interest. Both Bülow and Holstein found Eulenburg invaluable because of his influence upon the Kaiser. But Eulenburg and Holstein disagreed on how to deal with the Kaiser. Professor Johannes Haller in his two-volume life of Eulenburg has written: "Eulenburg wanted to stick to the system which in the course of six years had proved itself not wholly bad—namely, that of guiding and supporting the Emperor by the counsel, unanimous so far as might be, of his appointed officials, of retrieving his mistakes to the best of their ability, and arresting the fatal and growing influence of an irresponsible military environment. Holstein, on the contrary, strained every nerve to replace the tried system by another—that of rendering the Emperor innocuous. Eulenburg, to attain his end, tried to prevent, as far as he could, the occurrence of conflicts within the Government;

and if that proved impossible, to solve the problems without sensational public conflicts. Holstein, on the contrary, welcomed these crises. He sought to foment and embitter them in every way." This describes the situation at the time of Hohenlohe's chancellorship in 1895. For the subsequent conflict between Holstein and Eulenburg, see the material on Bülow in the Appendix, page 437.

FRANZ JOSEPH I, Emperor of Austria-Hungary (1830–1916), came to the throne at the age of eighteen in the revolutionary year 1848. Riots in that year drove Metternich, one of the chief figures at the Congress of Vienna, to permanent exile in England. Emperor Ferdinand I, a victim of epilepsy, abdicated in favor of young Franz Joseph, who reasserted the power of the House of Hapsburg and gained for Austria temporary ascendancy over Prussia. With the aid of Russia, he crushed an Hungarian revolt and then angered the Russians by supporting Britain and France in the Crimean War. But soon after, Austria lost all its Italian possessions, except Venice, and in 1866 suffered a serious defeat at the hands of Prussia, which became from then on the foremost center of German power in Europe. In 1868, the old Austrian Empire, which had attempted to Germanize its Slavic and Magyar subjects, became the Dual Monarchy, in which Hungary enjoyed equal status. But the Dual Monarchy contained more Slavs than Germans or Hungarians. Although Franz Joseph had lost wars and territories to both Prussia and Italy, he made an alliance with the new German Empire and with the new Italian monarchy; and although a devout Roman Catholic, he guarded the rights of his dynasty and his empire even against the Pope.

From the day Wilhelm II became German Emperor he looked ahead to the twentieth century and dreamed of enlarging the Reich. To the end of his life, Franz Joseph looked back at the eighteenth century, to which he felt he belonged, and tried only to hold his own. "The Austro-Hungarian Monarchy," he declared shortly after the turn of the century, "is no fanciful work of art but an absolute necessity for the present and future existence of her peoples. It is a refuge for those fragmentary nations of Central Europe which, without a common home, would have a deplorable existence and be tossed about by all their more powerful neighbors; whereas as long as they are joined together, they themselves constitute an imposing power." In Germany, the Kaiser worked with the new generation of coal and steel barons, shipping and banking magnates, traders, manufacturers, and promoters who organized their country's industrial power. In Austria, the Emperor tried to play the role of benevolent grandfather to his varied and unruly subjects. "God grants me this long life," he once remarked, "in order that the end of this ancient Empire may be delayed a little while. After my death it is sure to come." But he did not know or even try to understand the reasons for Austria's approaching doom. In his personal life he resisted modernity in all its forms. He refused to use a telephone. Only once in his life did he ride in an automobile, and then only to oblige King Edward VII of England. He slept on the cot of a common soldier, rose at four every morning, bathed in a wooden tub that attendants wheeled into his room. He dined at five and retired at half past eight. He agreed with his ancestor, Emperor Joseph II, who once remarked that if he were to avoid his social inferiors, he would have to spend his life in the Hapsburg burial tombs.

Just as Germany's delayed industrial revolution provided the drive that sustained the Empire of Kaiser Wilhelm II, so a more prolonged revolution in farming was undermining the Empire of the Hapsburgs. For the farm lands of Central and Southeastern Europe, from Poland down across Austria, Hungary, and on down into the Balkans, could no longer support all the people who lived on them. Nor could they compete against the growing efficiency of the Western Hemisphere and Australia. Moreover, the feudal system forced more and more landless peasants to seek jobs in the towns and cities or to emigrate overseas. Industry throughout most of the Austro-Hungarian Empire lagged far behind German industry, but population continued to increase, both in the cities and on the land. Nationalists, Socialists, and various demagogues appealed to this growing mass discontent. This was the kind of Empire and Franz Joseph was the kind of Emperor which had become Germany's one ally and the Kaiser's one true friend a full ten years before Sarajevo.

SIR EDWARD GREY (1862–1933) has long been regarded by German statesmen and historians as the villain of the 1914 tragedy. The Kaiser, at worst, is presented as a fool; at best as a well-meaning man, too naïve for his own good. As the Kaiser's official biographer, Kürenberg has chosen to represent Sir Edward Grey as he looked to the Kaiser—and in the light of what the Kaiser knew in July 1914 it is easy to see how he could convince himself that Grey had deliberately provoked the war. But abundant evidence has since come to light showing that if Grey erred, he erred in failing to follow the example Lloyd George set at the time of the Agadir Incident (which is also discussed in this Appendix), when strong words preserved the peace. Grey's memoirs, which he wrote after the war, show that some doubts still haunted him about the wisdom of the course he pursued in 1914. Even at the time, his critics accused him of not issuing a clear enough warning to the Germans. A quarter of a century later, at the time of the Munich crisis and afterward, even Neville Chamberlain went out of his way to avoid the uncertainty that Grey's handling of the 1914 crisis created. Whatever Grey may have done or left undone at that time, he was no warmonger when he observed, after Parliament had ratified the British declaration of war against Germany, "The lights are going out all over Europe; we shall not see them lit again in our time." Nor was he indulging in a theatrical display of hypocrisy when he brought his fists down on the table of the Foreign Office and groaned: "I hate war! I hate war!" Sir Edward Grey might be reproached for having failed, in his capacity as British Foreign Secretary, to transcend himself in July 1914. So might the Kaiser. In a drama that un-

folded with the inevitability of a Greek tragedy, those two were the only
major actors who seemed, now and then, to glimpse the possibility of
playing larger roles than fate had assigned to them—the Kaiser by issuing a sterner and earlier warning to his Austrian ally, Grey by issuing
a sterner and earlier warning to Germany. But the Kaiser felt constrained
by his alliance; Grey felt constrained by the democratic process under
which he lacked the authority to threaten war. But Grey emerged a
bigger man than the Kaiser. For Grey never satisfied his own mind and
conscience that he acted with perfect wisdom; the Kaiser never felt such
doubts.

PRINCE CHLODWIG KARL VIKTOR ZU HOHENLOHE-SCHILLINGSFÜRST
(1819–1901) served as Chancellor from the fall of Caprivi in 1894 until
the appointment of Bülow in 1900. Although a Roman Catholic, he had
supported Bismarck's position in the *Kulturkampf*. Like his brother, who
was a Cardinal, Hohenlohe opposed Pope Pius IX, who seemed to be
setting the Church up in opposition to the modern state. He referred to
the Jesuit Order as "the devil's society." Hohenlohe had a long history
of public service behind him when he became Chancellor at the age of
seventy-five and because of his advanced years let his two ministers of
foreign affairs, Baron Marschall von Bieberstein and Prince von Bülow,
do most of the speaking for his government. The years of Hohenlohe's
chancellorship were also the years when the Kaiser did so much to commit Germany to a program of colonial expansion and naval construction.
But the Kaiser did not impose this policy upon a reluctant or an unin-
formed people. In proclaiming himself the "Enlarger of the Reich," the
Kaiser was saying and doing what most German industrialists, shipping
magnates, bankers, traders, and manufacturers wanted him to do. And if
Hohenlohe was nothing more than the Kaiser's agent, it is no less true to
say that during his chancellorship the Kaiser was nothing less than the
figurehead for all those Germans who wanted for themselves and their
country a larger place in the sun.

BARON FRIEDRICH AUGUST VON HOLSTEIN (1837–1909) served for thirty
years as chief of the political bureau of the German Foreign Office,
where the power he wielded behind the scenes won him the title originally bestowed upon Richelieu—*Éminence grise*, or gray eminence. He
was a neurotic and an unmarried recluse who amassed a personal and
private equivalent of the "raw files" of the modern F.B.I., and used for
blackmail purposes the unevaluated charges he had accumulated against
various public figures. Bismarck regarded him as crazy and thwarted him
as long as he remained Chancellor. But with Bismarck's dismissal in
1890, Holstein became the real arbiter of German foreign policy. Although he met Kaiser Wilhelm II only once in his life, two of his protégés
rose to positions of the highest power—Bülow as Chancellor and Eulenburg as the Kaiser's intimate friend. Until Bismarck died, the fear that
he might return to power haunted Holstein. After the death of Bismarck,

Holstein bent most of his energies to trying to curb and even destroy the power of the Kaiser—not because he disbelieved in the principle of monarchy or the Hohenzollern dynasty, but because the Kaiser's constant interference in foreign policy frustrated some of Holstein's own designs. For further details on Holstein's conflict in this field with Prince Eulenburg, see Eulenburg in the Appendix (page 439), and for the final outcome, see the material on Bülow (page 437).

NICHOLAS II, CZAR OF RUSSIA (1868–1918). This is not the place for a full account of the life of Czar Nicholas II, but only for those aspects of his life that bear on Kaiser Wilhelm II. The Czar's wife, like the Kaiser, had Queen Victoria as a grandmother. Born the Princess Alix of Hesse, she was the daughter of a German father and an English mother. Because of her German birth, she was suspected during the first World War of exerting a pro-German influence on her husband and even operating as a German spy. Actually, the Czarina became more Russian than the Russians, succumbing to an extreme form of mysticism and always exerting a powerful influence on her impressionable husband. The Czar came to the throne in 1894 at the age of thirty-six and married his wife at his father's deathbed. Bad luck, of which he was intensely superstitious, haunted him. More than three thousand persons were crushed to death at his coronation, and during the ceremonies, the imperial chain on his breast fell to the ground. The Czar wielded more personal power than the Kaiser, but his weak, good-natured character made him ineffective. He and his wife both fell under the spell of the mountebank monk, Rasputin, and to a lesser extent under the influence of a French medium named Philippe. Personally, he was more disposed to the alliance with France and Britain than to establishing closer ties with Germany. He distrusted the Kaiser. The revolution of 1905 caused him to grant the Russian people a few democratic rights, but the influence of the conservative Premier Stolypin soon led to further repressions. Lack of character and will prevented the Czar from playing as great a part in Russian policy-making as the Kaiser played in the policy-making of Germany. The alliance with France, rivalry with Austria in the Balkans, and fear of Germany doomed in advance all the efforts the Kaiser made to play upon the Czar's concern for the survival of his dynasty. During the war, the Czar played an even smaller military role than the Kaiser, but Grand Duke Nicholas, his father's first cousin, held the post of Supreme Commander of the Russian Armies.

INDEX

ABOUT THE AUTHOR

JOACHIM VON KÜRENBERG *came of an East Prussian family, his father being stationed in Königsberg as an officer in the Prussian army in 1892, when the boy was born. As a young man he embarked on two careers—businessman and playwright—but World War I put an end to these budding activities. He served as a guards officer in Potsdam, and after the war was invalided out of the service.*

Thereupon, he was sent to the foreign office and served in diplomatic posts in Constantinople, Rome, and Vienna. His responsibilities in these cities left him time to study at the universities— study which proved to be useful training for his later career as a biographer.

The first of his twenty-three biographies, entitled Holstein, the Grey Eminence, *was published in Germany in 1930 and eventually achieved a sale of 220,000 copies. Other subjects that followed included Krupp, Johanna von Bismarck, Queen Victoria, Carol II of Rumania, and Voltaire. His works have been translated into most of the European languages and several Asiatic ones.*

For the writing of The Kaiser, *the author spent a good deal of time with his subject at Doorn. While the American edition of the book was on press, news came of the author's death at the age of 62.*

Da

Mr 21 63